Rebuilding Therapy

REBUILDING THERAPY

Overcoming the Past for a More Effective Future

MICHAEL GASS

PRAEGER

Westport, Connecticut
London

Library of Congress Cataloging-in-Publication Data

Gass, Michael A.
Rebuilding therapy : overcoming the past for a more effective future / Michael Gass.
p. cm.
Includes bibliographical references and index.
ISBN 0–275–95329–7 (alk. paper)
1. Reconstruction (Psychoanalysis) 2. Psychotherapy. 3. Brief psychotherapy. I. Title.
RC489.R39G37 1997
616.89′14—dc20 96–36360

British Library Cataloguing in Publication Data is available.

Library of Congress Catalog Card Number: 96–36360
ISBN: 0–275–95329–7

First published in 1997

Praeger Publishers, 88 Post Road West, Westport, CT 06881
An imprint of Greenwood Publishing Group, Inc.

Printed in the United States of America

The paper used in this book complies with the Permanent Paper Standard issued by the National Information Standards Organization (Z39.48–1984).

10 9 8 7 6 5 4 3 2 1

Contents

Preface

In practicing and developing Rebuilding Therapy for more than the past twenty one years, I have developed a psychotherapy which offers the depressed and managed care dominated mental health and chemical dependency community an innovative, breakthrough and cost-effective treatment modality on a short- to long-term basis for children, usually ages nine and over, adolescents and adults.

In doing so I have integrated portions of Transactional Analysis, primarily Structural Analysis and the influence of Script Analysis, and also Redecision Therapy, developed from Transactional Analysis into the psychodramatic process. To effectively assist in the uncovering and opening up process as needed, I have also utilized relaxation exercises or relaxation which can be referred to and is equivalent to hypnosis, and the influence of Bioenergetic Therapy, as needed. Psychodrama, which Rebuilding Therapy was developed from, remains a living part of Rebuilding Therapy.

Rebuilding Therapy is clearly not just an uncovering and cathartic approach, but is a holistic modality being uncovering, cathartic and cognitive in nature incorporating the past, present and future. My discussion of psychodramatic methods, which I refer to as Rebuilding Therapy methods is highly educational and easy to understand, while providing descriptive examples. I also have modified a number of these methods, while developing new methods. My discussion of prenatal and birth factors and my work in assisting persons to reconstruct themselves from their emotional wounds originating in this period helps to expand the dimensions of mental health treatment. I have also integrated talk therapy approaches and have relied on whatever aspects of personality theory and psychotherapy that I could utilize with my patients in an effective way.

Rebuilding Therapy, as needed, will take the patient into the depths of the mind where other modalities often won't dare to go, and when doing so assists the patient to do something healing and constructive with this therapeutic adventure.

Being a psychodramatic modality and more, Rebuilding Therapy believes that the person for the most part is good, is the product of his or her past and has God given healing powers to heal and reconstruct oneself from the past. It's emphasis on clinically reliving major abusive, rejecting traumatic or negative life experiences that have affected one's coping, relationship and functioning skills, gives the person the opportunity to connect to the causes of his or her problems and to rebuild oneself in the process. Although Rebuilding Therapy's major focus is assisting persons to rebuild from the parental mistreatment and dysfunctional upbringing of the past, it has application and can also be effectively used in rebuilding from other experiences and influences. In addition, although rebuilding is a relative process depending on the person and his or her situation, people no longer need to be the victims of their past and lives, but can become growing victors of their hardships opening up new doors for growth, healing, triumphs and a meaningful life. Rebuilding Therapy can also be effective when reliving work isn't done, though not to the same personality changing degree, in assisting persons to function, cope with stresses and to relate to others more effectively.

Rebuilding Therapy also encourages the involvement of the family as needed which is a necessary prerequisite when working with children and adolescents and some young adults. Its use of family therapy on an adjunct or primary treatment modality, along with reliving work and the use of Rebuilding Therapy methodology as needed, moves the family therapy process along in an effective way.

As the Rebuilding Therapy process is not only a laboratory to rebuild oneself from the past and to learn to function more effectively in the present, it is also a laboratory for experiencing the impact of one's dysfunctional, unhealthy or potentially dangerous behavior. In giving persons an opportunity, without of course actually doing this, to act out a robbery, a homicide or their own suicide, or to experience the impact of their drug or alcohol abuse, denial, hostility or lifestyle, effectively impacts the person with the implications of such behavior or attitudes on others and oneself. In experiencing this, the probability of the patient engaging in such behavior or continuing to act in a dysfunctional way is often reduced, or the effect and severity of the behavior is often decreased.

In being a power and breakthrough therapy, I have emphasized the importance of the patient's rights and his or her right to approve, disapprove or terminate any method, approach or part of the therapeutic process, and have discussed guidelines for this. It is essential for the therapist to respect the impact of the treatment methods he or she uses, while being sensitive to when and how they should be used, which Rebuilding Therapy certainly adheres to in integrating this into the rebuilding process.

Rebuilding Therapy has proved effective in clinical practice in dealing with a wide range of psychological and chemical dependency problems and has the potential to be used in other areas such as law enforcement, corrections, education, religion, business and in the areas of inner city, state, national and international conflict.

In my first book on this reconstructive therapy, I discuss its theoretical foundations, methodology and approaches to expand on the understanding of personality development and psychological functioning; to acquaint mental health, chemical dependency and related professionals with its value on a short-term and long-term basis; to operate as a text and training tool for those mental health and chemical dependency clinicians who seek training in Rebuilding Therapy; and to further expose this and related psychotherapies for use in other arenas Rebuilding Therapy and these other related therapies can be effectively used in.

Acknowledgments

I dedicate this book to the memory of Martin Haskell, a psychologist and a protégé of J. L. Moreno, the famed developer of Psychodrama. Dr. Haskell, as my beloved teacher, mentor and friend taught me Psychodrama, changing my course and direction as a psychotherapist. Without Dr. Haskell's influence this book would never have been written. Thank you Martin.

I also deeply thank my wife, Denise, my friend and colleague and a very talented and innovative mental health clinician for her ongoing sacrifice, support and consultation while I undertook this challenging and difficult journey writing this book. I also appreciate the understanding of my children Natalie, Lisa and Brandon and my father-in-law, Lyle Wiegand and other family members and friends. Lastly I thank my friend and colleague Dr. Tom Noyes, a very successful psychiatrist, for his support and consultation.

CHAPTER 1

The Need for Something with a Breakthrough Nature

PSYCHOTHERAPY: TOO OFTEN A BAND-AID PHENOMENON

Not infrequently, psychotherapists are unsuccessful in assisting their patients to significantly solve their problems and change their lives. This does not mean that the unusual or atypical psychotherapist is always effective. The major point here is that only a minority of psychotherapists are successful in assisting to bring about significant and lasting behavioral and personality changes. They do so as they use methods, techniques and themselves in ways that break through to the causes of the patient's problems, resulting in a significant overcoming of past and present experiences and reconstruction, rebuilding and rehabilitation.

Rather than assisting patients to make the significant and lasting changes they need to, too many psychotherapists and mental health practitioners often hold themselves righteously above their patients. They have little to offer them except superficial, weak, band-aid methods, which at best do no more than temporarily hold the person together before the next crisis.

TALK THERAPY

Talking about problems is the way psychotherapy is practiced in most cases across the spectrum of psychotherapies. However, in many cases, solely talking about problems is no more than an exercise in philosophy, intellectualization and futility. It may increase subjective insight, but insight alone has rarely resulted in significant personality changes, a more meaningful lifestyle or more intimate relationships in a lasting way. In fact, increased insight, without being able to do anything substantial about one's problems, increases agitation, stress and frustration as a person cannot resolve the problems he or she realizes exist. This isn't to say that talk therapy is not helpful, but more intensive breakthrough-type modalities are needed to get to the cause of a person's problems.

THE MEDICAL MODEL

The medical model in psychotherapy puts the therapist in the role of "mother or father" or authoritarian parent and the patient in the role of a sick person or child. Physicians have too frequently, been taught to "know it all," to be the strong savior and to believe that their patients are weak or sick and thus incapable of helping themselves on their own terms without the authoritarian intervention of the physician. This approach, however, is ineffective in most cases when treating psychological and relationship problems. A number of psychiatrists and to a much lesser, but still too frequent extent, some non-physician psychotherapists have adopted this philosophy. The psychotherapist using this method already knows what he or she is looking for in one's "neurotic or sick" patient. In this dictatorial way, the patient's feelings, thoughts and emotional strengths are secondary to what the psychotherapist feels and knows. However, it is a myth that the psychotherapist knows best and has the answers. The real answers and healing powers lie within the person's mind beneath the defenses erected for his or her survival. It is the psychotherapist's responsibility to assist the patient to find these answers and do something with them to solve one's problems and to change his or her thinking, behavior and lifestyle.

Another problem is the psychiatrist or nonpsychiatrist physician too frequently prescribing medication to medicate away the symptoms and the underlying feelings, thoughts and experiences that can resolve the problems. Prescribing medication may be a very helpful procedure if a patient is schizophrenic, suffers from a manic depressive syndrome, a severe depression, anxiety or phobic reaction or other mental health problems requiring medication, is unable to cope with life's stresses in some cases or is in a severe crisis situation. However, intensive psychotherapy that focuses on present problems, family issues, upbringing and past experiences is often necessary if significant and lasting personality and behavior change is to occur. Even where medication is needed, treating psychological issues is essential. Psychiatric medication and psychotherapy together can be very effective in some cases, but the treatment of choice should not be to use medication, if possible.

In a number of cases, medication would never be prescribed if the psychiatrist had greater confidence in the strength of the human mind to cope with stress and to make significant changes in lifestyle. The human mind can be penetrated effectively when the strength of the human being is recognized with empathy, sensitivity and respect and with a methodology that can reach the core of the person's problems, which often lies in the unconscious and the past. Psychotherapists too frequently have also fostered excessive patient dependence on them with this "I know best" and "the patient is weak" attitude. Rather than encouraging growth, this approach has fostered immaturity, a fear of being one's own person and has prevented persons from growing to their potential. Patients have the strength and need to put much effort into therapy to get to the core and causes of their problems, which involves "psychological" sweat, tears, perseverance, courage and again a lot of hard work. Psychotherapists also need to work hard in therapy to encourage this process and not retard their patient's progress. They must stop operating under the myth that the patient is sick, weak and incapable of intensive treatment or methods that can be helpful.

PSYCHOANALYSIS

Freud's Psychoanalytic Theory has been the cornerstone of psychotherapy. It has been instrumental in pointing out the importance of past upbringing and past experiences and the power and influence of the unconscious and repressed memories, feelings, thoughts and conflicts on behavior, interpersonal relations and lifestyle. However, in some quarters it has left the idea that "people are the helpless victims of their upbringing and unconscious," which is not a positive outlook on the human condition. This distortion has been further supported by the inability of most psychotherapies to effectively reach the repressed experiences and conflicts of the past and to assist the person to take control of these forces rather than being controlled by them.

From Psychoanalytic Theory evolved Psychoanalysis, a medical model treatment that is an arduous, long-term and expensive therapy available only to the minority rich. At its best, for the most part, Psychoanalysis assists this "lucky patient" to develop insight regarding his or her past, unconscious mind and coping with the past. However, it lacks the technology and methodology to effectively break through one's personality armor and defenses to get to the unconscious causes of problems and to fix and resolve them. Psychoanalysis, in providing intellectual, psychological and philosophical insight into the past's impact on one's functioning, is only a beginning and is not sufficient for significant and lasting personality change. As a result, Psychoanalysis and analytic methods have often not been effective in assisting persons to rebuild their lives from the wounds of their upbringing, past experiences and related conscious and unconscious conflicts to live more meaningful and productive lives.

POSITIVE THINKING AND COGNITIVE THERAPEUTIC APPROACHES

Those schools of thought that focus primarily on the positive aspects of the mind have gone to the other extreme, primarily emphasizing the positive elements of the person, including conscious free will, the power of conscious thought processes, positive thinking, love, creativity, concern for others and the great potential of the human being. However, this viewpoint, as cognitive therapy, has not given enough importance to the impact of one's past and the unconscious thoughts, feelings, conflicts and past experiences, which so powerfully influence human behavior. It falsely assures the patient that conscious free will, thinking in a positive way and one's positive attributes can direct and control "one's life" without significant interference from past experiences and one's unconscious mind. Although the human being has conscious free will and these positive characteristics, one's past and unconscious mind can easily overwhelm all the conscious free will, positive thinking, goodness, love, creativity and potential anyone has if not dealt with and treated effectively.

Cognitive therapeutic and related methods make the drastic mistake of believing that by trying to change conscious thinking in a rational, objective and reality-oriented way that this can overrule unconscious thinking, feelings and conflicts, family influences and the impact of the past on one's current behavior. If this was the case, all we would need would be an educational course on living in a rational, logical and psychologically healthy way. Unfortunately, to just tell oneself "I will think maturely, objectively and rationally" or "I will give up these unhealthy habits," or even trying to think rationally and maturely and then trying to live this out as part of one's lifestyle are not enough to create significant personality and lifestyle change. Rational cognitive thinking and insight is important and helpful, but not powerful enough to overcome the potent impact of the past and unresolved unconscious conflicts.

Messages from one's parents and others, as one is growing up, such as "You are no good," "You are unlovable," "I wish you were never born," "You shouldn't trust anyone," "You don't need anyone," "Be the best at any cost," and so on, strongly determine life decisions, the course and direction in life and overall behavior, superseding conscious, rational thinking, free will and any potential and positive characteristics the person may have. There is no way of getting around it. These past messages and decisions, which often become unconscious, need to be dealt with and overcome before the positive nature and conscious cognitive thought processes of the individual can control thinking and behavior. Once this is done, then and only then can conscious positive, mature, reality-oriented and rational thinking, positive and healthy attributes and conscious free will become a powerful force and influence in life. Of course, positive thinking and cognitive insight can be helpful in psychotherapy. However, it can also contaminate and inhibit one's trip into overcoming the past, if obsessively adhered to. A holistic approach, focusing, as needed, on conscious cognitive thought processes, positive thinking, one's present life and the impact of the family and past conscious and unconscious experiences are necessary for significant and lasting personality change and improved psychological functioning.

BEHAVIOR THERAPY

Behavior Therapy mistakenly believes that all behavior can be modified and that life can be significantly improved by only positively or negatively reinforcing behavior or providing no consequences at all. True, behavior may be modified, but the change may only be temporary. If the change is to be relatively long lasting, it is still necessary to struggle with, work through and overcome conscious and unconscious conflicts, present and past experiences and personal and family issues. Failure to address these factors will result in their continuously adverse effect.

Behavior Therapy is necessary and therapeutic, but it must work in a holistic manner, taking into account all factors affecting the person.

CHEMICAL DEPENDENCY PROGRAMS

The Alcoholics Anonymous (AA), Narcotics Anonymous (NA) and Cocaine Anonymous (CA) Twelve-Step philosophy has effectively helped to treat the chemically dependent person. In many cases, it has been the primary or sole helping factor in treating this person. However, this program when used alone primarily modifies only physical behavior, stopping alcohol or drug abuse and providing support in the process. The psychological problems and conflicts that caused or strongly contributed to the chemical dependency or addiction often remain. The person frequently becomes a "dry alcoholic or drug abuser," still behaving in similar ways to the practicing alcoholic or drug abuser, exhibiting such tendencies as denial, manipulation, blaming, not taking responsibility for his or her behavior, rationalizing and excuse making, having difficulty relating intimately with others and not being capable of living up to one's potential, though no longer abusing alcohol or drugs.

Even when AA, CA or NA is combined with a traditional comprehensive chemical dependency treatment program, the individual, group and family psychotherapy component is often superficial, not focusing sufficiently and effectively on the causative factors, including past experiences, upbringing and the impact of the family. Even when more intensive therapy focusing on the patient's upbringing and past experiences is utilized, it often isn't used until many months after he or she stopped using chemicals, when in a number of cases it can be used significantly sooner after a sufficient detoxification program. Integrating AA, CA or NA with programs and methods that assist the person to face, work through, overcome and rebuild oneself from the impact of present and past conflicts on current behavior and functioning, along with family therapy, is essential for a relatively complete and healthy recovery. However, the therapy must be powerful enough to accomplish this result.

EATING DISORDER PROGRAMS

Eating disorder programs too often have been programs primarily of symptom control and superficial psychotherapeutic methods rather than intensively facing the causes of these life- threatening problems, which so frequently lie in the person's family, upbringing, past conflicts and negative experiences, in addition to present issues. The person suffering from an eating disorder has frequently been regarded as fragile and unable to cope effectively with stress, whether it be internal or external. However, such a person, as do many persons, often has a stronger internal nature than appears on the surface. Knowing this and the life and death implications of getting to the causes of the eating disorder problem, as with chemical dependency, the psychotherapist may well be able to assist this patient to face and overcome this problem.

THE FAMILY UNIT

Family therapy modalities that focus primarily on the present communication, interaction and relationship factors in the family and neglect the impact of upbringing and past experiences on the family unit are neglecting an important part of the family member often contributing to family dysfunction. When this aspect isn't dealt with, improving present relationship skills is much more difficult, and frequently when progress is made in this area, it is often sabotaged by the impact of the family member's upbringing and experiences. Family therapy needs to be a comprehensive modality centering on both the present and past, when needed, to assist the family unit to improve its functioning and reach its potential.

THE MANAGED CARE PHENOMENON

What needs to be treated and dealt with in psychotherapy is far apart from what the environment is like for mental health and chemical dependency treatment today. This is due to the adverse revolutionary impact that managed care is having on psychotherapy. The managed care phenomenon has become a powerful force regarding what type of services will be delivered, in what way, how long, who will provide them, where and to whom treatment will be provided.

A managed care company or carrier is an organization or entity which administers and case manages a defined staff or network of health care providers to provide health care services in a cost effective and quality way. According to the American Psychological Association Practice Directorate (1996) this includes a Health Maintenance Organization (HMO), a Preferred Provider Organization (PPO) and even types of Indemnity Insurance coverage that incorporates certification and other type of utilization controls and mechanisms. The mental health provider is increasingly no longer operating as an independent practitioner, but must work within the guidelines and direction of the managed care organization he or she works in or contracts with.

The managed care organization is committed to cost containment while claiming to maintain quality of treatment. However, cost containment is of primary importance at the expense of the quality of treatment. As a result, much pressure has been put on mental health and chemical dependency practitioners to treat patients and families in the shortest period of time for the least amount of money. In addition, managed care carriers are strongly pressuring these practitioners to treat most patients on an outpatient basis, even when a person is severely disabled and formerly would have been treated in an inpatient or a residential program. If reimbursement is made for inpatient or residential programs, it is for a very brief and inadequate period of time.

Practitioners no longer have the luxury of inpatient mental health and chemical dependency treatment settings with large support staffs and diversified programs for the time periods once available, and in increasing numbers they are no longer available. Even though outpatient treatment, predominantly office visits and secondarily partial hospitalization and structured outpatient treatment (i.e., three hours per day three to five days per week), is the arena where most mental health and chemical dependency services are reimbursed by insurance coverage, the reimbursement is for short-term treatment and in many cases is not sufficiently available for the patient's treatment needs. In fact, insurance reimbursement is becoming much less available for mental health and chemical dependency treatment, with the future outlook worsening.

To further compound this issue, treatment now primarily focuses on cognitive-behavioral problem resolution, with the emphasis on teaching persons and the family to more effectively deal with their current stressors and problems, while leaving the underlying dysfunction intact. Although this approach provides for symptom reduction, the underlying psychopathology, in many cases, is likely to eventually overpower whatever progress has been made, with a return or partial return of the original symptoms or other symptoms.

WHERE DO WE GO FROM HERE?

Despite this environment, there is a tremendous need for innovative, breakthrough and effective psychotherapeutic modalities focusing on what works best and most productively and secondarily adjusting to managed care. Hopefully, the decision makers in managed care will adjust their policies to the "what works best method" rather than to profit-making and cost-efficiency policies, which won't save money in the long run owing to less effective treatment. This is why the power, uncovering, reconstructive and breakthrough therapies such as Psychodrama, Hypnodrama, Primal Therapy, Bioenergetic Therapy and now Rebuilding Therapy, which all can effectively treat the causes of problems, need to be looked at as models for the type of treatment that help bring about significant and lasting psychological and personality changes and growth and maximize the human potential. Such therapies require considerably less time and more effectively treat the causes of problems, often the patient's upbringing and past experiences, than talk therapies trying to accomplish similar goals. Besides Psychodrama, Hypnodrama, Primal Therapy, Bioenergetic Therapy and Rebuilding Therapy, the hypnosis-relaxation-age regression therapies have value and are effective, but other than discussed in chapter five are not discussed in other places in this book.

In a number of cases, the length of such therapies may still be compatible with the shorter term managed care guidelines for therapy, with some modifications, although such guidelines are becoming increasingly restrictive. When the length of such therapies is beyond managed care standards, it will be a good investment for the insurance carrier to at least partially reimburse such treatment. The option can be left open for increased reimbursement as it becomes clear that such therapies will reduce health care costs in the long run through less psychological dysfunction, improved parenting and family relations and improved physical health related to improved mental health.

Janov's (1991) Primal Therapy strongly supports the relationship of uncovering reconstructive therapy with improved physical health. In addition, considerable research has been done on supporting the relationship between improved mental health and physical health.

The power and breakthrough therapies also have a responsibility, without giving up their focus, to develop modified methods to fit the short-term managed care guidelines for the significant number of persons and families who will benefit from these modalities. This is not giving in, rather it is an acceptance of the need for innovation and the power of such therapies to get to the core of problems more quickly and effectively in a structured short-term managed care environment. This will require reducing the goals and expectations of therapy, but still working toward substantial psychological growth in a more limited way.

In summary, for significant and lasting psychological, personality and family changes to occur, treatment modalities should address whatever is needed, including assisting a person to rebuild from the damage of past experiences and integrating this into the present, dealing more effectively with present experiences, reducing symptoms and developing improved skills to resolve problems, to relate to others and to live a more productive life. Rebuilding Therapy has the capacity to do this effectively, relatively quickly and cost effectively in a supportive and intensive way, encouraging the strengths of the person and family, while being sensitive to the psychological wounds, problems and needs of each person and family being treated. In doing so, the Rebuilding Therapy therapist regularly evaluates its appropriateness and value for each patient, while respecting the contraindications for its use and those patients who are not ready or cannot be treated by this modality.

CHAPTER 2

What is Rebuilding Therapy? A Working Description

AN INTRODUCTORY DESCRIPTION OF REBUILDING THERAPY

I have been a mental health clinician for about thirty years. Currently I am a licensed psychologist, clinical social worker and marriage, family and child counselor in California and certified as a practitioner in Psychodrama, Sociometry and group psychotherapy. In my work in outpatient and inpatient settings on a full-time basis for more than the past twenty one years, I have developed, and have effectively practiced the psychotherapeutic modality of Rebuilding Therapy. In doing so, I have believed strongly in working with my patients in an uncovering and reconstructive way, when needed, in order to achieve the type of change the human being is capable of. My training in Psychodrama from 1976 through 1980 with the late M. Haskell and my work in Psychodrama are responsible for my pursuit of this direction as a psychotherapist. Psychodrama is what Rebuilding Therapy originated from, has strongly influenced its development and continues to be a significant and living part of it. In further developing the Psychodrama methodology I was using, I integrated Transactional Analysis (TA), primarily Structural Analysis and the influence of Script Analysis into Psychodrama, as I interpreted, refined, modified and developed this part of TA into the rebuilding process. I then also integrated Redecision Therapy, developed from and strongly influenced by TA, into Psychodrama and the rebuilding process. I have also integrated hypnosis or relaxation exercises, referred to as relaxation, and the influence of Bioenergetic Therapy, both as needed, into the rebuilding process to enhance the opening up process. Reparenting is also a developing influence in Rebuilding Therapy. Although relaxation and the influence of Bioenergetic Therapy, as needed, are helpful in the opening up process, with reparenting becoming a growing influence, the basic foundation of Rebuilding Therapy is an integration of Psychodramatic Theory and Therapy, Transactional Analysis, Redecision Therapy and Rebuilding

Theory and Therapy, including methods and approaches I have developed. These influences are discussed in chapters four and five. Though not using Primal Therapy in developing Rebuilding Therapy, it is referred to in chapters four and five as its theoretical framework and emphasis on reliving past experiences are similar and supportive to Rebuilding Therapy's focus and treatment to a certain extent. The modifications and additions I have made to existing theory and methodology are intended to strengthen the rebuilding process.

Rebuilding Therapy is conducted on an individual, group, individual family and multiple family group therapy basis with children, usually nine and older, adolescents and adults, though it has been used primarily with adults and adolescents. Although Rebuilding Therapy has been utilized with adults in the majority of the cases, with the involvement of their families as needed, it has also been used with a substantial number of adolescents and their families. Regarding children, although Rebuilding Therapy has been used infrequently with children and their families, it has much potential to serve this population in a more extensive way. Rebuilding Therapy has been used on an individual, individual family therapy and group therapy basis in outpatient and inpatient settings. Inpatient settings also include working with partial hospitalization patients. While Rebuilding Therapy has been used on a multiple family group therapy basis in inpatient settings it certainly can be used on a multiple family group therapy basis in outpatient settings. Rebuilding Therapy has been used effectively with a wide range of diagnostic categories and problems, including depression, anxiety and panic disorders, adjustment reactions, psychosomatic problems, dissociative disorders, personality disorders, post-traumatic stress reactions, eating disorders, chemical dependency, behavioral problems, law violating behavior, sexual dysfunction and addiction, workaholism, other addictions, family and relationship problems and other types of psychological problems. It also has application and much potential with the schizophrenic, psychotic and mildly neurologically impaired populations, although Rebuilding Therapy has been used on a very limited basis with these populations in a modified way. (See the last section of this chapter regarding the overall uses of Rebuilding Therapy.)

All the examples in this book are taken from individual therapy, group therapy, individual family therapy and multiple family group therapy in outpatient and inpatient settings. For the most part the specific setting of these examples wasn't given as these examples are typical of situations in outpatient and inpatient settings. Only in the examples of the suicide, crime and arrest methods and multiple family group therapy was the setting an inpatient one. This is because I have used the arrest, crime and suicide methods more frequently on an inpatient basis and because I have up to this time used multiple family group therapy on an inpatient basis, with the inpatient individual family therapy session in the second example in chapter sixteen being a follow-up session to the multiple family group therapy session in the first example in chapter sixteen. The names and identity of the patients in each example in this book have been changed, while the related specific circumstances and factors in these examples have been changed enough to fully protect the confidentiality of these patients. While confidentiality has been fully protected, the authenticity and accuracy of the issues, dynamics, problems, themes and outcome in each case in the examples in this book have been maintained. The examples are condensed excerpts from sessions to provide a description of the methods and approaches utilized.

Rebuilding Therapy is conducted on a short-term to long-term basis depending on such factors as the needs, problems, psychological functioning, background, motivation and the resources of the patient or family (see chapter seventeen). Rebuilding Therapy has been developed to help the individual and family to heal from the emotional and psychological wounds created by unhealthy upbringing, family dysfunction, mistreatment, any type of abuse, dysfunctional interaction, past and present experiences, other environmental factors or physical dysfunction without neurological impairment or with mild neurological impairment. Rebuilding Therapy is based on the belief that the human being, for the most part, is good and has the ability to love, interact, empathize, create, heal and rebuild. However, the human's natural ability to develop and actualize his or her psychological and social capabilities is damaged or crippled by physical abuse, psychological abuse and rejection, sexual abuse, neglect, negative parenting, family dysfunction, other traumatic events (i.e. a natural disaster, battle trauma, victimization in a crime, an accident, physical injury or illness, the death or loss of a loved one and so on) or other negative life experiences.

Rebuilding Therapy enables the person to rebuild his or her damaged personality; to overcome and grow from present and past experiences; to uncover and cleanse oneself of such contaminating feelings as anger, rage, despair, sadness, guilt, fear and unhealthy thinking; to release psychological pain; to cognitively reprogram and change dysfunctional thinking, negative decisions and belief systems to positive thinking, decisions and belief systems; to change negative life strategies and coping skills to positive life strategies and coping skills and to function more effectively psychologically and socially. Terms such as *rebuilding, overcoming, growing, cleansing, cognitive reprogramming, reprogramming, redecisioning* and related processes are relative entities and significantly powerful change processes related to the person or family and situation. When referring to the term *experience*, Rebuilding Therapy is primarily concerned with a major, key or significant life experience or experiences that vary in degree, though a minor experience or experiences are not ruled out. Though the term *significant other* is regularly referred to, what is discussed pertaining to a significant other in the singular or plural regarding the methodology used can apply to the methodology used with a nonsignificant other person or persons, as needed. In addition when the terms *significant or significantly* are used, though conveying the meaning of these terms, there are no statistical studies to support this which are referred to. With other persons often in the role of significant others, Rebuilding Therapy gives the person an opportunity to clinically relive and overcome abusive, rejecting, neglectful or negative experiences with such parental messages as "I wish you were never born," "You're no good," "The world is a terrible place" or "You can't trust anyone," which have impaired one's functioning and have made it less possible to effectively live up to one's potential. These experiences have caused such feelings as excessive anger, sadness, guilt, fear, anxiety, distrust and despair and dysfunctional thinking, belief systems and life decisions to the point where the person has become emotionally crippled.

The making of decisions is an unconscious process in the early years, usually becoming less of an unconscious process as the person matures, though still significantly an unconscious process regarding personality development. Some of the decisions made due to mistreatment and negative life experiences include "I'm no good," "I'm unlovable," "I won't ever amount to anything," "I'm nothing but a burden," "I never should have been born," "I want to die," "I won't assert myself," "I'll just please," "I must achieve to be liked," "I won't feel," "I must be tough and hard," "I must be in control," "It is okay to take advantage of others to get what I want," "I won't trust," "I don't need anyone," "I'll show them," "I'll get them before they get me," "I must be the best no matter what the price" or "I'll do anything to be loved, even being mistreated." The result is depression, anxiety and stress-related problems, panic disorders, psychosomatic problems, conversion reactions, psychosis, behavioral problems, alcohol and drug abuse, eating disorders, sexual dysfunction, marital and family dysfunction, chemical dependency, acting out behavior, law-violating behavior or violence or other psychological-related problems. Such decisions, often unconscious, are carried out in self-damaging life scenarios that seldom change except for the persons and situations.

By clinically reliving experiences that create these decisions, it is possible after uncovering, expressing and cleansing oneself of contaminating feelings thoughts and emotional pain related to these experiences to reverse or change these decisions to positive healthy decisions. For example, the person can change "I'm bad" to "I'm okay," "I won't trust" to "I will trust," "I won't love" to "I will love," "No one will love me" to "Someone will love me," "I'll get back at you " to "I'll use my energy to help myself," "I will die" to "I will live" or "I must control" to "Others need to have their say also." This process is hard therapeutic work, but certainly worthwhile. Psychodramatic methodology, referred to as Rebuilding Therapy methodology as part of the Rebuilding Therapy process, and hypnosis or relaxation exercises, as needed, are used to stimulate the reliving process.

When the person has the opportunity to relive significant life events, the process of redecisioning and changing major behavior occurs. In doing so, the patient in group or multiple family group therapy has the support and stimulation of the therapist (parental figure) and other group or family members (therapeutic brothers and sisters) and at times, though more often in multiple family therapy, the cotherapist (parental figure) or auxiliary agent (uncle- or aunt-type figures) assisting the therapist; the support and stimulation of the therapist in individual therapy; and the support and stimulation of the therapist and other family members in individual family therapy. This time the patient has his or her therapist or, if in individual family, group or multiple family group therapy, a few to an entourage of persons to accompany him or her when reliving a significant experience and refacing the significant persons who strongly influenced his or he life. After working through a rejecting experience, the patient will have the opportunity, if needed, to practice more effective ways of dealing with specific situations, with closure following, including a discussion of other's related feelings and thoughts in group or multiple family group therapy which can also occur in individual family therapy.

Integration and processing of what occurred in reliving a life event or events are always provided utilizing supportive and educational talk therapy approaches. The patient is encouraged to look at how each situation has affected one's life and current functioning, what progress has been made and other factors. Working on the impact of the past on the patient's functioning, while also working on improving his or her adaptive and coping skills and life in the present is encouraged. The patient's past, including his or her upbringing, is only worked with if needed, but so often this is necessary. Treatment goals, with time periods to achieve them, are an important part of therapy.

THE THERAPY TEAM

The therapy team includes the therapist, the co-therapist and the auxiliary agent, all of who are referred to as therapeutic agents guiding, helping and working with the patient in the therapeutic process. The therapist, being a licensed mental health professional such as a psychologist, psychiatrist, clinical social worker or a marriage, family and child counselor, is the leader or director of the session. The co-therapist, also a licensed mental health professional, assists the therapist, at times works in an equal capacity to the therapist and is able to take over the role of the therapist at any time. The auxiliary agent, usually a therapeutic assistant, intern or paraprofessional, is trained to assist the therapist and co-therapist in the therapeutic process. Assisting in the therapeutic process includes helping in the use of Rebuilding Therapy methods and approaches, acting or living out the role of significant others, as needed, and providing support and therapeutic stimulation.

Although I have had a co-therapist or auxiliary agent assist me many times in group therapy, usually one of these persons at a time, I have also conducted many more group therapy sessions alone or without a co-therapist or auxiliary agent owing to a lack of available therapeutic agents and support persons. When not having or having a co-therapist or auxiliary agent to assist me, I have also many times utilized nontherapeutic agent persons referred to as responsible persons, such as psychiatric nurses and mental health workers, in group therapy and multiple family group therapy sessions to provide supportive assistance and support for the patients and myself. As indicated, there have been many other times when I have functioned alone in group therapy. I have usually had at least one therapeutic agent assisting me in multiple family group therapy, where the size and nature of the group have made it more essential. Of course, it is always preferable to have a therapeutic agent assist the therapist in group therapy and is even more preferable in multiple family therapy. However, up to this point, because I have often had to function alone in group therapy or without another therapeutic agent and even when having a therapeutic agent available being most expert regarding this modality, while regularly functioning alone as a therapist in many individual therapy and individual family therapy sessions, has made it necessary for me to primarily function in the various roles of the patients' significant others and primarily to use the various methods and approaches by myself. When taking on various responsibilities in the same session, I have had to develop the ability to clearly define my roles and responsibilities and not to confuse or overwhelm the patient in the process. This has worked effectively for my patients who have usually responded well when I have, for example, moved from the role of the patient's rejecting significant other to his or her supportive double, as needed, or from the double to the role of the rejecting significant other, as needed. Of course the patient's needs, welfare, what is best for him or her and his or her willingness to take part in the rebuilding process have been of utmost importance. Whenever I have had a therapeutic agent to assist me, I have utilized this person's clinical skills wherever possible.

The significant other roles referred to are usually the major significant others in the patient's life acted or lived out by a therapeutic agent in the large majority of cases. The roles of minor significant others can be portrayed by other group or family members in the group setting, though, as discussed in chapter six, in some cases group members and to a lesser extent family members can live out the major significant other roles. In individual therapy and individual family therapy the minor significant other roles are utilized minimally, with the major roles given the primary focus in any setting.

When the term *therapeutic agent* is used alone, it incorporates the therapist as well as the co-therapist and auxiliary agent as these treatment team members have been utilized in clinical practice, though much less frequently than myself. However, the co-therapist and auxiliary agent can be used in such examples and discussion that are provided in this book depending on their specific training and education. Although there are examples in this book where I as the therapist have had assistance from therapeutic agents, I have been the only therapist and, as indicated, the primary clinician, as needed, utilizing the Rebuilding Therapy methods and approaches and functioning in the roles of the patients' significant others, including in the examples when only the therapeutic agent is referred to. When the terms *therapist* and *therapeutic agent* are used together, whether in the technical discussion or in the examples in the book, the term *therapeutic agent* includes the co-therapist or auxiliary agent. I have often referred to the therapist as the clinician utilizing methods and approaches and functioning in specific roles and ways in the examples that are provided, for it was necessary for myself as the therapist to function in this manner in such situations, as discussed in this section and the examples in this book, while also pointing out the therapist's ability to do so. In some examples, the roles of therapist and co-therapist have been described. (See chapter six for further discussion of the examples in this book.)

As Rebuilding Therapy is further developed and training becomes increasingly available, more therapists will become skilled in it's use and in turn will train others. Of course, training in Psychodrama, which provides the basic training needed to utilize Rebuilding Therapy, along with more specialized training in Rebuilding Therapy, is good preparation for skillful use of this modality. In addition, persons functioning as co-therapists and auxiliary agents as they are trained in Rebuilding Therapy will be able to assume the various therapeutic roles and responsibilities as needed.

I have also used the term *responsible person* to include, in addition to the therapist, co-therapist and auxiliary agent, other adults who are mature, objective and responsible persons and who are understanding and supportive of the Rebuilding Therapy process. Such adults can include nontherapeutic agent clinic, agency, residential facility or hospital staff members providing therapeutic support and supportive assistance for the patient and therapist. Other responsible persons, though not involved in the therapeutic support process as the staff persons just described, can include significant or nonsignificant other persons. These persons are not involved in the session for their own therapy, but are available, as needed, to provide support and supportive assistance such as taking a patient to or from a session, or being available to sit in or attend a session, to talk with the patient on the phone or to spend time with the patient for supportive purposes. Such a responsible person, as described, in addition to providing support and supportive assistance for the patient, therapist and therapeutic agents can also, as needed, be a reputable witness to further reduce the liability risks of the therapist, co-therapist, or auxiliary agent. Of course, therapeutic agents in the same session are witnesses for each other regarding possible litigation or liability risks. The responsible person can be utilized with or without a therapeutic agent in addition to the therapist in a session.

STAGES OF REBUILDING THERAPY

Rebuilding Therapy includes six stages: (1) The Warmup Stage, (2) the Living Out Stage, (3) the Catharsis and Ventilation Stage, (4) the Awareness and Reevaluation Stage, (5) the Practice Stage and (6) the Coming Together Stage. These stages are part of a session when reliving an experience or experiences occurs, with the practice stage being optional as needed. When an experience or experiences are not relived in the living out stage in a session because the patient isn't ready or it isn't the best time therapeutically to do so, what is described in these stages can still have application to a specific patient and session relative to the specific situation.

The Warmup Stage

A major part of the warmup stage was developed from the warmup phase of Psychodrama, as specifically described by Haskell (1975), which encourages the importance of warming up to whatever one is doing. (A discussion of the warmup phase in Psychodrama is provided in chapter five.) The overall warmup process reduces the patient's anxiety and discomfort level, acquaints the patient with other group or family members in group or multiple family group therapy, introduces the patient to the therapy process in a relaxed and comfortable way and prepares and stimulates the patient to move into the living out stage or into other intensive aspects of therapy. Though a number of the warmup methods have been primarily developed for group and multiple family therapy, in many situations they have application to individual therapy and individual family therapy. Other methods such as the double method, the therapeutic chair method and the visualization method utilized in the living out stage and at other times in therapy are also effective warmup methods. Some of these methods or techniques, that will now be described, are utilized as is any method, technique or approach as needed and therapeutic. Haskell described warmup methods 1, 2, 3, 6, 7, 8 and 9 specifically as warmup exercises.

1. An "introductory talk" by the therapist or group leader regarding a specific subject area such as parent-child relationships, rejection, neglect, the death of a loved one, assertion and communication.

2. The self-presentation method in which each group or family member is encouraged to introduce oneself in some comfortable way.

3. A "go around" asking each group or family member what he or she needs to work on such as "my relationship with my mother" or "my relationship with my husband."

4. The double method where the therapist or therapeutic agent sits beside the patient who is opening up in a soliloquy, and as the patient's double, expresses feelings and thoughts the patient may be feeling and thinking (see chapter seven for the double method).

5. The therapeutic chair or visualization method where each patient has an opportunity to perceive some significant person or situation that has had a significant impact on him or her as being in a chair or visualized in front of oneself in some specific way beginning to express significant feelings and thoughts to this person or situation. The situation involves a specific situation and the person or persons and human factors in it affecting the person. The patient may also be encouraged to see an aspect of oneself in the chair or visualized in the center of the room or in some way. (See chapter eight for the therapeutic chair and visualization methods.)

6. The pair or mini-group method where two to three members of the group, if the group is eight or more, gather together for a short time (five to twelve minutes) to discuss a specific problem area they would more likely discuss initially with one or two other persons than with the entire group. This is followed by a sharing with the entire group of at least one or more of the problems the mini-group chooses to share.

7. The subject-discussion method in which each group or family member discusses such subject areas as human behavior, human problems and relationships with others.

8. Poetry warmups which include reading a poem or an excerpt of a poem, short reading warmups which may include short articles and an excerpt from a newspaper column,

and music warmups which may include songs and music that arouse and bring out feelings, emotions, thoughts and inner conflicts.

9. Group exercises with the group as a whole, such as role playing to reduce anxiety, to increase one's comfort and belonging level and to stimulate the bringing out of emotions, feelings, thoughts and inner conflicts. Such exercises can also be adapted to individual and individual family therapy.

10. Hypnosis or relaxation may be used as a warmup, as needed, for the living out stage and the reliving of an experience or experiences and as a warmup in other ways. When this occurs a relaxation exercise will be used with the person's eyes usually closed. As will be discussed, the terms *hypnosis* and *relaxation* or *relaxation exercise* are used interchangeably in Rebuilding Therapy with the terms *relaxation* and *relaxation exercises* regularly used. At one time in group therapy a specific patient or some or all the group members may take part in a relaxation exercise, though only one patient is encouraged to relive an experience at a time. In multiple family therapy and individual family therapy usually one family member takes part in a relaxation exercise at a time. Though not occurring usually, there are a few times when a family member or members in a session may also take part in a relaxation exercise along with the patient who will move into the living out stage. Those other patients or family member or members who take part in a relaxation exercise usually with their eyes closed and who don't move into the living out stage are asked to open their eyes to take part in the session in a supportive role. In such a case this is a good warmup to move into the living out stage at another time or to more openly take part in the session. A person always naturally comes out of a state of relaxation or hypnosis during or before the end of a session. In the large majority of situations only one relaxation exercise is used in a group or multiple family group therapy session as one patient or family member reliving an experience or experiences or working on an issue is usually a good warmup for another patient or family member to do so. When needed a second relaxation exercise may be used in a session if a group or family member, for example, needs this as a warmup to move into the living out stage. This process is less complex in individual therapy where just one relaxation exercise is usually utilized with the patient in a session.

Though hypnosis or relaxation, as needed, is used in Rebuilding Therapy and other therapies in a specific and specialized way to assist the patient in the therapy process to achieve a psychological state that will allow therapy to proceed in an optimal way, it is not a magical or unnatural state. In fact as a state of heightened and focused concentration, where a person's mind is working in a highly effective way, it is a state patients may move into in varying degrees in psychotherapy when hypnosis or relaxation is not described as part of the process and when persons outside of psychotherapy tend to their tasks, responsibilities, activities and specific ways of living. And, as indicated, as persons move naturally into a state of hypnosis or relaxation they naturally move out of it. For the purposes of this book the terms relaxation and state of relaxation are used when a relaxation exercise is used to assist a patient to move into a state of relaxation or hypnosis, which when used, as needed, is helpful to the therapy process. In addition the relaxation or hypnosis process as needed is also part of the reliving stage and in some cases the practice stage. (See the section on hypnosis or relaxation later in this chapter and chapter five.)

The warmup exercises when used primarily in group therapy and multiple family group therapy, are used more frequently in the initial and beginning phase of therapy (first to third session), unless needed afterwards. Usually by the third or fourth session the warmup will involve group or family members briefly discussing what issues or problems they need to work on after, if needed, a brief initial discussion by the therapist. This will be followed by the selection of a patient, family member or family to work on a specific issue. When a family is selected a specific family member, usually after some interaction by the family members, may live out a specific experience or experiences related to the current family problems or the family may continue to work on present family issues without a family member reliving a past experience or experiences. The warmup comfortably leads to the living out stage, in which the patient or family member will begin to work on a major issue or conflict such as his or her negative relationship with one's mother. The choice and extent of the exercises used in the warmup phase depends on the needs of the therapeutic situation and is up to the therapist's discretion.

This warmup in individual therapy initially involves talk approaches where the patient discusses and talks about his or her present and past life situation. In the process the patient talks about and discusses his or her problems, feelings and thoughts. As the patient continues to open up other methods are introduced, as needed. For example, as the patient in a soliloquy further opens up, the therapist or therapeutic agent doubles with the patient, expressing feelings and thoughts the patient is or may be feeling and thinking to enhance the opening up process. The therapist may also encourage the patient to role reverse and become a significant other who has had a significant impact on the patient's life, in order to increase understanding of this person and his or her impact on the patient (see chapter seven for the role reversal method). Other methods such as the mirror method, playing back to the patient how he or she looks in the "eyes" of another person or others or the therapeutic chair or visualization methods can be utilized, as needed. These and other methods and approaches such as the poetry, reading or music warmups and other methods described in the book, at the therapist's discretion, can assist the patient to warm up to the living out stage.

There are patients who will resist or won't give themselves the opportunity to reach the living out stage. At the time, as such patients are often not ready to relive past experiences, the therapist needs to be very sensitive to this and treat the patient in a manner compatible with his or her needs. In such cases, traditional talk therapy while integrating such methods as described in this section and throughout the book, as needed, can still contribute to an effective therapeutic experience.

In individual family therapy the interaction of family members regarding present issues with the assistance, as needed, of the methods and approaches discussed in this section and in the book, at the therapist's discretion, is the warmup process for the living out stage, as needed for specific family members. This process usually takes a specific number of sessions usually ranging from three to four and in some cases at least six sessions before a specific family member is ready for the living out stage. (See chapter sixteen for the warmup stage in multiple family therapy that has application to individual family therapy.)

Though the living out stage is used less frequently in family therapy owing to the family's current needs, it is still a significant part of the family therapy process, as related to specific family issues when needed and as family members are ready to take part in the living out process. In those cases when a family is resistant or is not ready for the living out process, family interaction is encouraged along with utilizing specific methods and approaches described in this section and book, as needed, to effectively contribute to family growth and progress.

The Living Out Stage

The living out stage was taken and developed from the action phase of Psychodrama (see chapter five). The term *living out* is used because it accurately describes what occurs when a patient relives a specific experience and reexperiences a significant other or others' impact on oneself or when reliving an event that does not involve a significant other or others. Living out also accurately describes another person, such as a therapeutic agent, acting out, portraying or simulating the role of a significant other or another individual in the patient's life. As indicated when the term *significant other* is used, what is discussed about a significant other regarding the methodology used can apply to the methodology used when a patient needs to address a nonsignificant other in therapy. This stage is the essence of Psychodrama, which involves stimulating the patient to relive and reexperience major life events and experiences that have significantly affected the patient's functioning with another person or persons in the role of a significant other or others in these experiences, as the patient is ready and is needed and possible, in order to face and resolve conflicts arising out of these experiences. In the process, one's dysfunctional defenses have begun to weaken to allow the reliving experience to proceed. The reliving process enables the patient to face and heal from experiences and situations that strongly contributed to unresolved feelings and conflicts, emotional pain, unmet needs, dysfunctional thinking, decisions, beliefs and life strategies and the symptomatology and dysfunction that resulted. In doing so, the patient will reexperience his or her feelings, thoughts, dysfunctional decisions, emotional pain, unmet needs and conflicts associated with the relived experiences, a considerable amount of which have been partially or fully repressed, making this a significant uncovering process. It is also not unusual or uncommon for the patient to actually reexperience the physical pain of the relived experience.

Although one experience can strongly contribute to a dysfunctional decision, more than one experience usually creates or causes a dysfunctional decision. Even when a traumatic experience such as molestation or rape strongly contributes to unhealthy thinking and an unhealthy decision about life, usually this experience being repeated one or more times and other experiences contribute to this unhealthy thinking and decision. However, there are some situations, though much less so, when a traumatic experience such as molestation or rape can be the primary contributor to unhealthy thinking and a related decision without other experiences contributing significantly. Even if different experiences contribute to an unhealthy decision, they are still similar in that they are all rejecting or negative experiences with rejecting or negative messages. The number of different experiences, which include the messages from them, and the frequency of occurrence of these experiences contributing to a decision, primarily depends on such factors as the strength of the experience and decision and the environment lived in, although this is a complex process with individual variations. In addition, one experience usually contributes to more than one decision. Of course, a patient can clinically relive only one experience at a time, though living out more than one experience in a single session is common. As one major or key experience frequently represents some or a number of experiences like it or similar to it, it often is only necessary to relive major experiences representing other similar experiences, while, though occurring much less frequently, it is also necessary to relive singular major experiences that don't represent other similar experiences, which also have adversely affected the patient. In doing so, it may often be necessary to relive such experiences more than once, fully, partially or in another way than one did previously to effectively overcome them and for effective redecisioning. At times it may be necessary to relive a minor experience to warm up to the major experience. Usually a patient needs to relive a number of major experiences, which is the primary focus of the reliving and redecisioning process. The specific major experiences a patient relives depend on the patient and his or her life situation, with the motivated patient often allowing him or herself to experience what is needed. (See the redecisioning section in chapter five and the reliving process in chapter fourteen.)

When facing issues regarding one's upbringing, which usually involves issues of dysfunction, rejection and mistreatment, clinically reliving an experience involves reliving an experience with one's feelings and thoughts from that experience in the present tense again as it happened or is recalled, which is usually accurate, from the prenatal period, usually from about six months from conception and older in the womb, through adolescence. When reliving an experience from the prenatal period through the birth process and early childhood, the possibility of the patient believing what occurred, which usually relates to a specific event or situation or represents what actually happened or is symbolic of what occurred, is another possibility to directly recalling an experience, though it is also possible in this situation for there to be a combination of direct recall and the belief that an event occurred. Even when one relives a belief of what occurred, the reliving of this belief often stimulates the patient to connect in some way to the experience or situation the belief relates to or represents. When connecting to such an experience or situation, the patient is in the arena of what contributed to his or her dysfunction which can be very helpful to the rebuilding process as one relives this experience or situation. Reliving an experience involves reliving a major part or a significant portion of it in the therapeutic time available. The reliving work I have done with patients has only been with nonpsychotic patients, though in a few cases, with former psychotic patients who were able to effectively go through the reliving process. However, regarding actively psychotic patients, I believe that their delusional experiences and hallucinations are often likely representative or symbolic in some way of real life events or situations that did occur in their life. Although this is not the focus of this book, it is a discussion that can later be addressed regarding the use of Rebuilding Therapy with the schizophrenic or psychotic patient.

Reliving an experience is not reliving an experience totally as a child or adolescent again. Whereas the adult as a child or adolescent experienced this situation totally alone as a child or adolescent, the reliving process for the adult referred to here, without interfering with it, involves reliving an experience with the assistance of the patient's present mature self (Adult Nurturing Self for the adult) comprised of current rational, objective and reality oriented adult thinking (healthy Adult), nurturing self-parenting (healthy Parent) skills and other developed parts of the self (healthy Child) such as intuitiveness, creativity, inquisitiveness, spontaneity and the ability to feel and relate to the relived experience in a healthy way. In the process the present mature self or Adult Nurturing Self assists the person in the reliving process to interpret and make sense of what happened in the past and to change unhealthy decisions to healthy decisions. The person's adult thinking (healthy Adult) controls the present mature self's part in this process with its mature and healthy reasoning and being reality oriented, and in doing so the healthy Adult, often referred to as the Adult in this context, represents the present mature self (Adult Nurturing Self). In representing the Adult Nurturing Self, the Adult speaks for and as the person when reliving an experience without interfering, as the entire Adult Nurturing Self doesn't interfere, with what the person is reliving and is feeling and thinking while reliving this experience. When speaking as a child or adolescent again as an experience is relived, the healthy Adult with the healthy Parent and Child in the Adult Nurturing Self joins and is with the person again as a wounded child or adolescent (wounded Child). In the process while reliving an experience, the person is in one's self again as a child or adolescent and in one's wounded Child with the present mature self's (Adult Nurturing Self) help in assisting the rebuilding process. When the Adult is specifically referred to regarding its mature reasoning and reality oriented thinking in the reliving process, the healthy Parent and Child are also assisting in this process, as needed. The assistance that the current mature self gives to the reliving process depends on current development and dysfunction. For the child and adolescent the present or developing mature self's (Developing Nurturing Self) part in the process includes his or her developing mature thinking (Developing Adult), the developing healthy self-parenting (healthy Parent) skills and the developing healthy parts of the Child (healthy Child). The term *Developing Adult* is used for the child and adolescent to refer to the healthy and mature Adult that is developing with it's maturing thinking and functioning. Of course, one's psychological capabilities continue to grow throughout adulthood for the growing adult. The reliving stage also refers to an adult reliving a past rejecting, unhealthy, negative or traumatic experience at a younger age as an adult, when the person in varying degrees was often in a child-like or regressed state, with similar dynamics in operation. In summary, the present mature self joins the self in the past to help the patient repair and rebuild from the experience, without impairing his or her ability to relive the experience in an authentic and accurate way with the feelings, thoughts and pain of this experience. The reliving stage also includes reliving present stressful experiences with the most current mature self assisting in this process. (See chapter four for TA's Parent, Child and Adult ego states referred to as the Parent, Adult and Child and chapter eight for the joining the child with one's self method.)

An important part of reliving an experience also includes the therapist, co-therapist or auxiliary agent and others in attendance, with their present mature self and strengths, going back with and joining the patient to relive an experience providing stimulation, guidance and support to assist in this process without impairing the effective reliving of the experience.

As one patient relives an experience in group therapy, multiple family group therapy or individual family therapy, other group or family members may be warmed up and stimulated to relive their own experiences as this can be a therapeutically contagious process. Sometimes in group or multiple family therapy, this can be a chain-reaction type process. Though this can be therapeutic, the therapist needs to take control of this process to ensure where possible only one patient relives an experience at a time, while the other patient or patients ready for the reliving process are still receiving therapeutic support and stimulation. Such a patient or patients can be encouraged to double with the working patient or to assume the role of a significant other of the working patient until it is time for one of these patients to be the primary patient reliving an experience, if possible. When it is not possible for such a patient or patients to engage in the reliving process in a session, then he or she at least has been prepared to do so in the next or another session. If more than one patient relives an experience where the focus of the session cannot be directed to just one patient, which in the large majority of situations doesn't occur, then the therapist and therapeutic agent, if available, will do what is needed to therapeutically control the situation while assisting the patients in the process. This is a very powerful process that can be very therapeutic, but must be done in a carefully controlled and structured way. The physical and emotional well-being of the patient will always be protected in the reliving of an experience, as when using any therapeutic procedure.

Rebuilding Therapy methods and approaches that are taken from Psychodrama and, in a number of cases, further developed and originally developed by myself, are used in stimulating the accurate and authentic reliving of an experience and opening up of related feelings, thoughts and psychological pain and in the rebuilding and problem resolution process. The psychodramatic methods discussed are referred to as Rebuilding Therapy methods as they are used in the Rebuilding Therapy process. I in no way take credit for the development of these psychodramatic methods, although I have developed modifications of a number of these methods and have developed a number of new methods as indicated. The new methods have been strongly influenced by Psychodrama and are psychodramatic in nature. Some of the primary psychodramatic methods used as Rebuilding Therapy methods include the double where another person, such as a therapeutic agent, therapist or group member, acts as or "becomes" the patient expressing feelings and thoughts that the patient may feel or think, stimulating the patient's more open expression of feelings and thoughts; role reversal where the patient becomes or puts oneself in the place of a significant other (i.e., mother, father, etc.) in his or her life to increase empathy and understanding of this person's feelings, thoughts and behavior, to better understand and connect to the impact of this significant other on oneself, to experience how one looks in the mind of this significant other and to give the person acting or living out the role of this significant person a more accurate picture of how this person was or has been; and the mirror where another person, such as a therapeutic agent, therapist, group member or family member, acts or lives out a dysfunctional aspect of the patient's attitude and behavior as a "video replay" to demonstrate how one's attitude and behavior is causing problems and stresses in one's life and for others.

The therapeutic agent or therapist in the large majority of situations is utilized to act and live out the roles of significant others (i.e. parent, grandparent, sibling, spouse, etc.) in order to maximize the accurate and authentic reliving of these roles, which will stimulate greater recall of experiences, the more open expression of feelings and thoughts regarding the significant other and related issues and the further recall of related past experiences when reliving a specific experience. At times, though less frequently, another group member may live out the role of a significant other, or in less frequent situations than this, a family member may live out the role of a significant other, only after careful assessment, if in either situation it is beneficial to the patient and others in the session. The family member, of course, is a different person than the significant other the patient is addressing. The therapist in individual therapy and for the most part in individual family therapy needs to live out the roles of significant others as needed. As a result this needs to be taken into account when describing the living out stage or reliving process. At times a patient may not be ready to have a significant other lived out by another person. In such cases the patient can visualize the significant other in some way in an empty chair or visualize the significant other in some way using the visualization method or when being in a state of hypnosis or relaxation without the significant other portrayed by another person in any of these cases. The patient in such cases can address the significant other directly or think out loud in a soliloquy. Rebuilding Therapy methods and approaches can skillfully and creatively be applied in individual therapy, individual family therapy, group therapy and multiple family group therapy to assist the patient to make what progress he or she is capable of.

The Catharsis and Ventilation Stage

The third stage, an extension of the second stage and part of it, involves the experiencing, expression, ventilation and working through of rage, anger, sadness, guilt, despair and other feelings and dysfunctional thoughts associated with the patient's negative experiences. When discussing the expression of anger and sadness in this book, the expression of other feelings is also included as this has occurred. This stage allows the patient to begin cleansing him or herself of feelings, thoughts, conflicts and psychological pain that have contaminated one's thinking and perception. In doing so, the patient is assisted to begin becoming more aware of the impact of these feelings, thoughts and conflicts on him or herself and one's functioning. This process can also acquaint the person with positive feelings and thoughts, though the negative and unhealthy feelings, thoughts and thinking need to be faced, expressed and worked through before this usually occurs.

The Awareness and Reevaluation Stage

The second, third and fourth stages overlap, with the fourth stage also being a natural extension of the second and third stages and part of these stages. This stage involves the experiencing, acceptance and acknowledgment of unhealthy feelings, thoughts, emotional pain, conflicts, decisions, beliefs and unfulfilled or partially fulfilled needs resulting from past experiences. This occurs as the patient in the third stage, continuing to experience a weakening of his or her dysfunctional defenses, has begun the process of decontaminating and cleansing oneself of rage, anger, grief, despair, guilt and other feelings, unhealthy thinking and emotional pain which have blocked off and contaminated one's thinking, insight, awareness, beliefs and decisions related to one's past experiences. As a result the thinking and cognitive aspect of the individual's mind becomes less contaminated by unhealthy feelings and thinking, emotional pain and defenses. The patient then becomes in touch with and is able to experience and feel the impact of his or her negative decisions, beliefs and thinking on oneself and one's life. At this time, the patient can give up, let go of and change his or her dysfunctional thinking and decisions to healthy thinking and decisions and fulfilling life strategies, with stages two and three needed for this to occur after the warmup stage. In the process, the patient, by also becoming aware of and experiencing his or her unmet or only partially met needs, becomes aware of and experiences what he or she missed out on, had a right to have and has a right to have in a modified form in the present.

This process does not occur in talk therapy because talking about one's insight and problems is an "armchair" discussion, hypothesizing and philosophizing about feelings, thoughts, conflicts, unhealthy decisions, emotional pain and unmet needs one cannot feel, see or connect to. A person cannot fix or resolve something he or she cannot touch. However, in reliving an experience the patient can work toward fixing and resolving a problem, which this experience contributed to, as the problem and what related to it can be touched and experienced, including one's mistreatment, emotional pain, feelings, thoughts, dysfunctional decisions, unmet or partially fulfilled needs and what he or she had a right to have. In doing so, the patient can release emotional pain, feelings and thoughts and change his or her dysfunctional feelings, thinking, decisions, ways of living and dealing with life in a healthy way. This is why reliving an experience, which contributed to an unhealthy decision and frequently represents similar or rejecting experiences, is necessary for effective redecisioning and changes. This is an ongoing process that often must be worked on a number of times, reliving the same or similar experience again fully or partially or in another way, as indicated, or other experiences that contributed in a major way to a dysfunctional decision. One can't, of course, relive every life experience, but one can relive the major ones that also represent similar experiences. In addition, one experience or type of experience can contribute to more than one decision, as indicated. Significant learning often occurs after a catharsis and the open expression of suppressed and repressed conflicts, emotional pain, feelings and thoughts related to an experience, as one's mind has become increasingly cleansed and decontaminated. Once this occurs, the person's mind is more receptive and open to the information, stimuli and input coming from outside and inside oneself.

The Practice Stage

The fifth stage, taken and developed from Haskell's work, involves practice, role training or active rehearsal, which is the active teaching and practicing of new and more effective ways of relating and dealing with persons and situations in one's life. Haskell discussed and effectively used role training, which he also referred to as role playing. Through active practice, the patient can learn more effective methods and ways to communicate and relate to others and to resolve problem situations. This stage is utilized as needed in a session. Therapists, therapeutic agents, other group members and, less frequently, family members act in the roles of other important persons (i.e., spouse, children, parents, siblings, friends, coworkers, employees, employer), living out the roles of those persons one is practicing to deal with. The double, role reversal, the mirror and other methods are utilized to assist in this process. Active practice also includes the process of mental rehearsal, which enables the patient to actively rehearse in his or her mind how to relate more effectively to other persons, to resolve problem situations and become more confident in specific situations. A person will often learn more effectively by practicing and experiencing what he or she needs to learn and making it part of one's behavioral patterns. This is an effective way to practice carrying out healthy new decisions. Talking about how to function more effectively is, of course, needed to assist in this process.

Active practice can also occur on the patient's own outside of the therapy session. Practicing on one's own can include the patient role playing oneself and another person or persons he or she is practicing to deal with, utilizing family members or friends to live out the role or roles of the person or persons the patient is practicing to deal with or mentally rehearsing dealing with a specific person or persons. As when practicing in a session, the patient is learning on one's own to more effectively relate to other persons and to resolve situations of a problem nature. Taking this a step further, living out in one's life what one has practiced to do will provide the patient ongoing practice and rehearsal for improved functioning as one walks down the path of a more fulfilling and productive life.

Although the examples, in this book, don't focus specifically on stages 5 and 6, they are important aspects of the rebuilding process.

The Coming Together Stage

The coming together stage, taken and developed from the discussion phase of Psychodrama, is the final opportunity to bring the patient down from the intensive, cathartic and open reexperiencing he or she has just gone through. The "coming down" process usually starts in the awareness and reevaluation stage as the patient is in the process of changing his or her thinking and a major life decision or decisions to healthy thinking and a healthy life changing decision or decisions and then continuing in the practice stage as needed. This stage encourages the group or family members, including the therapist and therapeutic agent, if assisting, to share in discussing experiences, problems, feelings and thoughts that relate to those experiences and problems worked on by a specific patient or family member or patients or family members during the session. As this occurs, the group or family members are stimulated to come together and relate with each other and their major life issues with support, encouragement and companionship. The discussion stage provides warmth and support for the patient who has just actively worked on oneself, to other group or family members, creating a sense of belonging and support as they prepare to deal with their unresolved problems, and to those group or family members who feel isolated or fearful to address their problems. The therapist can provide the type of closure needed for the patient and family in individual and individual family therapy, respectively. It can also be a creative stage in which the therapist utilizes his or her creativity and spontaneity, as can also be used in other stages, to assist in bringing closure to the session and preparing for future therapeutic work. (See chapter five for a discussion of this stage.)

REBUILDING FAMILY THERAPY

Another important aspect of Rebuilding Therapy is working with the family, as needed, which is often the case. The family and family members worked with usually include the married or unmarried couple with or without children, other immediate or involved family members (parents, siblings, etc.) and important nonblood persons involved with the patient. Family therapy originates as an extension of the patient's problems and treatment or with the family as the initial presenting problem. Rebuilding Family Therapy is conducted on an individual family therapy and multiple family group therapy basis. When the patient is the initial person involved in therapy, then the family members taking part in therapy are significant others the patient is actually involved with from the above family-type unit, with the patient being a significant other to the other family members. Of course, when the family is the initial presenting problem all family members taking part in this process are all significant others to each other. The term *significant other* refers to any family member or close nonblood relationship. All participants in family therapy are considered patients, though usually referred to as family members besides the initially designated patient and when the family is the initially designated problem.

When the individual adult patient makes progress, the involved family members need to make significant changes, as needed, or the patient will be pressured to regress to former dysfunctional patterns in order to adjust to his or her dysfunctional family unit, or, when possible, the patient may need to terminate, reduce or change one's involvement with those dysfunctional family members refusing to change in order to maintain his or her progress. This, of course, does not include terminating relationships with minor children or abandoning specific responsibilities. The involvement of the family or family members in the therapy process, as needed, will usually increase the adult patient's progress. Unfortunately, children and adolescents are usually at the mercy of their family dysfunction, with some young adults being victims of this, and usually won't make progress unless their family or at least one parent or significant parent figure does, though there are some exceptions as in any case. In addition, when the family is making progress, the patient is often making progress. As a result, Rebuilding Therapy encourages the rebuilding of the entire family system and the family members in the patient's life. In doing so, it encourages each involved family member, as needed and possible, to rebuild aspects of his or herself by overcoming negative experiences that have contributed to one's dysfunction and in doing so, improving his or her functioning individually and in the family unit. This process improves the prognosis and the likelihood of more significant progress by the designated patient or other family members. Optimally, such change by family members should be mandated, but practically it can only be encouraged. Unfortunately, not infrequently even involved family members resist helping themselves. Each family member, where possible, needs to make constructive changes to increase the likelihood of rebuilding the family system in an effective way or at least acknowledging and beginning to work on his or her issues and problems and improving his or her interaction in the family unit to some degree. For those who don't it will be difficult for them to interact in the family in a healthy way.

At times, though not necessary and not occurring as much as it should, it is also helpful to bring in the adult patient's parents and siblings (family of origin) into the family therapy process, even on a limited basis, in order to increase insight and understanding which can be helpful in the patient's own rebuilding process and improving relationships with his or her family of origin members as a by-product. In some cases, such family members may already be involved in the family therapy process, especially if the patient is relating to them in a significant way, which often involves a certain degree of dysfunction.

With children and adolescent patients it is always essential, when possible, to involve at least the parental figures, while this is needed at times with young adult patients, for the family unit in these cases is where the problems are created and further influenced and reinforced.

Though the rationale for the Rebuilding Family Therapy process described up to this point involves family therapy in an adjunctive role, it is a powerful process in its own right and can be used as the primary treatment modality with the support of individual and group therapy for specific family members as needed. In the process, due to the various factors involved in Rebuilding Family Therapy, the boundaries are sometimes blurred regarding whether the family therapy process is an adjunct or primary treatment modality. Nevertheless, what is most important is for family members to improve their individual functioning family interaction and relationships, which the Rebuilding Family Therapy process can effectively contribute to.

Rebuilding Family Therapy has two major phases. The first phase involves rebuilding from past rejecting and negative experiences through the reliving process, for before a family member can understand, communicate, empathize and relate to other family members as effectively, as he or she is capable of, one must be able to relate to oneself, understand oneself and be in the process of resolving his or her own internal issues and conflicts. This can occur in individual family and multiple family therapy as related to a specific family therapy issue, or as needed in individual and group therapy. The second phase involves stimulating and teaching family members through methods such as doubling, mirroring, role reversal and active practice or role training, in addition to talk family therapy approaches, to communicate, empathize and relate to each other in more intimate, open and emotionally healthy ways. Those family members who don't take part in or resist engaging in the first phase, as needed, have much more difficulty engaging in the second phase.

Though these two phases appear clear-cut on the surface, it is a complex process. As the first phase is a very helpful prerequisite for the second phase and is considered the first phase for this reason, the family therapy process requires considerable focus on present dynamics, communication and interactional factors to at least assist the family to begin functioning in a healthier way. As a result the reliving process, though utilized and of significant importance in the family therapy session, as it relates to specific family issues, is utilized less frequently than in individual and group therapy. This is why it is often necessary for specific family members to also take part in individual therapy or group therapy to substantially improve their functioning in the family unit. As this occurs, Rebuilding Family Therapy not only encompasses the process of the individual family therapy and multiple family group sessions, but also the involvement of specific family members in individual or group therapy to improve their individual functioning and then their functioning in the family unit. As such, it looks beyond the family therapy session and takes a holistic approach to the family therapy process, taking into account whatever factors will improve the family unit. In doing so this increases the likelihood of a successful and lasting treatment outcome. (See chapter sixteen for a discussion of Rebuilding Family Therapy.)

TRANSACTIONAL ANALYSIS

Transactional Analysis, (TA), primarily Structural Analysis and the influence of Script Analysis, as it has been interpreted, refined, modified and developed, has been incorporated into the rebuilding process. Rebuilding Therapy has also relied on Redecision Therapy, developed from TA, in further developing its focus on redecisioning and changing unhealthy decisions to healthy decisions. (See chapter four for a discussion of TA and chapter five for a discussion of Redecision Therapy.)

In addition, Rebuilding Therapy has incorporated the reparenting school of Transactional Analysis into it in a limited and developing way. Reparenting is the process of parenting the patient again, partially or completely. This process is carried out by the therapist, therapeutic agent or the patient to provide the type of parenting one has not received and needs in some partial and specific way. (See chapters five and thirteen for a discussion of the reparenting method.)

Rebuilding Therapy doesn't focus on the TA language and method as the traditional TA therapist, but integrates it into the therapy process for the therapist's understanding, while incorporating it into its work with patients as needed on a limited basis. The dialogue in the examples in this book, except in the joining the child with one's self and reparenting methods on a limited basis, doesn't describe this limited use of TA with patients. The focus of TA in Rebuilding Therapy is on the structural and intrapsychic workings of the human mind and the impact of parental and other influences on psychological functioning.

Again, any refinement, modification and development of any existing theory and methods has been done to improve the rebuilding process.

ANOTHER UNCOVERING MODALITY: HYPNOSIS OR RELAXATION

Other uncovering methods such as hypnosis or relaxation or relaxation exercises are also utilized, with the patient's approval as with any method or approach, when therapeutically needed and the patient is ready to assist in the uncovering process. I use the terms *hypnosis* and *relaxation* interchangeably, but regularly use the term *relaxation*. I also regularly use the terms *relaxation* and *relaxation exercise* interchangeably. The induction or relaxation exercise utilized to achieve a state of hypnosis or relaxation can be left to the discretion of the therapist. When psychodramatic methods are used while a patient is in hypnosis or relaxation, the modality is referth psychodramatic or Rebuilding Therapy methods and in the reliving process, the term Hypnodrama is not commonly used in the Rebuilding

Therapy process. Hypnosis or relaxation has been primarily used with adult patients, though it has been used with some adolescent patients.

The role of hypnosis or relaxation in relaxing the patient in a way where the patient's defenses, impairing his or her perception and repressing his or her underlying memories, conflicts, feelings, thoughts, decisions and pain, are weakened and the patient's concentration powers are maximized is often very helpful in the reliving, redecisioning and rebuilding process. Hypnosis or relaxation assists the patient to bring specific unconscious memories and experiences, partially or relatively in whole, into one's consciousness or for one's conscious mind to join these unconscious memories and experiences to relive, reexperience, work through and to heal from. As such, a major role of hypnosis or relaxation, as needed, is as a warmup and stimulus to assist in the uncovering and reliving process with the receptive person.

A relaxation exercise to induct a patient into a state of hypnosis or relaxation is usually done with the patient's eyes closed, with the therapist guiding the entire therapeutic process. The therapist usually asks the patient to give a signal, such as a finger signal, or some type of indication he or she is beginning to relive an experience. The patient's eyes will still usually be closed when he or she begins to relive an experience, with the patient at the supportive request of the therapist, opening his or her eyes at the time when he or she is ready and first viewing a significant other or others, portrayed by another person or persons, makes a major impact on the patient. In essence, when reliving an experience, a patient will usually continue to keep his or her eyes closed if a period of time needs to pass until it is therapeutic, the best time and the patient is ready to begin viewing a significant other or others portrayed by another person or persons. Though more than one significant other may be portrayed, usually more frequently in a group session as other persons are available to portray these persons, in most cases there will be one major significant other such as a mother or father who will be the primary focus of the patient's attention. When a patient opens his or her eyes in this situation, he or she will continue to be in a state of relaxation or hypnosis usually until after the therapeutic work is completed or a significant amount of therapeutic work has been completed in a session, with the Rebuilding Therapy process, after the patient opens his or her eyes, continuing to assist and stimulate the patient to face and resolve his or her issues. The patient will usually open his or her eyes during the reliving of the first experience in group therapy, which could be, though it may not be, the only experience the patient relives in the session. When a relaxation exercise is used, a patient in a group therapy session will usually open his or her eyes sooner than in an individual therapy session as there are more stimuli in a group session, including another person or persons besides the therapist to act out the role or roles of a significant other or others and to assist in other ways, to effectively stimulate the patient without adversely affecting his or her concentration or taking the patient out of a state of relaxation. A patient who is not ready at any time in a session to view a significant other or others portrayed by another person or persons is usually not ready for a Rebuilding Therapy group session. When a patient is asked to open his or her eyes when a relaxation exercise is used, there will always be sufficient and significant time in the session for the patient to effectively interact with a significant other or others portrayed by another person or persons. A patient will usually keep his or her eyes open, once doing so, although there may be some times when a patient needs to close his or her eyes again to deepen his or her state of relaxation to engage in the reliving process more effectively. A therapist by him or herself in an individual session is more limited regarding the stimuli the patient can be provided, needing to rely more on the patient's internal way of stimulating oneself to relive a situation, though the therapist alone still has significant ability to stimulate the patient in an effective way, as is often needed. As a result it is not uncommon in individual therapy for a patient to keep his or her eyes closed in a state of relaxation for the entire reliving process, though it is also common in individual therapy for a patient to open his or her eyes while still in a state of relaxation to continue the reliving process. When a patient opens his or her eyes in individual therapy to continue the reliving process, he or she may have relived one or two experiences or a portion of these experiences. It is best for the patient to keep his or her eyes closed in a state of relaxation for the time period the therapeutic work occurs in individual therapy if he or she isn't ready to view a significant other or others portrayed by another person or persons or if it is therapeutic in this case. Though occurring much less frequently, in specific cases such as reliving a prenatal or birth experience, it is beneficial for the patient to keep his or her eyes closed in a state of relaxation throughout the reliving process whether in group or individual therapy, although, for example, when a patient is living out being delivered into the world either while reliving a birth experience or living out a healthy rebirth, he or she may or may not open one's eyes depending on the situation. When a patient has his or her eyes closed usually in a state of relaxation reliving an experience or situation, a significant other or others will be acted out in an audible way by another person or persons or the patient will just reexperience a significant other or others without the significant other or others portrayed by another person or persons. In such a situation with a patient in a state of relaxation, he or she is stimulated in the large majority of cases by a significant other or others lived out audibly by another person or persons and by specific Rebuilding Therapy methods, as needed; without the stimulation of a significant other or others acted out audibly by another person or persons but by specific Rebuilding Therapy methods as needed; or in the large minority of situations without the stimulation of a significant other or others portrayed audibly by another person or persons and without specific Rebuilding Therapy methods other than the therapist interacting with the patient. When hypnosis or relaxation is used in individual family therapy or in multiple family group therapy to assist in the reliving process, though used less frequently in family therapy, appropriate modifications are made to the process described.

Relaxation or relaxation exercises may or may not be used when the methods and approaches described in this book are used, depending on the specific situation, and when used with a specific method or approach relaxation or a relaxation exercise is utilized in a way to maximize and not inhibit the effectiveness of the method or approach used. Though the use of relaxation is described in the examples in chapters fourteen and fifteen, the therapist can use relaxation as needed. However, when reliving past experiences the combination of a relaxation exercise or relaxation with Rebuilding Therapy methods is often preferred when possible, therapeutic and the patient is ready, as this combination of modalities often stimulates the more effective reliving of past experiences and rebuilding from them, though Psychodrama alone without a relaxation exercise, which I have also used in many cases, is still a strong and effective modality in the reliving of past experiences, and itself often can induce a state of relaxation or hypnosis. When psychodramatic or Rebuilding Therapy methodology is used without hypnosis or relaxation, it is usually utilized with the patient's eyes open, unless used with such a method as the visualization method.

Hypnosis or relaxation is very difficult to use and usually not feasible with the patient who is denying, resisting or sabotaging treatment efforts. Relaxation or hypnosis is also used, as needed, when the patient mentally rehearses in his or her mind ways to problem solve, function more productively and relate to others more effectively. It is also used in the reparenting process, as needed. Whenever hypnosis or relaxation is used, the patient is highly alert and very much in control of him or herself, always capable of rejecting any method, procedure or approach or whatever is objectionable. A patient will always come out of a state of relaxation or hypnosis when the therapeutic work it has assisted the patient to do is done. (See the hypnosis and Hypnodrama sections in chapter five.)

ANGER REDUCTION USING PHYSICAL EXERCISES

Anger reduction methods and approaches using physical exercises, when needed and appropriate as the patient is ready, stimulates the patient with support and safety to express anger at a high level of strength and release. The anger mat release method, described in chapter seven, where the patient hits on a mat with one's hands to release anger is an example of this. These methods stimulate and encourage the more open expression of anger and rage, and often sadness, despair and other feelings, thoughts and conflicts, assisting in freeing one of the contamination that such buried and unresolved feelings, thoughts and conflicts have created. (See chapter seven for the anger mat release method and other anger release exercises.) Bioenergetic theory advocates that as the tension in the muscles and body is reduced and as a person breathes more freely through physical exercise, there is a more open expression and uncovering of underlying feelings, thoughts and conflicts. Though these methods and approaches are powerful anger releases, other Rebuilding Therapy methods and approaches are also effective in stimulating the expression and release of anger.

CONFRONTING RESISTANT AND SABOTAGING BEHAVIOR

Rebuilding Therapy also utilizes methods, using psychodramatic methodology, to confront the patient with the impact of his or her dysfunctional defenses and resistant and sabotaging attitude and behavior which impairs the patient's ability to become aware of, face, work through and overcome his or her problems and to live productively. The goal is to reduce or eliminate such defenses, behavior or attitudes, by acting or living out the impact of these defenses, behavior or attitudes on one's life and others. The patient can reject the use of these methods at any time. An example of these methods is the denial method where the patient is confronted with one's denial of his or her feelings, thoughts, behavior or past experiences. When using the denial method, the therapeutic agent or therapist becomes the patient's denial, acting or living out how the patient's denial is adversely affecting oneself or others or where the patient acts or lives out his or her denial to experience its impact on oneself and others. The denial and hostility methods are a form of the mirror method, but are geared to a specific problem. Other methods confronting the patient's dysfunctional and sabotaging behavior are the spell and silent night methods. (These methods are described in chapter ten.) Such methods don't solve a person's problems, but encourage the patient at least to begin to face and experience how he or she is adversely impacting oneself and others and to see what he or she needs to begin doing to resolve this problem.

CONFRONTING DANGEROUS AND INAPPROPRIATE BEHAVIOR

Rebuilding Therapy has also developed methods, using psychodramatic methodology, to prevent or reduce the probability of a person behaving in a dangerous or inappropriate way, which includes suicide, homicide, assault, law-violating behavior or other damaging behaviors. The methods utilized encourages the patient to clinically act out and simulate the potential behavior or incident such as suicide, homicide or a robbery to give the person the opportunity to experience its impact on others and oneself if such an act is actually committed. The patient is in no way encouraged to actually live out a crime or an inappropriate behavior. As with any method, the patient can reject the use of such methods at any time. These methods include the patient experiencing the damaging or destructive effects on others and oneself, the irreversibility of such behavior, going to jail or prison if this behavior violates the law, the guilt and despair it would create, what the person or others would miss out on or lose, and so on. The primary goal is to convince the patient to change one's mind and not to behave violently, self-destructively or inappropriately. One of these techniques is the suicide method described in the case example of Susan in this chapter and in chapter eleven. The drug, crime and arrest methods are described in chapter twelve. The therapist is always responsible for adhering to existing laws regarding reportability and protecting the welfare of others, while protecting the rights of the patient.

CASE EXAMPLES

Rebuilding Therapy assisted Susan to rebuild from the psychological damage and wounds that had led to her self-destructive, suicidal and self-damaging tendencies, severe depression, strong feelings of hopelessness and helplessness, moodiness, "poor me" attention seeking behavior, overcompetitiveness, anger and rage and her inability to love and live a meaningful life. Susan, 26, was severely rejected by her mother and father from the time she was an infant. Her mother never wanted her, having at first decided to abort her, she felt Susan was a burden and never let Susan forget this throughout her upbringing. According to Susan, her mother was very sadistic, physically and emotionally abused her, threatened to kill her, beat her, constantly criticized her, called her stupid, dumb and retarded and frequently told her that she would never amount to anything. The basic messages from her mother were "I wish you were never born," "You're no good," "You ruined my life," "You will ruin everyone else's life" and "You will never make anyone happy, including yourself."

Susan grew up believing she was no good, ugly, retarded, stupid, unlovable, would never amount to anything, was a "no good" burden and would be better off dead. She spent her entire life trying to overcompensate and manufactured herself into becoming a highly successful and presentable person professionally, but she was very unhappy in the process. Her mother's physical and mental abuse continued to plague her to the point where she broke down emotionally, becoming actively suicidal as an adult.

Before therapy was to proceed further in assisting her to overcome her past rejection and mistreatment it was essential for Susan to confront herself with her strong desire to die. To assist her to do this, while still an inpatient, she was stimulated in group therapy to act out her own death wish and suicide, while still being alive of course. This gave her an opportunity to experience and determine whether death was what she really wanted and, hopefully, to change her mind and to decide to live. She acted out cutting her wrist, the dying process and its impact on herself and loved ones with the assistance of the therapist, a therapeutic agent also in the session and other group members. While lying on the floor in her "death postion" and in a closed "psychodramatic coffin" with a sheet over her still wanting to be dead, she experienced the grief stricken and angry reactions of how loved ones would have likely rsponded to her. As she allowed herself to experience the impact of her suicide on herself and others around her, she began to cry openly. At this point she was stimulated to reverse her death wish to one where she wanted to live and live a meaningful life. A major factor in reversing her death wish was her realization of the irreversibility of death and what she would lose and miss out on in her life if she died. This became convincingly clear to her when she tried to get up out of her "death position" and "psychodramatic coffin," while still lying on the floor with the sheet over her as she was held down for a period of about one minute by the therapist and the therapeutic agent demonstrating the irreversibility of death to her. In trying to get up, she yelled out, "I can't breathe! I can't breathe! I want to live! I want to live!" Representing the "Spirit of Death," the therapist replied, "I am death and when you die, you can't breathe and there is no coming back. Sorry. Sorry. It's over. It's over." Once the impact of this was felt, she was encouraged to get up. When she got up and took the sheet off her, she clearly looked like she had come out of her "coffin" and from "death." She stated emotionally that she wanted to live and did not want to die anymore. Of course, this patient was agreeable to this therapeutic process and was never in any danger when the sheet was on her or when she was being held down therapeutically. The use of the sheet is optional depending on the patient and the situation. (See the suicide method in chapter eleven.)

Susan, after no longer wanting to die, had another chance to live out her potential to love, achieve and enjoy life. However, before she could accomplish her goals, and fulfill her potential, she needed to work on overcoming the abuse, rejection and neglect in her life and reinforce her decision to want to live. Rebuilding Therapy gave her this opportunity by stimulating her to relive those major experiences in her life when she was mistreated. She did so initially on an inpatient basis and then on an outpatient basis, mostly in individual and group therapy, while doing some reliving work in individual family therapy with her husband encouraging and supporting her. In a following session, by going back to relive a specific childhood experience, one of a number of experiences she had relived, when her mother threatened to kill her and severely rejected her, she had a second opportunity to face and overcome the impact of her mother's rejection at this time. This experience represented many rejecting experiences, and their impact on her overall feelings, thinking, behavior and functioning. In working on overcoming this experience, she was also working on overcoming these other similar experiences. However, she first needed to go through the first stage, the warmup stage. As she did, she reduced her anxiety and tension level, preparing her for the second stage, the living out stage. The living out stage involved reliving this experience, giving her the opportunity to face, confront and reexperience it. This was followed by the third stage, the catharsis and ventilation stage, stimulating her to express, externalize and decontaminate herself of her feelings of rage, sadness, despair, guilt and fear, unhealthy thinking and emotional pain which had influenced her and contaminated her thinking and feelings. Of course, the decontamination was a relative process, relative to what she was able to release and cleanse herself of in this session. Following this in the fourth stage, the awareness and reevaluation stage, her mind was cleansed to the point in this session where she became more aware of how her mother had affected her thinking and behavior, including her beliefs, decisions and the coping styles she developed because of her mother's rejection. Such decisions from the experience just described and other experiences included, "I want to die," "I'm no good," "I won't trust anyone" and "I'll show them all." This led her to continue reevaluating the validity of these decisions, beliefs and strategies and to continue changing them in healthy ways. Her changing thinking included such new beliefs and life decisions as "I want to live" (reinforcing her decision to do this), "I am okay," "I am a good person," "I will trust," and "I don't really need to prove anything in an excessive way or show them." This was followed by the fifth stage, the practice stage, where she had an opportunity to think out, visualize and psychologically experience through mental rehearsal, role training and practice more effective ways of carrying out her new decisions and life strategies. In the sixth stage, the coming together stage, she was provided with therapeutic support from other group members, the therapist and therapeutic agent through the sharing of mutual experiences, feelings and thoughts.

In the example provided, Susan had an opportunity to change more than one dysfunctional decision related to this typical rejecting experience, which was a theme of her upbringing. In addition, she needed to relive this experience more than once, as most patients need to partially, fully or in another way to most effectively rebuild from this type of negative experience. Susan could not easily have achieved this in traditional talk therapy alone, where she only would have had an opportunity to discuss her feelings, thoughts, problems and emotional pain, rather than reexperiencing her feelings, thoughts, problems and emotional pain and rebuilding herself from this, as she needed to. At best, she only would have had an opportunity in talk therapy to look at her life as on a movie screen, but with no power to do anything about it. In talk therapy alone, very likely, her increased insight, without being able to do anything about it, would probably only have aggravated her, further increasing her frustration and despair.

Rebuilding Therapy, through the reliving of experiences she had as the one just described, stimulated Susan to walk back into the despair and trauma of her past rejection and to overcome its negative impact on her. Having this opportunity to do it on her own, with the stimulation and support of therapy, enhanced her sense of control and independence, while giving her the opportunity to redecide, reconstruct and rebuild herself from the damage created by her past experiences. This renewed Susan's hope, reversed her childhood decision to die, further strengthening her desire to live, enhanced her self-image and trust and allowed her to begin taking control of her life. Once this occurred she was able to begin utilizing her potential more effectively to live a more fulfilling and meaningful life. Other forms of parental mistreatment are not as direct or as openly traumatic, but are still devastating and damaging. Examples will be presented throughout this book.

Rebuilding Therapy has also been used extensively in family therapy, in this case multiple family group therapy. Henry and Joan, a couple in their middle thirties, were having serious problems in their marriage and with their 14-year-old daughter, Linda, who was abusing drugs. Joan, a dominating and critical mother, whose father had been rejecting and overbearing, was encouraged to clinically reexperience major life events with her father to give her an opportunity to overcome her father's unhealthy influence and improve her functioning and parenting skills. Once this began to occur, Linda became more comfortable, realizing that opening up was acceptable, and she willingly allowed herself to clinically reexperience events when her mother Joan rejected her to begin her own healing process. When this occurred, Linda's parents observed in a supportive way, glad she was helping herself. As this rebuilding process effectively unfolded, the family unit became ready to face and were assisted to effectively work through present family issues and conflicts that they needed to resolve. However, these family members had to begin resolving their own past conflicts before they could sit down and work effectively on present issues. Linda's father also worked on his own personal issues from his past to improve his functioning as a husband and father.

THE OVERALL USES OF REBUILDING THERAPY

In summary, Rebuilding Therapy is effective in stimulating and assisting persons to psychologically rebuild from and overcome physical, sexual and psychological abuse and mistreatment, neglect, faulty parental upbringing, family dysfunction, any type of damaging experience including battle trauma, victimization by a crime, an accident, a natural disaster (i.e., earthquake, hurricane, tornado, etc.), an illness or injury, the death of a loved one, divorce or other losses or other traumas and negative experiences. It also assists people, who desire to grow and rebuild aspects of their personality and life, to progress to a more fully functioning and meaningful lifestylentative therapy utilized when a person is considering or is a likely threat to commit suicide, homicide, a law violating behavior or a dangerous or dysfunctional action by stimulating the person to act out and experience and confront the impact of this behavior on others and oneself. Of course no one will actually be harmed in this clinical process. An example is the use of the suicide method with Susan in the preceding case example. It also uses methods that confront the resistant patient with his or her dysfunctional behavior and habits, with the goal of reversing this behavior.

Rebuilding Therapy also assists persons and families to develop more effective communication, relationship, intimacy and problem solving skills. It encourages the integration of the past with the present, by assisting family members to overcome issues from the past or at least to begin confronting these issues and understanding them better. Rebuilding Therapy also utilizes traditional talk therapy methods to develop rapport, provide integration and support and educate and assist the patient, when talking solely is necessary, and for those who are not ready or willing to deal with more active methods.

As indicated, in the beginning of this chapter Rebuilding Therapy has been used with a wide range of diagnostic categories and problems, and in the process has been effective. When Rebuilding Therapy has been used in a very infrequent, modified and limited way with the schizophrenic, psychotic and mildly neurologically impaired populations regarding most present issues and some past issues relative to their capablility, it has also been effective. J. L. Moreno (1939 and 1940b) and Z. Moreno (1978) referred to the use of Psychodrama with psychotic patients, which are among some of their writings that are not limited to the psychotic and schizophrenic patient. Z. Moreno (1965), in further discussing J. L. Moreno's work with psychotic patients, described the use of Psychodrama as a way for the patient with psychosis to develop some degree of control of his or her situation by voluntarily reentering the psychotic state he or she was in to develop skills and resources to prevent the reoccurrence of such an episode. J. L. Moreno's 1939 article more specifically discussed this process. Of course, such an approach is only utilized in a highly structured and supportive setting by the director or therapist with the help of his or her associate or associates, if available. A number of other authors refer to the use of Psychodrama with the psychotic and schizophrenic patient, which is referred to in the *Bibliography of Psychodrama* (1995) edited by Sacks, Bilaniuk and Gendron.

Rebuilding Therapy can be utilized independently in outpatient, in-home, day treatment, partial hospitalization, residential or inpatient settings and can be integrated and used creatively in conjunction with other therapeutic methods and programs. It also has potential use in related fields such as law enforcement, corrections, education, business and industry and religion and in the community, state, national and world arena to reduce conflict, resolve problems and improve relations with others. (See chapter seventeen.) Sack's, Bilaniuk and Gendron's *Bibliography of Psychodrama* contains references in these areas where Psychodrama has been used. These various areas can be the subject matter for a later book.

CHAPTER 3

Guidelines for Rebuilding Therapy

THE STRENGTH AND HEALING POWER OF THE HUMAN MIND

The strength and healing power of the human mind has frequently been demonstrated throughout my years of rebuilding work with patients. The natural human mind allows the person to heal if treated effectively and if not inhibited or cut off by lack of motivation, fear and resistance or well-meaning mental health clinicians, relatives and others who have no confidence in the person's strength to deal with past experiences, don't want to upset themselves by the patient's reliving of these experiences or simply don't believe in or comprehend the value of uncovering past experiences and underlying feelings and thoughts necessary for healing and rebuilding. Uncovering and reconstructive therapy does work effectively, providing clinicians practice it in a highly supportive, structured and ethical manner, while also taking into account the contraindications for its use.

INFORMING THE PATIENT AND FAMILY OF THE REBUILDING THERAPY PROCESS

As with any type of therapy, the patient needs to be well-informed regarding his or her treatment. The patient and the parents or guardians of children and adolescents need a detailed discussion of Rebuilding Therapy, its stages, goals, methodology and approaches and use in individual, group and family therapy. Other family members involved in treatment will also benefit from a discussion of the Rebuilding Therapy process. Though this type of patient is treated very infrequently in Rebuilding Therapy, an adult patient with a conservator or guardian should also be provided with a discussion of the Rebuilding Therapy process in a way he or she can comprehend, while the conservator or guardian of such a patient should also be provided with a detailed discussion of Rebuilding Therapy. The process of informing the patient regarding the treatment process will be done in a manner which meets the patient's needs and takes into account the patient's psychological functioning, while protecting his or her rights. An informed consent should be provided to the patient, the parent or parents or guardian or guardians of a child or adolescent, the conservator or guardian of an adult patient and family members taking part in family therapy regarding a discussion of Rebuilding Therapy, including its rationale, its methodology, what it is, contraindications, limitations and alternative forms of treatment. As I have worked with so few adults with a conservator or guardian I do not refer to this situation when further discussing the patient's rights and the rights of a conservator or guardian of an adult. This in no way minimizes the importance of such a situation, for the rights of the adult with a conservator or guardian and of the conservator or guardian will always be strictly adhered to. In fact although I have utilized Rebuilding Therapy very infrequently with chronic adult patients, Rebuilding Therapy has much potential to assist such patients. The term *parent* is used for the term *guardian* when discussing the treatment process when the guardian is in the role of a parent with a child, adolescent or a young adult needing this. Often parents of children, adolescents and some young adults are involved in therapy themselves or usually are at least part of the family therapy process. The patient and family will also benefit from information and recommendations regarding what to expect and do between sessions, including if past memories and related feelings and thoughts of the patient or a family member surface or if just feelings and thoughts surface. In addition, the patient and family need to know that help and support will be available if the patient or a family member become distressed between sessions related to the uncovering of past experiences or whatever issues or concerns exist. The patient is also requested to get a physical, as needed, or to continue ongoing evaluations with his or her physician, as needed, with this also applying to involved family members or family members jointly taking part in family therapy. Whatever is discussed regarding the patient applies to family members involved in the treatment process, who in actuality are patients themselves.

THE PATIENT HAS ULTIMATE CONTROL

The patient should know that he or she can terminate therapy at any time, though with the child and adolescent, their parent or parents have the right to terminate treatment. However, in addition to the adult patient, the child or adolescent's desire to terminate therapy needs also to be carefully looked at regarding what is best for the patient. Although the person or persons legally responsible for the child or adolescent can approve or reject any part of the therapy process, the patient's rights need to also be respected within the framework of what the patient and parent approve of. The patient should always have ultimate control, having the right to approve and consent to or to terminate a specific method or procedure and to approve and consent to working on or not to work on or to stop working on a specific experience, conflict or issue. At any time the patient has the right to tell the therapist that he or she wants to stop the therapeutic process and the therapist needs to immediately respect this wish. When this occurs, the therapist gives the patient an opportunity to look at why he or she wants to stop and what it means, with the patient having the opportunity to resume therapeutic work or to stop working on whatever he or she was working on at least for the session, for a period of time after the session or permanently. If the patient chooses to stop working on a specific issue that he or she had been working on, the therapist will then provide therapeutic support, integration and a processing of what occurred. Regarding the desire to terminate therapy, the same process will be followed, enabling the patient to explore why and the meaning of his or her desire to terminate therapy in order to reconsider and continue in therapy or terminate in a therapeutic way. The patient's confidentiality is always protected with respect to the patient's rights and what is best for the patient. Of course, the applicable laws and legal rights of anyone involved in the psychotherapeutic treatment process need to be adhered to.

MOTIVATION AND THERAPEUTIC READINESS

The patient's motivation and therapeutic readiness are significant factors, for no patient should be worked with in a specific area or direction if he or she chooses not to or is not ready to do so. Especially when working in an uncovering and reconstructive way, any doubt or resistance the patient exhibits needs to be looked at and examined jointly with the patient before proceeding further. Even a slight indication that the patient is not comfortable with a specific method or dealing with a specific issue needs to be taken very seriously, with the patient's feelings and thoughts explored thoroughly, before proceeding in the therapeutic process. The patient always needs to be in control of his or her destiny and situation, with the therapist doing whatever is necessary for this to be accomplished. The dangers of proceeding too quickly or against the patient's resistance can become significant, causing the patient to feel that he or she is not in control of one's own destiny as was the case when a child or it becomes another painful antitherapeutic situation for the patient. The therapeutic situation needs to be a safe and secure place in which the patient feels free to face the psychological pain and issues in his or her life with the therapist's support and stimulation. Of course, whenever a patient chooses to give "up control" relatively and to explore the depths of one's mind, he or she has the ultimate control to go as far as one wants and to stop when he or she wishes to.

Being a supporter of the strength of the human mind, I believe that most persons are capable of doing some type of uncovering and rebuilding work ranging from light to intense, as needed. This has clearly been demonstrated in my more than twenty years of doing uncovering reconstructive therapy. The ability to do this effectively, while providing for the safety and security of the patient, will depend on the same factors determining the methods and approaches and direction and focus of therapy, that includes the patient's motivation, readiness, needs, problems, condition, personality strength, the therapist's skills, the financial and insurance resources, the amount of therapy that can be provided and the setting.

WORKING WITH THE PATIENT'S RESISTANCE

Working with the patient's resistance is an important part of therapy, along with respecting the patient's boundaries and limitations. Through exploration of the patient's resistance, it may be possible to better understand why he or she is resisting dealing with a specific situation, with there always being some type of legitimate reason. Patients need to be given credit that they are not just lazy, cowardly or unwilling to help themselves. Usually, there is a reason behind the patients resistance, which the therapist needs to explore and work through with the patient to help him or her eventually face and resolve specific issues and problems. It is always easy to conclude that the patient does not want to help him or herself, but the human mind is more complex than oversimplifying the patient's motivation or lack of it. The timing of any intervention or specific method is essential. The patient and therapist need to walk hand in hand, with the therapist a fraction of an inch ahead of the patient, always sensitive to where the patient "is" emotionally and psychologically.

PATIENT AND THERAPIST COMMUNICATION

The patient and therapist must communicate regularly regarding the patient's progress and treatment, also including his or her resistance and feelings and thoughts about future treatment. This should be done regularly every specific number of sessions. In doing so, guidelines can be developed, including the number of sessions needed for specific goals to be attained, with flexibility for additional sessions. In this way, mutual agreement regarding termination time can also be reached, reducing the possibility of premature termination by either the patient or therapist.

THE COURSE OF TREATMENT

Whether individual therapy, group therapy, individual family therapy or multiple family therapy, the length of treatment, how treatment is utilized and the goals of treatment depend on the patient, family member or family's problems, level of functioning, motivation, needs, and resources and the age of those persons taking part in therapy. The length of treatment will also have a significant influence on the treatment plan depending on what the patient, family member or family need and is motivated and capable of accomplishing, and also what is anticipated about the length of treatment when it starts and continues. Of course, in a number of cases, it is not possible to know if there is going to be a premature termination, and when it is known the period of treatment will be limited or will be for less sessions than is anticipated, appropriate modifications will be made. Whenever possible treatment should be provided in the shortest period of time with specific goals in specific time periods relative to the needs of the patient, family member or family and other factors just mentioned. With these factors and variations in mind, I have provided some general guidelines to offer the reader regarding the course of outpatient treatment for the adult patient in Rebuilding Therapy.

These guidelines can also apply to adolescents and some young adults mostly up to about twelve weeks of therapy, though there will be specific variations depending on the patient and family with usually more variation the younger the patient in this age category. In addition these guidelines may apply to some adolescents and specific young adults who are in outpatient treatment longer than twelve weeks. Regarding children, ages nine to twelve, these guidelines can apply to this population for a number of such children up to twelve weeks where individual therapy, individual family therapy and multiple family therapy is used with much variability also expected. Though there are variations in treating any patient and family, the variability in treating children, adolescents and specific young adults also relates to such factors as their dependence on their family to change, the instability or dysfunction of their upbringing and family of origin they are often still living in and their varying maturational levels. Again, the various factors coming into play in the treatment process contribute to much variability regarding the course of treatment, making it essential for the therapist to individualize treatment to each patient and family's needs, though the presentation of such general guidelines will give the reader a general outline to follow.

What has been discussed for outpatient treatment can apply to inpatient treatment, partial hospitalization, day treatment (i.e. three days a week, three hours a day) and other settings with appropriate modifications. In such settings the course of treatment may be speeded up in a number of cases as the patient is ready, where in other cases a patient may need more time to prepare for the reliving process, as needed. In addition, not all patients will be ready, willing or able to take part in the reliving process. Though Rebuilding Therapy methods and approaches are used extensively in Rebuilding Therapy, talk therapy approaches are used as needed.

When it is known that a patient will be in therapy for about six weekly individual outpatient therapy sessions, many of the Rebuilding Therapy methods and approaches, along with talk therapy approaches, can be used when a patient is assisted to deal with present problems or relationships. An individual therapy session usually is forty-five to sixty minutes, though in some cases it can be longer if the need arises. The patient's reliving of present experiences to assist in resolving present problems can be done in six weekly individual outpatient therapy sessions. The type of uncovering of past experiences which, in the large majority of cases, should be done within this time period should be of a lighter nature primarily relating or connecting the past to the present. In this time period when the patient is ready, the therapist or therapeutic agent may live out a parent or significant other's mistreatment and message or messages from the past or present, without the patient specifically reliving an experience, to connect the patient to this mistreatment, though this approach can also be used in other longer therapeutic time periods. (See chapters six and fourteen regarding the delivery of the message, chapter eight regarding the blending the past with the present method and chapter ten regarding the spell method. A modified form of the cage method described in chapter nine, with it being used in a less intense way can also be utilized.) Another way to connect the patient to past mistreatment or negative messages is to encourage the patient to visualize this mistreatment in an empty chair or without an empty chair or role reversing with a parent or significant other moving from chair to chair or position to position as oneself and the significant other in a dialogue regarding this person's mistreatment or message or messages. In this case, the patient will usually remain in the present, dialoguing with the significant other sometime in the past or in the present. In some cases, however, the patient may engage in a dialogue with his or her significant other at the time this conflict occurred. During this six weekly individual therapy session period, only when needed and as the patient is ready, will a patient be stimulated to relive past experiences in one's life in a way modified to this time period, usually in the third to fifth session. In this case, the patient will be given closure to effectively prepare him or her to carry out what progress is made without continued therapy.

In therapy that is to last for seven to twelve weekly outpatient individual therapy sessions, the reliving of past experiences, as needed, in addition to present experiences is encouraged as part of therapy. Such reliving is encouraged from about the third to tenth session, as the patient is ready, in a twelve session time period to ensure an adequate warmup and closure period.

Usually weekly outpatient group therapy, as needed, should take place when there are at least twelve weeks of therapy starting at about the fourth to sixth week often along with weekly individual therapy for the twelve-week period, if therapy is anticipated to be for a twelve-week period, though there can be variations such as whether individual therapy will continue or will decrease once group therapy starts. Usually a patient is ready for the reliving process when he or she takes part in group therapy, which often will start in the second group therapy session for a specific patient. The length of a group therapy session is from about ninety minutes to one hundred and twenty minutes, and can be longer depending on the need. Group therapy, after a sufficient period of individual therapy, is an ongoing process with patients moving in and out of group therapy for the period of time they need, while also connecting to some other patients on a supportive basis.

When there is a significant possibility that therapy will last for more than twelve weekly individual outpatient therapy sessions, the reliving process can begin in about the third session or whenever the patient is ready after this and proceed as long as is possible and as the patient's best interest is served with an appropriate closure period. The length of outpatient treatment can extend to six months or more with weekly individual and group therapy often done concurrently for a significant period of this time, with group therapy starting from about the seventh to twelfth weekly individual therapy session or later, though, as indicated, there can be variations in the treatment plan depending on the patient's needs, including just individual or just group therapy being the primary treatment modality at different time periods during the course of treatment. There are also a number of times when individual therapy or individual family therapy may be the only treatment modality ranging from short-term to long-term treatment. Integrating individual family therapy or multiple family group therapy, as needed, on an adjunct basis into a primary treatment program which involves, for example, individual and group therapy can maximize the treatment process in a way which isn't excessive with substitutions of one modality for another, as needed. However, as managed care and financial factors dictate the need for shorter term therapy, therapists may increasingly use group therapy, for example, in a twelve session treatment program that can include six individual therapy sessions and six group therapy sessions or four individual therapy sessions and eight group therapy sessions. As mentioned, treatment can be varied depending on the patient's needs including the frequency of sessions and the spreading out of sessions, especially near the end of treatment. (See the short to long-term treatment section in chapter seventeen which also includes Rebuilding Family Therapy which will now be discussed.)

The involvement of family members or significant others, though not essential for therapeutic change for adults, can be an integral part of the patient's therapy, as needed. The young adult ranging in age from eighteen to twenty-five even more often requires the support and involvement of family members, and in some cases for this age group family involvement is a necessary prerequisite for success in therapy, as with the child and adolescent population. Family support ranges from family members supporting the therapeutic process to improving their own functioning and making psychological changes depending on their need and involvement in therapy. This includes the family member's involvement in family therapy or one's own personal therapy, as needed. The involvement of the family in family therapy, as needed, is an integral part of Rebuilding Therapy. The positive involvement of family members can only enhance the patient's progress, as well as the family's progress. However, at times, dysfunctional family members are likely to adversely affect the patient's progress, unless the adult patient can break off or significantly reduce or change his or her relationship with these family members; a process which is very difficult to impossible for the child or adolescent and some young adults.

Individual family therapy on an adjunct basis or, less frequently, as the primary treatment modality for about six weekly outpatient sessions primarily focuses on present interactional and relationship dynamics. Various Rebuilding Therapy methods and approaches, and talk therapy as needed during any aspect of Rebuilding Therapy, can be utilized to improve the family's functioning. Though less so than in individual therapy, family members will only be stimulated to relive past experiences in a way modified to this time period, usually in the third to fifth session, as it relates to present family issues. An individual family therapy session is usually forty-five to sixty minutes, though it can be longer depending on the need.

When utilized as the primary modality on a short-term basis, outpatient individual family therapy is more frequently carried out for about seven to twelve weekly sessions. The reliving process for specific family members in this situation, as needed related to present family issues, is encouraged starting from about the fourth session and continuing to about the tenth session, but is done so less frequently than in individual therapy due to the need to deal with present family dynamics. When there is a significant possibility outpatient individual family therapy won't be limited to twelve sessions, then the reliving process for specific family members, as needed related to present family issues starting in about the fourth session or later with an adequate closure period, will be more frequent but less so than in outpatient individual therapy of the same frequency and length.

Outpatient multiple family group therapy should usually be introduced after about the sixth weekly individual family therapy session, which can, for example, be held concurrently with individual family therapy amounting to eighteen sessions or in place of individual family therapy amounting to twelve sessions. The reliving process is also a part of multiple family group therapy, but to a lesser extent than in group therapy, again due to the need to focus on present family issues. The length of a multiple family group therapy session is usually from about ninety minutes to one hundred and twenty minutes, though it can be longer depending on the need.

The length or number of sessions of individual family or multiple family group therapy can be increased depending on the family's needs. In these cases, the reliving process as it relates to family issues will occur more often, though less often than in individual or group therapy as discussed. As indicated, family therapy can be used on an adjunct basis or as a primary treatment modality. Individual therapy or group therapy, as needed, may also be integrated on an adjunct basis into a family therapy treatment program with this done in a way which maximizes the family members and family's treatment without overwhelming anyone, and making substitutions of one treatment modality for another as needed. (See chapter sixteen on Rebuilding Family Therapy and the Rebuilding Family Therapy section in chapter seventeen.)

PRACTICE AND ROLE TRAINING

Practice and role training to assist the patient to resolve problems, to be more assertive and to cope with life stressors and relate to others more effectively can be an integral part of short term therapy and, of course, of therapy of any length. Actively rehearsing and experiencing healthier ways of functioning is an excellent learning tool in the practice stage of Rebuilding Therapy.

THERAPEUTIC SUPPORT AND CLOSURE

Whenever Rebuilding Therapy methods and approaches are used, as in any therapy, therapeutic support and closure are always necessary. The need for therapeutic support and closure increases as the intensity and strength of the uncovering method and approach increases. The last part of the session should be spent integrating and processing what has occurred in the session and supporting the patient or patients who worked on specific issues and other patients or persons in the sessions. The length of the comedown and closure period depends on such factors as the personality strength of the patient, patients or others involved, the intensity of the uncovering process and the session. This comedown and closure period should usually range from fifteen to twenty-five minutes in a two hour or more group therapy or multiple family group therapy session to ten to fifteen minutes in a one hour individual therapy or individual family therapy session. In some cases, the closure period may be longer. The term *hour* refers to any therapeutic time period from forty-five to sixty minutes.

When more than one patient works on oneself in a group session, the comedown and closure period for the first working patient may be shorter than discussed above, as another patient will follow working on his or her issues. The closure period at the end of such a session will be as it has just been described. A short closure period may be necessary after the first patient works therapeutically to keep the intensity going for the next patient working. The first working patient may also actually come down as the session continues and will have more of an opportunity for a closure period in the last part of the session. Though there is a comedown and closure period, a patient will often start coming down before this in the awareness and reevaluation stage.

TOUCHING

Therapeutic touching of the patient is a complex issue for therapeutic and ethical legal-liability reasons. Even simple hugging of a patient or holding a patient's hand for supportive purposes is risky, if done alone by a therapist from a liability-litigation standpoint. (This issue is further discussed in chapters eleven, twelve, fourteen and fifteen.)

SELF HELP PROGRAMS

Another important part of therapy is to encourage the patient to develop a self help program outside of the sessions, involving such activities as reading, esteem building exercises, goal setting exercises, communication-relationship exercises, coping-adaptive-assertive exercises and exercises for whatever situation the patient will face. Exercises to support, reinforce and prepare the patient for further reliving work in therapy are also encouraged. Patients are also encouraged to see their physicians regularly, to exercise and to eat a healthy diet.

SUPPORTIVE ASSISTANCE FOR THE PATIENT OUTSIDE OF THERAPY

A specific procedure is required to provide emergency or out-of-office support services for the patient. This procedure needs to include persons to contact in order of priority if the patient finds oneself in an emergency, a life threatening situation or in a situation that requires the assistance of a helping person. In an emergency, it is always in the patient's best interest to have a supportive significant other, a sponsor if involved in AA, CA or NA, a telephone hot line and lastly, his or her therapist to call on for help, usually in this order as available. The therapist should be the last person to contact so that the patient will be encouraged to deal with life's stresses, including emergency situations, as independently as possible.

MUTUAL PATIENT-THERAPIST TERMINATION

Although patients in any type of therapy not infrequently terminate prematurely, it is also important, if possible, that therapy terminate in a positive and therapeutic way with both therapist and patient in agreement. The likelihood of this occurring is positively related to the patient's motivation, trust, lowered resistance, therapeutic input and working diligently in therapy, patient-therapist communication, family involvement as needed, the patient's resources, the setting and the effectiveness of therapy.

FOLLOW-UP PROGRAM

An effective follow-up plan is essential, ensuring that the patient will have a strong and realistic self help program, a strong family or significant other support system, helpful community resources and programs to turn to and an open door policy regarding the patient being able to contact the therapist or return to therapy for a session, a limited or more extended number of sessions. Information pertaining to follow-up services should be provided early in therapy, and in actuality, is provided when introducing the patient to the importance of utilizing self help resources, supportive help outside of therapy and significant others for assistance, as needed. This also provides the patient who prematurely terminates therapy with information regarding follow-up services. The therapist should, when possible and therapeutic, contact or correspond by mail with the prematurely terminated patient to let this person know that the therapist is concerned and is available to help, and to ensure this person has information regarding follow-up services. In addition, the therapist should provide this service to patients who don't prematurely terminate therapy.

CONTRAINDICATIONS

As indicated in chapter two, Rebuilding Therapy is effectively used with a wide range of diagnostic categories and problem areas. The primary contraindications lie with such factors as patient motivation, willingness, psychological-therapeutic readiness, how much a patient can tolerate and the possibility of symptomatic regression. Factors such as these need to be assessed individually and for each patient as a whole clinically.

The patient's psychological condition, mental state and functioning needs to be assessed daily. Though, a patient may in a number of ways lack motivation to help oneself and resolve his or her problems, he or she by willing to take part in a specific method or approach is communicating his or her willingness to do so. A patient consenting to take part in a confrontation method is an example of this. In addition, while assessing contraindications, the patient and family's strengths need to always be concurrently looked at.

Other factors regarding contraindications should be looked at. The therapist needs to regularly evaluate his or her skill limitations, as well as the skills and limitations of the therapeutic agents assisting him or her. The psychological functioning, capabilities and limitations of group and family members when assisting the therapist needs to be regularly assessed, also.

Throughout the book, it is clear the Rebuilding Therapist is always sensitive to the needs, welfare, safety and well-being of the patient. The patient's physical safety is never risked or is the patient ever put in any type of dangerous situation, physically or psychologically.

CHAPTER 4

Theoretical Foundations Contributing to Rebuilding Therapy

A BRIEF LOOK AT PERSONALITY DEVELOPMENT

The theory underlying Rebuilding Therapy is referred to as Rebuilding Theory. Rebuilding Theory claims that the person, without significant neurological impairment which would prevent healthy personality development, is conceived with the ability to grow into an individual who can love, empathize, relate effectively and harmoniously with others, create, function productively and meaningfully, and heal and rebuild, if needed, if given the opportunity. However, this potential, as described more specifically in chapter two, is damaged by faulty and dysfunctional upbringing, rejection, neglect or other negative experiences and influences in the person's life. A major premise of Rebuilding Theory is that the person is a product of his or her history from prebirth to the present. Personality development is an unconscious process in the early years, usually becoming less of an unconscious process as one matures, though the unconscious mind continues to have a significant influence on the person throughout his or her life, varying in degree depending on the person. The more powerful psychological and environmental influences on personality development, psychological functioning and psychopathology occur from prebirth to about ten to twelve years of age, usually decreasing in strength as one grows older up to this time and through adolescence, and relatively leveling out in adulthood, except for unusual or traumatic factors. Also to be noted is the period of old age when environmental factors often increase in strength regarding their effects on psychological functioning when the person regresses psychologically and physically. Personality structure is relatively in place by age ten to twelve with adolescence being a time, in preparation for adulthood, to further develop personality and to adjust to the dysfunction and psychological wounds created by earlier upbringing. Although adolescence is an important time to accomplish this, the damage created at earlier ages needs to be repaired through psychotherapy. In addition, the adolescent's degree of psychological dysfunction will vary directly with his or her degree of psychopathology previous to adolescence and will be further influenced by the degree of dysfunction in the adolescent's environment. This is not to discredit the importance of the adolescent period on psychological functioning and further development, but again the preadolescent factors need to be accounted for as the primary factors affecting personality development. The younger a person is, usually the more powerful environmental influences are on one psychologically as the child is weaker, more helpless and more suggestible, with the decisions the child makes usually being stronger the younger the age. Janov (1991) pointed out that the system is most naive and fragile during the prenatal period when the impact of trauma is the highest. If a child is rejected from prebirth throughout his or her childhood, the rejecting experiences usually are more powerful from the earliest or first rejecting experiences in the womb. Similarly, if a child's negative experiences started at two or seven years of age, the experiences at these ages usually are the most potent influences on the person. Negative experiences such as physical mistreatment, molestation, neglect, severe criticism or conditional love repeated after the earlier mistreatment or rejections further reinforce the earlier mistreatment and are still powerful influences in themselves. Although in doing uncovering and rebuilding work, it is most helpful to work with the earliest rejecting experiences, if possible, among other experiences, later experiences can still be worked with effectively in therapy as they often represent earlier experiences and may be the only experiences which the patient and therapist have access to. In addition, if the degree of rejection was greater at a later age, this is a profound factor, in itself, and must be treated therapeutically.

Any influence or event, whatever the age, on a person's life that has a significant effect on psychological functioning and needs to be dealt with in therapy should be treated, while it is essential to treat the previous factors, if needed and possible, for the person to maximize his or her progress in therapy.

Experiences or events occurring after age sixteen to eighteen, especially traumatic events such as rape, battle trauma, the death of a loved one, sexual harassment, an injury or accident, a traumatic job loss, marital conflict or a divorce, can have a strong influence on the person's psychological functioning and adjustment, but usually aggravate existing personality dysfunction rather than cause such dysfunction. In this regard, personality foundation, character and makeup, which have developed previous to a traumatic or negative experience, will have a strong influence on how effectively the person responds, adjusts and heals from this experience. A person who has experienced mistreatment and dysfunction in his or her upbringing will often have more difficulty than a person with a healthy upbringing adjusting to and overcoming such a negative experience as this person usually has been more impaired. In addition, one's unhealthy upbringing and its related psychological wounds that have been unconscious will often become conscious again in various degrees or will continue to affect the person unconsciously, inflicting ongoing pain and conflict on the already suffering person, making it more difficult to overcome the current traumatic or negative experience. Rebuilding Theory stresses the importance of all factors affecting the person and family and in doing so Rebuilding Therapy will address these factors as needed and possible.

Eric Berne's Transactional Analysis, discussed later in this chapter, has contributed strongly to Rebuilding Theory's discussion of one's upbringing, past, decision making and psychological functioning as related to psychological and personality development. Goulding and Goulding's Redecision Therapy (1979), which originated from and has been strongly influenced by Transactional Analysis, has also contributed significantly to Rebuilding Therapy regarding the redecisioning process. (See chapter five regarding Redecision Therapy.) Prebirth or prenatal experiences and factors and the birth process, as they affect personality development, have also contributed significantly to Rebuilding Theory in addition to, of course, postnatal experiences and factors.

PRENATAL DEVELOPMENT

Prenatal factors and their influence on personality development is a relatively new area of interest for Rebuilding Theory and Therapy. Although this area has not been the major focus of Rebuilding Therapy, it has increasingly become an area of attention regarding its impact on personality development, warranting considerable attention in the review of the literature.

Janov (1991) claimed that after twelve weeks of gestation the fetal nervous system is fully organized and can fully react to, code and store trauma. Fodor (1949) supported the influence of prenatal factors on the human mind and that the unborn's mind could only be looked at through the study of postnatal dreams. He postulated that there is a record of the influences on the fetus in the womb and the unborn child's adaptation to these influences. Fodor theorized that the blueprint of these influences or impacts is preserved in an organismic memory and could be consulted. He asked how could adaptation in the womb take place without an organismic mind or organismic consciousness which controls the relationship of the growing fetus to the maternal environment. In asking this question, Fodor appeared to answer it affirmatively stating that the organismic consciousness may be the bedrock of the unconscious mind ordinarily beyond our reach, but an ever present entity without which the mind could not be developed.

According to Fodor, no two persons are closer than the unborn child and the mother, that telepathy may exist between mother and child and that the mother's expectations and thoughts may have a profound impact on the developing fetus. Fodor's discussion is theoretical and speculative, but merits consideration regarding the influence of prenatal factors on personality development.

Berne (1972) discussed the powerful impact of the parent's prebirth wishes, aspirations, feelings, thoughts, beliefs and the like on the child's development. He believed that a child was likely to have a good start in life and become a winner if he or she was planned and wanted and if the parents had positive aspirations for the unborn child. Berne referred to the conceptive attitude, the parental attitude at the time of conception, as having a potent influence on the child's personality and development. According to Berne, conception resulting from sex and passion, an accident, rape or violence, spite, resignation, ambivalence or a loving plan clearly determines the conceptive attitude. He focused on such prenatal influences as the following: Was a baby wanted? Was an abortion contemplated during the pregnancy? Were there previous abortions or attempted abortions in previous pregnancies? Was the third child not wanted with two children being the plan? Was the child planned to be the heir to a fortune? Was the child planned warmly or coldly? Was the child supposed to be a scholar, athlete, scientist, mother or businessperson? What was the expectation of the child's role in life if born first, third, youngest or boy or girl? and so on. These influences, Berne stated, could not be documented or identified until after birth when the parental and child's behavior and interaction could be identified.

In discussing the influences of prenatal factors, Berne expressed some skepticism and pointed to the speculative or only theoretical aspects of prenatal influences. He claimed that script programming or programming that strongly affects development begins after birth in the nursing period between mother and infant. The lack of direct empirical evidence apparently led Berne to this conclusion.

In recent years, there has been growing clinical and empirical evidence that prenatal psychological influences have a powerful effect and influence on personality development. Barnett (1987) reported that a number of researchers have found buried memories of life before birth, that there is much evidence to support the validity of such memories and that the unborn child is able to experience and record events before birth. Barnett also claimed that most of the memories uncovered in hypnosis are factual.

According to Givens (1987), a person's experience from conception is recorded in the unconscious mind and is preserved without censorship. Givens claimed that the fetus has a consciousness that stores maternal experiences, but does not have analytical awareness.

Van de Carr and Lehrer (1988) reported that a number of investigations, such as by Chamberlain (1983), have suggested that hypnosis can bring out prebirth and birth memories, which are of quite specific content and nature. They reported that such memories are primarily singular and are indicative of traumatic experiences uncovered during therapy.

Anand and Hickey (1988) stated that long-term memory requires the functional integrity of the diencephalon and limbic system, which are well developed and functioning during the newborn period. If this part of the body is developed at birth, is it possible to assume that it is developed significantly in the late fetal period from six or seven to nine months of pregnancy? They also contended that the cellular, synaptic and molecular changes necessary for memory and learning depend on brain plasticity, which is known to be highest during the late prenatal period and neonatal periods of life, further supporting the ability to recall in the late prenatal period and at birth.

Chamberlain (1990) claimed that the origin of memory stretches back to the womb. In hypnosis, Chamberlain reported prenatal recall is almost as common as birth memories, comes without request and sometimes can be verified as true. According to Chamberlain, memories close to birth or in the third trimester are easy to explain, for the physical equipment of the child in place at birth is likely to be in place a little earlier, whereas recall in the first two trimesters needs a different explanation. Chamberlain referred to other hypnotherapists like himself encountering prenatal memories and referred to Van Husen (1988) writing about forty-eight survivors of attempted abortion and how the patients taught her to value and work with these prenatal memories, with some of the stories confirmed by the mothers. Whether some of these patients had previously been informed of this is not clear, although Chamberlain's findings implied that the patient had no prior knowledge. Chamberlain also referred to Ferrant (1986) who in "repeated primals" discovered that his mother tried to abort him, with his mother confirming this occurrence. To further support the validity of early recall, according to Chamberlain, "is the reactivation of forceps bruises or a blue area on the throat where a person had been choked by the umbilical cord" (1990, p. 179) and that these marks came and left with the memory. Chamberlain also cited other findings (Grof, 1985; Laing, 1982) that, under certain conditions, persons can access information of their early gestation. While Chamberlain also reported that some of his patients recalled events around the time of their conception, such findings and related findings require further investigation. Again, whether such recall is affected by previous knowledge of the events, partially or fully, is open to question. Chamberlain claimed that memory may be a right of all persons, whatever the age, and seems to track experiences even when under situations of damage to the senses, anesthesia, brain injury and coma.

Verny (1994) stated he believes that there are two separate, but complementary systems serving memory: (1) cerebral memory, which depends on the development of mature neurological networks that make up the central nervous system and is operative by the end of the second trimester or six months after conception, and (2) cellular memory based on a "holographic" model in which each cell knows what every other cell knows, but also carries some additional information specific to that cell. According to Verny, this bipolar model of memory explains the existence of validated memories from before the third trimester. Chamberlain (1990), supporting the existence of memory in the first two trimesters of pregnancy, stated that "memory is possible without cells and endures while cells do not" (p.186).

Janov (1991), the developer of Primal Therapy, stated that after twelve weeks of prenatal life, "the fetal nervous system is fully organized and can fully react to, code and store trauma" (p. 142). According to Janov prenatal experiences, such as trauma or psychological or physiological maternal influences, result in changes in the cellular functioning where "the memory is 'held' by these changes in the various systems" (p. 143). In addition Janov stated "that possibly the very genetic structure of cells in the central nervous system is changed as a result of early imprints (p. 143). Janov pointed out that reliving the memory and connecting to consciousness alters the "cellular changes back to normal" (p. 143). In further discussing this Janov claimed "every cell in the body holds memory" (p. 143) and that is why there are "major changes in the function of cells after the imprint is relived and resolved..." (p. 143).

According to Verny, pushing back the conventionally held age barrier for the recall of memories is responsible for beginning a major revolution in psychology. However, he warned against a narrow orthodox method, and instead called for moderation and open-mindedness, applying this understanding rationally and responsibly. Verny also developed the Gestational Model for systematically studying material from the birth and prenatal periods which is uncovered in psychotherapy. This model is divided into six stages: the primary germ cell, conception, overduct, implantation, uterine and labor and birth stages.

The issue of prenatal memory, previous to six months from conception, is a wide open area for future investigation and should not be ruled out as far fetched fantasy, though it is questionable and raises various questions. The six to nine months from conception period offers more fertile ground for investigation at this time. The findings, claims and views made in the literature review in this chapter regarding the prenatal and perinatal periods and its effect on personality development need to be looked at in an open-minded, prudent and questioning way, with a tremendous need for future research in this area. Clearly, psychological development during the prenatal and perinatal periods needs to be fully investigated, with such issues as professional concern and doubt regarding the ability to recall during these age periods needing to be respected. As a psychologist I clearly support and respect current knowledge regarding the physiological functioning of the human body, and provide what the writers have presented in this literature review as information to look at in the psychological and related fields. Additionally, the physiological aspects of memory recall in the prenatal and perinatal periods, though certainly not the focus of this book, is an area of utmost importance. Janov's (1991) discussion of the physiological aspects of memory recall is worth looking at.

According to Chamberlain (1992), there is intelligence before birth. He claimed that research findings indicate that the fetus has intrapersonal intelligence, being able to experience and express a range of feelings and to discriminate among them, and interpersonal intelligence, being able to notice and distinguish from other persons their feelings, moods, intentions and motives.

Barnett referred to Liley (1972) who claimed that the unborn child has distinct personality characteristics and is a dominant partner with the mother in the pregnancy process and is not just a passive entity.

Chamberlain (1992) claimed that life in the womb is an activity or practice in relationships, referring to Church (1988), Marnie (1989) and Verny and Weintraub (1991) that bonding between the child and parents begins in the womb. According to Chamberlain, mutuality in the womb is unavoidable where the mother and fetus breathe, eat and sleep together and perhaps even smoke together if that's what the mother does.

Turner and Turner (1993), in their whole-self therapy, claimed that the newborn child's psychological makeup is a synthesis through the mother of the parents' emotional state and experiences or the parents' emotional DNA during the nine months or so of pregnancy. According to Turner and Turner, the nine months of gestation is a time when psychological capacities develop, grow and practice. They also cited the ultrasound research findings of Piontelli (1992) that by thirteen weeks the fetus is indicating behavioral and psychological traits that continue after birth. In further supporting the influence of prenatal factors they reported that studies suggest that prematurity and pathology can be due to the parents psychological and interactional activities during pregnancy. In support of this, Janov (1991) claimed that "high stress levels in the mother cause both prematurity and immune system damage leading to later disease" (p. 142).

Gilmor (1989) referred to A. Tomatis, a noted French physician and specialist in otolaryngology, who was convinced that listening began in the womb. Gilmor claimed that among the sounds the fetus hears as early as four and one half months after conception is the mother's voice and through its rhythm and intonation the mother's voice communicates her feelings, stimulating the fetus's desire to communicate or discouraging it. Gilmor claimed that the sense of warmth and welcome in the mother's voice encourages the fetus to seek it out, whereas being in an emotionally insecure environment will encourage the fetus to withdraw.

Chamberlain (1992), cited Humphrey (1978), claiming that feelings of fear, hurt and anger are likely manifested in the earliest fetal cries documented back to twenty one weeks after conception. According to Chamberlain, it would not be fair to assume that fetuses don't feel, don't have anything to cry about or don't care. Chamberlain referred to Goodlin (1979) who thought that with air available, the fetal cries would be heard often.

Van den Bergh (1990) cited a number of research studies some of which included Ottinger and Simmons (1964), who reported that two to four days after birth children of high anxious pregnant women cried significantly more than children of low anxious pregnant women; Farber, Vaughn and Egeland (1981) who found that such infants showed a deviant behavior on the Brazelton Neonatal Behavior Assessment Scale; and that these infants, according to Vaughn et al. (1987), were seen by their parents as having a difficult temperament. Also supporting these findings is Chamberlain (1992) who referred to research conducted by Zuckerman et al. (1990) with over 1,000 infants and mothers at term, demonstrating that mothers who had been depressed during their pregnancy were more likely to have newborn infants who cried more than normally and were not consolable. Van den Bergh's results support these findings, claiming that "it may be concluded from our results that the influence of maternal emotions has been established in the prenatal period" (p. 127), with fetuses of high anxious women tending to be more active than fetuses of low anxious women for both acute situational anxiety and more chronic anxiety. She claimed that there is a certain amount of continuity existing between prenatal and neonatal behavior, with active fetuses having a high activity level after birth; that mothers' emotions during pregnancy are correlated with newborn and postnatal behavior; and that the correlations found indicated that children of high anxious pregnant women cry frequently, have gastrointestinal problems and are seen as having a negative temperament. Van den Bergh claimed that the findings should be interpreted with caution. The influence of prenatal and neonatal factors on psychological functioning needs in all cases to be examined in an openly cautious way, with further research needed to provide stronger additional findings.

Barnett in his clinical work using hypnosis, and research and findings regarding this, supported the influence of prenatal experiences on personality development and psychopathology. He also reported, frequently, that guilt and other uncomfortable feelings began prior to birth and that some patients even heard their mother or father expressing strong opposition to them, which appeared from my review of Barnett's article to occur before birth. This was mostly experienced as being deeply felt rather than actually heard. Barnett also reported that Frank (1966) believed that a mother carrying an unwanted child may be so depressed and emotionally disturbed that she may have a hostile uterus. In addition, Barnett cited Netter (1982), who reported that the rejection of pregnancy caused by psychoneurotic factors was associated with the infant's later development of aggressive or regressive tendencies. The rejection of pregnancy will often communicate to the fetus that he or she is not wanted. Barnett also cited Verny's (1977) review of the literature, reporting many examples of the effect of maternal stress on the fetus and that many researchers attributed infantile autism to the mother's intense anxiety during pregnancy.

Ward (1991) evaluated the relationship between prenatal stress and anxiety and the development of psychopathology in severely emotionally disturbed children and adolescents, some of who were developmentally disabled. In evaluating his data, Ward claimed there are important risk factors for child psychopathology, with his findings also applying to emotionally disturbed adolescent patients and developmentally disabled patients in his study. These prenatal risk factors included the pregnant mother being unmarried, the pregnancy not being planned, there being family discord during the pregnancy, the mother being unhappy about being pregnant, the pregnant mother emotionally rejecting pregnancy and the pregnant mother experiencing more physical problems than would be expected.

With regard to the power of mother-fetus communication, Riley (1988) discussed the process of transuterine communication from mother to fetus in unwanted pregnancies pioneered by family counselor B. Findheisen. Findheisen, who used a modified Gestalt technique for teaching these mothers to talk to the consciousness of the unborn fetus, reported that spontaneous miscarriages often resulted after such communication. Riley also referred to Watkins (1986), who used hypnotic visualization to help the mother communicate with the fetus to decrease the trauma of abortion, with some of these mothers reporting spontaneous miscarriages and all reporting it as a way to begin grieving before the loss of the fetus.

Chamberlain (1990) cited Feldmar's (1979) discovery that suicide attempts among four adolescent patients, who made previous attempts, corresponded to the month when their mothers had tried to abort them and that they used a method of suicide similar to the method of the attempted abortion.

Barnett also referred to James (1969) claims that illegitimate infants were a greater risk of being stillborn, indicating that the mother's psychological stress may be responsible for some of this greater risk. In addition, Barnett reported that Stewart (1955) found three times as many perinatal deaths and twice as much prematurity among children conceived out of wedlock. In both studies, the issue of the child not being wanted is likely in a number of cases.

Unwanted children often receive the message "I don't want you" and on some primitive level they may give up on themselves and wish themselves dead. This position has been supported by my own findings, where some of my patients who were not wanted by their parent or parents, while in hypnosis or relaxation reexperiencing themselves in the womb from about six to nine months from conception, the age period during which patients have appeared to reexperience themselves in the womb, wished they would not be born, that they would die or that they had never been conceived. Although my patients did not die prematurely, they had a strong wish to die, which could have been the case of some of the unwanted unborn fetuses referred to previously who did die prematurely. Premature death in the womb or premature birth, though due to physiological factors which may include inadequate prenatal care, in some cases may also be due to the unwanted fetus feeling unwanted on a primitive level, contributing to the "push" and need to get out of the womb which contributes to a premature death in the womb or premature birth. Although unwanted unborn children are more likely to be the victims of poor and inadequate medical and physical treatment, the issue of the fetus not being wanted and its psychological effect on the fetus needs to be further evaluated.

The fifteen adult patients I have worked with when reexperiencing life in the womb while in hypnosis or relaxation, believed and felt they were actually in the womb again. When reexperiencing life in the womb, the patients appeared to regress to the age of about six or seven months months from conception and older. Based on the literature review and my clinical experience, it is likely that these patients directly recalled prenatal experiences or that this was what they believed had occurred in the womb or a combination of these factors. In addition, though the birth experience will be discussed in the next section of this chapter, based on the literature review and my clinical experience with adult patients who have in hypnosis or relaxation relived their birth or the birth process, this same recall and reexperiencing process is also likely operating. In these cases, even if a patient's reliving of an experience was a belief, the patient's belief could usually only have occurred if it related to a specific event or situation or represented or was symbolic of some real life event or situation that actually occurred. As indicated, it is also possible there is a combination of direct recall and the belief of what occurred in the prenatal period or during birth when a patient reexperiences this time period.

I have worked with patients in relaxation who have psychologically regressed back to the womb reexperiencing maternal messages regarding their mother's pregnancy with them, which have included the mother's emotional and physical state while pregnant, wanting or not wanting her child, wanting to or wishing she could abort or get rid of her child, wanting to give her child up for adoption or wanting her child primarily to obtain meaning and satisfaction in her life, to take the place of a deceased child, for her spouse's satisfaction or to be a boy or a girl. The patient's adult mind assisted and interpreted this process, with the help of other healthy parts of the mind which occurs when reliving any past experience. (See chapters two and eight for the reliving and joining process.) Although occuring with much less frequently, some of these patients when a father was available in the prenatal period, appeared also to have received paternal messages of acceptance or rejection and messages related to his emotional state often communicated through their mother. They mostly appeared to become aware of their father's message when role reversing and becoming their mother while reexperiencing being in the womb. In a few cases, when role reversing to become their father while reexperiencing being in the womb, patients have connected to their father's feelings and thoughts regarding them as a fetus, as interpreted by their adult thinking. Despite this paternal influence, the mother's psychological effect on prenatal development appears to be more powerful, for she is the first person to influence the fetus and as her messages are in closest proximity to the fetus.

Because most prenatal recall, or what the patient believed happened in the womb or a combination of these factors has been of the mother's influence on the fetus in my work and is what the literature has primarily focused on, I have mostly dealt with the mother's influence during this period of development. For the same reasons the mother has been the primary area of focus during the birthing and delivery process. However, I believe the father's influence during these periods certainly should not be discounted, while further investigation of paternal influences during these periods is needed. In fact the issue of paternal influences during the prenatal and perinatal period was discussed in the example provided regarding the prenatal-birthing-rebirthing method in chapter fifteen.

I have also found that the unborn child may make decisions on a primitive and elementary level regarding prenatal life. Patients in hypnosis or relaxation clinically reliving life in their mother's womb have reexperienced feeling, thinking and the making of major decisions such as "I don't want to be born," "I wish I would be aborted," "I wish I would die," "I'm not loved, it will be terrible out there," "I'm not lovable," "I'm a burden," "I can't trust," "I'm bad," "I'll be so good. I'll just please" or "I'll hide or escape." Again, the patient's adult mind was interpreting and speaking for itself as a fetus, as he or she was reliving, feeling and thinking as a fetus from one's recall or at least from what he or she believed one was reliving, feeling and thinking as a fetus or a combination of one's recall and belief. The fetus cannot think or decide this in verbal terms, but, much more likely in the six to nine-month period after conception, appears to be able to feel, think and decide on some primitive and elementary level in response to the mother's message. Such primitive and elementary thinking and decision making appears to often have a powerful influence on the birth process and post-birth psychological development and functioning. These decisions are often supported and reinforced by the patient's birth experience and postnatal life of dysfunction, rejection and neglect. (The decision making process is discussed later in this chapter and in chapter five.)

Children can be born happy, sad, angry or fearful, but the reported etiology and causes of this mental attitude have often likely been mistaken for genetic rather than environmental factors. Parents may say "He was born angry," "She was born sad," "She was born loving," "He was born irritable," "She was born curious," "He was born fearful" or "She was born withdrawn." These remarks often are followed by "He is just like his father" or "She is just like her mother or aunt," more frequently relating these traits to genetic factors. Despite this genetic bias, my clinical experience and the literature review support such remarks as being indicative of the prenatal psychological environment having a strong influence on the developing child. The importance of the prenatal environment should not be underestimated, although much research is needed in this area. (The prenatal and birth periods are discussed further in chapter fifteen regarding the prenatal-birthing-rebirthing method.)

THE BIRTH EXPERIENCE

The birth experience has a major impact on personality development. According to Barnett, birth experiences can be recalled in hypnosis, and recall is often factual. On occasion, Barnett had the opportunity to confirm the birth experiences with the subject's parents. Barnett reported that Chamberlain (1980) compared the birth memories of ten mother-child couples and reported they shared a large amount of factual detail in most of the cases, concluding that birth recall is real, though the possibility of falsification does exist. Chamberlain affirmed that the content and quality of these birth memories give clear evidence of the newborn child's ability to experience, understand, learn and develop relationships, which previous findings indicate start in the womb on some elementary level.

Barnett also cited Meltzoff and Moore's (1977) findings that a newborn has a detailed awareness of his or her environment right after birth that can reasonably be assumed to have begun prior to birth. In addition, Barnett also referred to Harris (1967) who cited evidence that the events of birth and infant life are recorded, though not remembered.

For some theorists birth in itself is traumatic. Janov (1970) referred to O. Ranke, who wrote about birth trauma in the early twentieth century, believing birth itself is traumatic as the newborn leaves the warmth and security of the prenatal environment. Fodor (1949), claimed that birth is traumatic in almost every situation. According to Fodor, after nine months of tranquil development, the fetus "is forced into a strange world by cataclysmic muscular contractions which like an earthquake shake its abode to the very foundations" (p. 3). Fodor stated that the fear of dying began at birth, and that if the fear of destruction had not been so overwhelming at birth, it would not have been repressed in the unconscious. According to Fodor, the length of labor and the shocks or injuries the child receives influence the intensity of the birth trauma, and the love and care the child receives after birth is decisive in the persistence and severity of the birth trauma's impact.

Janov claimed that a birth is only traumatic if it is traumatic, that birth is a natural process and that anything natural is not traumatic. According to Roedding

(1991), Lake (1982) claimed that the process of birth for most people may be tough, though tolerable, and that for some it can be a devastating, suffocating, tearing, twisting, crushing traumatic experience in which the will to live may be destroyed. Roedding stated that the varying severity of nearly experiencing a death-like experience at birth differentiates the nature and degree of acting out for suicidal and nonsuicidal persons.

Barnett in his findings claimed that the birth experience has an important effect on personality development and psychopathology and that a negative birth experience in a large number of cases is related to the influence of prenatal experiences. In addition, Barnett referred to L. Feher (1981) who claimed that every person is made up of all that came before birth as well as what follows, for birth is a bridge to a new part of life. Feher also related certain personality structures to specific experiences of birth.

According to Rebuilding Theory, each birth should be regarded individually, assessing its psychological effect on the person and strongly taking the prebirth experience into account, for the birth experience is a natural continuation of the prebirth experience. The more the fetus's parents or parent want him or her, provide good prenatal care, are well adjusted, have not experienced negative or traumatic experiences of a physical or psychological nature during the pregnancy, have communicated messages of love and acceptance to the fetus and no physical complications for the fetus arise, the greater the possibility that the fetus will have a healthy psychological birth and a positive psychological "start" in life when not taking into account a traumatic or negative birth experience if this occurs independent of prenatal factors. Where there is a negative or traumatic prebirth psychological environment due to nonacceptance, rejection, family dysfunction, the physical or psychological problems of the parent or parents, poor prenatal care or the fetus having physical problems, the more likely the fetus has been damaged psychologically and will more likely have a difficult and negative psychological birth and poor "start" in life when not taking into account the effects of a traumatic or negative birth experience if this occurs independent of prenatal factors. If a traumatic or negative birth experience occurs this will likely add to the negative influences on the person psychologically. In addition, if during a mother's pregnancy, the less receptive she is to her child and the greater her psychological impairment, the more likely she will have difficulty functioning psychologically during her delivery and immediately after when looking at the delivery and birth process. Since I am a psychologist, my focus is on the psychological aspects of how persons are affected by the prenatal and birth experience, whether caused by psychological or physical factors.

According to Barnett, the newborn child is apparently capable of making decisions that will have a significant effect on his or her future. He claimed these decisions remain repressed, affecting the person's psychological functioning, and if these decisions can be reached in hypnosis they can be modified appropriately.

Barnett, in some cases, was able to obtain a verbal description of the negative birth experiences. This included the person as a baby feeling guilty for the mother's distress during delivery, the mother being unconscious during the delivery and not able to welcome the newborn in a positive way and the child not being wanted. Barnett also pointed to the frequency of depression among adopted persons. When referring, previously in this chapter to the issue of the fetus not being wanted and other psychological factors affecting the fetus, this process often carries over into the birth process, as has been discussed, and into the child's life.

Janov (1970) gave two examples of a traumatic birth, in one of which a woman relived her birth bunched up in a ball, almost choking, gurgling, spitting up fluid and then straightening out and crying like a newborn child, and in the second example, a person reexperienced his mother in labor for almost 20 hours. In the second case, Janov's patient stated, "'It was like my mother was going to make it hard on me from the beginning'" (Janov, p. 88). The birth experiences of these persons had a significant impact on their psychological development.

According to Janov (1991), birth trauma is coded and stored in the nervous system, and the way birth ends or a person responds to birth is a prototype reaction that remains permanently in physiological and psychological ways influencing personality tendencies in a broad and powerful way. Janov claimed, that "the pain surrounding birth is imprinted as a prototype (an original model on which something is patterned) that affects a variety of related behavioral traits" (1991, p. 147). Janov pointed out that if the neonate is heavily anesthetized during birth, due to the mother's anesthesia, the newborn is born in a passive way, which is stamped or imprinted as a prototype affecting him or her physiologically and behaviorally resulting in passivity, futility resignation and despair. According to Janov, the whole superstructure of a person's personality depends on the prototype, with prototypic behavior being "the memory of the beginning of neurosis" (1991, p. 150). The prototypic behavior, passivity or aggressiveness, for example, will become manifest only if it is reinforced in later childhood.

Hendricks and Hendricks (1987) reported diagnostic indications of birth trauma, which included feeling stuck, jammed or not able to get out, frustrated by rapid changes, having histories of respiratory illness or distress such as bronchitis, strep throat, chronic colds and allergies, developing nausea, head pressure, headaches or dizziness in stressful or energetic situations and having an extremely rigid body, for example, related to a forceps delivery. They also found that persons who were heavily anesthetized during birth tended to get sleepy during stressful situations supporting Janov.

Roedding, on the relationship between suicide and birth trauma, referred to Salk et al. (1985) and Jacobson's (1988) studies that both "found birth trauma to be a high risk factor for later suicidal behavior" (Roedding, p. 146). Salk found that birth trauma was the highest of forty-six risk variables, which included social and environmental factors, and that the most significant correlation leaned "toward prenatal and birth conditions in the obstetrical histories of the suicides under study" (Roedding, p. 146). In addition, Salk found that out of ten perinatal risk factors, respiratory distress, chronic maternal disease and no prenatal care "had the highest prevalence in suicides when compared to two matched control groups" (Roedding,

p. 146), with these risk factors occurring independently in 81 percent of the suicides evaluated. Jacobsen cited specific correlations between methods used to commit suicide and specific birth imprints, finding asphyxiation during birth to be four times higher in suicides of hanging, drowning and strangulation. Jacobsen found that mechanical injuries during birth involving the neck and head such as breech birthing, knotted umbilical cords and forceps deliveries were present in twice the percentage of suicides than in the controls. Roedding also cited Grof (1985), providing specific correlations between suicide methods and psychobiological recall of birth pain, referring to the tendency to hang oneself to be based on previous and strong feelings of choking and strangulation easily recognizable in the birth process. Other research, according to Chamberlain (1992), are correlations between birth complications and mental illness as found by Zitron, Ferber and Cohen (1964), Feldman (1981), Reading (1983) and Batchelor, et al, (1991).

The birth process has a significant impact on psychological development and functioning, though further research is needed as regarding the prenatal period. As with prenatal factors and other areas, the literature review in this book has been presented in a way to be informative to the reader with questioning of what had been presented and further examination encouraged. What occurs immediately after is also very significant, including the post-birth process and further postnatal development. Barnett reported the findings by Klaus and Kennell (1972) that infants who bonded with their mothers became more self sufficient and outgoing than children who were taken from their mothers immediately after birth before bonding could be developed. Of course, where affection and bonding take place, healthy psychological adjustment is more likely to follow. Much more can be said about this process, which will not be discussed here. However, the importance of welcoming the newborn child into the world in a loving and nurturing way is an important contributor to psychological health and well being.

POSTNATAL CHILDHOOD INFLUENCES

Infantile, early childhood and later childhood influences have been discussed and documented in great detail by Freud, analytic therapists and others. Such influences profoundly affect personality development and behavior, which is strongly supported and documented by the use of Rebuilding Therapy. Where there is a healthy psychological prenatal, birth and postbirth environment, the more likely the person will develop in a healthy way, psychologically, whereas if the psychological environment is unhealthy during these periods the person is more likely to have an unhealthy psychological development.

TRANSACTIONAL ANALYSIS FROM A REBUILDING THEORY PERSPECTIVE

Transactional Analysis, primarily Structural Analysis and the influence of Script Analysis, as developed by Berne (1961, 1963, 1964, 1966, 1967, 1972) has contributed strongly to Rebuilding Therapy. James and Jongeward (1971) claimed that Transactional Analysis was originally developed as a psychotherapy method preferably utilized in groups. Berne, Harris (1967), James and Jongeward, Steiner (1966, 1974), Goulding and Goulding (1976, 1979) and others' discussion of Transactional Analysis, as well as and my interpretation and modification of it as it applies to Rebuilding Theory and Therapy, will now be discussed.

Structural Analysis, according to James and Jongeward, is the analysis of the individual personality and "is a method of analyzing a person's feelings, thoughts and behavior, based on the phenomena of ego states" (p. 16). Script Analysis, according to James and Jongeward is the analysis of specific life scripts or dramas which the person compulsively lives out.

The Ego States

An ego state is "a consistent pattern of feeling and experience directly related to a corresponding consistent pattern of behavior" (Berne, 1966, p. 364). James and Jongeward referred to Berne's (1966), claiming ego states are the natural way one experiences and records events in totality. Ego states represent actual experiences and behavior, not hypothetical constructs such as the psychoanalytic id or superego. Berne identified three ego states: the Parent ego state or Parent, the Child ego state or Child and the Adult ego state or Adult, distinguishable by the person's thinking, mannerisms, posture, facial expression, voice tone, volume and quality, other physical characteristics and behavior. According to Steiner (1974) "every ego state, being a substructure of the ego, is in its own way an adaptive organ having as its function adaptation to the demands of reality" (p. 40).

According to Steiner, a person functions in one of the three distinct ego states at any one time which has the executive power to control the person's functioning. However, Steiner claimed it is possible for another ego state, though not in control, to become conscious and able to observe and dialogue with the controlling ego state and eventually gain control and significantly influence the person. Steiner claimed that this can occur with two ego states at a time and that the rate of alternation between ego states, pertaining to which one is in control, varies. In doing so Steiner referred to inner dialogues between ego states in every day life. In interpreting what Steiner said, this involves all three ego states interacting, with two of them appearing to interact at a time. It appears this interaction occurs at the rate and in the way the situation dictates as the three ego states influence each other and interact in every day expereinces. Whatever concious dialoging is occurring is always influenced by unconcious dialoging between the ego states, the extent of which depends on the person and situation. This interaction and internal dialoguing between ego states can be expanded to the person's overall psychological functioning, though when it does it becomes more complex, which will be described later in this chapter. As with any personality theory questions will be raised and other questions will be unanswered, though the door is always open for further research, study, explanation and theory. The ego states, as taken from Berne's TA, will now be described. See figure 4.1 for a structural description of the ego states.

Figure 4.1, Structure of Personality

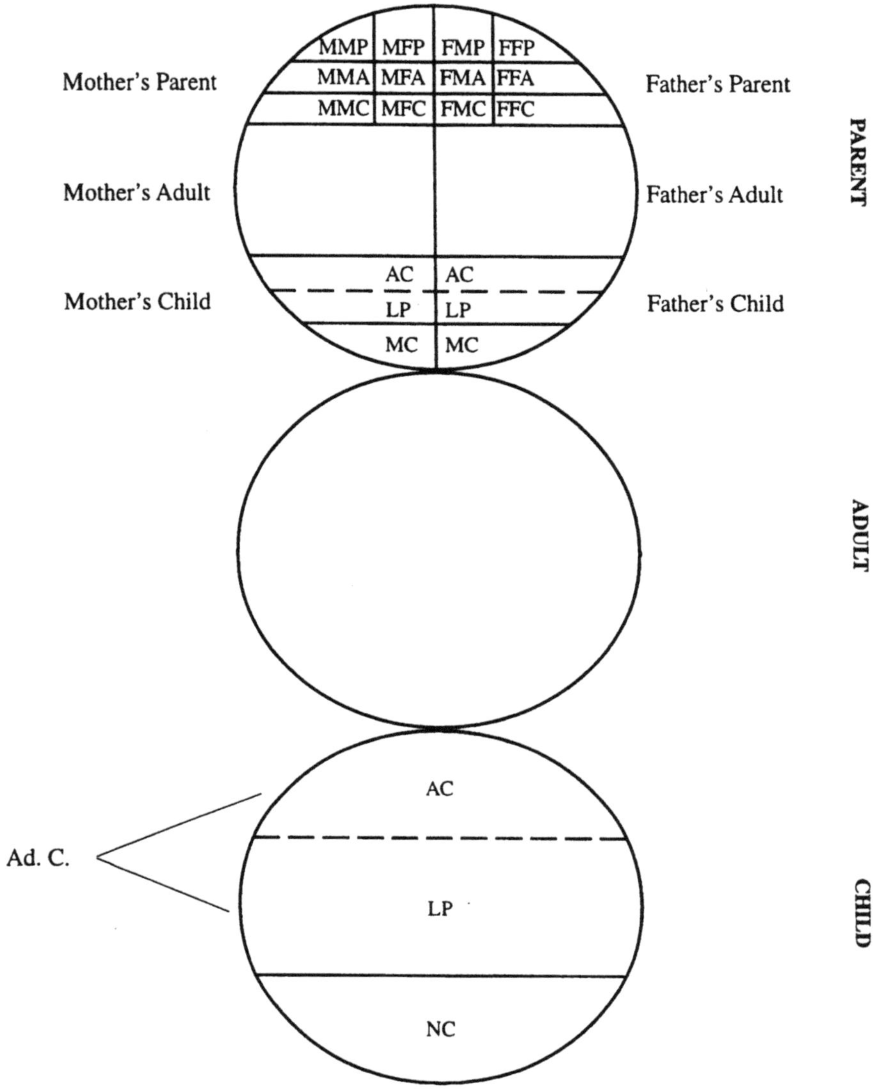

Ad. C.	Adaptive Child	MFA	Mother's Father's Adult
AC	Adapted Child	MFC	Mother's Father's Child
LP	Little Professor	FMP	Father's Mother's Parent
NC	Natural Child	FMA	Father's Mother's Adult
MMP	Mother's Mother's Parent	FMC	Father's Mother's Child
MMA	Mother's Mother's Adult	FFP	Father's Father's Parent
MMC	Mother's Mother's Child	FFA	Father's Father's Adult
MFP	Mother's Father's Parent	FFC	Father's Father's Child

Ego States of Person: Parent, Adult and Child

The Parent

The Parent is made up of behavior, messages, feelings and teachings incorporated, internalized and copied in whole without editing or modification from one's parents, relatives, teachers, clergy and other parental or authority figures in one's life. The Parent, according to Harris, is a large collection of recordings of imposed or unquestioned external events predominantly regarding one's parents or parent substitutes perceived by a person, or everything the child saw his parents do and heard his parents say in roughly the first five years of life. In other words, one's parents become internalized in one's Parent of what he or she as a child observed and heard them to do and say, according to Harris. I would add that this parenting process stems into adulthood as one continues to be exposed to parental influences, although their impact decreases as one grows older into adulthood and usually continues in adulthood in a slowly evolving way with the influence of such persons as parental figures, mentors and teachers and one's own self parenting. Steiner (1974) claimed that the Parent is a video replay of one's mother and father or whoever filled these roles. According to James and Jongeward, the Parent is comprised of the Parent, Adult and Child ego states of one's own parents and other parent figures. In addition, the Parent of one's father and mother is comprised of the Parent, Adult and Child of one's father and mother's parents and on and on, accounting for how traditions, customs, attitudes and behaviors are passed on from generation to generation. Thus, it is very natural for parents to treat their children as their parents treated them. It is not a thinking, cognitive or perceptual entity and preserves permanently its teachings, messages, beliefs, outlooks and whatever is stored in it. However, it is not a completely fixated ego state and has the potential to change. The Parent can change as the person finds new teachers and parental figures one admires and incorporates specific teachings, messages and values, although the earlier influences of one's parental figures remain significantly more powerful interacting with the Child until treated in therapy. The recordings of parental rejection in the Parent cannot be erased, yet the strength of such recordings can be increasingly weakened by strengthening the Child's thinking and decision making to counteract the Parent and by incorporating healthy messages and teachings into the Parent through reparenting.

Transactional Analysis therapists and writers generally refer to the Parent developing after birth. Harris wrote of the Parent developing in about the first five years of life, as indicated, whereas, James and Jongeward stated the child's first adaptations to the environment begin before birth in response to the mother's emotions, chemical makeup, nutrition and health. Such prenatal adaptations develop in the fetus in response to one's parent, for the most part the mother, and secondly the father or others close to the mother primarily through the mother. The strong support in the literature regarding the influence of prenatal factors supports the position that the Parent and Child and the developing Adult, the Little Professor, start in the womb on a very elementary basis. Woollams (1973) claimed that the Parent "is being recorded from the earliest of times..." (p. 32), and as Stuntz (1972) claimed, activates the Adapted Child in the Child. Whether the Child or the Parent develops first is open for further investigation as they both appear to need each other to come into existence. When exactly these ego states begin in the womb is also open to further investigation, although this process is likely to begin at least at about five or six months from conception.

The Child

James and Jongeward claimed that "the Child ego state is the inner world of feelings and experiences and adaptions" (p. 139). According to Harris, as the Parent is made up of the recordings of perceived external events primarily of one's parents or parent substitutes, the Child is the recordings of internal events which is what one perceived, heard, felt and understood in response to these external events or parental behavior and statements in about the first five years of life. However, as indicated, I believe this process starts in the womb and extends significantly beyond the first five years. What the child perceives, hears, feels, thinks and understands becomes more advanced and sophisticated as the child matures.

The Child develops in response to the Parent as the child matures. According to Steiner (1974), "the Child ego state is essentially preserved in whole from childhood" (p. 34). The Child is made up of three parts: the Natural Child, the Little Professor and the Adapted Child in traditional TA literature. However, I refer to the Child as being comprised of the Natural Child and Adaptive Child, the Adaptive Child made up of the Little Professor and Adapted Child. The healthy Child is the psychologically healthy part of the Child, while the unhealthy or wounded Child is the psychologically unhealthy part of the Child. Whenever the person is affected by negative and dysfunctional influences in his or her life and the term *Child* is used it refers to the wounded part of the Child, though the healthy part of the Child as part of the Adult Nurturing Self is assisting in the rebuilding process.

The Natural Child

The Natural Child, according to James and Jongeward, is what the Child would be naturally if it would not be further influenced. It is the center of feelings, including love, contentment, anger, hate, fear, joy guilt and so on. The Natural Child is also where one's needs such as those for care, security, love, sex, attention and self expression develop from. It is also the source of psychological energy and of dreams. The Natural Child is the very young, untrained, impulsive, curious, expressive, sensuous, affectionate, loving, uncensored and spontaneous very small child inside the Child. It is also selfish, self-centered, rebellious, aggressive, willful and fearful, pleasure seeking and pain avoiding and experiences itself as the center of the universe. The Natural Child is capable of feeling content, satisfied, dissatisfied, taken care of or not taken care of. James and Jongeward indicated that fantasy and imagination start in an uncensored way in the Natural Child, becoming more sophisticated as one grows older. The Natural Child's influence contributes warmth, caring, love, spontaneity, charm, the ability to fantasize and imagine, curiosity, self-centeredness, aggressiveness, anger and resentment to a person's personality along with the characteristics described.

The Little Professor

The Little Professor, according to James and Jongeward, is the emerging Adult in the Child and is intuitive, relatively capable of sensing and figuring out what is going on in its environment, creative and manipulative. Although James and Jongeward also claimed the child often develops wrong conclusions and makes wrong decisions, this is according to adult reality and without adult resources. There is no question that the more mature Adult can respond to its environment in a more rational, objective and accurate way than the less mature Little Professor and that the Little Professor is more limited the less mature it is and becomes increasingly sophisticated and advanced as it matures. However, thanks to how the mind has been made, the Little Professor, without being adequately experienced and knowledgeable about life, is still relatively accurate for the most part relative to the particular situation, in intuiting, sensing and figuring out what is going on in the child's world, including the verbal and nonverbal messages from one's parents and others and what is loving, accepting, rejecting, abusive, neglectful, guilt provoking or fear provoking. In doing so, the Little Professor makes relative sense out of one's childhood reality, learning to adjust, problem solve and survive, and makes decisions about life which often guide the child most effectively through childhood, relative to the situation, carried out by the Adapted Child, though some of these decisions may also be self-destructive and very self-damaging. These decisions are difficult to change and unfortunately often are dysfunctional when the child grows up in a dysfunctional and rejecting environment, being wounded and with less maturity and more limited resources than the adult to adjust to his or her experiences. When referring to decisions "often are dysfunctional when a child grows up in a dysfunctional and rejecting environment" or where the meaning is the same, it refers to a person usually making a number of dysfunctional decisions among the decisions made in a dysfunctional environment, the number, extent and frequency depending on the person and his or her life situation. When the child lives in a rejecting world, then he or she spends much more energy on manipulating his or her world in order just to survive. The manipulative skill of the Little Professor, related to specific decisions, includes such behaviors as whining, playing sick or "poor me," overpleasing, dominating, rebelling, bullying or having a temper outburst to get what one wants and withdrawing, and continues into adulthood for a large number of people. This manipulation also involves the Little Professor manufacturing acceptable reasons, rationalizations, excuses, projections, denial and other defenses, even if unhealthy and dysfunctional, to deal with and accept what is going on in the person's environment and to protect against and avoid his or her inner pain. The need to survive, defend and manipulate in a dysfunctional environment takes energy away from the creative, imaginative and healthy side of the Little Professor and leads to a dysfunctional and unhappy life, if one continues, as one grows older, to depend on these ways.

The Little Professor can create something original without guilt or fear and may not stay within the boundaries of things, but can develop new boundaries and a new creation, according to James and Jongeward. This creative ability, if unhampered, continues into adulthood. It can make a doll house into a loving home or a toy baseball game into a major league production. The Little Professor's belief in magic contributes to its ability to fantasize and imagine, which in turn is necessary for creativity. As James and Jongeward indicated, the ability to fantasize and imagine starts in the Natural Child. The Little Professor adds more reality and sophistication to one's imagination and fantasies. However, according to James and Jongeward, the fantasies of the Little Professor can be realistic or nonrealistic. James and Jongeward claimed that young children also attribute magical powers to parental figures fearing they have the power to turn them into ugly ducklings or snakes or make them disappear, with children learning to think of their parents as powerful witches or giants to be outwitted and of themselves as powerless. Of course the point that James and Jongeward made is that parents are perceived as very powerful in contrast to the weaker child. Positive fantasies of the Little Professor include becoming a famous actress or model, a doctor, a famous athlete, an attorney, having a happy family and so on. James and Jongeward claimed that believing in magic continues into adulthood. Wishing and waiting for a magical event to improve one's life, which many do, can develop into chronic disappointment when such a fantasy is unrealistic, such as hoping for the love of a rejecting parent, or seeking it out through others or one's achievements. When the person for the most part realizes that specific fantasies or wishes are not possible, he or she can grieve over this disappointment and develop realistic wishes and expectations for success. However, allowing oneself to fantasize in a healthy way provides direction to work toward in some way, even if the wish is only partially fulfilled or achieved in another or related way. Even when it can't be achieved, it is something a person can cherish or have for a short period of time as a source of strength, as long as it is not dominating one's life and one is following realistic expectations.

The Little Professor's intuitiveness, creativity and ability to wish and fantasize, if allowed to develop, can contribute to a healthy functioning and more fulfilled adult, whereas a dysfunctional parent continuing to adversely affect the growing child's Little Professor will contribute to ongoing psychopathology.

The Adapted Child

James and Jongeward claimed "a child's adaptations result in what Berne calls the Adapted Child" (p. 157).The Adapted Child is the child's adaptations to his or her environment, primarily one's parents and authority figures. Although the child's environment can provide love and security, it also places demands and stresses on the child while communicating direct and indirect messages. All too frequently this environment can be rejecting and neglectful. These adaptations, in the Adapted Child according to TA, are the child's attempt to survive, to find acceptance and approval and to avoid rejection. The Little Professor and Adapted Child require each other's assistance to operate. The Little Professor does the childhood intuiting, thinking and decision making, and the Adapted Child then carries out these decisions in a behavioral way through the beliefs and attitudes in these decisions that influence behavior. These adaptations will become healthy or unhealthy depending primarily on one's upbringing and background. As these adaptations must occur with the interaction of the Little Professor and Adapted Child, I believe a clearer description of this part of the Child is one where the Little Professor and

Adapted Child are merged into an Adaptive Child rather than two separate entities. The TA literature does not appear to provide a clear description of where the Little Professor's role stops and the Adapted Child's role begins, which Rebuilding Theory tries to clarify. (See the section later in this chapter on the processing of parental messages into decisions.)

The Adaptive Child

The Adaptive Child is made up of the Little Professor and Adapted Child and their interaction. It begins developing in a rudimentary way in the womb as the fetus adapts to the prenatal environment. The primitive Little Professor begins intuiting and making sense of its prenatal environment, responding to its messages, attitude and nature and the developing Natural Child's input and signals, and directs the primitively developing Adapted Child to behaviorally adjust to its environment in the least stressful and most comfortable way. This process continues, through birth and afterward as the child matures. The Little Professor's adaptation to its environment sets in motion its thinking, decision making and decisions that guide and direct the Adapted Child to carry out these decisions and to adjust to its environment. These decisions set into motion the course and direction of the person's life, unless effectively changed by therapeutic intervention, when needed. As a result Rebuilding Therapy sees the Adaptive Child as that part of the Child where the decision making process is carried out and completed. The Adult also has a decision making process that is more developed, sophisticated, mature and adultlike, and that eventually needs to take control of this person's life for healthy psychological functioning.

The Adaptive Child also accounts for the child's identification with and modeling from one's parental figures. This process, mostly unconscious, in which a significant amount of personality development takes place, is so powerful that it can overpower a person deciding that he or she is never going to be like one's dysfunctional parent. The child's decision to conform to and to model from his or her parents often is so strong that one's parents become embedded in his or her personality in a manner that appears to be of a genetic and physiological nature. This process occurs as the parent is the "world" to the child and represents everything to the child. How Mom or Dad feels, thinks and acts is the way "you're supposed to feel, think and act" as the child models oneself after his or her parental figures. In addition, to be like Mom or Dad is frequently interpreted by the child as the way to be accepted and loved. Also, the parent often looks strong and powerful to the child, and to be like one's parent also is the way to be strong and powerful. Although the Adaptive Child will also rebel, fail to meet parental expectations or make decisions that conflict with those of the parents, he or she still will identify with one's parents in varying degrees.

The Adult

James and Jongeward claimed the Adult, not related to a person's age, is oriented to the present reality and the objective gathering and taking in of information. While being organized, intelligent and adaptable, it operates by evaluating what is real, estimating probabilities, computing objectively and making decisions on this information or data. The Adult reasons, evaluates stimuli, problem solves, stores information for future reference and allows a person to survive independently, according to James and Jongeward. When the person is operating from the Adult, according to James and Jongeward, he or she evaluates before taking action, takes complete responsibility for his or her feelings, thoughts and behavior and uses what is okay from one's Parent and Child. Harris claimed that the Adult develops a thought concept of life in contrast to the Parent's taught concept of life and the Child's felt concept of life.

James and Jongeward referred to Berne (1963), who stated that the Adult is "'an independent set of feelings, attitudes and behavior patterns that are adapted to the current reality and are not affected by parental prejudices or archaic attitudes left over from childhood...The Adult is the ego state which makes survival possible'" (James and Jongeward, p. 248).

The development of the Adult begins on a primitive basis in the womb with the development of the Little Professor. The Little Professor is the precursor to the Adult and, in actuality, is also the emerging or Developing Adult. It remains the Little Professor in two ways: (1) being the healthy Little Professor providing creativity, intuitiveness and the ability to wish and fantasize with some type of sophistication and (2) being the Little Professor fixated and dysfunctional with unhealthy thinking, decisions and defenses. The primary distinction between the Little Professor and Adult, which continues to develop into and through adulthood as does the Little Professor within its limitations, is the Adult's ability to respond to and process more objectively, rationally, accurately and validly the stimuli, information and reality in its internal and external environment, with its more developed and advanced thinking and greater knowledge and experience, in contrast to the Little Professor's response to and processing of reality in a more immature way and often its strong defenses to maintain this. This does not mean that the Little Professor is unable to process reality effectively, for the Little Professor, as discussed, has the ability for the most part to respond congruently and with relative accuracy to its environment it knows, relative to its maturity and specific situation, intuiting and figuring out whether the child is treated well or mistreated and what is occurring in order to survive and often making the best adjustment to one's situation. Although it is usually easy to distinguish between the Little Professor and the Adult there is also a gray area between the Little Professor and Adult. However one can still usually tell when the Adult or Little Professor is in control.

James and Jongeward claimed that every person has the potential to place the Adult in executive control of the Parent and Child. This allows for a more objective and reality oriented processing of information, more effective decision making and a higher level of functioning. The functioning of the Adult and the quality of its decisions depend on how knowledgeable it is and how effectively it can choose, process and use information and data from its external environment and from the Parent and Child. This is a complex process, however, and depends on the development of the Adult, the interaction of the ego states and the contamination of the Adult by the Parent and Child. As this book is geared toward treating dysfunction and psychopathology, the dysfunctional interaction of the ego states and the contamination of the Adult, and the effect of this process on the Adult's development will now be discussed.

Interaction of the Ego States and Dysfunction

In the dysfunctional adult, the dysfunctional interaction between the Parent and Child that started in childhood, continues into adulthood and continues to result in the Child's direct impact on a weakly developed Adult and its direct contamination of the Adult due to the Parent's influence and direction. This is largely an unconscious process which the person usually becomes more conscious of as he or she matures, heals and rebuilds from, though the unconscious mind continues to have a significant influence on psychological functioning, varying in degree depending on the individual. The degree of dysfunctional interaction between the Parent and Child varies directly with the degree of childhood rejection, psychopathology and fixation, with the degree of childhood psychopathology and fixation also varying directly with the degree of dysfunctional interaction between the Parent and Child. The greater the degree of dysfunctional interaction between the Parent and the Child which is high in the dysfunctional Adult, the more the Adult is contaminated by the Child due to the Parent's influence and direction, further hampering the Adult's development and weakening its influence on the Parent and Child and entire self. The part of the Child having a direct impact on the Adult is the Adaptive Child, for when the Parent and Child interacted in childhood the Adaptive Child adapted to this process and continues to have a strong impact on the dysfunctional person into adulthood.

The dysfunctional interaction of the ego states just described briefly in which the poorly developed Adult has an inhibited influence on psychological functioning, results in dysfunction whereby the Adaptive Child's decision making, influence and identification with dysfunctional parental figures continues to strongly influence and significantly control the person's life into adulthood. The decision making process of the Adaptive Child to the dysfunctional parental messages is the way the child adjusts to the parent's impact, with these decisions, often dysfunctional, usually having a significant and lasting dysfunctional effect on the person's life into adulthood unless treated. Though this process will be discussed further in this chapter, it effectively describes briefly the dysfunctional interaction of the ego states. Figure 4.2 further illustrates this process.

The inadequate or incomplete development of the Adult and its contamination prevent the person from growing up emotionally, leaving it in the hands of a dysfunctional Parent and Child. Nonetheless, a part of the Adult develops in a healthy way, depending on the degree of dysfunction. The inadequately developed, contaminated, weak and unhealthy Adult and the healthy part of the Adult which exist, concurrently, still make it possible for the large majority of persons to live independent and conventionally acceptable lives with families, jobs and some fulfillment in life, though with varying degrees of dysfunction and psychopathology.

Figure 4.2, Decision Making Process Resulting in Dysfunction in the Adult

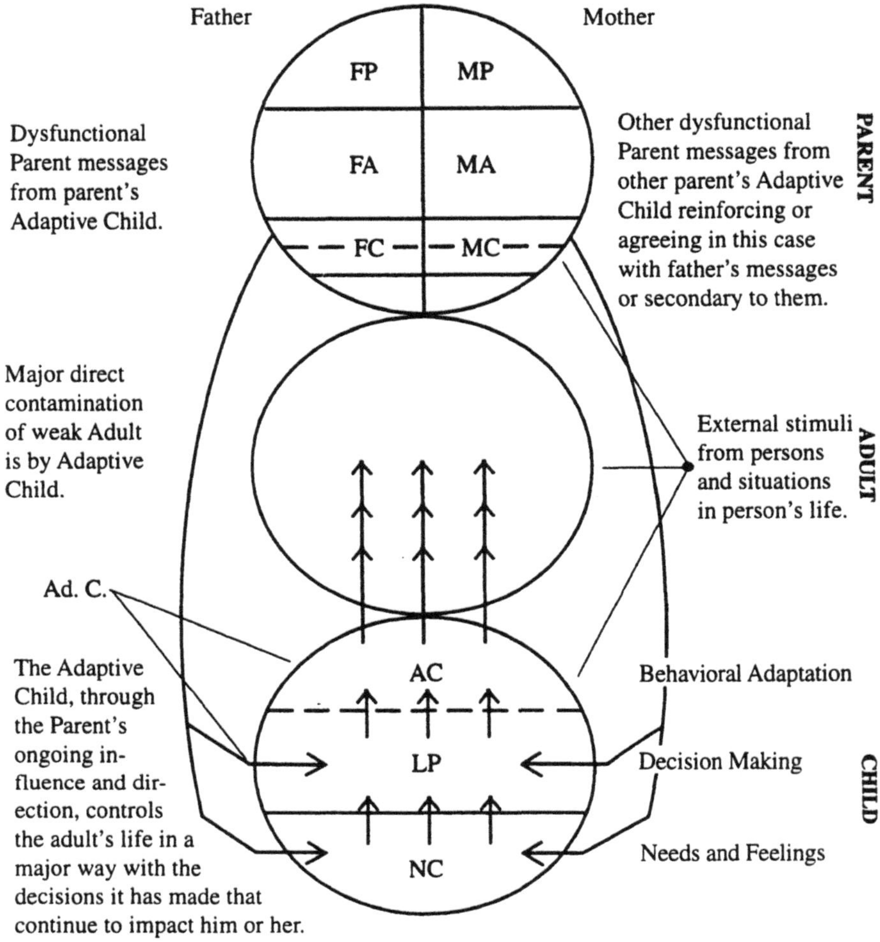

The adult when a child made major dysfunctional decisions to rejecting Parent messages, given directly or implied, resulting in dysfunction that continues unless treated. The direct contamination of the Adult by the Parent in the present is secondary to the major direct contamination of the Adult by the Adaptive Child. The healthy input into the Adult that is available from the environment and the Parent and Child, and the healthy operation of the Adult strongly depend on the degree of dysfunction.

Ad. C.	Adaptive Child	MA	Mother's Adult
AC	Adapted Child	MC	Mother's Child
LP	Little Professor	FP	Father's Parent
NC	Natural Child	FA	Father's Adult
MP	Mother's Parent	FC	Father's Child

Dysfunctional Interaction of the Ego States.

The degree of dysfunction depends on the degree of healthy Adult development and Child and Parent dysfunction and healthiness.

As the child develops, the primary interaction between ego states is between the Parent and Child, for the Adult is only a developing entity and minimally existent in the early years in a maturely functioning manner. The Little Professor in the Adaptive Child, as the forerunner of the Adult, is operative but in a childlike way. In childhood the Child, specifically the Adaptive Child, is the overt executive ego state directed and dominated by the Parent. When the child has been seriously mistreated, which often continues into adolescence, the rejecting and unhealthy Parent, within the chronologically growing person, continues to interact significantly into adulthood with the person's Adaptive Child or wounded dysfunctional Child without the significant and strong enough assistance of the Adult, retarding psychological maturation and health and often resulting in psychopathology and conflict. The Adult, in this case, has not been nurtured and parented adequately to develop and function in a healthy way, whereas the person's Parent and Child remain dysfunctional, dominating the person's functioning from the Adaptive Child. The dysfunctional Parent's and Child's role will decrease and yield to the Adult as the person matures, though they will remain powerful in the dysfunctional adult. Such a maturing process usually requires intense psychotherapy for the dysfunctional adult.

Although the role of the wounded Child is strong in the dysfunctional person, the Parent is more powerful as it originates and sets the policy and direction of this person's life, which the Adaptive Child has responded to and continues to respond to through its thinking and decisions in response to the direct and implied parental messages. The dysfunctional Parent is like a C.E.O., president or dictator in a in a dysfunctional person, whereas the Adaptive Child is the lower level sergeant, running back or receiver carrying out the policy of the Parent. Woollams agreed with Stuntz that the real influence on an individual's behavior lies in the Parent and that the Adapted Child is the middleman. Regarding this, Woollams was referring to the formation of the script, which can set up a life plan and scenario of dysfunction. The script is discussed later in this chapter. Further supporting the Parent being the primary influencer of the script, which involves a number of parental messages, Berne (1972) claimed that the script message from the parent is inserted into the Adapted Child like an electrode causing the Adapted Child to automatically respond to the parental message. Steiner (1966) provided an example, supporting Berne, referring to mother's Child giving the message "Don't be a Man" being lodged in her son's Adapted Child, causing him to avoid masculine behavior. This boy's nonmasculine father further strengthened the mother's message by communicating "How to be a non-Man" to him, which also became lodged in his Adapted Child. This, of course, leads to significant dysfunction in adulthood. Although Rebuilding Therapy believes that the child has some options in responding to parental mistreatment and rejecting parental messages, the decisions resulting from these options will often still be dysfunctional. The degree, extent and number of dysfunctional decisions to dysfunctional parental messages primarily depends on the degree of parental dysfunction, rejection and mistreatment in the child's environment. Though negative or traumatic experiences in one's childhood not involving parental figures can contribute to dysfunctional decisions, the parental messages are usually the primary contributors to unhealthy decisions and personality development. The degree of healthy factors in the child's environment, such as healthy parental messages and healthy messages from persons other than parents, can decrease the degree of unhealthiness in dysfunctional decisions, as can healthy decisions, but when the dysfunction and mistreatment is significant, which is the case when describing it in this book, such healthy factors only have a minority, limited and toning down effect on the dysfunction. This is not to say that healthy parental and nonparental influences don't have a major positive influence in other ways on personality development and functioning. However, the dysfunctional factors are very poisonous and need to be addressed in treatment if one is to heal from such factors and reduce or eradicate them in a major way. While the child has decision making abilities, as Holtby (1976) states "parents are still 'to blame' for dishing it out in the first place" (p. 372) when rejecting their children. The child would not have to make decisions to rejecting parental messages or be stuck with these messages and decisions if the parent didn't give these messages in the first place. Certainly, the child would be much better off without rejection and dysfunctional messages and, as mentioned, is often bound to make dysfunctional decisions to dysfunctional messages. For example, the parental message "You're no good," usually contributes to different decisions such as, "I'll never amount to anything" (functioning very marginally to giving up), "No one will love me" (withdrawing), "I'll show him. I'll be the best" (overcompensating and competing), "I won't trust" (not trusting others) or "I want to die" (giving up, escape and in some cases self-destructive behavior or suicide). See Figure 4.3 to further illustrate this. In addition, more than one parental message usually contributes to a decision. The specific workings of the decision making process are described later in this chapter with further clarification given in Figures 4.2, 4.3 and 4.4 to summarize this process.

In summarizing this process up to this point, the dysfunctional Parent strongly interacts with the Child in the dysfunctional Adult. The major direct interaction with the rather weak Adult comes from the Adaptive Child, which directed by the Parent, significantly controls the person's behavior and attitude. This is moderated, toned down and modified by the Adult relative to the Adult's strength, but in a minority nonmanaging role. There may be individual differences in the way the child responds to parental mistreatment, but the Adaptive Child will often respond in a dysfunctional way, usually making a number of dysfunctional decisions among the decisions it makes. In this process, the Parent's direct influence on the Adult in the present is secondary to the Adaptive Child's impact on the Adult, though the Parent is still directing the Adaptive Child in the dysfunctional adult.

As the adult in psychotherapy heals, rebuilds and matures in a healthy way, the unhealthy interaction between the Parent and Child decreases, with the Parent and Child becoming healthier, allowing for the freer development of a healthier Adult.

Figure 4.3, Roger as a Child Deciding

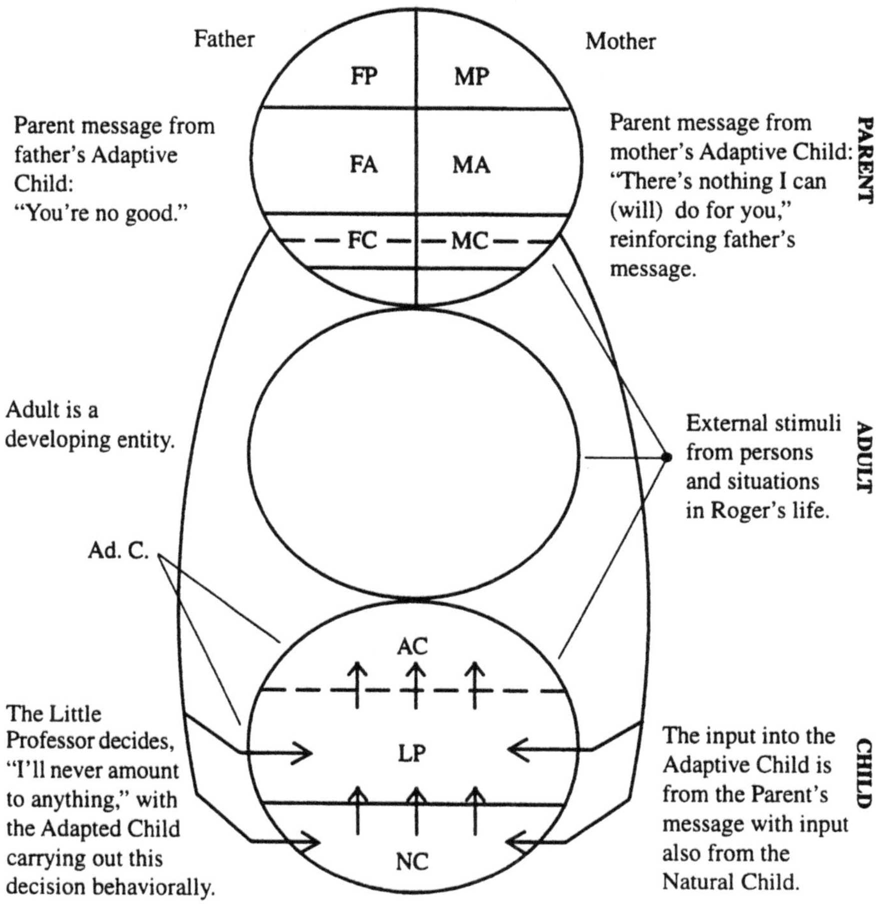

Roger making a decision to parental messages, given directly or implied, with both parental messages being major ones. The Adaptive Child is responsible for decision making resulting in an active and living decision. More than one parental message usually contributes to a decision, which may include other parental messages in addition to the parental messages in this example. One parental message also usually contributes to more than one decision.

Ad. C.	Adaptive Child	MA	Mother's Adult
AC	Adapted Child	MC	Mother's Child
LP	Little Professor	FP	Father's Parent
NC	Natural Child	FA	Father's Adult
MP	Mother's Parent	FC	Father's Child

Figure 4.4, Tamie as a Child Deciding

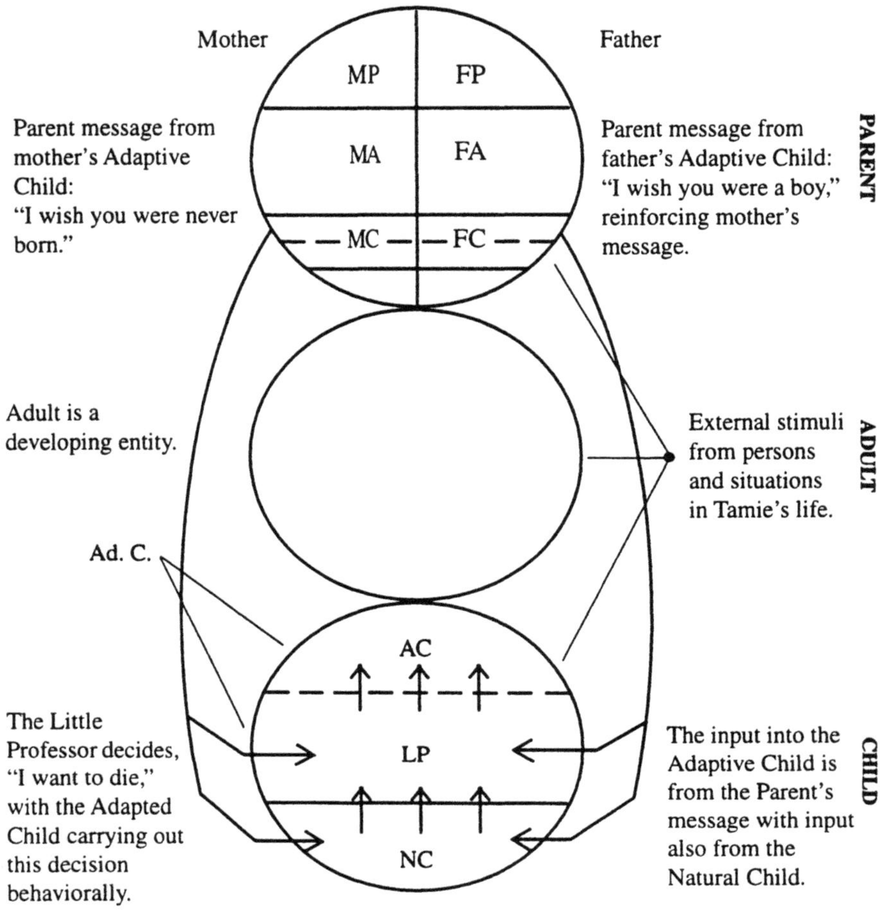

Tamie making a decision to parental messages, given directly or implied, with both parental messages being major ones. The Adaptive Child is responsible for decision making resulting in an active and living decision. More than one parental message usually contributes to a decision, which may include other parental messages in addition to the parental messages in this example. One parental message also usually contributes to more than one decision.

Ad. C.	Adaptive Child	MA	Mother's Adult
AC	Adapted Child	MC	Mother's Child
LP	Little Professor	FP	Father's Parent
NC	Natural Child	FA	Father's Adult
MP	Mother's Parent	FC	Father's Child

The healthier Parent's interaction with the Adult increases, and in a healthier way, while the Adaptive Child's dysfunctional impact on the Adult and its contamination of the Adult decreases. In the process, the Child's interaction with the Adult becomes more healthy and mature as the person grows. In addition, as the Adaptive Child has less influence, through the Parent's direction, the Adult has more involvement with the Natural Child and in turn is in more control of the person's feelings whether anger, sadness, love or joy and his or her needs such as for nurturing, affection, security and self expression. In this case, the stronger and more developed Adult is in the majority role, relying on its interaction with a more mature and healthier Parent and Child, and giving the person the opportunity to live a more fulfilling and productive life. To create a healthy functioning Parent, Child and Adult in a dysfunctional person, a therapeutic decontaminating, cleansing, reprogramming, rethinking and redecisioning process must occur, along with the informal reparenting process of therapy and, as needed, formal reparenting. In such a case, the Adult will become the chairman of the board and chief operating officer, with significant interaction and input from the healthier Child and Parent directly. The discussion of a child or adolescent's progress in therapy can also be provided referring to the interaction of the ego states. This discussion of the overall interaction between the ego states and the examples provided, sets the stage for a specific discussion of the decision making process in the Child, which in turn will set the stage for an understanding of the redecisioning process.

The Decision

As in Goulding and Goulding's Redecision Therapy, the decision is a major theoretical concept and therapeutic issue in Rebuilding Therapy. Of course, the parental message, direct or implied, is the strongest influence contributing to the original decision, but it is the decision that is the centerpiece of attention as it is instrumental in contributing to psychological development and functioning and is an entity which something can be done with, changing it. A decision may be major, powerful and broad affecting the entire life style of the person as the TA's script or it may be more limited and less powerful as the TA's counterscript. Major, powerful and broad decisions affecting the person's entire lifestyle are primarily made from the prenatal period through ages ten to twelve in response to one's experiences. Such decisions made during this period are made on an unconscious level in the early years, with decision making usually becoming less unconscious as the child matures, though still significantly affected by the unconscious mind with the degree of this depending on the child and situation. Major, powerful and broad decisions affecting the rest of one's lifestyle can also be made in response to traumatic or major events and situations after age twelve. Although the making of major decisions after age twelve usually continues to become less of an unconscious process as the person continues to mature, the making of major decisions is still affected by the unconscious mind, often in a major way, the extent depending on the person and situation. Of course traumatic or major experiences can occur at any age. Less powerful and significant decisions in response to life experiences usually occur after age twelve, and are more likely to be of a conscious nature, especially as a person continues to mature and isn't impaired organically, though one's unconscious mind still has an effect on the quality and maturity of such decisions depending on the person and situation.. Such decisions may still have an important impact on a person in some way, but are more limited in nature, though major decisions can also be made after age twelve as one grows into them or develops them including from more limited decisions. In addition, as the person matures and becomes emotionally healthy the Adult takes on more of the decision making operations from the Adaptive Child.

Rebuilding Therapy is not concerned with TA's concept of position, a term regarding how one perceives oneself and others, believing the decision encompasses the position it creates. A brief discussion of the script and counterscript is helpful for a better understanding of decision making.

The Script

James and Jongeward defined a script "as the life plan, very much like a dramatic stage production, that an individual feels compelled to play out" (p. 42) related to the early decisions and positions taken by the child, in the Child, through the person's interaction with his or her parent or parents. The script, according to Steiner (1974), is made up of the person's decisions early in life based on parental messages, injunctions and attributions. The prevailing TA view is that the parental message or "the injunction is the most important part of the script apparatus and varies in intensity" (Berne, 1972, p. 113). Steiner (1974) also claimed that injunctions vary in intensity, range, area of restriction and malignancy, with some injunctions only affecting a small range of actions or behavior, whereas others are very comprehensive in their range.

Berne (1972) described the injunction or parental script message as "a prohibition or negative command from a parent" (p. 443). Steiner referred to the injunction as a parental curse, prohibition or inhibition of the child's free behavior. Campos (1970) concurred with Steiner, claiming that "parental injunctions have a power and malignancy of supernatural witchcraft and often are received as 'curses' by the child" (p. 52). Rebuilding Therapy regards such messages as major dysfunctional parental messages contributing to the person's dysfunction.

Goulding and Goulding (1979) referred to parental injunctions as parental "don't messages" giving their "basic list: Don't. Don't be. Don't be close. Don't be important. Don't be a child. Don't grow. Don't succeed. Don't be you. Don't be sane. Don't be well. Don't belong" (p. 35).

Steiner (1974) also referred to attributions as the parent's message from the Adapted Child of the parent of what to do, with the injunction being the message of what not to do to remain in the parent's good graces. According to Steiner, attributions can be positive or negative parental messages predicting a child will be healthy or unhealthy, smart or stupid. However, I believe there really isn't any need to refer to attributions, for injunctions, being prohibitions, can apply to any rejecting parental message including such messages as "You're stupid," meaning don't be smart; "You're no good," meaning don't be a winner; "I wish you were dead," meaning don't live; "You're crazy," meaning "Don't be sane," "You're a child, what do you know," meaning "Don't think" or "You can't trust anyone," meaning "Don't trust."

Steiner (1974) claimed that the injunction is for the most part nonverbal, is not communicated in explicit words and is often implicitly given by disapproval or approval of certain types of behavior. However, Woollams claimed "with further work which leads to uncovering of early memories the negative injunctions ordinarily turn out to have been quite verbal and repeated often" (p. 33). In doing uncovering therapy for many years, I have often experienced patients directly recalling the verbal rejecting messages of their parents as it happened for the most part or what closely resembled it, while in other cases the message was implied. Implied parental message or messages are messages which imply a meaning from a specific verbal message or from such factors as facial expressions, posture, mannerisms, the tone and volume of the voice, a specific attitude or attitudes, a specific behavior or behaviors or the absence of a specific attitude or attitudes or a specific behavior or behaviors.

Berne (1972) claimed that for an injunction to be solidly locked in the child's mind, it must be repeated frequently and transgressions punished or in exceptional situations be from a singular traumatic experience. Steiner (1966) stated the script is pre-Oedipal, pre-conscious, nonverbal and visceral, though it can also be verbal or interpreted verbally. Goulding and Goulding (1979) and Steiner (1974) indicated that injunctions are given out of the parent's wishes, fears and anger, with Goulding and Goulding (1979) adding out of the parent's pains, sadness and disappointment. Holloway (1972) claimed that the injunction is utilized to reduce the stress and conflict in the Child of the Parent, to which the child has contributed.

McGee (1973) described the occurrence of double and contradicting injunctions when the script injunction from both parents differs. However, Berne (1972) claimed that most persons who marry have compatible injunctions. I have found that often both parents give out similar injunctions or script messages, or when they differ one of the parent's messages are usually more powerful and dominant. The child receives a number of script messages, usually from both parents or the more influential parent, although there are often major or key parental messages. When there is only one parent primarily in the child's life, parental messages may be implied through the other parent's absence.

TA theorists, such as Berne (1972), Steiner (1974) and Holtby, referred to the injunction as coming from the Parent in the Child of either parent or the Adapted Child of either parent. I believe the Adaptive Child of either parent is responsible for the injunction or message no matter how disturbed the parent is. The more pathological the injunctive or parental message, the more dysfunctional and unhealthy the Adaptive Child of this parent is.

The clearest term describing the parental message contributing to the script is the script message, if one chooses to use the script as a focus of concentration, which Rebuilding Therapy does not. I refer to these messages as parental messages, for most of them come from a parent or parental figure. When an influencing message that has a significant impact on the person comes from a nonparent figure, which is much less frequent, it is just referred to as a message. Of most importance is the meaning and significance of the parental message including if there is more than one meaning, and its intensity or strength. The strength of a dysfunctional message depends on the degree of parental pathology, the intensity and nature of the dysfunctional feelings and thoughts of the parent related to the message, the punishing verbal or physical action inflicted on the child or adolescent when delivering this message or after delivering it when the consequence is related to the message and the frequency of these factors as parental rejection is usually a repeated process. The rejecting parental message is of primary concern for it is the primary message contributing to psychopathology. The healthy parental message from one's parent can be looked at after dealing with the negative parental message, which will usually overpower the healthy parental message until dealt with. The healthy parental message is contrasted with the unhealthy parental message, in the winning life method in chapter eight, to help bring out the patient's feelings and thoughts regarding the rejecting message and what needs the patient had and has a right to request fulfillment of.

The Counterscript

Another parental message, the counterscript, helps clarify the nature of the parental message further. Steiner (1974) described to the counterscript as a reversal of the script, with parental counterscript messages coming from the Parent or Nurturing Parent of the parent contradicting the parental injunctions and attributions (both script messages) and being "an acquiescence to the social and cultural demands that are transmitted through the Parent" (p. 104). The counterscript message is the primary component of the counterscript. The counterscript message is usually a more positive message such as "Be a loving and good person," "Treat others equally," "Save your money" or "Don't drink," and is a conventionally held view regarding what people should do. Goulding and Goulding (1979) described counterscript messages as counter-injunctions, as being restrictive and, if followed, may prevent spontaneity and growth, including giving examples from Kahler and Hedges (1974, p. 38) such as "'Be strong,' 'try hard,' 'be perfect,' 'hurry up,' and 'please me.'" In addition, Goulding and Goulding referred to counter-injunctions as racial, religious and social stereotypes passed on from generation to generation. In this case, it may be negative or prejudicial. James and Jongeward claimed that counterscripts are frequently based on slogans or mottos that are like prescriptions for the child. Berne (1972) gave examples of other counterscript messages or prescriptions such as "'Work hard!' 'Be a good girl!' 'Don't eat starches!' 'Never sit on a public toilet seat!'" (p. 118).

Steiner (1966) claimed the counterscript, with its counterscript message, is post-oedipal, conscious and verbal. The counterscript becomes meaningful later in one's upbringing, whereas the script is inserted earlier in childhood, according to Berne (1972). (See the section on the decision earlier in this chapter.)

Most TA theorists claim that the counterscript message originates in the Parent or Nurturing Parent in the parent. However, Woollams stated that the Nurturing Parent may be the Parent or Adult in the Parent and sometimes the Child in the Parent. It appears that the Nurturing Parent or nurturing parental message originates from all three ego states in the Parent, the healthy Parent with its nurturing, caring and positive teachings, the healthy Adult with its reasoning and reality orientedness and the healthy Child with its intuitiveness, inquisitiveness, curiosity, creativity, spontaneity and ability to relate to the child or person the message is given to, with the healthier counterscript message occurring when the healthy parts of the three ego states contribute to this message.

According to Steiner (1974), the person will basically follow the script message because it is much more powerful and meaningful to the person's life than the counterscript message, which is temporary and usually brittle and unstable. Berne (1972) stated that while the script controlled the person's ultimate destiny, the counterscript determined the person's lifestyle. Woollams maintained that the counterscript message is communicated less intensely from the parent's Parent, which feels less intensely than the parent's Child from where script messages originate. The script message also has more impact than the counterscript, for it is delivered earlier in childhood when the child is weaker and is less able to deal with this message, except to be dominated and programmed by it. Steiner (1974) gave an example of the script message being "Don't cry and feel" and the counterscript message being "Be a loving man." In such a case, this person will probably have difficulty relating intimately, but may try to show affection by respecting others and giving love through material things. Steiner also gave an example of a woman with a loveless script after a brief period of well being in a relationship while in her counterscript, once again found herself loveless. The alcoholic who identifies with her mother's drinking, but is able to remain sober between binges is responding to her mother's script message to drink and counterscript message to be sober. Although there can be an alternation between the script message and counterscript message, the script message will prevail. It is very clear from these examples of the power of the script message over the counterscript message. However, the counterscript message does moderate the power of the script message and gives the person temporary reprieves from the script message or from as strongly carrying out the script message, although the script message is still carried out in varying degrees depending on the strength and pathology of the script message, the strength of the counterscript message and the strength of the person.

Steiner (1966 and 1974) and Berne (1972) all agree that the Adapted Child receives the script and counterscript message leading to a decision as part of the script or counterscript, although decisions in themselves, without referring to them as leading to a script or counterscript, are often very script or counterscript like. This leads to the parental message and the decision as Rebuilding Therapy views this.

Parental Messages And Decisions

Rebuilding Therapy doesn't distinguish between the injunction or script message and the counterscript message, just as it doesn't focus on the script or counterscript, preferring to focus on the decision. It looks at the parental messages from one's experiences as ranging from healthy to rejecting and neglectful to abusive and is concerned primarily with the dysfunctional rejecting, neglectful and abusive parental messages that contribute to dysfunctional decision making and are the focus of redecisioning. However, once the redecisioning process has occurred, Rebuilding Therapy is also interested in the healthy parental messages which the person can rely upon as part of his or her psychological growth. Even when the person wasn't exposed, for the most part, to healthy parental messages they are utilized as part of the therapeutic process, as needed.

Where this message comes from in the Parent, depends on the degree of its dysfunction. The dysfunctional rejecting, neglectful and abusive messages come from the parent's dysfunctional Adaptive Child, whereas the healthy messages usually come from the parent's healthy Parent, Adult and Child with the Adult in control. The healthy messages contradict the unhealthy messages from the same parent or other parent. However, the unhealthy and dysfunctional message usually prevails, when there is such a contradiction, because it is usually delivered with more intensity and power from the parent's Adaptive Child, especially having more impact when delivered to the weaker younger child. In such a case, the more powerful dysfunctional parental message, prevailing, contributes to an unhealthy decision. As indicated, the healthy parental and nonparental messages can have a toning down effect on the dysfunctional decisions and can contribute to healthy personality development and functioning in other ways. The parental messages are the primary messages referred to as they are the primary messages the person receives whether rejecting, neglectful, abusive or loving and usually have the most impact on the person. Sometimes the messages of a rapist, molester or individual who is not the person's parent, any of whom have abused the person, are also major messages. Healthy messages from nonparents can have a considerable influence on the person in some cases, but usually are less influential than the healthy parental messages. As mentioned earlier in this chapter, both parents often give out similar messages or when they are different one of the parent's messages are usually stronger and more dominant. Although one parental message can strongly contribute to a dysfunctional decision, more than one parental message usually contributes to the creation of a dysfunctional decision. However, in some cases, though much less frequently, a powerful parental message can be the primary contributor to a dysfunctional decision, without other messages contributing significantly. If looked at in another way a powerful parental message often encompass weaker messages which are also delivered. The number of parental messages and their frequency of occurrence, as with the experience, contributing to a decision, primarily depend on such factors as the strength of the parental message and the decision and the environment the person grows up in. Some parental messages may not be strong enough and delivered frequently enough in combination with other parental messages to have a significant impact on the person, but still appear to be stored by the person. If such messages have any influence on the person it is in a minor way. As with the experience, which the message is part of, this is a complex process with individual variation which needs to be further assessed and looked into as with any aspect of personality theory. Each parental message, which is usually repeated, contributes to a tentative decision, usually developing into the final living decision. As indicated, more than one decision usually results from a parental message with this usually being more pronounced if it is powerful, such as "I wish you were never born." However, with such a message the parent is likely to deliver other rejecting messages, such as "You're so ugly," "You're such a burden" or "You can't do anything right." Such messages may be part of this message or independent though this is a different process to determine. Less powerful parental messages, if they can be processed to make a decision, will usually result in less powerful or weaker decisions, with the stronger decisions prevailing in directing one's life. The weaker contradictory decisions can have an impact on the person in the way that the counterscript does. One or both parents may deliver any of these messages. As indicated, parental messages, direct or implied often overlap with stronger ones often encompassing weaker ones, while decisions also often overlap, often including weaker decisions.

A decision can affect a person's entire life or only part of it, can incorporate subdecisions and be script-like or counterscript-like. Decisions can range from "Whites (Blacks) are," "I will never work for anyone," "I won't show my anger" or "A man (woman) will take care of me" to "Winning is all that matters," "I don't want a family and children" or "I don't need anyone" to "I'm no good," "I will never amount to anything" or "No one in the world can be trusted" to "I want to die," "I'm going to kill myself," "I want to murder him or her" or "I will murder him or her." Broader, more powerful major decisions, such as "I'm no good," may include subdecisions such as "I won't apply myself," "I'm unlovable," "I won't get close to anyone," "I'm ugly" or "I don't have a right to express my feelings." Sometimes such a decision can contribute to a more powerful decision, such as "I want to die" though the parental message is the primary causative factor. Whether a major decision may result in the development of subdecisions, or more limited decisions may contribute to a major decision, again the parental messages are the primary causative factors in decision making.

Whatever the decision, the decision making process is the same for each decision, whether a major decision, a subdecision or a limited decision, following the same process as script and counterscript formation, which involves decision making regarding the development of the script and counterscript.

Decisions contribute to specific attitudes, beliefs and behaviors with specific behaviors having an emotional-cognitive component.

Processing of Parental Messages into Decisions

As has been discussed, the Parent has the primary influence on personality development and on decision making, although the Adaptive Child through its decision making process tries to make the best of its childhood world.

The parental ego state needing to have the primary influence on its offspring for healthy psychological functioning is the Adult, with the assistance of its healthy Parent and Child. However, when the parent has an unhealthy Child, his or her Adaptive Child significantly controls the parent, through the influence and direction of his or her unhealthy Parent, and in the process will negatively influence one's offspring with unhealthy parental messages, who in turn will often make unhealthy decisions regarding living life and will usually become dysfunctional in the process. The child's processing of the parental message into a decision will now be described. Although the focus of this book is on unhealthy decisions, the child also makes healthy decisions in this way.

As the parental message is communicated to the Child, it impacts the Natural Child responding with specific feelings and needs. The message also impacts the Little Professor responding in a cognitive and reality oriented way relative to the child's capacities regarding what this message means and what is happening, and then, after also assessing the Natural Child's feelings and needs, works toward making a decision regarding this information. The Adapted Child then stores the Little Professor's decision making work for behavioral action and usually lives it out in some way directly or indirectly when ready with the approval of the Little Professor. One decision can contribute to one or more specific attitudes, beliefs and behaviors. Though each behavior has an attitude and belief component or an emotional-cognitive component that affects a behavior, the relationship between the emotional-cognitive component and a specific behavior depends on the person and his or her situation. The Adaptive Child is the entity responsible for the overall decision making impacting and influencing the person's life, with both the Little Professor and Adapted Child needed for the making and living out of a decision, respectively. Although the Little Professor initially makes the decision, its value or impact is implemented by the Adapted Child, leading this author to refer to the Adaptive Child as making and being responsible for the completed decision or decisions. In this light, and as the Little Professor is part of the Adaptive Child, the Adaptive Child is often referred to when discussing decision making and redecisioning in the context of psychological functioning as this author describes it. The Adaptive Child, as indicated, will usually make more than one decision in response to a parental message. See Figure 4.2 for an illustration of this process.

Holtby's interpretation is similar, except that he didn't postulate the parental message directly impacting the Natural Child, although he claimed that the Little Professor does take into account the needs data of the Natural Child.

Woollams gave the Adapted Child more strength, claiming that the decision or decisions in response to parental messages take place in the Adapted Child with the help of the Little Professor in response to the feelings of the Natural Child. I agree with Holtby that the Little Professor is the centerpiece of the child's decision making rather than just assisting the Adapted Child, whose primary role is to carry out behaviorally what the Little Professor decides in response to parental messages. This has much to do with the development of the Adaptive Child to avoid this confusion and referring to it as making the completed active living decision, without devaluing the input of the Little Professor. For example, the parental message "I wish you were never born," whether implied or made directly, may contribute to such decisions as "I want to die or I want to disappear" (some type of escape, self-destructive behavior or suicide), "I will not be a burden" (withdrawing and not being assertive), "I'll do everything to please and never upset anyone" (overly conforming and burying one's feelings), "The world is bad. I'll get him or her before he or she gets me" (antisocial and sociopathic behavior) or "I'll be the boy you want me to be" (female denying her femininity) also in response to the parental message "I wish you were a boy" with the Adapted Child carrying out these decisions. The parent inflicting the message "I wish you were a boy" to his or her daughter is also communicating to her, "I wish you were never born." As mentioned, more than one of these type of decisions are usually made by the same child to a parental message and more than one parental message usually contributes to a decision. Also, different children may make different or similar type of decisions to the parental message "I wish you were never born, though usually more than one of these type of decisions to such a parental message." See Figure 4.4 to further illustrate this. Figure 4.4 is also a good description of the decision making process that originally occurred with Edna in the example provided in chapter fifteen. Although the Adaptive Child has been developed to avoid what disagreement may exist regarding the role of the Little Professor and Adapted Child, the Little Professor and Adapted Child are still referred to because of their discussion in the literature and because it is beneficial, as in this context, to describe their interaction at times.

James and Jongeward claimed, after referring to Berne (1964), that an individual's "experiences are recorded in the brain and nervous tissue" (p. 17) and that these stored video tape-like recordings can be replayed, recalled and reexperienced. These recorded experiences include such factors as what one experienced in childhood and internalized from parent figures and one's perceptions and feelings related to these events according to James and Jongeward. Taking this a step further with the support of my literature review, experiences occurring at any time in a person's life can be recorded in this way.

Holtby also pointed out that the parental message sent into the Child is not necessarily the message that is received. The accuracy of the Little Professor's interpretation of the script message, according to Holtby, can be questioned on two bases: that the Little Professor had insufficient and incomplete information at the age the message was incorporated and that the Little Professor's conclusions regarding the parental messages were based on primary thought processes that are more elementary compared to the more sophisticated secondary thought processes of the Adult. Holtby also pointed out that the Little Professor's interpretation of the parental injunction does not account for the parent's motivations, which are mostly positive and which could account for the child misinterpreting the parental message. However, even if a parent is positively motivated and well intentioned, delivering this message to the child in a rejecting way will primarily communicate rejection rather than a loving message.

Although the Little Professor's interpretation of the parental message may not be totally accurate, or an overreaction or inaccurate at times, according to adult standards, it still usually is on target intuiting and knowing when the child is loved or unloved, wanted or unwanted, approved and accepted or a burden or disappointment, or whether a message is healthy or unhealthy. The Little Professor also has the ability to intuit and know when a major nonparental experience is healthy or unhealthy or positive or negative, though the child's response to the parental message is the primary focus of this discussion. Even when the child overreacts, according to adult criteria, to the parental message, this is not unexpected with his or her immature mind being less developed in contrast to the "big" and powerful adult. Holtby supported this in giving the example of a mother's message "You're even worse than your father," who had killed himself, being interpreted by the child's Little Professor to mean "Don't be." Goulding and Goulding 1979 claimed the child can also fantasize, invent, and misinterpret, thereby giving him or herself one's own injunctions or messages. The Gouldings referred to the example of a child believing his own jealousy magically caused the death of a sibling and giving himself a "don't be" message, which in actuality is deciding not "to be." Even in those cases when the Little Professor's interpretation of a parental message, according to adult reality, is significantly inaccurate, it must be respected and accepted based on the child's reality, feelings and thinking at the time, especially since an important decision was likely influenced by it which significantly affects the person's life and usually needs to be changed in a healthy way. In summary, though the child's Little Professor does respond inaccurately at times to parental messages or situations and does not respond as rationally, objectively and as accurately to its environment as the Adult, in my clinical practice, assisting patients to explore the depth of their mind on the road to rebuilding, I have found that the child's Adaptive Child (Little Professor deciding and Adapted Child carrying out the decision) for the most part responds congruently and with relative accuracy, relative to the specific situation, to parental messages regarding what it perceived, heard, felt and understood, often making the most effective decisions at the time relative to the situations the child experiences. Despite this, the Adaptive Child, being wounded and with its less mature and more limited resources, will usually make a number of dysfunctional decisions in response to parental mistreatment, rejection and dysfunctional messages. The degree, extent and number of dysfunctional decisions primarily depends on the degree of parental rejection, mistreatment and dysfunction. Although such decisions, as indicated, often are the most appropriate ones at the time relative to the situations the child experiences, they often are unhealthy compared to the healthy way the child would most often respond in healthy situations and will usually continue to influence, direct and control the person's life as he or she develops chronologically unless treated. This process also applies to the adolescent in varying degrees, depending on the family dysfunction and his or her maturity and psychopathology. In addition, in psychotherapy, whenever a patient clinically reexperiences a specific event, the patient's Adult has the opportunity to add adult reality to one's recall to further clarify it, usually resulting in one's recall being accurate, even if one's interpretation wasn't accurate, while assisting the patient as part of the Adult Nurturing Self's overall help to make a healthy new decision or decisions.

AN OVERVIEW

The human being from the fetus, from about six months from conception and older in the womb, to the adult, relative to the situation, has the capacity to respond accurately to stimuli in the environment and to the treatment one receives, intuiting and knowing when he or she is loved or unloved or if something is okay or not okay. Personality development is an unconscious process in the early years of life, that usually becomes less of an unconscious process as the person matures, though the unconscious mind continues to have a major influence on the person's life, varying in degree depending on the individual. The person brought up with love and respect from the prenatal period through adolescence is more likely to become well adjusted and psychologically healthy with healthy decision making, whereas the person brought up from the prenatal period through adolescence in a dysfunctional and rejecting way is more likely to become dysfunctional and psychologically unhealthy with unhealthy decision making he or she is stuck with having to make. Knowing this, the mind is very predictable and needs to be treated as such when understanding personality and psychological functioning and healing and rebuilding the human mind. Of course, the degree of dysfunction and psychological health for the dysfunctional person and healthy person will depend on the specific person and his or her overall life situation. Further research and study is clearly needed regarding psychological functioning in the prenatal and perinatal periods, though further research and study is also needed in other areas of personality development and personality theory, as well as in the area of psychotherapy.

CHAPTER 5

Other Therapies, Methods and Theories in Relation to Rebuilding Therapy

REDECISIONING

Berne's Transactional Analysis has made a significant contribution to the development of Rebuilding Therapy, as discussed in chapter four. Berne (1961) claimed that "The ultimate goal of Transactional Analysis is the structural readjustment and integration" (p. 224) of the personality, with the optimal situation for this requiring "an emotional statement from the Child in the presence of the Parent and Adult" (p. 225). This optimal situation, in interpreting Berne, occurs in his regression analysis, which Berne appeared to coin, where the Child ego state is revived in an experiential way, while being at the disposal of the patient and therapist for detailed evaluation. It is an attempt to assist the patient to experientially understand one's Child's effect on oneself and to deconfuse and clarify the Child's thinking. Berne claimed that this revival of the Child is more than an abreaction and a working through, where the Child is treated like a real child gently nurtured and turned over and over until previously unseen features are perceived and unfold. Regression analysis appears to involve more of an experiential understanding of a part of the Child with the help of the therapist, rather than a specific programming or reprogramming of the Child. In discussing this approach, Berne pointed out that the therapist's Child, by relating to the patient's Child, is helpful to the therapist's Adult in assisting the patient to better understand his or her Child's impact on oneself when reexperiencing a specific situation before eight years of age. Berne's description of regression analysis needed further clarification, while he acknowledged it was in its rudimentary stages in 1961.

Gellert (1974) described regression analysis as the process whereby a young Child ego state is cathected in the presence of the patient's Adult. Although regression analysis has had potential from Berne and Gellert's description of it, it has needed significant development and refinement. It appears that regression analysis was never further developed, at least in name, although others such as Goulding and Goulding (1979) and those doing age regression work, as I, have been doing this type of work without calling it regression analysis. Its contribution is its description on an elementary level of what needs to occur in redecision work to a significant extent.

With regard to the effectiveness of redecision work, Gellert (1976) distinguished key scenes from early scenes as being necessary for effective redecision-type therapy. According to Gellert, redecision work may be ineffective when a person goes back to an early scene which will not account for one's present individual's feelings or behavior, with the person in future sessions likely going back to the same scene or event in an impasse. Gellert claimed that when the past key scene and decision associated with it are reached, it will usually have a heavy emotional content, may approach a primal in its intensity and will account for and explain the individual's feelings and behavior over a series of life events, including the present.

Goulding and Goulding's Redecision Therapy, which helps the patient change unhealthy childhood decisions to healthy decisions (redecisioning), appears to be a further development of regression analysis or is at least closely related to this process. Goulding and Goulding (1979) claimed that no one is scripted and that injunctions or parental messages are not placed in people's heads like electrodes, as Berne claimed. According to Goulding and Goulding, a child makes decisions in response to parental messages and influences in his or her life. Goulding and Goulding (1979) stated that the person writes one's own script and can rewrite it with the assistance of a strong Parent he or she builds within oneself, rather than being scripted and needing to incorporate a strong Parent in the therapist to change the script. However, as indicated, the original script writing or decision making and development is strongly influenced and is at the mercy of the powerful parent in the child's attempt to survive and adjust to parental treatment, demands and messages. The individual child's response, as Goulding and Goulding (1976) claimed, may be unique. However, such unique responses in a dysfunctional environment are often unhealthy compared to how the child would most often respond in a healthy way in an emotionally healthy family and remain dysfunctional as the person grows older if not changed. The rewriting of the script occurs in therapy where the patient has an opportunity to redecide from the Child according to Goulding and Goulding. I advocate that the therapist, as a surrogate parent, will assist in this process, but it is the patient oneself who is changing his or her thinking and decisions in the Adaptive Child with the help of the healthy Adult's understanding of reality, the healthy Parent's nurturing and teachings and the healthy Child's intuitiveness, spontaneity, creativity, sensitivity and ability to relate to the wounded Child's feelings and needs. As indicated, Rebuilding Therapy refers to this assistance or helping entity as the Adult Nurturing Self, comprised of the healthy Adult, the healthy Parent and the healthy Child working together, assisting the wounded Child in the redecisioning process.

Redecision Therapy does not utilize the script in a detailed way and is concerned mostly with the injunction or parental message, decision and redecisioning process with which Rebuilding Therapy is also primarily concerned.

Redecision Therapy involves the patient finding a childhood scene or experience related to his or her present problem, where an injunction or unhealthy parental message was given and an unhealthy decision was made and then, while reexperiencing this event, making a healthy redecision in the Child and rejecting the injunction one formerly accepted. However, this is a complex process, as usually more than one injunction or parental message and more than one experience, from which the messages come from, contribute to a decision, while usually more than one decision are strongly influenced by a parental message and experience. As a result it is necessary to relive whatever experiences are necessary to change unhealthy decisions to healthy decisions. This, however, does not mean that the patient needs to relive every experience and in the frequency which they occurred that contributed to a decision, for, as discussed in chapter two in the living out stage, one major experience frequently represents some or a number of experiences like it or similar to it. In the process to change unhealthy decisions to healthy decisions and to rebuild oneself, the patient will often only need to relive major experiences representing other experiences similar to it and, when needed, though occurring much less frequently, singular major experiences that don't represent other similar experiences. The reliving process may include, as needed, reliving the same experience again fully, partially or it another way than the patient did previously. The particular major experiences the patient relives depend on his or her specific life situation, with the patient often allowing oneself, when motivated, to experience what is needed. As indicated, also, in chapter two, sometimes it may be necessary to relive a minor experience to warm up to the reliving of a major experience.

According to Goulding and Goulding (1979), for successful resolution the patient involves oneself in his or her memories, reexperiencing in his or her Adapted Child the memory of one's significant others, the place, how they looked, sounded and felt, feeling intensely the same feelings one did when making the original decision. Experiencing one's adaption to his or her past experience makes the patient's redecision very powerful as he or she knows the difference between the original decision and adaption and the new healthier one according to the Gouldings. They point out, emphasize and mirror the patient's gestures, moves, words and tones, which reinforce the patient remaining a victim, in order to stimulate the patient to fight back. This process helps the patient experience the impact of his or her past experience on oneself and the context of how and why the decision was made and in experiencing the unhealthiness of this assists him or her to change this decision. Although Rebuilding Therapy is concerned with the patient's mannerisms, gestures and moves, it focuses primarily in the living out process on the patient experiencing, expressing and cleansing oneself of his or her unhealthy feelings and thoughts and emotional pain, followed by healthy redecisioning. If this process is blocked by the patient's unhealthy defenses, then the patient may be stimulated to look more deeply at these defenses (unhealthy thinking and behavior) related to the relived experience to stimulate the patient to become more connected to these defenses and then to begin giving them up. The patient then can return to the reliving process to accomplish the redecisioning, if possible. Rebuilding Therapy's mirror and confrontation methods that stimulate the patient to experience the impact of his or her behavior and symptoms on oneself and others, have been developed to confront the parents dysfunction and related decisions.

According to Goulding and Goulding (1976), if patients get in touch with the power they had as children to make decisions, while realizing they were the ones to decide to be unhealthy, unloving, distant or "all work" they could change this. Although the Gouldings seem to be giving more power to the child than he or she actually has, not taking into account the tremendous power of the parent, what is important is that the child has a decision making mechanism that the patient needs to connect to in one's Child. This also underlines the importance of making the redecision in the Adaptive Child in the reliving process as a child again, when and where the original unhealthy decision was made, for as one is reexperiencing oneself making an unhealthy decision one is experiencing the mechanism and power one had to do this. In experiencing this decision making mechanism in one's Adaptive Child, the person realizes and experiences he or she has had the power in the Adaptive Child to think, evaluate and make decisions, including a healthy decision. Thus, as a person had the power to make an unhealthy decision, though stuck with it at the mercy of the parent in the less developed and weaker state of a child and victim, the person now in one's Child again, and with the help of one's Adult Nurturing Self, is connected to the Adaptive Child's power of decision making and dismantling his or her original decision and making a healthy decision. Reliving experiences, one at a time, for the most part the major experiences, and the parental message or messages from each experience that contributed to an unhealthy decision, is also necessary as one needs to connect to the unhealthiness, poison and dysfunction of this situation to know and feel throughout oneself what one is dealing with that helps make it possible to repair and rebuild oneself. Once realizing the capability to make decisions, while also being connected to the experience and its message or messages that contributed to a decision, a person now has the ability to put one's hands on what one has been dealt, needs to change and rebuild. If an experience contributed to more than one decision, this can also be addressed as is therapeutic. This same process can occur when original decisions were made as an adolescent, though the major and most powerful decision making is usually done as a child from prebirth through age twelve. Traumatic experiences, as indicated also have a significant effect on decision making. Adults reliving a traumatic rejecting or negative experience in their life when they were still adults usually were in a regressed state when originally experiencing this situation. The extent of which ego state was in control at this time depends on the situation at the time and the psychological functioning of the person. What is important is that the adult in this case also has the opportunity to connect to his or her decision making mechanism at the time the event occurred and with the help of the Adult Nurturing Self can work toward healthy redecisioning to assist in rebuilding from this situation. The process discussed here also applies to the child and adolescent. (See the living out stage in chapter two and the reliving process in other chapters.)

The Gouldings primarily practice one to one therapy in the group for it is easier for the patient to remain in the Child and make redecisions if the past experience is kept simple and the active participants are minimized. In addition, the Gouldings pointed to an advantage of family therapy being that the parents and children make their redecisions together. The Gouldings discourage negative or positive transference and dependence, and are interested in intrapsychic change rather than group process, interpersonal relationships or the analysis of transactions. Redecision Therapy is short term ranging from a weekend to a month or so.

In Redecision Therapy, the patient is the star of the drama that is plotted carefully to end in victory, while interested in positive endings and looking for a specific way for the patient to be a victor. The Gouldings (1979) stated, "we begin planning the happy ending even before we know the scene" (p. 212). Although this sounds great, an ending that may be premature may bring on pseudo-happiness, which may mask one's underlying problems, with the patient later overwhelmed by these problems, if they are not resolved in therapy. Similarly, the Gouldings' (1979) claim that "redecision work is fast, often fun and curative" (p. 214) appears positive, but fast may not be best, possibly overlooking specific issues, conflicts and factors that need to be dealt with before an actual redecision can occur. A problem I find with Redecision Therapy is that it appears to be too wish fulfilling and not as uncovering, intense, nor as cathartic as therapy needs to be to achieve effectiveness on a relatively lasting basis. It doesn't appear to go far enough into the roots of the decision which need to be "uprooted," defused and dismantled to be most effectively redecided, or the original decision will soon grow back from its roots and what significant parts of the decision are still there. Of course, not having the opportunity to experience the Gouldings' work leaves the door open for further assessment and examination of this method.

Rebuilding Therapy, however, largely, agrees with the concepts and approaches of Redecision Therapy, going a step further from the information I have in being more undercovering, deeper and reconstructive in its process. Rebuilding Therapy, in addition to individual and individual family therapy, usually works with one patient or one family at a time in the group process with the assistance of those persons in the group, discourages the transference, is primarily interested in intrapsychological and family change and is much less interested in group dynamics, interpersonal group relations and analysis of the group transactions, unless at times necessary. Redecision Therapy is short-term, whereas Rebuilding Therapy can make a major impact on a short-term basis, while also giving the patient an opportunity to make major personality changes on a longer-term basis, though in a significantly shorter time period than the long-term talk therapies trying to accomplish this.

REPARENTING

The reparenting school also needs specific attention, for it has made a significant contribution to resolving dysfunction related to faulty parental upbringing and mistreatment. Moroney (1989) referred to Schiff (1970 and 1975) as the therapist most closely associated with reparenting, developing her total regressive reparenting method in the mid 1960's to heal schizophrenics and further developed by Schiff and her associates. Schiff's total regressive reparenting is worth looking at and can be used with other diagnostic categories, but it is not very practical, for the most part, if used in its pure form. Moroney described Schiff's reparenting involving the complete giving up of and the exclusion of the patient's unhealthy Parent, which is replaced by a new Parent developed from a parent child relationship with the therapist taking several years. Schiff (1969) described this method in detail, giving M. Schiff, her husband, and her credit for it. It involves the patient living in the therapist's home (i.e., Schiff's home), giving up his or her natural parents and family and usually not reestablishing a relationship with them. During this therapeutic period, the patient is totally regressed to infancy and is cared for by a married couple, such as the Schiffs, who parent the child-adult in a healthy way through the developmental stages, with significant nurturing and consistent structure and discipline until the child-adult is ready to leave home. In Schiff's work, through the regression and reparenting, the patient is encouraged to act out and work through early childhood conflicts in the supportive and nurturing family environment. The patient's conflicts are resolved through as a child again acting out within limits, expressing whatever feelings and thoughts are necessary and then receiving healthy support, clarification and guidelines and experiencing one's developmental needs being met. Physical contact, as a healthy parent makes with one's child, is also provided. The Schiffs also maintained that it was acceptable to spank or slap the child, though I strongly disagree with any type of physical punishment. The patient also learns healthy thinking and reality testing and effective social and adaptive skills, as he or she is reparented.

Moroney also referred to Wilson and his associates (1982 and 1985) reparenting in time limited regression sessions with schizophrenic adolescents and adults in a hospital setting. Like the Schiffs, Wilson and his associates' goal is the complete exclusion of the original Parent and its replacement with a new Parent coming from the therapists, while advocating that the bonding the patient receives from kinesthetic nurturing is essential to treatment. Unlike the Schiffs, instead of using a complete 24-hour regression for an extended time period, Wilson's patients were described taking part in five two-hour therapy sessions weekly. In these sessions they spent forty five minutes in an autohypnotic regression, with the therapist providing intensive primitive parenting, including holding and bottle feeding and for the rest of the session working in groups of six to eight, developing cognitive understanding of their regression. For the rest of the day the patients are expected to operate responsibly from their Adult in a highly structured environment and may be treated during this time with behavioral or family methods and medication. Like Schiff's reparenting, Wilson's reparenting takes a number of months of in-house treatment referring to one patient experiencing twenty months of inpatient treatment, which is also often not practical as the Schiffs' reparenting.

Osnes (1974) spot reparenting is less time intensive and is also discussed by Moroney. It involves his patient reliving a negative experience to the point of negative parenting, when faulty or rejecting parenting occurred, with the therapist, co-therapist or group member providing the nurturing and caring needed in the original life experience. Osnes stated that this process reconstructed a part of the Parent and deconfused a part of the Child, resolving an archaic problem in the child. The problem with this approach is that instead of the patient working through one's feelings and thoughts, the intrusion of the therapeutic parent to nurture is done prematurely preventing the necessary expression, cleansing and working through of feelings and thoughts, cognitive reprogramming and redecisioning. Once this process occurs, then effective reparenting can occur, unless a limited form of reparenting is also needed before or during the redecisioning process to strengthen a person for redecisioning.

James' (1974) self-reparenting is compatible with the type of reparenting provided in Rebuilding Therapy and is also described by Moroney. James pointed out that the person's Adult is in charge during the self-reparenting process, even when techniques to regress the child are utilized, which I strongly support. This method of reparenting encourages the person to take responsibility for his or her reparenting rather than relying on the therapist. James pointed out that a drawback of the Schiff method is that the therapist may transmit unsolved problems into the person's new Parent. The person's Adult, according to James, creates a new Parent to balance off the negative characteristics of the old Parent, but not to get rid of the original Parent. The rationale for creating a new Parent as part of the old Parent is that a new Parent can defuse the negative parts of the old Parent. James claimed that the Parent for the most part has a mix of positives and negatives and that the positives can be consciously used. She stated that persons, except in rare situations are stuck with their Parent and parents within it. However, according to James, developing a new Parent in the old Parent, carefully designed by the Adult with the help of the person's creative Child, changes the overall Parent, increasing its options, and provides the opportunity to incorporate influences from many sources, including real and fictitious models, attending classes, reading books on parenting and observing other parents. Like James, I believe that it is very difficult or even impossible to completely or even significantly eradicate the old Parent, but that it can be modified in a healthy way with healthy reparenting.

Moroney also discussed reparenting, using parents of origin or the actual parents whenever possible as reparenters, referring to Del Casale, et al. (1982) and his associates from the Argentine School of TA and their reparenting work with schizophrenics. Moroney claimed the goal is not to completely decathect the original Parent, but to affirm its healthy aspects, correct its negative parts and decontaminate the person's distorted and incomplete view of one's parents. Such a method, according to Moroney, increases communication between parents and patients, with the parents giving the patient the permission and affirmation he or she needed at each stage of early development. Despite what therapeutically is done in the present, as with any reparenting approach, redecisioning and rebuilding work needs to be done to repair the damage of faulty parental upbringing and mistreatment or other forms of rejection.

Mellor and Andrewartha (1980) advocated reparenting of the Parent by utilizing a Parent interviewer interviewing the patient as one's parent with three fully functioning ego states, assisting the patient's Parent to make effective decisions and changes supporting Child redecisions already made or to be made. Mellor and Andrewartha provided an example of this with a patient as her father dialoguing with the therapist and dialoguing with her father as herself in her Child and as her father to her. In doing so she, as her father, in her Parent, first giving her Child permission and then as herself in her Child, decided to handle anger in a healthy way. Reparenting methods can also be helpful, according to Mellor and Andrewartha, for example, when one needs an effective way to deal with anger, inserting assertiveness thinking in one's Parent, or to provide healthy instructions and teaching to offset dysfunctional Parental thinking.

Mellor (1980) was impressed with the congruency and complementary philosophy between redecisioning and reparenting, which I concur with, pointing out the importance of differing methods being able to contribute to the effectiveness of helping others.

I support Mellor's claim that redecisioning is preferable with specific early high impact scenes or experiences. However, Mellor's claim that reparenting is preferable when an impasse or a conflict is a result of ongoing day to day childhood experiences occurring one after another is overly simplistic, for such experiences can lead to unhealthy decisions and can be addressed in the redecisioning process if the therapist, for example, can effectively assist the patient to focus on one of these day to day experiences as representing a number of similar experiences. When redecision work isn't possible, Mellor's claim that reparenting could be effective, for example, with the workaholic needing parental permission to relax followed by redecision work has merit. In this case, the reparenting process, encouraging the patient to relax, can stimulate the recall of past experiences, contributing to effective redecision work. Mellor wisely claimed that when patients resist using redecision methods, feeling hopeless about the outcome, reparenting work can provide a positive experience encouraging hope regarding redecision work. He gave an example of a patient who froze when trying to do redecision work regarding a long traumatic birth. To resolve this impasse, the patient had a therapeutic experience of being reborn into a warm, approving atmosphere, an experience that gave him the confidence needed to reexperience his traumatic birth. In addition, Mellor insightfully pointed out that reparenting will meet with significant resistance when early decisioning, such as not to listen to one's parents, requires redecisioning before effective reparenting can be done.

Redecision work in the wounded Child, to rebuild the wounded Child, should precede reparenting whenever possible. Reparenting used alone doesn't produce effective redecisioning, which is usually a necessary and essential prerequisite for effective reparenting work. The process of redecisioning is not specifically focused on in reparenting work and can only be a by-product of the reparenting process. However, even as a by-product, at its best, the reparenting school appears to diffusely deal with the redecisioning process and often does not appear to touch or focus on it in any significant way, leaving an impaired Child. Though through healthy reparenting alone the patient has appeared cured or healed, it is likely that one's conflicts weren't adequately resolved, but were only partially addressed due to the lack of focus on specific childhood experiences, their parental messages and the Child's related feelings, thinking and decisions. This could only result in a partial healing through the reparenting process due to remaining conflict and psychopathology stemming from the inadequately treated Child wounds and the dysfunctional decisions and infectious feelings and thoughts related to this. These dysfunctional decisions and related feelings and thoughts would continue to infect the person and sabotage reparenting or any therapeutic process.

Due to the position presented here, I strongly support the use of the redecisioning process through reliving work, when possible, as the major focus and work of therapy, for it is the wounded Child, through the strong influence of the disturbed Parent, which so powerfully affects the person's life and must first be, when possible, treated, in the process of significant healing and strengthened if effective change and reparenting can occur. As the Child becomes healthier, the Adult becomes less contaminated and healthier, with this process significantly weakening the impact of the unhealthy Parent in the area worked on. In most cases this can be done, except when reparenting first needs to be done as only a door opener for later redecision work. In such a case reparenting provides the confidence and hope, as Mellor claimed, to allow effective redecisioning work to occur. However, in no way can this door opening reparenting provide the necessary and lasting reparenting that the person needs. This usually won't occur until one's Child is relatively on its way to making healthy redecisions and repairs, becoming more receptive and less resistant to reparenting because unhealthy decisions from the wounded Child will fight off and sabotage the best of reparenting or any therapeutic work, as indicated. Without such redecisioning work, a cure or significant life change will never occur, for the causes of one's pathology must be treated and relatively overcome for significant and lasting change to occur. Although the dysfunctional Parent continues to direct the wounded Child in the dysfunctional person, the wounded Child is where the infection and unhealthiness are lodged that are directly affecting the person, and in this sense is the most treatable cause of the person's dysfunction and so must be treated, as discussed. As this occurs, the Adaptive Child makes major redecisions, becoming healthier, and with the growing, stronger and less contaminated Adult is better able to take control of the unhealthy Parent and oneself. As this occurs the person is increasingly receptive to reparenting as needed. In this process as it continues, the Adult eventually takes control while the Parent is also strengthened along with the strengthening of the Child. This process, having clear application to the adult, can apply to the child and adolescent relative to the particular situation and in terms of the child or adolescent's psychological development.

Although I see redecision work as the core and foundation of the rebuilding process, reparenting is also essential, as needed and possible during the course of therapy, most often after redecisioning work in a session when redecisioning is first possible. Reparenting can achieve a limited degree of success without redecisioning work, though it will usually be much less effective than if redecisioning work is done. In addition, though developing adaptive skills throughout therapy is helpful it is usually much more effective as redecisioning work is progressing. The Rebuilding Therapy reparenting method is not as extensive as Schiff's or Wilson's method, but it relates to Osne's spot reparenting though after redecisioning work when possible, and to James's self-reparenting. (For a discussion of reparenting in Rebuilding Therapy, see the reparenting method in chapter thirteen.)

HYPNOSIS

Hypnosis, relaxation or relaxation exercises are part of the Rebuilding process in a number of cases. The term hypnotic induction as a procedure and pathway to a hypnotic state is used interchangeably with hypnosis. The terms *relaxation* or *relaxation exercise* are used regularly for the term *hypnosis* in Rebuilding Therapy.

Hypnosis is a well established psychotherapeutic procedure in its own right and is also an adjunct to other methods and psychotherapies. However, it has been engulfed in controversy, many definitions and theoretical frameworks regarding what is hypnosis and what contributes to it.

Kohn (1984) stated that there is no consistent and concise theory of hypnosis.

Udolf (1981) claimed that it is difficult and likely impossible to find an explanation of hypnosis that all experts agree on.

Lynn and Rhue (1991) noted that there is no simple single definition and that there is far from agreement on how to describe hypnotic phenomena. Referring to Sutcliffe (1960), they mentioned that different schools of hypnosis make very different assumptions, take up different methods and accept differing data as allowable evidence.

Zeig and Rennick (1991) claimed that most experts have tried to define hypnosis from their pre-existing theoretical frameworks. They cited eight traditional hypnosis definitions, giving credit to Zeig (1988) for his summary of these definitions.

1. Disassociation (Janet near the end of the nineteenth century and Hilgard, 1977)
2. A role people play acting as if hypnotized (Sarbin and Coe, 1972)
3. Defined according to nonhypnotic parameters of behavior, including task motivation and the act of labeling the process as hypnosis (Barber, 1969)
4. A state of increased suggestibility (Weitzenhoffer, 1953) and a type of influence by one individual exerted on another person through suggestion (Weitzenhoffer, 1989)

5. "Regression in service of the ego" (Gill and Brenman, 1959)
6. A state of relaxation (Edmonston, 1981)
7. A biological capacity (Spiegel and Spiegel, 1978)
8. A special internally directed "altered state of functioning" (Erickson, Rossi and Rossi, (1976).

Udolf noted some of the same definitions as well as to others not mentioned, including a narrowing of the person's perceptive field and total concentration on a single entity, with Kohn supporting this. Zeig (1988) defined hypnosis from the patient's perspective "as a state of focused awareness on whatever is immediately relevant, in which previously unrecognized psychological and physiological potential are accessed to some avolitional extent" (p. 278).

Zeig and Rennick, Ericksonian supporters, claimed that it may not be necessary to have one definition of hypnosis. For them, hypnosis is a multifaceted process involving a system of interpersonal interaction, and by broadening the definitions taking into account a variety of viewpoints, hypnosis can be demystified and viewed as an interpersonal process.

Ericksonian Hypnosis

Erickson (1980), describing to the aim of hypnotherapy, stated that "the induction and maintenance of a trance serve to provide a special psychological state in which patients can reassociate and reorganize their inner psychological complexities and utilize their own capacities in a manner in accord with their own experiential life" (p. 38).

According to Erickson and Rossi (1979), therapeutic trance or hypnosis is a period when the limitations of a person's habitual and usual beliefs and frame of reference are temporarily interrupted, stopped, distracted and "altered so one can be receptive to other patterns of association and modes of mental functioning that are conducive to problem solving" (p. 3). Erickson (1980) claimed that hypnotherapy provides the opportunity to work with the unconscious independently without being hindered by the resistance or the inability of the conscious mind to accept therapeutic gains. Erickson and Rossi pointed out that the trance initiates an unconscious search and facilitates unconscious processes to arrive at a new association or frame of reference. Zeig and Rennick noted that Erickson found hypnosis useful in allowing the conscious mind's operations to recede and the functions of the unconscious to surface. Hypnosis weakens one's defenses to reach the unconscious areas of the mind, such as buried memories, that are not otherwise accessible with the healthy Parent, Child and Adult operative, as needed to assist in reevaluating, reeducating, rebuilding and healing.

Udolf claimed that there are many examples of spontaneously induced mental states which are similar or identical to hypnosis, such as daydreaming or being completely absorbed in a book, excluding everything else around. An example is Psychodrama or the reliving of a past experience, which often results in a state of significantly increased concentration, a narrowing and focusing of attention and a suspension of present intervening stimuli, bringing on an authentic age regression back to this experience. Once it was found possible to induce a trance or hypnosis with induction techniques, hypnosis became a potent tool in psychotherapy. Erickson and Rossi reported that trance induction is not a standardized process, but a personal experience in which the therapist assists the patient to find his or her own individual way. They pointed out no technique always works with all persons or even with the same person at different times. Zeig and Rennick suggested that formal trance induction is optional and that assisting a patient into hypnosis involves individualizing various means to get there. What is important to Rebuilding Therapy is that the patient is in a state of relaxation or, even more specifically, a state of therapeutic readiness, where his or her defenses are relaxed and concentration is sufficiently focused to effectively relive a past experience, if needed, and to effectively take part in the therapeutic process. The hypnosis or relaxation process is the vehicle, when needed, to get to this state.

Erickson (1980) in his discussion of hypnosis stated "too often the unwarranted and unsound assumption is made … whatever develops from hypnosis must necessarily be completely a result of suggestion and primarily an expression of it…. Contrary to such misconceptions the hypnotized person remains the same person. At the most the therapist can influence only the manner of self expression…. Hypnosis does not change people nor does it alter their past experiential life. It serves to permit them to learn more about themselves and to express themselves more adequately … hypnotic psychotherapy is a learning process for the patient, a procedure of reeducation. Effective results in … hypnotherapy derive only from the patient's activities. The therapist merely stimulates the patient into activity, often not knowing what the activity may be, and then guides the patient … while the patient's task is that of learning through his own efforts to understand his experiential life in a new way" (pp. 38-39). Zeig and Rennick stated that Ericksonian hypnosis encourages the patient's control of one's destiny. Udolf supported this position by asserting that all hypnosis is self-hypnosis produced by the subject, with the hypnotherapist being a facilitator, guide and teacher.

Hypnosis As An Uncovering Tool

The use of hypnosis in the uncovering and dealing with repressed and past memories is well documented. Wolberg (1964) stated that hypnosis is valuable in uncovering and expediting the recovery of repressed experiences. Also Maldonado and Spiegel (1994) maintained that hypnotic age regression assists in the recall of dissociated or repressed memories.

Spiegel and Cardena (1990) asserted that "hypnosis can be an effective adjunct to psychotherapy facilitating access to and working through of dissociated traumatic memories" (p. 42), which otherwise may be kept out of consciousness, with post traumatic stress disorder (PTSD) patients, including abuse victims, who are highly hypnotizable and responsive to hypnosis.

Maldonado and Spiegel pointed out that exposure to stressful events may naturally lead to developing high hypnotizability. They referred to their experience that some victims of trauma may accidentally learn to use hypnotic-like mechanisms to avoid the total impact of a traumatic experience. Maldonado and Spiegel cited Nash and Lynn (1986) and Spiegel and Cardena (1991) reporting "a positive correlation between severity of punishment during childhood and hypnotizability" (p. 229). According to Maldonado and Spiegel, it is possible that the impact of the stress experienced by victims of early sexual or physical abuse stimulates a more productive use of self-hypnosis. They noted that the need and frequent use of self-hypnosis due to repeated exposure to abuse may prevent its extinction later on in life, accounting partially for the high level of hypnotizability observed in adults who were once victimized by abuse. As support for this position, Maldonado and Spiegel cited Kluft (1984, 1992) and Spiegel, Detrick and Frischolz (1982). Although victims may use hypnotic-like mechanisms to avoid the total impact of their trauma, these hypnotic or relaxation skills can be used in therapy to face, recall and overcome their past abuse in an effective way.

Maldonado and Spiegel believed that hypnosis should be utilized in psychotherapy to facilitate the controlled recall of traumatic events. They cited Kluft (1992 and 1993) and Spiegel (1981) stating "that when abreaction is not done within the context of cognitive restructuring and before new defenses are in place it can lead to further traumatization of the patient" (pp. 231-232). This view was supported by Wolberg who encouraged the use of hypnosis with respect to what one's defenses are capable of tolerating as underlying material is uncovered. This is the accepted viewpoint among psychotherapists. Erickson encouraged at a pace the patient can handle the integration of the unconscious with the conscious or of making the new insight in the unconscious fully accessible to the conscious mind upon need.

Spiegel and Cardena concluded that it is critical the patient use his or her controlled access to buried memories to cognitively and positively restructure them, perceiving the information from a new viewpoint, a basic goal of uncovering work and Rebuilding Therapy.

Relaxation: The Basic Ingredient In Hypnosis

With regard to the similarity of hypnosis and relaxation, Edmonston (1991) stated: "Again, again and again clinical applications of relaxation and hypnosis yield no appreciable differences in their effectiveness. Why? Because, at base, they are one and the same process and are so perceived by the clinical patient" (pp. 216-217). In 1977 he reported a survey revealing that hypnosis as perceived by patients primarily involves relaxation and its related sensations and feelings, that data from physiological studies supported "the equation of neutral hypnosis = relaxation" (p. 73) and that the content of induction procedures and the response to them support this equation, whether objectively or subjectively measured. Edmonston (1977) claimed that as induction procedures involved verbal and physical suggestions of relaxation, that it isn't too surprising that patients respond with relaxation responses and appropriate perceptions of the relaxation process. Edmonston (1991) reported a substantial amount of findings and "compelling evidence for a basic physiological similarity between hypnosis and relaxation" (p. 222), with him going beyond this in his findings to claim an overall similarity between hypnosis and relaxation or relaxation procedures. In 1981 Edmonston reviewed the literature regarding the impressive similarities in therapeutic effectiveness between hypnosis and nonhypnotic relaxation techniques. Among some of the studies he reviewed, Edmonston reported that in the treatment of anxiety, insomnia and addictions to alcohol and tobacco that nonhypnotic relaxation yielded results that were similar to the results of hypnosis. It is clear from Edmonston's review of the literature through 1991 that there is much clinical and physiological evidence of similar results regarding the effectiveness of hypnosis and relaxation. Edmonston (1981) wrote "just as hypnosis focuses attention, so does relaxation; just as hypnosis enhances patient motivation, so does relaxation; just as hypnosis is an effective treatment of a variety of disorders, so is relaxation; and just as hypnosis influences patient's perceptions, so does relaxation" (p. 118). In further supporting the similarity or equivalency of hypnosis and relaxation, Edmonston (1991) referred to Coleman's (1976) conclusion, after starting out with this hypothesis, that the only difference between hypnotic induction procedures and relaxation procedures is the name that is given them. In support of Coleman and Edmonston, Kirsch, Mobayed, Council and Kenny (1992) reported that their findings indicated "traditional hypnotic inductions produce a state of consciousness that is indistinguishable from nonhypnotic relaxation training" (p. 657).

Lynn and Rhue cited Edmonston claiming that "it is not dissociation or psychological regression but relaxation that proceeds and 'forms the fundamental basis of subsequent phenomena associated with the term hypnosis'" (p. 7) and that relaxation is such a basic process that other mechanisms such as psychological regression and dissociation are secondary to it. Put simply, Edmonston claimed "relaxation is the basis for all that follows in hypnosis ..." (1991, p. 227). Edmonston (1991) proposed that the outmoded term of hypnosis be replaced with the term *anesis* the noun form of the Greek verb *aniesis* ("'to relax, to let go'") (p. 228), for a lot of what is observed in present hypnosis is due to the relaxation inherent in it and as anesis accurately explains and summarizes the literature he reviewed. My clinical work together with Edmonston's position have led me to use the term *hypnosis* and *relaxation* or *relaxation exercise*, interchangeably. In addition, I use the term hypnotic induction interchangeably with the term hypnosis, for hypnotic induction is a procedure and pathway to a state of hypnosis just as the relaxation exercise is to a state of relaxation. I prefer relaxation or relaxation exercise because it more clearly defines the relaxation process facilitating the relaxing, weakening and decrease of the inhibiting influences of one's defenses, age regression, as needed, and the significant increase in concentration and focusing of attention, relatively free of intervening stimuli. Relaxation utilized in this context does not mean one does not face his or her emotional pain. To the contrary, in relaxation, through the weakening and decrease of one's defenses and the inhibiting factors working against the uncovering process, the patient is assisted to uncover and relive past painful experiences and the emotional pain and conflicts of these experiences to help in rebuilding and healing oneself. The effectiveness of the method, whether referred to as hypnosis or a hypnotic induction procedure or relaxation or a relaxation exercise, depends on the clinician's skills and the patient. Relaxation is also free of the misconceptions and multiple definitions of hypnosis.

Edmonston (1991) also discussed physical activities as a way to achieve hypnosis or relaxation, with it appearing from his discussion of this matter that significant research is needed in this area. He stated that perhaps the bringing together of a passive and active form of induction is in their basic similarity, which is relaxation. In doing so, Edmonston (1991) referred to Hilgard that "there are multiple pathways to hypnosis, including physical activities and verbal relaxation instructions, and that they all lead to one condition: the basic fundamental condition of *anesis* (p. 227). This also lends support to my discussion in the Hypnodrama section later in this chapter, that the active psychodramatic process often can lead to a state of hypnosis or relaxation where a patient's defenses are relaxed and decreased enough to enhance the uncovering process and one's concentration and focus of attention is increased to effectively deal with the uncovered experience and material. Combining relaxation or a relaxation exercise with Psychodrama will often increase the level or state of relaxation or hypnosis, often resulting in a deeper and more effective uncovering and rebuilding process. (See the Hypnodrama section later in this chapter.) In addition, through the use of a physical exercise, such as hitting on a mat (the anger mat release method described in chapter seven), a patient's defenses often relax with increased concentration and focusing of attention on the issue being dealt with. The Bioenergetics process of relaxing one muscles and breathing in a freer and a more open and relaxed way through physical exercises such as this, contributes to the reduction of one's tension and defenses and a more focused and active uncovering process, which hypnosis and relaxation encourage.

PSYCHODRAMA

Haskell (1975) made a significant contribution to my discussion of Psychodrama. Haskell a protégé of J. L. Moreno, the developer of Psychodrama, trained me in Psychodrama at the California Institute of Socioanalysis in Long Beach, California from 1976 to 1980. He was effectively assisted by his wife R. Haskell, also a practitioner and trainer in Psychodrama, who has been very helpful and supportive to me throughout the years. Of course, due credit is given to J. L. Moreno for developing Psychodrama and who is its foremost writer. Moreno's writings are extensive, including some of his works included in this book's bibliography (1939, 1940a, 1940b, 1944, 1946, 1956, 1968, 1969 and 1975). Z. Moreno, Moreno's wife and colleague, has also written extensively on Psychodrama, (1956, 1959, 1965, 1969, 1975 and 1978). She co-authored books with her husband in 1956 and 1969. Other writings include Treadwell, Stein and Kumar's (1990) discussion of psychodramatic action and closure techniques and Kellerman (1984) and Blatner's

(1985) discussion of catharsis as part of the therapeutic process in an integrated way. Sacks, Bilaniuk and Gendron's (1995) extensive *Bibliography of Psychodrama* is an excellent reference tool.

Haskell's description of Psychodrama will now be presented without discussing the techniques. The psychodramatic techniques developed in Psychodrama, which Rebuilding Therapy uses, are called Rebuilding Therapy methods, which in a number of cases I have developed further. These techniques or methods and the method's I have developed are discussed in the following chapters.

According to Haskell, Moreno developed Psychodrama in the Theater of Spontaneity, which Moreno started in Vienna, Austria in 1921. As Haskell reported, Moreno developed the "Theater of Spontaneity from the Greek Tragedians who recognized that drama, when it presented incidents arousing pity or fear to a large audience, produced catharsis of these emotions" (p. 155). After viewing the drama, audience members appeared to be free from fear, with the theatrical performance credited with freeing them. Members of the audience in the Theater of Spontaneity, after being involved in a discussion of items in the news, reenacted on the stage one of the events reported in the newspaper that day, with Moreno functioning as the director. What appeared to occur in this situation was that the personal problems of the audience members who did not participate on the stage, as well as those who did, influenced their selection of topic and the reenactments on the stage, while the perceptions of important events of all those involved were influenced by their experiences and needs. Following an enactment, persons in the audience engaged in a discussion based on it. The enactments and the following discussions resulted in catharsis, with the participants who performed on the stage and the audience who didn't participate on the stage relieved when they left the theater. It was from this that Moreno developed Psychodrama.

Haskell claimed that the essence of Psychodrama is the reenactment of past experiences, the acting out of oneself in the present or experimenting experientially with future actions one may take. He believed that each person is responsible for assessing one's own experiences in the past, present and future and finding alternative solutions to unresolved problems. What was important to Haskell was that Psychodrama provided a method whereby a person could examine one's life and relationships and experiment with alternative modes of action. Elaborating further on this, such alternative forms of action regarding one's past experiences involves new thinking, decisions and actions that one would have taken if given a second opportunity to reexperience the past, whereas the present and future alternative actions involve more effective thinking, decisions and actions regarding present issues, problems and relationships and preparing to live more effectively in the present and future.

The resolution of one's conflicts as they relate to past and present experiences is a primary focus of psychodrama. Yablonsky (1976) stated that Psychodrama provides an opportunity to encounter one's conflicts and psychological pain in a setting that more closely approximates one's real life situation than most other therapeutic methods can provide. According to Yablonsky, a person who is having conflict with a parent can talk directly to one's parent (acted out by an auxiliary ego), act out one's fantasy or reality of anger or love and experience one's pain or primal emotions in direct relationship to a significant other who contributed to this pain. Yablonsky also noted that going through an intensive Psychodramatic experience does not require lengthy discussion or analysis, for the person (protagonist) has learned about the theme of one's problem in the action of the psychodramatic session.

Another significant aspect of Psychodrama, according to Yablonsky, is being a mirror of life for both the primary person reenacting an aspect of one's life situation and for the other group members. For the person reenacting major experiences, Yablonsky stated that "the real world is slowed down and the time can be taken to explore critical emotional issues by acting out key life scenes" (p. 5), which often helps in resolving problems and providing a clearer perspective on one's life. Group members, according to Yablonsky, are encouraged to experience parts of their own lives that become apparent in the ongoing session.

Though primarily a group method, Psychodrama has also been utilized on an individual basis. It has also been used effectively in individual family therapy and in multiple family group therapy. I have utilized Psychodrama in all four contexts.

According to Haskell, the benefits of Psychodrama include catharsis, insight, spontaneity which is the development of new approaches and more effective solutions to specific problems, and improving in "sociometric status" or choosing relationships with more persons and being chosen more frequently by others. Psychodrama is instrumental in assisting the person to improve and further develop his or her interpersonal skills and relationships with others.

The Instruments of Psychodrama

The five instruments of Psychodrama are the stage, the director, the protagonist, the auxiliary ego and the group or audience. I refer to the protagonist and group members as patients, although Haskell did not do so, believing that the term *patient* was a disrespectful role or way of looking at the person being worked with. I believe the patient is a very respectful role as long as the patient, therapist and others involved conduct themselves in a manner that encourages the respect and dignity of this role.

The Stage

The stage is the first instrument. If practical, which is usually not the case, the stage is generally constructed ovally on three levels. When the patient moves from the group to the first level he or she starts to present one's problem, with movement onto the second level representing the patient's intention to present his or her problem in action. With movement to the third level the person becomes the protagonist acting out his or her relationships and problems toward some type of resolution. Few props are necessary, according to Haskell, with a table and a few chairs being sufficient and an attempt made to simulate symbolically, at least every object in the situation remembered by the patient. Haskell stated that a lighting system is used to reflect the mood of the protagonist's feelings, with brightly colored lights representing happier experiences and dimmer lights representing depressing events. In reflecting one's mood, lighting is helpful in further stimulating the expression of one's feelings. If a stage is not available, which is usually the case as indicated, the session can be conducted in any feasible place or location.

The Protagonist

The second instrument, (which Haskell called the third instrument) is the protagonist, the person who acts or lives out on the stage or in the action area one's specific experiences leading to problem resolution. According to Haskell, a past experience is enacted in the here and now and not in terms of looking at it from the present to the past. There can be more than one protagonist in a psychodramatic session, with there usually being one or two protagonists in a one and one-half hour to two-hour session and one to three protagonists in a two and one-half hour session.

The Director

The third instrument, (which Haskell referred to as the second instrument), is the director. According to Haskell, the director is the producer and expert, who focuses the production on the protagonist's problems, while maintaining rapport with the group members. The director is an expert in the psychodramatic method and is the catalyst stimulating the working through and resolution of specific issues and conflicts. Haskell claimed the functions of the director are as follows:

1. Planning each session taking into account the needs and interests of the group members.
2. Encouraging a permissive and warm atmosphere where group members are free to express themselves.
3. Warming up the group to decide on goals and proceeding toward them.
4. Assisting the group in the selection of the protagonist.
5. Stimulating the involvement of group members while the protagonist is reenacting specific experiences and in the discussion whenever practical.
6. Assisting the protagonist in setting up each experience and then to act it out.
7. Providing the protagonist with techniques that will be effective in dealing with relationships and problems.
8. Protecting the protagonist from the confrontation and criticism of other group members which should occur toward significant others in the Psychodrama session.
9. Leading a group discussion after the action part of each session.
10. Summarizing the action and discussion that can be a prelude to the next session.

Haskell called himself a protagonist-centered director, where the group members select the protagonist who initially is asked to select an experience to reenact and persons in the group to act as significant others such as parents or spouse.

According to Haskell, while the protagonist-centered director may give suggestions, the decisions regarding experiences or sequences to reenact are made by the protagonist. Although the use of other group members to assist the protagonist or patient and to act out the roles of significant others is encouraged, the use of trained persons is needed, wherever necessary, to maximize the patient's treatment and when if not utilized would impair the patient's progress. In this light I have relied heavily on the trained clinician, which in most situations has been myself. However, when helpful I involve other group members and family members, though utilizing family members less so, to assist in the reliving of an experience and with such methods as the double. I have relied heavily on myself to act or live out the roles of significant others and to use specific methods, techniques or approaches, for I have often been the only clinician available or have been the most capable person to do this. Although the director or therapist, as myself, will make recommendations and encourage the patient in a specific direction, all final decisions on experiences to relive are left to the protagonist. The protagonist is always in control and can reject any suggestions, recommendations or the use of any specific technique or method.

The Auxiliary Ego

The fourth instrument is the auxiliary ego, who acts or lives out the role of the protagonist's significant others or other persons in the protagonist's life and assists the director in the use of specific techniques and in specialized roles. Haskell also referred to the auxiliary ego assisting the protagonist to deal with future situations, such as in the role of a prospective employer, or raising issues that the protagonist would face regarding choosing a specific occupation or making a major decision. Haskell claimed that the auxiliary ego can be helpful in showing the protagonist more effective or alternative ways of dealing with specific situations. Rebuilding Therapy refers to the auxiliary ego as the auxiliary agent or therapeutic agent.

The Group or Audience

The fifth instrument is the group or audience, which to Haskell represented all persons in the session who do not participate, though, of course, the protagonist is part of the group. The group is a more accurate name in that a good director will encourage the active involvement of the group members. Haskell claimed that the members of the group represent the persons in the protagonist's natural groups, the world at large and public opinion. The group provides support, stimulation, education, insight and approval for effective change and problem resolution for all involved. According to Haskell, it is during the discussion that the group members, directly, most often assist the protagonist, although he also encouraged their involvement as auxiliary egos and in the action phase of the session when practical. The group members can learn significantly from the protagonist and each other regarding their own problem areas and relationships. Haskell stressed the importance of group members sharing their own experiences in the discussion phase rather than analyzing or criticizing the protagonist in some way.

The Phases of Psychodrama

The three phases of Psychodrama are the warmup, action and discussion phases.

The Warmup Phase

The warmup phase assists the group members to become familiar with the psychodramatic process, warms them up to specific problem areas or issues they may wish to involve themselves in, results in the selection of a protagonist who could be more than one if there is time for this and warms up the selected protagonist to move into the action phase. There are a number of different types of warmups and warmup methods.

Haskell used the initial warmup in the first session. The first session, to Haskell, focuses on the development of group goals and the involvement of the group members, familiarizing the group with Psychodrama and preparing for future sessions. Haskell claimed the initial warmup includes a ten minute talk by the director of the psychodramatic method and its application, and the director personally welcoming each group member and asking about their acquaintance with Psychodrama and what they want to achieve. According to Haskell, the action phase of the initial session should focus only on preparing the group for future sessions, not on the group member's personal problems. I have regularly conducted first sessions in which patients have worked on their personal problems, though less intensively than in later sessions. The initial session, according to Haskell, can also include the group members becoming acquainted with each other, role playing nonthreatening situations and introducing some of the psychodramatic techniques. This is followed by a discussion of what occurred in the session.

Haskell most frequently used the group centered warmup, after the first session, which he considered to be the most effective way of helping a group focus on a problem, common to a significant portion of its members and assisting in the selection of a protagonist whose problem areas were most representative of the other group members problems. There are three portions of this warmup according to Haskell. The first portion is a ten minute discussion by the director regarding, for example, problems people have in relationships in a general way. This is followed by the second portion briefly interviewing each group member, for example, about any relationship he or she would like to better understand or improve. The third portion is the selection of the protagonist to work on one's personal problems, which is done in a democratic manner by the group members.

Another type of warmup, described by Haskell, is the directed warmup. The primary difference between a directed warmup and the group centered warmup is that in the first type the director decides on the topic of his or her introductory ten minute talk, with the goal that this topic will be pursued in the action portion of the session. For example, according to Haskell, if a group resisted dealing with the issue of parents, he would then focus on this issue in his introductory talk, with the aim of selecting a protagonist to focus on an issue with one's parent. As one person initially talks about an issue in the introductory presentations other group members often follow, even if initially resistant. Similarly, if one group member initially works on an issue that the group was resistant to, others will often follow.

A number of projective techniques may be used as a warmup. Haskell discussed the person projection that stimulates the projection of specific types of feelings and thoughts toward a significant other. For example, to project guilt Haskell asked a female auxiliary ego to sit in front of the group in a guilt provoking way; to project fear, he asked a male auxiliary ego to stand in front of the group with a belt in his hands; and to project anger, he asked a male or female auxiliary ego to sit or stand in front of the group with a disdainful or angry look on his or her face. He then asked group members to identify who this represented in their lives, with a protagonist selected from this process. In a modified version of this method, I ask two therapeutic agents, if available, or one therapeutic agent and a group member or two group members to sit in front of the group, informing the group members that they represent a male and female significant other or person who has had an impact on them, to then identify this male and female person and express "something" briefly to this person. If a group member can only address one of these persons, he or she is encouraged to do so, with of course this process being voluntary. The group members who represented the significant others are then given the opportunity to warm up this way with, for example, other group members in the chairs as significant others. Only group members who are ready to be the projected significant others are asked to do so. Two empty chairs can also be used to represent the projected significant others, with the group members asked to express "something" to the visualized significant others in the chairs. I use the empty chair or person in the chair, depending on the situation when using this projective warmup method. This results in the selection of a protagonist, moving the warmup process on more quickly. Though the warmup phase prepares the patient for the action phase, the phase in which a catharsis will occur most of the time when it occurs, a patient can have a catharsis during the warmup phase, with the therapist then stimulating the patient to move into the action phase or bringing closure to this process if it is not the right time to move the patient further.

Haskell also described music projections using recordings of popular songs and poetry projections of various poems or essays, which, as the music projections, stimulate the uncovering of specific feelings, thoughts, issues and problems and assists in selecting a protagonist.

Haskell discussed a number of other warmup techniques that will not be described in the present volume, but can be referred to in his book.

In practicing Rebuilding Therapy, I have used modifications of a number of Haskell's warmup methods. I give an introductory talk about the Rebuilding Therapy process in the first group meeting and usually when at least two new patients join the group in subsequent sessions, unless done individually as therapeutic. After the first session, I may give a five to ten minute introductory talk about a general or specific problem area depending on the situation. For ongoing groups after the first few sessions, asking each group member what they are initially feeling and what they want to work on has been an effective warmup procedure. The projective warmups have also been effective and powerful warmup tools. (See chapter two for a discussion of the warmup stage in Rebuilding Therapy and chapter sixteen for a discussion of the warmup process in multiple family group therapy, which is not limited to multiple family therapy with appropriate modifications.)

The Action Phase

The action phase involves the protagonist acting out his or her present or past experiences or those experiences anticipated in the future. A major part of the action phase involves reliving or reenacting past experiences regarding significant relationships and issues in life which have adversely affected or influenced the protagonist in some way. The action phase, through reenacting or reliving past experiences, gives the protagonist or patient the opportunity to reexperience, reface, express, work through and relatively cleanse oneself of contaminating emotional pain, feelings and thoughts related to these experiences and to reevaluate and change one's thinking and decisions associated with these events. In doing so, the patient empowers oneself to overcome these rejecting experiences one at a time and to find more effective ways to deal with present and future relationships and situations. Of course, one rejecting experience can represent many similar rejecting experiences. As the protagonist often goes through a catharsis, some other group members may be stimulated to experience a catharsis of their own. This is my description of the action phase as I have psychodramatically used it and developed it into the Rebuilding Therapy living out stage.

Yablonsky saw Psychodrama as an opportunity to act out correcting past negative experiences or frustrations, including being rejected, injured or past mistakes. This can be accomplished, he stated, by reenacting the rejecting experience and then acting out the situation as one wishes it had occurred or what the protagonist could do about it. Although Yablonsky claimed that in most cases a correction of a past experience is beneficial, the person doesn't usually experience a significant healing when wishing for something that didn't occur. What first needs to happen is the catharsis, expression and cleansing of one's pain, feelings and thoughts related to the experience, followed by the rethinking and redecisioning process in a healthy way. I will usually not have a patient relive his or her parents treatment of him or her in the way wished for, for the patient needs to give up hoping for the success of this wish and rebuild oneself from this. Experiencing the love one never received from a therapeutic parent (therapist, co-therapist or auxiliary agent), not representing one's actual parents as part of the reparenting process, is helpful after the negative or rejecting experience is relived and worked through. (For further discussion of the action phase see chapter two for Rebuilding Therapy's living out, catharsis and ventilation, and awareness and reevaluation stages.)

Haskell did an excellent job in utilizing role training or practice techniques for preparing persons to more effectively deal with present and future relationships, issues and situations.

The Discussion Phase

According to Haskell, the discussion phase provides an opportunity for all group members, through their own sharing, to offer assistance to the protagonist and themselves in developing an understanding of their relationships and conflicts. This phase is also a way of stimulating group members to begin looking at feelings, thoughts and conflicts they were not aware of and preparing to work on a specific issue or issues as a protagonist. A nonprotagonist group member may also experience a catharsis of some extent during this phase, as well as during the action phase. In addition, this phase is a way of coming down for the protagonist and group members from the intense action phase and provides support and closure in the process. Although the discussion phase usually begins after the action phase, besides what discussion occurs in the warmup phase, a discussion can occur at another time in the session, if needed though strongly discouraged during the action phase. (See the group or audience previously in this chapter and Rebuilding Therapy's coming together stage in chapter two for further elaboration of the discussion phase.)

Psychodrama is a very intense form of psychotherapy often stimulating the patient to move into a hypnotic-like state reexperiencing a past event in one's life in the here and now of the past and being "totally" involved in this reexperiencing process. The specific integration of Psychodrama and hypnosis is discussed in the following section.

HYPNODRAMA

Moreno (1950) defined Hypnodrama as "a synthesis of psychodrama and hypnosis" (p. 164). Greenberg (1977) claimed that Hypnodrama combines the power of Psychodrama with the sensitivity of hypnosis. In doing so it goes a step further, strengthening the uncovering process of therapy. Perline (1968) pointed to Moreno (1950) and to Supple's (1962) claim that the major principles of Psychodrama are applicable to Hypnodrama. According to Greenberg, Hypnodrama was invented by Moreno in 1939 and independently developed by J. Ennes, a disciple of Moreno, in 1948. The development of Hypnodrama has been limited because few therapists have developed the joint skills of the psychodramatist and hypnotherapist.

Greenberg claimed that in Hypnodrama the protagonist along with the director, auxiliary egos and group members can be hypnotized. He conducted Hypnodrama both under hypnosis and not under hypnosis, whereas Moreno, according to Greenberg, never conducted a Hypnodrama session under hypnosis. I believe that it is highly preferable for the therapist and his or her team not to be in a hypnotic state and that this is not necessary. The essence of Hypnodrama is the patient being in a hypnotic or relaxed state while Psychodrama is being utilized. It is also beneficial for other group members to be in a similar state to facilitate their opening up if they get the chance or at least to possibly experience some uncovering of a past experience, even if briefly. In addition, a group member in a hypnotic or relaxed state may be more open to assist the working patient as a double to express feelings and thoughts, to live out the role of a significant other or to stimulate or support the working patient in other ways. Again, the term *relaxation* is defined here as being a state equivalent to hypnosis. Although, patients who have not gone through hypnosis or relaxation in a session often open up deeply in Psychodrama and assist and support each other, hypnosis or relaxation can facilitate this process.

However, there are some persons who can open up and assist others as well without an hypnotic induction or relaxation exercise because they are highly hypnotizable and are likely in a hypnotic or relaxed state in the Psychodrama experience. Greenberg pointed out that due to the action and emotion Moreno stimulated, many of his protagonists and some of the audience in his group likely slipped into a hypnotic state, which may have been the beginning of Hypnodrama. Supporting Erickson and Rossi in their discussion of hypnotic responses earlier in this chapter, Scott (1977) stated there were reports suggesting that "hypnosis does occur without conscious intent" (p. 303) citing Orne (1964) and Scott (1968). Scott claimed in some cases that Psychodrama can lead one into hypnosis and be viewed as a prelude to hypnosis.

In essence, the psychodramatic process often is an induction into a hypnotic state, for when a person is reliving a past experience with a relaxation of his or her defenses not focusing on anyone or anything in the present and is very much in the past experience, he or she is likely in a state of hypnosis or relaxation. However, Hypnodrama provides this state initially and frequently more quickly, without having to use Psychodrama to accomplish this, with the use of hypnosis initially taking the patient to a depth in his or her mind sufficient and deep enough to allow the uncovering process to effectively begin, often allowing the patient to operate, along with the impact of Psychodrama, at a deeper level and in a more effective way than in Psychodrama or hypnosis alone. Supple's findings, as noted by Perline, pointed out that many patients participating in Hypnodrama revealed much deeper levels than in Psychodrama. Perline cited Moreno and Ennes's (1950) claim, that in Hypnodrama, hypnosis serves as a psychological starter in the warming up process freeing the patient from many inhibiting defenses, prepares the patient to move to greater spontaneity, brings out the patient's deeper self early in therapy, assists in the assessment of the patient, bases treatment more directly on the patient's needs and achieves therapeutic results in a relatively short time period. Perline also discussed Moreno and Ennes's claim that Hypnodrama can be useful when other methods have not been effective in achieving catharsis and successful treatment outcome, while speeding up the therapy. Greenberg supported these claims stating Hypnodrama can be helpful in breaking through many of the patients defenses and dealing with repressed events. Therefore, hypnosis or relaxation synthesized with Psychodrama will often increase the level or state of hypnosis or relaxation and along with the interacting effects of these modalities will often stimulate the uncovering of partially repressed or repressed memories and their associated feelings and thoughts more quickly, deeply, openly and fully and the rebuilding from them more effectively than when using hypnosis or Psychodrama alone. This primarily occurs as hypnosis or relaxation is a good warmup, frequently, moving a patient quickly into a deeper level of the mind sufficient to effectively begin the uncovering process, and then along with using Psychodrama further stimulates the uncovering and working through of the experience. Also to be noted, is even when a person is aware of a past experience there usually are partially repressed or repressed factors associated with the experience which need to be addressed and worked through. In summary the combination of relaxation and Psychodrama or Rebuilding Therapy methods often give the patient the opportunity to get closer in touch with the relived experience to more authentically relive it and to more effectively rebuild from it.

Often Psychodrama used alone can be very effective therapeutically in dealing with rejecting experiences and repressed events, which it can uncover and assist patients to effectively resolve. However, whenever possible, therapeutic and the patient is ready owing to the reasons discussed, I prefer to use hypnosis or relaxation with psychodramatic or Rebuilding Therapy methods to facilitate the likelihood that the patient will relive past experiences and rebuild from them more effectively and will also aid the therapist to more effectively assist the patient to rebuild him or herself from these experiences. This in no way discounts the psychodramatic process, for I have also utilized psychodramatic or Rebuilding Therapy approaches specifically without hypnosis or relaxation many times since 1976 and will also continue to do so in Rebuilding Therapy as needed.

BIOENERGETICS OR BIOENERGENTIC THERAPY

Bioenergetics, developed by Lowen (1967, 1970 and 1975), also contributes to Rebuilding Therapy, relating the body to the mind by incorporating direct wok on one's body into psychotherapy. Bioenergetic Therapy operates on the premise that the mind and body are functionally identical and that what occurs in the mind reflects what is occurring in the body and visa versa. Bioenergetics advocates that emotional stress from one's environment and repressed feelings and conflicts results in chronic muscular tensions, which need to be reduced therapeutically in order to release such stress, feelings and conflicts, and followed by a therapeutic working through is necessary for a more psychologically fulfilling and productive life.

Lowen (1975) mentioned that "It is an important thesis of Bioenergetics that changes in personality are conditioned on changes in bodily functions—namely deeper breathing; increased motility; fuller and freer self expression" (p.115). Bioenergetics claims that as the person breathes more freely, is physically less tense and is more relaxed, he or she is more and better able to open up psychologically and make significant psychological changes.

According to Lowen (1970), the goal of Bioenergetic Therapy "is to restore the natural motility of the body" (p. 48). For Lowen motility refers to the involuntary or spontaneous movement of the body, with a person's motility reflected in the aliveness of one's facial expression, the quality of one's gestures and the range of emotional responsiveness. According to Lowen, Bioenergetic Therapy starts with breathing, for this provides the energy for less inhibited and more spontaneous bodily movement that enhances the expression of feelings. In Bioenergetics attention focuses on patterns of muscular tension and their relation to breathing, movement, posture and emotional expression, which are related to a person's emotional background reflecting early childhood relationships. As a result, Bioenergetic

Therapy works through body work and physical exercises to improve breathing and to increase awareness of muscular tension and to reduce it, which results in an uncovering of underlying feelings, thoughts, experiences and conflicts that can then be worked with therapeutically.

For example, Lowen advocated kicking and hitting exercises on a bed or mat. He also recommended the patient expressing verbally his or her feelings such as "I won't" or "no," which brings on deeper breathing and adds an emotional quality to the exercise, while integrating the mind and body.

Verbal exploration of psychological conflicts and their relation to one's personal history is also an important part of Bioenergetics. Lowen (1970) also claimed Bioenergetics uses exercises or "movements which express tenderness, affection and desire" (p. 54).

PRIMAL THERAPY

Neurosis, according to Janov (1970), is one's defense system covering up one's inner wounds and hurt or Primal Pain related to unmet needs caused by faulty parenting or mistreatment. I am interpreting the term *Pain* to mean repressed hurt or pain. Janov's Primal Therapy specializes in reliving the traumas and negative experiences that neuroticize the person. The cure for neurosis or getting well from neurosis according to Janov is the Primal experience, which is an engulfing "total feeling thought reliving experience from the past" (p. 86), which allows the person to release the buried or unexperienced hurt or pain. Each Primal, according to Janov, breaks open new buried memories leading to additional Primals, with the patient going further back into childhood. He noted that the body will only allow itself to feel a certain amount of uncovered pain or hurt at a time, and if the patient is not hurried this will occur in an orderly and safe sequence. Forcing a patient to feel more than he or she is ready to handle will only have one shut down again, according to Janov. (The discussion regarding Janov and Primal Therapy in this section is from his book *The Primal Scream* [1970].)

According to Janov, once a significant amount of painful memories are released, "memories of post Primal patients begin within a few months of birth" (p. 87). Janov described two patients who clinically relived traumatic birth experiences, (see chapter four), and he also gave an example of a woman who couldn't cry until she relived a tear duct operation at one year of age.

Janov pointed out that trauma appears to be laid down in the nervous system and is recalled organismically and that one's physical system is aware of being traumatized, though there is no consciousness of this effect. Janov claimed that it is insufficient to know about one's traumas and that "they must be relived and *experienced* fully in order to be resolved from their continuing effect on the organism" (p. 88).

According to Janov, one's Primal style is unique for each individual. Some patients talk their way into their feelings, whereas others start with a bodily feeling, associating it with a memory. Reactions just before the main connection to the Primal may include grasping one's stomach, grasping the couch, rolling one's head, perspiring or teeth chattering. No two Primals are alike with there being fearful ones, quiet ones, sad ones or angry and violent ones. Being out of control totally, according to Janov, permits connection of the feeling to the source, whereas self control usually means suppression of one's self. Janov claimed that once the patient is into experiencing his or her Primal, the therapist needs to do little except to remain quiet as the patient is "back there" reliving the experience, reexperiencing the aroma, sounds and bodily processes that had occurred, and that any talk in the present by the therapist may bring the patient out of it.

While in a Primal, the person often uses the words of a young child and loses track of time. Janov claimed patients described Primals as a conscious coma knowing they could come out of them at any time they chose, but they preferred not to. Patients know what is happening and where they are, but when they are in the Primal they are reexperiencing their past history while being engulfed by it. Feeling more of one's infancy and childhood results in increased maturity. Janov's stated that the Primal places the past back where it should be, allowing the patient to finally live in the present.

Janov's Primal Scream is a scream from the buried wounds and hurt that underlies rejecting experiences. The person screams for the many humiliations and beatings he or she received and couldn't express oneself about. The curative process, according to Janov, is the expression of one's hurt, resulting in the disappearance of the pain which one screams out or expresses as one faces the truth. Although the scream is the most usual response to the pain, it is not the only or the perennial reaction to hurt from the past, as indicated. Some patients thrash about, writhe, groan and moan.

According to Janov, Primals vary based on the age one split from one's real self into one's neurotic self to cope with his or her mistreatment and the depth of the repressed pain. Some patients can go directly to the major scene or experience where they felt the split, whereas others take months to do so. Janov claimed some patients report that they never get to one specific scene and that with many experiences have equal weight in producing their neurosis. He also noted that if the split or related major scene is early and the buried pain is great, the patient may relive one experience many times. I have found a similar process of patients reliving experiences in Rebuilding Therapy.

In referring to the healing process, Janov mentioned that feelings themselves don't hurt, rather, defending against the feeling is what appears to hurt. Though not denying there are painful feelings when reliving a negative childhood experience, he pointed out the more one feels these painful experiences of unmet needs and rejection, the less hurt one will experience or hold onto.

With regards to psychosomatic problems, Janov claimed that physical pain is the result of repressed early emotional pain, and when this hurt is felt, physical symptoms move away. Janov stated that repressed memories too painful to face "are laid down in the brain and stored below the level of awareness, sending messages to the body" (p. 93), and that the related feelings are coded into one's muscle system in a symbolic way, resulting in physical pain or tension. In one of Janov's examples a repressed impulse to hit back at a rejecting parent resulted in tense arm muscles, which was resolved once this impulse to strike out was faced and related to the muscle tightness, as Bioenergetics advocates.

According to Janov, "the explanatory process of conventional therapy may make the patient *more* neurotic" (p. 241) describing irrational behavior in terms of some theory and manipulating the patient into believing one is better because there is understanding, which is one more layer of protection from the underlying pain. As he strongly advocated, patients need to face feelings, not explain them. According to Janov, as long as the feelings are buried, the therapist and patient are guessing at what lies within the patient. For Janov, insight should never precede the underlying feelings and hurt, for it is the result of experiencing one's underlying pain and the connection between feeling and thought. As long as one's repressed pain blocks insight, there is no change, according to Janov, advocating the importance of stripping away the lie the patient is living to bring out the truth.

According to one of Janov's patients, Primal Therapy "'seemed to have taken out the whole tumor and everything fell into place'" (p. 244). The statement "'Everything fell into place'" (p. 244) is a typical feeling among Janov's patients, including ideas and the body both falling into place with sharper perceptions and increased physical coordination. Janov also pointed out that when reliving painful childhood experiences, the patient undergoes no reflecting, processing or reasoning of what he or she is doing and what is happening, but a total participation in the feeling process, becoming his or her feeling and pain. I have found in my work, although the patient is not stopping to think about what is going on and is reliving the total experience, his or her thinking and feelings are interacting in the healing process. Even in a highly cathartic process, the patient is connecting to his or her mother or father not wanting him, one's feelings of worthlessness, isolation, helplessness, hopelessness and so on related to his or her parent's rejection and soon relates this to one's dysfunction. According to Janov, the uncovering of buried pain can lead to several hours of insight, with everything the patient will become knowledgeable of being inside his or her mind.

Rebuilding Therapy, in emphasizing the importance of the reliving process, has advocated and supported Janov's discussion of it and the therapeutic process with modifications. Accordingly, Rebuilding Therapy focuses on the expression and release of feelings, thoughts and pain and the insights and redecisioning that result once this occurs, which are powerfully change inducing. Though not focusing specifically on the body's reaction, this at times is looked at as the patient discusses it and as obvious changes are noticed. Although positive physical changes are likely occurring as one rebuilds oneself, not being a physical healer has led me to leave the physiological side of health to the physician, chiropractor and other physical healers, though clearly respecting the interaction of the mind and body. In this light, I regularly consult with physical healers, though the possibility of further integrating the physical domain into Rebuilding Therapy is an open matter.

Primal Therapy, according to Janov, takes patients into an arena that is rarely if ever seen by other psychotherapists. It is a systematic, ordered, step-by-step journey of a person into one's self. Janov stated that when patients finally get to the early tragic feeling of knowing they were hated or never understood and experience the feeling of aloneness, they perfectly understand why they turned off. In Primal Therapy, as in Psychodrama, Hypnodrama, Bioenergetics and Rebuilding Therapy, the patient experiences the essence of his or her dysfunction, significantly lets go of the pain and hurt and starts healing. This is a lot of hard work involving reliving a number of rejecting experiences, that also often includes the same ones in similar or different ways to eventually reach psychological health. Reliving an experience in different ways refers to reliving different parts or aspects of it. Of course, the reliving of any experience involves the major and key parts of it.

Janov claimed the patient is asked to discuss his or her history and background, encouraged to stay with his or her feelings, to breathe effectively and eventually to address one's parents directly, rather than just talking about them. The patient soon moves back into the past reexperiencing, through the Primal, specific experiences with one's parents and significant others and opening up to them at that specific age. This process occurs over a number of sessions. Janov did not explain any specific techniques utilized to stimulate the patient to relive major life experiences. He described the patient's defenses as increasingly breaking down during the course of therapy enabling the patient to relive significant experiences, followed by the further weakening of the patient's defenses to relive other significant experiences and this process continuing until it is no longer therapeutically necessary. Yablonsky reported various devices, such as six foot cribs, baby bottles and machines to simulate birth experiences are used to assist a patient to face one's pain, that bags are hit or punched, and a range of primal physical activities are encouraged to stimulate the expression of feelings.

Primal Therapy does not deal with the transference, shutting it off. It does not permit this type of neurotic behavior as it turns off feelings, according to Janov. Instead, Janov stated that the patient is encouraged to confront his or her parents directly and to experience one's early feelings toward them which will remove the neurosis and transference. Janov claimed that the patient-therapist relationship is ignored and that analyzing the transference process seemed to be "a discussion of derivative, displaced and symbolic behavior rather than getting at basic need" (p. 246) or the core of the dysfunction. Rebuilding Therapy minimizes the transference, primarily assisting the patient, when possible, to directly face the causes of his or her problems, most often one's parents and significant others, past rejection or other negative experiences. Rebuilding Therapy is concerned with the patient-therapist relationship to stimulate trust and the patient opening up and providing support and reparenting.

The major therapeutic work in Primal Therapy of disassembling the defense system is achieved by the end of the third week, with major changes seen in symptomatology and personality, although the patient still has a good deal of repressed conflict and hurt to face and work through. At this time the patient is placed in group therapy, with individual sessions provided as needed. The focus of Primal group therapy is internal, with almost no sharing of feelings and thoughts about each other among group members. The major goal is to stimulate group members into reliving significant experiences. Janov claimed that one person experiencing a Primal may stimulate others to experience Primals. It is not uncommon for six or seven Primals to occur at once during a three hour group session, as each patient is oblivious to his or her surroundings, being so involved in his or her memories and feelings. The average Primal lasts a half hour, with the patient spending another hour making connections and processing. There is a discussion period at the end of each group during which the participants discuss what happened to them, including how a repressed feeling or conflict related to a specific symptom.

Janov stated that a patient is usually psychologically well or healthy by the time he or she reaches the eighth month, although some patients may need from ten to twelve months to achieve this level of progress.

According to Janov, once a person's major defense system has been broken one has no choice but to get healthy, which is inevitable as long as the patient remains in treatment, as I inform my patients. In other words, there is no turning back once the defenses are down. The patient knows the difference between health and neurosis, usually not wanting to return to a dysfunctional life, though he or she still has the choice to not get healthy by terminating therapy or not working effectively in therapy.

Like myself, Janov pointed out that neither loving parents, stepparents, lovers, warm psychotherapists nor kindness can undo the neurosis of one's past, which cannot be reasoned, placated, loved or threatened out of existence. Its pathological processes appear to eat up anything in its path according to Janov. Clearly, an intense and powerful process such as Primal Therapy, Psychodrama, Hypnodrama, Bioenergetics or Rebuilding Therapy is needed to effectively treat neurosis and unresolved problems. However, the degree of recovery will depend on the degree of impairment and the patient's problems, the involvement of the family as needed, how productively treatment is used, remaining in treatment long enough, the therapist and treatment team, if the treatment team is also utilized, the effectiveness and success of therapy, the setting and the financial and insurance resources.

Janov claimed that Primal Therapy has application to all neuroses and expresses cautious optimism regarding its use with the psychotic person. The therapeutic process of ridding one of psychosis, according to Janov, is similar to the treatment of neurosis, although "the psychotic, however, differs from the neurotic because of the tremendous amount of underlying Pain and the fragility of the real self" (Janov, p. 383). Janov noted that it may take two to three times longer to treat the psychotic, while it will be necessary to protect his or her environment during treatment to protect against external stresses. He pointed out that if a person can make interpersonal contact he or she is likely to be treatable. Psychodrama has also been utilized with the psychotic patient.

Janov also stated that when an adult has someone to assist him or her to feel and understand one's feelings and provide support in the process, there is no way a break into psychosis can occur. According to Janov, "he can only break down into himself—which means health, not sickness" (p. 381). He gave an example of the treatment of a psychotic woman who was assisted to face and feel what made her fall apart, which was the agony and horror she ran from, and then healing and becoming whole. I have regularly informed my patients that they can't go crazy if they give up control, but will only come more to their *senses* regarding what they feel and think and who they are and in the process will gain more control.

Yablonsky claimed that many psychodramatic techniques would be very useful during the early part of Primal Therapy to break down patient defenses to reach deeper feeling levels. According to Yablonsky, the incorporation of psychodramatic techniques and the use of the group for stimulation and supportive purposes into Primal Therapy can be very helpful.

Moreno, according to Yablonsky, made reference to the Primal experience in many areas of his discussion of Psychodrama, but used different terminology. Yablonsky stated that "in hundreds of psychodramatic sessions I directed, protagonists have expressed their primal pain, made the connect, clarified their emotions and in some measure resolved their problems" (p. 161). He claimed Psychodrama is more powerful, for the protagonist is stimulated to react to the basic source of his or her Primal Pain, such as one's parent reenacted by the auxiliary ego. Psychodrama, according to Yablonsky comes closer than any other method to delineate the original situation that created the neurosis. He noted that the addition of the represented significant other provides a situation conducive to the Primal experience. I strongly concur with Yablonsky, though sometimes a patient reliving an experience is only ready to visualize his or her significant other without an auxiliary ego or is better off not having an auxiliary ego as a significant other if "totally" into reliving one's experience without this. However, in many cases introducing psychodramatic techniques and approaches or Rebuilding Therapy methods and approaches in a timely and therapeutic way can further enhance the reliving and integration process.

AN OVERVIEW

Psychodrama has been the most powerful influence in the development of Rebuilding Therapy, while integrating the process of Structural Analysis, the influence of Script Analysis and Redecision Therapy developed from the TA school, as interpreted and developed in the rebuilding process. Hypnosis or relaxation has been added to this process, when needed, to assist in the uncovering and reliving process, in reparenting and mental rehearsal. Bioenergetic Therapy has also added its influence regarding Rebuilding Therapy's use of some physical exercises, primarily hitting on a mat, although it can be a bed or large pillow, to assist in the release of anger and related feelings. However, it is to be noted I learned about such physical exercises in my Psychodrama training and then in Bioenergetics workshops. Reparenting from the TA school has also been a significant influence as it has been interpreted and developed for Rebuilding Therapy. Primal Therapy, though not utilized in the development of Rebuilding Therapy, strongly supports what occurs in the reliving process and in Rebuilding Therapy. As with other methods, Primal Therapy needs to be looked at seriously to further develop and improve the rebuilding process.

In this light, Rebuilding Therapy has been developed, using for its methodology existing psychodramatic techniques, referred to as Rebuilding Therapy methods, further developing them in a number of cases and devising original and new psychodramatic or Rebuilding Therapy methods or at least not knowledgeable that these methods existed while I was developing them as original methods. As mentioned, the Psychodramatic techniques that are utilized are called Rebuilding Therapy methods as they are used in the rebuilding process. However, in no way, do I take credit for any technique or methodology developed by others. Hopefully, the use of methodology and theory that Rebuilding Therapy has relied on, may further develop and refine what others have so ingeniously created.

Although the major theoretical and therapeutic influences on Rebuilding Therapy have been presented in chapter four and this chapter, this doesn't rule out other theories.

CHAPTER 6

Acting and Living Out the Specific Roles

The skill of acting, acting out, dramatizing, simulating or living out the roles of the primary significant others who mistreated or affected the patient in some way, in order to strongly stimulate the patient to effectively relive life experiences and open up regarding his or her experiences, relationships, conflicts, and issues, as in Psychodrama, is an important part of Rebuilding Therapy. As the patient is living out his or her life experiences, the therapeutic agent, therapist or others, living out the roles of significant others, need to be effective and skilled actors and knowledgeable and sensitive of the psychological dynamics of the persons in these roles to portray the patient's significant others as accurately and authentically as possible. In doing so, this will stimulate the patient's more open expression of feelings and thoughts regarding the experience being relived and the more effective reliving of this experience, and will contribute to maximizing the uncovering of another experience or other experiences and related feelings and thoughts. Though using other persons in the roles of significant others is not always done, it is done in the large majority of situations and when done, as the patient is ready, it usually stimulates the most effective reliving of an experience when other factors such as the patient, relaxation and the effective use of Rebuilding Therapy methodology are contributing to the reliving process. Although the therapeutic agent or therapist in the large majority of cases will live out the role of a significant other, at certain times, another patient or group member in group therapy or, less frequently, a family member in individual family or multiple family group therapy will live out being a significant other when, in any of these situations, this relates to the group or family member's experiences and issues, the group or family member is ready and capable of doing this and it is helpful to him or her, it is helpful to the patient and won't create negative therapeutic side effects. The family member in this case is not the same significant other who mistreated or affected the patient in some way whose role is being lived out and which is the subject of discussion here. An advantage of using another group or family member who relates to the working patient and his or her experiences is that this person has personal experience and knowledge of this role and if ready can effectively live it out. Disadvantages are that another group or family member hasn't been trained and can easily allow one's conflicts and defenses to contaminate or inhibit living out the role of the significant other. It is also essential that any nontherapeutic agent utilized in the role of a significant other be willing and supportive of this process. The issue of utilizing other group members, or in less frequent situations, other family members in the role of significant others is discussed further in the latter part of this chapter. However, living out the role of a significant other is often more effectively done by the therapeutic agent or therapist as he or she is trained to do so, with the therapeutic agent or therapist taking on this role in the large majority of situations, as indicated.

When selecting among trained clinicians, ideally it is preferable to utilize a trained co-therapist or auxiliary agent rather than the therapist to free the therapist to guide and direct the session. Even so, I have often found myself in the position of being the only therapeutic agent available, or the person most effectively able to act or live out the role of a significant other. As a result, I have learned to be very versatile, while still effectively directing the session.

The therapeutic agent or therapist's personal and psychological readiness to live out being a significant other is essential. The power of this approach will likely stimulate the uncovering or at least the conscious awareness of past negative experiences or unresolved conflicts in the therapeutic agent or therapist. If this occurs, the therapeutic agent or therapist needs to be psychologically ready to cope with this situation and not get into a countertransference relationship with the patient. The therapeutic agent or therapist needs to freely and spontaneously live out the significant other's role without any interference, resistance or sabotage from his or her emotional conflicts or lack of readiness to do so.

There are several common roles regarding specific types of mistreatment and rejection that the therapeutic agent or therapist need to learn to stimulate the reliving process. It takes considerable practice to master these roles and to live them out as authentically and accurately as possible. Any variation of these roles relative to the circumstances of the patient's life can also be lived out. It is also essential that the major messages of these roles and types of rejection be lived out and communicated to the victimized patient, whether they were directly said or implied, for this is what is important and significant when recalling and reliving an experience. In this light, although it would be preferable to recreate the exact wording of rejecting messages, it is important not to get bogged down in too many specifics; instead, focus should be on the meaning and significance of the message, including if there is more than one meaning in it. These rejecting messages were not only inflicted at the time they occurred, but also remain in the patient's mind, continuing to influence him or her until dealt with in therapy.

The power of these rejecting messages is so great that in addition to using them when a patient relives an experience, in a number of cases to expedite the opening up process or when the patient isn't ready to relive or live out a specific experience, an effective approach is for the therapist or therapeutic agent to live out one or more of these rejecting messages in the manner that it was delivered. This process not only stimulates the patient to open up, but in some cases stimulates the patient to relive the experience or experiences the message or messages were delivered from, even when the patient wasn't initially ready to do so. Usually one or a few or a related number of messages are delivered when using this approach, so as not to confuse the patient. The example of the cage method in chapter nine illustrates the effectiveness of delivering these messages. Such rejecting messages may include "You're no good," "You'll never amount to anything," "I wish you were never born," "You're nothing but a burden" or "You can't trust anyone in this world. You have to get them before they get you." The messages of the various types of rejection and dysfunction described in this chapter can be lived out in this way. (See chapter fourteen regarding this approach.)

Though the focus of Rebuilding Therapy is, for the most part, on the rejecting and dysfunctional roles of significant others in the patient's life, what applies when living out these roles also applies when living out healthy roles of significant others.

A number of the major rejecting roles are described in this chapter with examples. The roles of the major significant others in the examples provided in this and other chapters have been acted or lived out by the therapist, co-therapist or auxiliary agent in this order, though primarily done so by myself. These persons are referred to as the therapeutic agent, unless they are more specifically mentioned in these examples. As indicated, when the terms *therapist* and *therapeutic agent* are used together the term *therapeutic agent* refers to the co-therapist or auxilary agent. The examples did not include other group or family members in the major roles of significant others. The significant others portrayed in the examples were the major significant others affecting the patient in the relived experiences, for the most part one major significant other per example. Other significant others were also portrayed by other persons in the sessions, as needed, though not discussed in the examples.

It is also usually in the patient's best interest to deal with one major significant other and one major issue at a time as the focus of the session to not overwhelm the patient, though another significant other or others, as needed, may also be acted out by another person or persons in the reliving of an experience or experiences pertaining to this significant other and issue. More than one significant other is more frequently portrayed in a group session as other persons are available to act out these significant others, though more than one significant other can be portrayed in an individual session, as needed. Sometimes the patient can address two parental figures or two major significant others in a session, if needed and therapeutic, though in the large minority of situations. The therapist at times, when not having other persons available to assist him or her in a session and needing to act out the significant other or others, as needed, can portray the second major significant other as this is therapeutic. As with any approach or method used, acting or living out the role of a significant other requires much skill, sensitivity and timing, with the therapist needing to adapt to the therapeutic situation and resources available to him or her.

The therapeutic agent needs to practice the rejecting roles presented in this chapter and other major rejecting roles, while learning to function in them effectively. Various major rejecting roles will now be described.

DIRECT REJECTION

Direct rejection is abusive in some way and includes physical or direct emotional rejection and abuse. Whereas physical abuse is always accompanied by emotional abuse, emotional abuse does not necessarily imply physical abuse. Sexual abuse, a type of direct rejection, including rape and molestation, is included under sexual mistreatment, which is described in chapter fourteen. Physical abuse involves any type of physical assault on another person, including hitting a victim with a belt, "switch," and so on, punching, slapping, throwing, pushing, shaking or choking the victim. Direct emotional rejection and abuse include verbal threatening such as "I'm going to belt the hell out of you" or "Shut up or else," name calling such as "You're so stupid," "You're so dumb," "You're so lazy," "You bitch" or "You bastard," severe criticism such as "You'll never amount to anything," "You're no good," "You're nothing but a burden" and other type of sadistic remarks such as "I wish you were never born" or "I wish you were dead." An example is Steve's, age 44, rejecting father, portrayed by a therapeutic agent, abusing him for not trying harder and doing better in a Little League game as a child.

Father: "You're no good, you're a klutz. You play just like a girl. I've tried to show you how to hit, but you just don't have what it takes" (loudly).

Steve: "I tried, but I'm just not that good at baseball. I don't like baseball that much, Dad" (upset).

Father (in an angry and rejecting way): "You can't do anything right! You're nothing but an embarrassment to me. Why couldn't I have a son who makes me proud?"

Steve (starting to cry): "Please Dad, don't be so mad at me. I'm sorry."

Father: "You're just a big disappointment. You're nothing but a burden, a pain in the ass. I wish you were never born" (yelling louder and having a temper outburst as he throws insults and psychological "knives" at and into his son's mind).

These messages can also be delivered in a stern, firm or even a relatively calm voice. What is communicated, however, is clearly contaminating and poisonous.

Another example of direct rejection is physical abuse of a child. As with any type of rejection, this needs to be acted or lived out as authentically and as closely as it occurred in the patient's life. Of course, no actual physical discipline or harm is inflicted on the patient as the abuse is lived out and simulated clinically. The therapeutic agent also verbalizes the emotional abuse that accompanied the physical treatment as authentically as it occurred. Various ways in which physical abuse is simulated are described here.

One way of simulating physical abuse is for the therapeutic agent to hit and smack on a mat placed on a table next to the patient. Such a mat should be firm enough for the patient, group or family member to feel, visualize, hear and believe that something is being hit to assist in uncovering a memory or memories of being physically mistreated if this was the case.

If the patient was beat or hit with a belt, then the therapeutic agent using a large enough belt slams it down on a mat, making sure that the sound of the belt hitting the mat is loud enough to make an impact and sounds like it could be hitting a person. This is the most powerful and effective way of reproducing a "belt hitting" because of the booming noise of the belt hitting the mat and because the visual and emotional experience of a belt hitting a mat in close proximity to the patient approximates being hit with a belt. The therapeutic agent can also slam the bottom part of his or her flat hand down on the mat to simulate a belt hitting the patient. This alternative should be used only when no belt is available, when the patient isn't ready for the belt to be used or when the patient would "shut down" more than is therapeutically helpful if a belt were used.

Another way of reproducing the patient being beat or hit with a belt is for the therapeutic agent to hold the belt with one hand and slap the belt into the other open hand. This is often the least powerful or effective way of simulating belt abuse, although visually it most closely approximates this type of abuse, as the sound of the belt hitting the hand has less impact on the patient than the louder noise of the belt or the hand hitting the mat. However, some patients are affected differently; the therapeutic agent therefore needs to be flexible in providing the most effective stimulation.

The therapeutic agent can also use the mat to simulate or live out the patient being slapped or punched. If the patient was punched or slapped, then the therapeutic agent needs to hit on the mat with his or her fist or the bottom part of one's open hand respectively.

If a mat is not available to assist in simulating or living out a patient being hit by a belt, fist or open hand, a firm mattress, a cushion on a couch or a large pillow can be used in this order of effectiveness. The firmer the object, the louder and more powerful the impact will be when it is hit and on the patient psychologically, and in turn will often more effectively assist in uncovering the rejecting experience.

Another way of simulating or living out the patent being slapped or punched is for the therapeutic agent to live out slapping or punching his or her right hand against the left open hand. The therapeutic agent acts as though one's right hand will hit the patient's face or wherever the patient was approximately slapped or punched, but stops oneself with his or her left open hand. The therapeutic agent uses the right hand as the primary assaulting limb, because most persons are right-handed. If the perpetrator is known to be left-handed, however, the therapeutic agent should use the left hand as the primary assaulting limb, acting this out in the same manner as when using the right hand with appropriate modifications. Usually, this process is the more powerful way to more authentically stimulate the patient to relive being slapped or punched and elicit the more open expression of feelings and thoughts. However, this may not always be the case, for the louder sound of the hand or fist hitting the mat rather than hitting one's other hand can sometimes more effectively reproduce this type of mistreatment clinically. Also, the patient experiencing the therapeutic agent's open hand or fist hitting the mat can in some cases stimulate the patient to feel oneself being the "mat" as it is being slapped or punched.

Another way of simulating the patient being slapped or punched is for the therapeutic agent to act out the hand and bodily motions of slapping or punching the patient. The therapeutic agent in acting out mistreatment in this way doesn't make physical contact with the mat or his or her other hand. Because no physical impact occurs when simulating abusive behavior this way, it is usually the least powerful process for acting out this type of rejection. However, this may be all that the patient is ready for, as it is essential not to overwhelm or overly threaten the patient's sense of control or to stimulate the patient to withdraw or resist facing his or her past rejection.

The therapeutic agent needs to be comfortable, not overly threatened and not over one's head when living out the significant other's mistreatment of the patient. This occurs as the therapeutic agent is adequately trained and psychologically ready. Examples of physical abuse are provided in the discussion of the rejecting alcoholic.

LESS DIRECT REJECTION

Less direct rejection is less abusive appearing and sometimes more subtle. It is often difficult to deal with this form of rejection because it is less direct, isn't as obvious, is camouflaged and is communicated in a more socially acceptable and even outwardly loving way. One would have difficulty even arguing with this type of communication and treatment at times. This type of rejection is "crazy-making" and often creates a tremendous amount of confusion, guilt and shame, weakening the victim's ability to defend oneself and blinding his or her perception regarding what the perpetrator is doing. It also invalidates the person's confidence in his or her judgment regarding whether he or she is accurately and justifiably upset and in asserting oneself appropriately against the mistreatment of another person. Susan, 43, was subtly rejected by her mother for years. Her mother professed to be a loving person and tried to appear this way, but she was skillfully manipulative, critical and emotionally abusive. An example of this type of rejection is described which Susan reexperienced at age 8, with a therapeutic agent as her mother.

Mother: "Susan, I love you dearly, you are intelligent and you're pretty, but you're always seeming to put your foot in your mouth. I just don't understand you. I don't know what the problem is" (patting her shoulder in a condescending and patronizing way).

Susan: "But Mom, I do the best I can. It seems like things just don't go right for me."

Mother: "It was so easy for me when I was your age. It's so hard to understand how you just don't understand simple things and do them right. I just don't know. I size up a situation and I just know what I need to do. You? Well, I don't want to sound negative, but sometimes you have two left feet."

Susan: "But I try so hard" (crying).

Mother (putting her arm on Susan's shoulder appearing to console her but continuing to throw knives in her): "Some people have the talent to deal with life's situations, but maybe this is not what you're cut out to do. I love you anyway, but you just can't help the way you are."

This interchange continued with her mother constantly throwing out double messages. The "I love you" often is the bait before the shot that is not communicated from the heart; it is in reality the camouflaging preparation for the real blow that will come after. There is often a compliment followed by a "but" and then the intended message of abuse. This less direct rejector is an expert manipulator in placing blame on his or her victim, leaving the person little recourse to defend oneself.

GUILT PROVOCATION

Guilt provocation is one of the most potent forms of rejection and is one of the conditional love syndromes in which the parental figure only accepts the child if he or she agrees with the parent, does what the parent wants or pleases the parent in some way. It involves much criticism and rejection and can be accompanied by physical abuse. The victim is often caught in a symbiotic relationship with his or her parent with parental guilt, suffocation and the parent's unrealistic need to have the child fulfill his or her needs and in some cases one's life. Along with this, the child or adolescent's insecurity and fear of losing his or her parent's love and being alone on one's own contribute to a poisonous and unhealthy relationship. This form of rejection gives the victim such messages as: "You're no good," "It's your fault," "Look what you're doing to hurt me," and in some cases, "You're killing me." The victim is held responsible for the abuser's welfare and happiness, with it being impossible for the victim to meet the perpetrator's demands. It also involves a significant amount of camouflage and deceit as the perpetuator operates from an underdog-victim position in controlling the actual victim, making it easy for the victim to feel sorry for the abuser and not want to hurt him or her. A person of any age can be inflicted with guilt provocation, as with any type of rejection. An example of this type of abuse is described regarding Bob, 26, and his mother, lived out by a therapeutic agent, which he reexperienced at age 14.

Mother: "Don't you care about me? Do you know what I'm going through because of you? I've been sick because of you. I have lost sleep because of you. I can't eat over you. You're killing me. You're killing me" (crying in a "poor me" type manner).

Bob: "I don't want to hurt you, I'm just doing what is best for me. I wanted to go out for football and be with the guys."

Mother: "If you cared about me, you'd do what I want. You'd put me first. I've always wanted you to get the best grades and when you play football you don't apply yourself."

Bob: "But I have to care about myself, Mom. Football and being with my friends means a lot to me, and my grades are okay."

Mother: "I'm your mother; I gave birth to you. I made your life possible. I've sacrificed for you, and you talk to me like this. Your grades have not been that good. You just don't care about me. You just care about your father because he lets you play football."

Bob: "I love you both, Mom, but I like to have fun too. I apply myself in school, too. I'm trying. You don't even care about what matters to me" (beginning to cry).

Mother: "Don't you know how embarrassed I am over this? What are people going to say about me if you continue getting poor grades you? You have no idea what you're doing to me."

Bob: "I'm sorry, Mom" (crying).

Mother: "You're not sorry. If you were sorry you wouldn't do this to me" (continuing to cry in a pathetic "poor me" way, as she emotionally slapped, punched, and beat up her son).

The power of guilt provocation is that the abuser realizes to a certain extent that the victim is dependent on him or her and uses this against the victim, knowing that the barrages of guilt provocation will wound him or her badly without a strong defense. The victim of guilt provocation is often saying to his or her assailant, "Please, love me. Just give me a break. There is only so much I can do." This type of scenario occurs in conditional love in varying degrees.

OVERPROTECTION

In overprotection, the overprotective parent does not allow his or her child or adolescent to be exposed to healthy life relationships, experiences and situations. This parent makes it difficult for the child or adolescent to learn to relate to others effectively and intimately, to deal effectively with specific life situations and experiences and to develop effective coping skills. Overprotection is suffocating, stifling the child or adolescent's creativity and potential and not allowing him or her to grow emotionally.

Sally, 16, an example of this, was severely overprotected by her mother to the point where she never developed her own personality or the ability to live in an effective and meaningful way. Following is an interchange relived at age 7 with a therapeutic agent as her mother.

Mother: "Sally, you're such a good little girl. You're so special. Mommy is always going to take care of you. You have nothing to worry about. You're not like the other girls who get themselves dirty and get in trouble."

Sally: "But I want to play with Sonya. She's having two other girls over to her house."

Mother: "You can stay home with Mommy, and I'll take care of you. If you go out there and play, you'll get hurt. Something will happen to you."

Sally: "I'll be okay, Mommy. It's safe. Please, Mommy."

Mother: "Her brother will call you names. I've heard a lot about him. He's a real bully."

Sally: "He won't bother me. Please, Mom" (beginning to cry).

Mother: "I'm just afraid for you. You can't trust anyone. I just want to make sure nothing happens to you. I want to take such good care of you. You're such a special little girl. Let me comb your hair. You look so pretty. You're so special" (in a suffocating way).

Sally: "But, Mommy, I want to go out and play. The other girls have so much fun. I want to be like them. Please, please, Mommy" (crying).

Mother: "Don't you want to make Mommy happy and stay home with me? I'll comb your hair and I'll bake cookies for you."

Sally: "But, Mommy, the other girls make fun of me when I stay home. They tell me I'm a baby."

Mother: "Don't worry about them. See how fresh they are? I will take care of you. You don't have anything to worry about. They're no good for you. You stay home with me" (in a subtly firm voice as she put her tentacles of overprotection into Sally's being).

Sally: (her crying decreasing and inhibited by mother's suffocation): "Okay, Mommy. I'll stay with you" (giving into her mother's overprotective suffocation, tyranny and rejection).

Such a parent operates with a considerable amount of guilt provocation and a strong need to have one's needs and often one's life fulfilled through his or her child. As with the guilt provoking and perfect child type parents, this child or adolescent doesn't have the right to develop one's own identity and must psychologically stop breathing, feeling and thinking and become his or her parent's robot.

THE PERFECT OR GOOD CHILD SYNDROME

The perfect or good child syndrome is a form of a rejection in which the child is compulsively pressured into conforming. This is also referred to as conformity rejection. When the child is not overprotected and is allowed to engage in normal, acceptable age appropriate activities, he or she is mandated to do so in an obedient, conforming and "good boy or girl" manner and to achieve some type of success primarily to meet the parent's needs. This type of rejection, as any conditional love or rejection, also stifles and inhibits creativity, risk taking, assertiveness and free thinking, reduces the ability to function independently and maturely and retards psychological growth. It is a powerful form of rejection, for it hides under the disguise of social acceptability, where the "good child" often has a high rating in his or her parent's and community's eyes. The "perfect child" is often well behaved, polite, inhibits his or her feelings and thoughts, is a good student and may be a good athlete, which endears him or her to adults. This is the type of child about whom a parent would say: "He's such a wonderful boy. We never have any trouble with him. We are so proud of him." An example of this type of parenting is provided in chapter seven when describing the role reversal method.

WORKAHOLISM

Another form of rejection involves workaholism. The workaholic neglects his or her family primarily because of an addictive obsession with work or activities. This person doesn't allow enough time to parent and interact with his or her family in a loving and healthy way, working excessively away from the home or preoccupied with other activities in or out of the home. The workaholic will use a significant amount of denial, stating that he or she is working for one's family to give them the "things" in life they need or that will bring them happiness. The theme of the workaholic's denial is that "I am doing this for you and I am sacrificing myself because of you," making it difficult to fight against. The workaholic is often working to gain the acceptance of others as substitutes for his or her own rejecting parent or parents, strives for parental acceptance to no avail and uses work or activity as an escape from intimacy and from one's feelings, thoughts, stress, emotional pain and one's self. The workaholic, often contaminated with stress and conflict, may also be directly or indirectly rejecting to one's family during his or her infrequent contacts with them. The neglect and mistreatment inflicted by the workaholic are often supported and enabled by a co-dependent spouse who allows it to go on, as with other types of rejection in other cases. An example is Carol's, 15, father who worked excessively throughout her life to the point that she did not know him and never really had an intimate conversation with him, while her mother reinforced his workaholism. Carol's interaction with her parents, who were portrayed by therapeutic agents, is relived at a younger age in her childhood.

Carol: "Dad, could you come to my dancing program today? You're always so busy all the time. The other kids have their dads there. Please, Dad?" (reaching out to him with all she had).

Father: "I'm sorry, Carol, I'm just going to be so busy. I have a meeting to go to, but you know I would love to be there."

Carol: "But Dad, can't you not go to the meeting this time?"

Father: "I must go. It is very important. I can't miss it. It involves a big contract."

Carol: "But what about my dancing, isn't that important?"

Father: "It's important, but this meeting is important, you know you're Daddy's girl."

The therapeutic agent then portrayed Carol's father, thinking quietly, turning himself away from Carol and thinking out loud for reliving purposes. Carol may never have directly heard this thinking spoken by her father, but she received many nonverbal or indirect messages that her father felt this way.

Father (thinking out loud): "I can't miss this meeting. This is just a stupid dancing program. This meeting means a lot of dollars for our company and maybe a bonus for me. This meeting is what's important to me not a dumb dancing program" (and then turned to Carol) "Look, Carol, another time" (of course, lying again).

Carol: "But Dad, you never go to my performances and you promise and you never come."

Father (in a guilt provoking way): "But I'm busy, I'm working for the entire family. My hard work buys your dancing costume and shoes. It buys your clothes, the games that you have and this pretty house we live in."

Carol (crying): "But I want my Dad to watch me like all the other kids. They ask me where you are. Mary even made fun of me saying I don't have a Dad. Susan said you're too drunk to come. Joy said that you probably have a girlfriend."

Father: "Now, stop the crying. I can't go to your dancing program. That's the way it is. I need to go now" (walking out the door with Carol continuing to cry).

Carol (as her father walked out the door, she yelled out): "I hate you. I hate you. I wish you weren't my father anymore. I hate you."

Mother (in a guilt provoking way): "How can you talk to your father like that? He would rather be home with all of us. He works so hard for us. If it wasn't for him we wouldn't have all the wonderful things we have, those pretty clothes, the vacations we go on every year. I'd be gone a lot more having to work more. What's wrong with you? Show some respect. He loves you. If he didn't love you, he wouldn't work so hard. He does it for all of us. I don't want to ever hear you say anything against your father again. Do you understand?"

Carol: "But Mom, he never comes to my performances and I want him to be proud of me. Sometimes I feel like he isn't even my dad" (crying).

Mother: "I've had it with you. Go to your room and I don't want to hear a sound from you" (very angry).

Carol (still crying): "Okay Mom".

The workaholic message, "you are not worth my time," and its open guilt provocation, if the child, adolescent or family member become unhappy with it, are a common theme. Although the co-dependent parent or family member is partially described, a more detailed discussion of this person is provided later in this chapter.

ALCOHOLISM

The alcoholic person is addicted to alcohol, just as the workaholic is addicted to his or her work. This type of person must have alcohol to cope with life, to increase his or her confidence, to escape, to tranquilize him or herself from one's problems or to get some type of "high" in life. The alcohol is what he or she is really married to, and this person won't let anyone or anything get in its way. The alcoholic person may also be abusive, rejecting, withdrawing, sleep excessively or act inappropriately and in embarrassing ways, often being a negative factor in the home.

The therapeutic agent's ability to live out the role of an alcoholic with its symptomatology is helpful in bringing out the feelings, thoughts and conflicts it elicits. Various forms of alcoholic mistreatment will be described. As alcohol is a drug, what is described regarding these types of alcoholic mistreatment can also apply to the drug abusing person with specific variations relative to the type of drug and its related rejecting behavior. Rebuilding Theory takes the position that psychological dysfunction, psychopathology and family dysfunction contribute strongly to alcohol and drug abuse.

Direct Alcoholic Rejection

In this form of alcoholic mistreatment, direct alcoholic rejection, the alcoholic abuses in a physical and emotional way, although it may just be emotional abuse, though still very serious. Here Buddy, 22, relived an experience, at age 7, with a therapeutic agent acting out being his father.

Buddy: "Daddy, can you play a game with me? Please, Daddy."

Father: "I'm relaxing. I'm watching television. Will you leave me alone" (sipping another beer).

Buddy: "But, Daddy, you promised to play with me."

Father: "Why don't you play with your mother. Just leave me alone. I'm busy right now. I'm trying to relax. I've had a hard day" (very harshly).

Buddy: "Can't you play with me, Daddy?"

Father (getting up out of his chair and acting out smacking Buddy): "Buddy, I told you to leave me alone. I told you I was tired! Now get the hell out of here! I'm busy. I don't want to do anything with you! And if you don't stop that crying, I'll give you more to cry about!" (as he acted out slapping him again and again with Buddy crying hysterically).

Usually such a person is already disturbed, with alcohol worsening the situation.

Alcoholic Argumentativeness

Another form of alcoholic mistreatment is alcoholic argumentativeness. This person, already a rejecting person in some way, inflicts a stronger degree of mistreatment on others when he or she is intoxicated. An example is presented with the therapist mirroring and acting as Charlie, 41, in a joint marital therapy session (individual family therapy) with Charlie and his wife, Rose, 39. Charlie was an alcoholic who had an answer for everything, would not listen and was constantly arguing.

Charlie: "Nobody tells me what to do. If I want to spend my hard earned money on some beer, that's what I'm going to do. If I want to drink with my friends, that's what I'm going to do. No woman, nobody tells me what to do! I put a roof over your head. I put food on the table and clothes on your back and if I want to go out for awhile, that's what I'm going to do. If you don't like it, it's too bad" (in a very authoritarian way).

Rose: "But you're hurting the kids. You're never home during the evening. They miss you. You're not even a husband anymore. I feel like I've lost you" (crying).

Charlie: "Stop the crying. I give you everything. I don't go out on you. I don't beat you. What do you want from me?"

Rose: "I just want you to be a husband. I can't take this anymore."

Charlie: "If you don't stop nagging me, I'm going to leave. Do you understand? I don't have to listen to this. I could be out with the boys enjoying myself instead of listening to you".

Rose: "I can't even talk to you anymore. I don't know what to do."

Charlie: "I'm not putting up with this. I'm leaving" (walking out, slamming the door).

Observing himself and his wife's despair, Charlie was visibly upset, knowing now he needed to help himself, and eventually decided to enter a rehabilitation program.

Alcoholic Outrageousness

In another form of alcoholic mistreatment, alcoholic outrageousness, the alcoholic engages in inappropriate, bizarre and outrageous behavior that is embarrassing and poisonous to anyone in contact with him or her. Such behavior can also produce much fear, anxiety and worry, especially if this alcoholic exhibits dangerous behavior, gets sick or passes out. An example is Tom, 33. A therapeutic agent mirrored and lived out his behavior in the present to confront Tom with the impact of his drinking.

Tom (walking in the door, falling over his feet and slurring his speech): "I'm home. Where are all of you?" (falling down). "I guess I had too much to drink" (his speech slurred). "My head hurts real bad. Oh, I'm sick. I feel like throwing up" (simulating and living out the throwing up process, letting out gulps and noises as a person does when throwing up and then passing out).

Tom's daughter, Mary, 10, was portrayed by another therapeutic agent to further confront him with his impact on his family.

Mary (crying): "Daddy get up, get up. What's the matter, Daddy? Are you drunk again?" "Daddy, Daddy" (starting to cry). "Mommy, Daddy's passed out again!" (hysterically). "I'm scared. I'm scared my Daddy's going to die!" (The therapeutic agent as Tom laid passed out on the floor in front of her while Tom observed).

At this point, Tom began to cry, stating he didn't want to continue hurting his daughter and family this way. If his daughter had been in the session she likely would have reacted in a similar way.

Alcoholic Seclusiveness

In another type of alcoholic mistreatment, alcoholic seclusiveness, the alcoholic becomes very seclusive and withdrawn. An example is provided by a therapeutic agent, as the alcoholic mother of Gertrude, 35, when Gertrude was reliving an experience as a young child. The therapeutic agent lived out the alcoholic seclusiveness of Gertrude's mother, portraying her sitting on the couch sipping a drink, with each sip slumping down in a more lifeless manner and becoming increasingly more a part of the couch as she mumbled to herself.

Mother (mumbling and slurring her speech): "I really don't feel like doing anything. I don't want anyone bothering me. I just want to be left alone."

Gertrude (appealing to her to stop drinking): "Mom, please stop your drinking. I need you to take care of me, to play with me" (crying).

Mother: "Just let me be. Get away from me. Stop bugging me. Nothing bothers me this way. I can get away from everything, all of you. I don't have to put up with any of you" (continuing to avoid Gertrude turning herself further away from her).

This session stimulated Gertrude to face and work through a significant amount of sadness and anger she had been holding onto, followed by a continuing healthy reprogramming of her thinking. In other cases, this type of alcoholic will be portrayed as eventually going to sleep or continuing to avoid significant others in some way. The therapeutic agent will act or live out the significant other's pathological behavior in whatever way it manifests itself.

No matter what type of alcoholic behavior has occurred, it is essential that the primary alcoholic message, as with any message, direct or implied, is communicated to the victim or patient in the reliving process, to the patient, if mirroring one's attitude and behavior or to whom it needs to be communicated to in the specific therapeutic situation.

CO-DEPENDENCY

In co-dependency, the co-dependent parent or person also is often a rejecting individual. The co-dependent is one who lives through another person, who the co-dependent is excessively dependent on and derives one's strength and meaning in life from. Often the co-dependent person is dependent on a dysfunctional person or perpetrator who is rejecting, manipulative or neglectful of him or her and other family members and may also be addicted to alcohol, drugs, work or "something." The co-dependent person makes excuses for, enables, rescues and tries to rationalize away the inappropriate or rejecting behavior of the perpetrator in one's life. The co-dependent is overpleasing, has difficulty asserting oneself, lacks self-confidence and lives as an underdog and victim. However, the co-dependent person will often pay back, counterattack or act out against his or her perpetrator in passive aggressive, indirect or underhanded ways, further provoking the perpetrator's mistreatment. Often a co-dependent mother, for example, is an accessory to her abusive husband's rejection of their children. In the following example, the co-dependent parent is portrayed by a therapeutic agent, while Matt, 15, relived an interaction with his co-dependent mother at age 8.

Mother (thinking to herself): "Even though he drinks, yells and screams and sometimes goes overboard in disciplining the children, he's still a good man. He really loves us and does good things for us. He badly criticizes me, but he doesn't hit me or have affairs on me. He needs me and I need him. He provides a living for us, puts a roof over our heads and feeds us. Where would we be without him? How could I take care of the children and myself all alone?"

Matt: "Daddy just slapped me in the face. He said I was a sissy and shouldn't cry. I hate him. Why don't we leave him? I just want to live with you and Mary" (his 6-year-old sister.)

Mother: "You shouldn't have got him angry. I told you what he would do to you."

Matt: "But, Mom! He's always yelling at me. He scares me. I'm scared of him. He hits me so much. He's so mean! I hate him. I'm going to run away."

Mother: "He can't help it. He's not that bad. You just upset him too much. He's your father. He really loves you. You must respect him. Look at all the nice things he does for you. What would happen to us if we didn't have him."

Matt: "I hate him. Mom, please, can't we find another place to live? He hits all of us. Why can't we leave, Mom?" (crying).

Mother: "There would be no place for us to go. I couldn't support all of us. We wouldn't be able to live in as nice a house or have all the things we have."

Matt: "I just don't want him to hit me and yell at us so much. I can't take it, I can't take it" (continuing to cry).

Mother: (slapping his face and angrily telling him): "Go to your room and don't come out until you appreciate what you have."

Matt: "But, Mom, it's not fair. It's not fair."

It is sometimes also necessary, as in this case, to emphasize the specific theme of the parent's message to further stimulate the expression and working through of the patient's feelings and thoughts. This approach is illustrated with the same therapeutic agent as his mother.

Mother: "These material things are very important to me. At least I have security, more than I've ever had in my life. He may not treat us well at times, but I'm not giving up the house, clothes, and money I have. So when I say we wouldn't have a nice home to live in and who would support us, I'm really saying to you I have to think of myself. I don't want to give up what I have even if it means sacrificing you. So if I have to choose between you or me, Matt, I'm choosing me. You are on your own with your Dad. I'm not jeopardizing my welfare for you."

The therapeutic agent, as mother, may stop here or may continue communicating this message depending on what therapeutic stimulation the patient needs. In this case, it is continued:

Mother: "There's nothing I will do. Don't upset him so much. If he does hit you or yell at you just accept it the best way you can. I'm sorry. There's nothing I can do. There's nothing I will do for you, I'm abandoning you with this. You're on your own with this" (walking away from him or in some cases walking out of the room to further emphasize her rejection, though of course coming back into the room after the point has been made to continue the session).

Matt: "But what about me, Mom? Don't I matter?" (crying for her to help him to no avail and being at the mercy of two rejecting parents).

OTHER POINTS REGARDING LIVING OUT THE ROLE OF A SIGNIFICANT OTHER

While the therapeutic agent is living out the role of a significant other as accurately as possible, he or she needs to put oneself entirely into the significant other's self, experiences, feelings and thoughts to stimulate the most authentic and realistic reliving of this role. This in turn will stimulate the more authentic and realistic reliving of an experience associated with his significant other and will maximize the patient opening up. Experiences that are not previously recalled that are brought out and not actually worked on because of a lack of time or the patient isn't ready can be dealt with further at another time.

It is also essential that the therapeutic agent be flexible and spontaneous in living out these roles as they occurred rather than according to a script or even the authentic acting out of a script. Reliving these roles must be in accordance with what actually happened through the patient's experience and perception. The therapeutic agent needs to be versatile enough to relive authentically and accurately whatever mistreatment the patient's perpetrator inflicted, even if not specifically trained to live out a specific rejecting role or a similar role.

The therapeutic agent needs also to develop the ability to live out healthy roles, for these roles and parts of these roles may overlap with dysfunctional roles. Healthy roles are also portrayed briefly when using the winning life method in chapter eight to demonstrate to the patient what needs weren't met in the patient's life and the contrast of his or her mistreatment with the healthy treatment that others have experienced. The patient needs to be exposed to healthy roles to know what one had a right to experience and needed to experience. Healthy roles are also important in the reparenting process. Being exposed to healthy roles also provides a beginning model for what the patient needs to encourage oneself to experience in its age appropriate form in the present.

LIVING OUT THE ROLE OF A SIGNIFICANT OTHER BY A GROUP OR FAMILY MEMBER

As indicated, in the large majority of cases, the therapeutic agent or therapist is utilized to live out the role of a significant other, who mistreated or affected the patient in some way. In some cases, however, another patient or group member or, less frequently, a family member of the patient is selected to live out a significant other's role if he or she relates to the patient in some way and can effectively live out this role. Again, the family member is not the same significant other who mistreated or affected the patient in some way which is being worked on therapeutically. However, this will not be done if it significantly hampers or prevents the patient from authentically reexperiencing a previous event or situation or if it impairs the patient, group or family member in some way. Usually, living out the role of a significant other has significance for the group or family member selected. For example, Joe was severely rejected by his father and would benefit from living out the rejecting role of Tom's abusive father in group therapy if ready to. In doing so, Joe would have an opportunity to experience and put himself into his father's feelings, thoughts and self while he was in the role of a rejecting person such as Tom's father. This would deepen Joe's understanding and awareness of what his father's rejection and poisoning of him was all about, as experienced through his father's mind. It would also further uncover and bring out Joe's feelings and thoughts regarding this situation. Although Joe was a victim, he also learned to be abusive from his father and carried it out with his children. This process would also give Joe the opportunity to experience his own feelings and thoughts contributing to his abusive behavior, while stimulating him to become further alienated from this behavior. A patient such as Joe, in some cases, may live out the role of the rejecting parent, Tom's father in this case, for part of the session or for a short time with a therapeutic agent taking over this role. In such a case Joe can then effectively double with Tom, relating to Tom as he does.

If Joe was Tom's brother in family therapy this process would be especially helpful if Joe and Tom were open and ready for it, though this would occur in infrequent situations. If they were adults, as in this example, they could be taking part in an individual family session involving adult siblings pertaining to problems, one of which is their upbringing. However, a much more likely possibility is for Joe and Tom to be adolescents or young adults in individual or multiple family group therapy. In such a case Joe would be even more in touch with the feelings, thoughts and behavior of Tom's father than another group member who was mistreated in a similar way and possibly could more effectively portray this role for they both would have the same rejecting father. In addition, a family member such as Joe, as if Joe was a group member, in some cases may only be used for a short time period to communicate the parental message or messages, for this may be what is most therapeutic while giving Joe the opportunity to double with Tom and assisting both of them in the process. Joe would benefit from this experience as an unrelated group member would, but likely to an even greater degree if the patient he was assisting was a sibling or close relative, if both were openly and ready to pursue this as indicated.

It is likely in some cases that Joe as the adult could live out an aspect of Tom's father's rejection of him even more authentically and accurately than a therapeutic agent or therapist as Joe had experienced it, first hand, as the victim and then as the perpetrator. Joe as the teenager or young adult, while being a victim of abuse, but not a perpetrator of it, could still in some cases live out an aspect of Tom's father's rejection of him more authentically and accurately than a therapeutic agent or therapist. Optimally, and whenever possible, it would be therapeutic if a significant other's role could be lived out by another group member or even a family member in a specific situation because this could also be part of his or her own therapeutic experience and would prepare the group or family member for working directly on oneself. However, this is not often the case due to the skill needed to live out a significant other's role and as the group or family member has not yet become sufficiently aware of his or her significant other's effect on oneself, is still too defended, isn't ready to deeply experience his or her feelings and thoughts regarding the significant other or isn't ready to live out such a rejecting role. When this does occur, such a group or family member often has been in therapy for a while; has made progress in therapy; is relatively aware of his or her feelings and thoughts regarding the mistreatment he or she experienced as a victim or as a perpetrator who inflicted abuse on others; is ready, motivated and has the courage to become more aware of such feelings and thoughts; and can effectively live out the role of the significant other.

As indicated, a family member is used less frequently in the role of a significant other, (different person than him or her) and only when he or she is ready, when this will enhance the patient's ability to open up, won't adversely affect the patient's relationship with his or her family member or impair the family member's functioning. A family member rather than another group member is used in this role in multiple family group therapy only when doing so would be more effective. All necessary therapeutic factors are considered when choosing the appropriate person to function in the role of the significant other who the patient is addressing while reliving an experience.

CHAPTER 7

Basic Rebuilding Therapy Methods

The double method, the multiple double method, the role reversal method and the mirror method are basic methods often used in a Rebuilding Therapy session. Though these methods are psychodramatic techniques they are referred to as Rebuilding Therapy methods, as other psychodramatic techniques, when they are used in Rebuilding Therapy, with due credit given to their development. Each of these methods, as any of the methods taken from Psychodrama, are described, interpreted and utilized as I believe they should be used. I have further developed them when applicable to best meet the needs of the patient. The double anger method and the anger mat release method, both anger release methods, are also basic Rebuilding Therapy methods and have their origin and roots in my Psychodrama training. While giving due credit to my training in Psychodrama, I have further developed them for Rebuilding Therapy. Bioenergetic therapy, a body-mind psychotherapy, supports and encourages the use of the anger mat release method. The methods and approaches need to be utilized in a way which maximizes the patient's progress relative to the patient's needs and specific situation.

THE DOUBLE METHOD

The double method is used to stimulate the more open expression of feelings and thoughts. It does so (1) by stimulating the patient to express feelings and thoughts he or she hasn't been sufficiently ready or comfortable to express, needs to become more aware of or needs further stimulation or reinforcement on and (2) by stimulating the inner examination of issues, conflicts and experiences the patient needs to become more aware of and further explore. The person doubling or the double, in effect, becomes the patient he or she is doubling with—standing or sitting beside the patient in a similar physical manner as the patient, if possible, and moves into the mind of the patient, feeling his or her feelings and thinking his or her thoughts as closely as the patient is. When doubling, the double speaks in the first person "I" to personalize the doubling rather than in the less personal third person. Doubling is primarily a catalyst to stimulate the patient to open up with his or her inner feelings, thoughts, conflicts, strengths and resources, and in no way does the double take the place of the patient.

The patient is informed that he or she can reject or disagree with anything being expressed by the double and that any expression or statement of the double is considered to "be" the patient's feelings or thoughts, unless he or she objects. The double may also ask questions in the first person to stimulate the more open expression of feelings and thoughts. This includes such questions as: "How I feel is," "What I'm afraid of is," "What is making me so mad is," "What saddens me is" or "What confuses me is."

The double can be the therapist, co-therapist or auxiliary agent, referred to as the therapeutic agent. The specific type of therapeutic agent is referred to for clarification purposes as needed throughout the book. In group or multiple family therapy, in dealing with present or past experiences, the double can also be another patient or group member, and in some cases, though less frequently, a family member of the patient. In individual family therapy, in some situations a family member of the patient can double with the patient. In any case, the family member or significant other is not the person who mistreated or adversely affected the patient who the patient is addressing in the session. When the double is a therapeutic agent, he or she is trained, making it easier to control or guide the doubling, while being expert in its use and other methods. The value of having another patient or group member or family member double or assist with this method or the multiple double or mirror (which is discussed later in this chapter) is that this person often relates to the patient working and has insight regarding the patient. This person can, therefore, effectively assist the patient, while the working patient can stimulate the doubling person to become more aware of one's own conflicts and issues. This can be especially helpful when the double is a relative, such as a sibling, and experienced the same or similar treatment from the same significant other or was exposed to it. In addition, whether a group member or family member, he or she must be supportive of the patient and willing and ready to double, as when involved in any method or approach. In a number of cases, however, as with the multiple double, other family members or significant others of the patient may not be used as doubles because they may be less objective and not helpful due to their own problems, feelings, thoughts, conflicts, defenses or relationship with the patient. Similarly, any group member who is not ready to double won't be used.

Most importantly the various methods must be utilized most effectively in the patient's behalf and for all involved, as needed, in the treatment process. The therapeutic agent, being trained in using specific methods and living out specific situations and roles, is utilized more regularly and frequently than another patient or group member or family member. However, involving another patient or group member, and in some cases though less frequently, a family member in utilizing the double or multiple double is encouraged, whenever possible, if the effectiveness of treatment and the welfare of all involved are not adversely affected. Usually, another patient or group or family member can more readily be used to double rather than in the role of a patient's significant other, who mistreated or affected the patient in some way. This is because doubling is a role one may be more ready, able and less resistant to assume and easier to function in. Whenever another patient or group or family member is used to assist in the therapeutic process, the therapeutic agent needs to be prepared to assist or take over at any time. This process, as any part of therapy, requires ongoing evaluation regarding what is best for the patient and everyone involved.

The double should speak in a voice that is slightly stronger than the patient's voice, though relatively indistinguishable from it. In doing so, the double needs to be a "fraction of an inch" ahead of the patient, while still "walking together" with the patient. As this occurs, the double becomes so sensitive to the patient's feelings and thoughts that he or she "becomes" the patient to the point that the patient "doesn't" realize the double is even there stimulating him or her.

The double must not overpower or overload the patient in too loud, excessive or strong a way. This will only inhibit or retard the expression of feelings and thoughts. Verbalizing in too loud or strong a fashion may scare and push away the patient, or be too "out of touch" for the patient to identify with.

Another form of overstimulation is talking too much. This may reduce the patient's ability to express feelings openly, reinforce or encourage intellectualization, confuse the patient or even lose the patient in the process.

Overstimulation may also occur when more than one double is used. At times, more than one double is encouraged if the patient needs further stimulation or other group or family members are relating to the patient working on oneself. This may result in the patient becoming overstimulated with too many voices coming at him or her from too many directions.

Understimulation of the patient may also be a problem. This may result when the double speaks too low, softly or weakly, doesn't say enough, doesn't present information or stimuli on target or provides effective information or stimuli in an untimely way too soon or too late.

The therapist uses corrective measures when the patient is overstimulated or understimulated or doubling is ineffective. The first measure is for the therapist to also double with the patient, providing demonstrative guidance for the double. This can continue until the double no longer needs it, or at times, when it continues to be helpful to the patient. Corrective measures may also include asking the double to lower or raise the volume of his or her voice, to say less, to get right to the point or to politely ask the person doubling to stop doing so if he or she is not doubling effectively. In the latter case, the therapist may need to take over and become the double for the patient if this will improve the therapeutic process.

I have assisted the double based on therapeutic need and the effectiveness of the doubling. In addition, I have frequently functioned as a double owing to not having another double or an effective double available (see the therapy team section in chapter two).

The double stimulates the patient with as few words as possible. For example:

Double: "I'm mad at you because you betrayed me," instead of: "I'm mad at you because you 15-25 words," or "I'm so sad, you really hurt me," instead of: "I'm so sad, you hurt me so bad when you 15-25 words."

The double or doubles must primarily stimulate the patient rather than other doubles, and must not primarily interact with a therapeutic agent, for example, acting as a significant other. For example, in group therapy if when reliving an experience Frieda is expressing feelings to a therapeutic agent acting as her mother, she will have two stimuli, her own double and the person acting as her mother. Frieda needs to be given a chance to respond to either her double or the person acting as her mother. Only when there is a pause and Frieda isn't responding to her double or the therapeutic agent acting as her mother is it appropriate for the double and therapeutic agent as her mother to respond directly to each other to stimulate the patient to open up again.

Another example occurs in multiple family group therapy when there is a double for Amy (wife) and another double for Todd (her husband), where there usually is a co-therapist or an auxiliary agent or group or family members assisting in the doubling. It is essential that the doubles not primarily interact with each other, nor should Amy or Todd primarily react to their spouse's double, but instead to their own double or each other. If Amy or Todd is stuck or there is a longer than necessary pause, Amy's double can double and interact with her or Todd's double can double and interact with him regarding their feelings and thoughts for a short period of time until one of them begins to respond. If both spouses fail to respond to their doubles, the doubles can have a brief interchange, or either Amy or Todd can interact with the other's double, stimulating Amy or Todd to open up again. The patient is the star and needs to be the primary focus of "everyone's" concern.

The patient's physical expression, including posture, facial expressions, gestures and specific body movement is important for the double to identify with and approximate as it signals the expression of feelings and thoughts. This assists the double to relate to the patient more closely with the patient often experiencing this, encouraging the patient to open up more. The double's bodily movements also will act as a mirror, signaling the patient to be more sensitive to what his or her bodily movements are telling him or her, while stimulating the patient to open up further perceiving one's bodily movements in action. When feelings are more subtle and less openly expressed, the skillful doubling of posture, bodily movement or facial expressions becomes more important, along with the doubling described. However, it is important not to get bogged down with the patient's bodily movements, which could inhibit his or her open expression of feelings and thoughts.

The examples of the double and other Rebuilding Therapy methods and approaches provide the reader with a description of how these methods are used, though the clinician can make modifications and use this methodology creatively and skillfully within the context of his or her therapeutic practice. The therapist as the director of the session guides the therapeutic process, including when the methodology is used by others. An example of the double, while Bill expressed his feelings in a soliloquy to himself in group therapy, is provided next. Bill, 29, was reexperiencing a time at age 11 when his father did not attend his baseball game. As in any reliving experience, Bill's healthy Adult, the managing ego state, his healthy Parent and his healthy Child as his Adult Nurturing Self joined his wounded Child to assist him, while he reexperienced this event in his wounded Child. (Refer to chapter eight for a description of the joining method).

Bill: "I am mad at him for not coming to my baseball game. He just doesn't spend any time with me" (beginning to cry).

At this time, it was clear that he was primarily sad, which the therapist, being the only therapeutic agent available, as the double stimulated him to express. The stimulation of anger would be left for another time.

Double: "I am so sad. He's never here for me."

Bill: "He never comes to my baseball games. The other kids have their fathers here" (breaking down further in tears). "I've just hit a single that won the game for my team. Everyone is congratulating me, but my dad isn't here. He's too busy working" (continuing to cry).

At this point the double, knowing significant life decisions are often made during experiences like this, in a very sad and low voice, said:

Double: "What's the use? Why try?" (stimulating Bill to feel and think whatever was in his mind, was having difficulty bringing out or wasn't aware of, knowing he would only respond to what was in his mind and would reject what didn't apply).

Bill (crying): "What's the use of trying? If my dad doesn't care about me, then I'm not really important to anyone. Maybe I'm just no good anyway."

From age 11 until he entered therapy at age 29, Bill gave up on himself, quitting baseball, becoming a behavior problem, not applying himself, abusing drugs and alcohol and losing a number of jobs because of his uncaring attitude. He lost his wife and two children, followed by an attempted suicide. Knowing Bill's history and that he needed to begin deciding he was okay and needed to care, the double assisted him to continue opening up and to accomplish this. Because Bill began making unhealthy decisions before age 11, he would have more therapeutic work to do, but this was a key experience regarding the emergence of his decisions in an active way. As the session continued:

Double: "I'm so sad. I'm so sad."

Bill (crying more openly for more than five minutes, saying periodically): "He's never been a father to me. He's never been a father to me. Why try? Why try? I give up. I give up."

At this time, at an open and vulnerable point, Bill was ready for someone to reach out to him and also continue stimulating him. The double put his hand on Bill's shoulder for a short time to provide needed support until Bill no longer needed this support, while Bill continued to open up. After continued doubling with Bill, Bill reached the point of redeciding.

Double: "I'm really a good person even if he isn't here for me. It's his fault, not mine."

Bill: "I'm not really bad. He's the one who's hurting me and not being a father to me."

Double: "I really am okay. I really am special."

Bill: "I am a good person. I'm a very good person."

Double: "He's not worth giving up over."

Bill: "I'm giving myself a chance again. I deserve to. No more! I've been a fool to hurt myself over him. No more!" (also integrating his Adult thinking and the thinking of the double).

The therapist looked to the group, asking them, "Is Bill okay? Is he good?" The group replied, "Yes, he is a good person," and made other positive statements. Bill smiled, feeling the group's support reinforcing his redecisions that he was okay and to care about himself.

The double helped Bill to face and work through an aspect of his sadness regarding his father's neglect and to change his thinking from "I'm no good" to "I'm okay" and "There's no hope for me" to "I'm going to give myself a chance." This was only the beginning, however, for he had to begin practicing and carrying out these new decisions and to further work through and decontaminate himself of the poisonous anger, sadness, guilt, and other feelings and thinking he had harbored from other experiences that had contributed to his original decisions, while continuing to reprogram his thinking. As indicated, earlier, the double method in this case was used in a soliloquy, with the double stimulating Bill to express his feelings and thoughts alone and to himself, not in direct interaction with a significant other. Both Haskell and Yablonsky describe the soliloquy and other psychodramatic techniques in a helpful way. Although the double is used effectively in its own right in a soliloquy, the soliloquy, with the double usually assisting, is a good warmup for the patient to directly deal with and confront a significant other or another person in whatever therapeutic situation. The double is then used while the patient is directly interacting with a significant other or another person, acted out by someone else or visualized in an empty chair or in a specific way, when reliving a life experience; is interacting with this person in any of these ways therapeutically when not reliving an experience; or is interacting with this actual person directly in family therapy. In an individual therapy session a few days later which the previous session was preparation for, the therapist doubling, stimulated Bill's expression of anger, while reliving an experience at age 10 when his father rejected him. Being an individual therapy session the therapist portrayed Bill's father.

Father: "What's wrong with you? Can't you ever listen to me?" (yelling).

Bill: "But, Dad" (and then being cut off by his father).

Father: "What do you know? You're just a stupid kid" (in an overpowering way).

Bill: (Shocked, initially wondering what to say followed by interaction with his father, with the double's assistance, until he reached the point where he was ready to express his anger).

Double: "You don't respect me."

Bill: "You never respect me. It's always your way. You're always right" (becoming angry).

Double: "My views mean nothing to you."

Bill: "My opinions never mean anything to you. I feel I mean nothing to you when you don't accept what I feel" (becoming angrier).

Father: "I'm only trying to help you. I know what is right. You have to listen to me."

Bill: "You never accept my opinions. You never do. They're nothing to you. They're crap to you. I'm crap to you."

Father: "You can't talk to me like this. Who do you think you are?"

Bill: "I'm your son, but you don't treat me like your son."

Double: "And I deserve to be respected."

Bill: "I do deserve to be respected" (rebounding from his silence).

Double: "You just keep hurting me."

Bill: "You don't give me any confidence. You just keep putting me down and hurting me."

Father: "If you'd listen to me, I wouldn't have to yell or say these things to you."

As there was a pause and a silence, the double intervened to stimulate the opening up process.

Double: "I'm angry at you. You have no right bullying me" (stimulating his anger).

Bill: "I'm so upset with you. You keep bullying me around. That's not right. It's wrong."

Double: "I'm very mad at you. I hate you for this."

Bill: "I hate you. I hate you" (spending about ten minutes working through his anger, with the double's assistance, including releasing his anger by hitting on a mat on a table next to him with the anger mat release method described later). "I will never let you or anyone discount me" (he continued).

Double: "No more! No more! I deserve much better."

Bill: "You or no one will ever do this again. I deserve better. I really do!"

Though another step forward, he, as other patients, had other experiences he still needed to relive, including earlier ones to continue rebuilding himself. At times, a patient may work through primarily anger or sadness, both feelings or more than two feelings in a session, depending on the situation and what the patient can handle and is therapeutic. When a primary feeling such as anger is worked on in a session, other feelings such as sadness, guilt or fear may also be experienced to a certain extent.

THE MULTIPLE DOUBLE METHOD

The multiple double is used in the same way as the double, but specifically when the patient's feelings and thoughts are ambivalent, confused or are going in different directions (i.e., love-hate, like-dislike, excusing-accusing, positive-negative).

The multiple double can be used with one therapeutic agent or person as the double, doubling on both sides of an issue. In some cases when it is important to further stimulate and emphasize the polarity or difference in feelings and thoughts, the person, as the multiple double, may move physically from side (positive) to side (negative) to further point out the differences. The use of one person as the double, when utilizing the multiple double, is the only alternative when utilized in individual or individual family therapy or in a group where the therapist is the only viable double due to availability or expertise. In group therapy or multiple family group therapy where it is more likely for there to be a co-therapist or an auxiliary agent and other group members, it is possible to have two persons acting as doubles. In some cases, this format can be preferable to one person, with another person adding feelings and thoughts to support the opposing position.

When there are two doubles, each double doubles the opposing feelings and thoughts or the opposing direction of feelings and thoughts, with each double sitting or standing depending on the patient's position, on opposite sides of the patient. At times, it is helpful if the doubles are patients or group members doubling on the side which is helpful for them in working through their own ambivalence, conflicts, feelings or thoughts. For example, in group therapy, Sally, 19, needing to further uncover, work through and let go of her anger toward her father, doubled on the side of 28-year-old Irene's anger for her father as the Anger Double. Steve, 44, having difficulty acknowledging his underlying sadness and love for his mother, doubled on the side of Irene's love for her father as the Love Double. The following example is part of a reliving of the time when Irene's father slapped her in her face at 5 years of age. Irene told him she hated him for overreacting to her when she didn't pick up her toys to his expectations.

Irene: "I hate you! It has to be your way or you're never happy!"

Sally, Anger Double: "You're never happy with me."

Irene: "I try so hard to please you and you're still disappointed!"

Steve, Love Double: "I love you so much. I just want you to be happy with me."

Irene: "All I want is to try to please you!" (starting to cry).

Therapist as Irene's Double: "I'm confused."

Irene: "I don't know what to do. I love you, but I can't please you."

Therapeutic agent as Father: "Then clean up your room the way I told you to" (yelling).

Irene: "I'm doing my best!"

Love Double: "I try so hard, I just want you to be happy with me."

Irene: "I'm getting sick trying to please you."

Father: "It's not good enough! It's not good enough!" (continuing to yell).

Anger Double: "It's never good enough! You make me so mad!"

Irene: "I hate you! I hate you!" (her anger escalating, spending more than five minutes ventilating and letting go of some of her anger as both Irene and Sally [Anger Double] pounded on the mat and screamed out the rage and anger they had been harboring for their fathers with the therapeutic agent, as Irene's father continuing to throw out rejecting remarks).

Irene and Anger Double: "I hate you so much for never being happy with me." (being the theme of their resentment. Following her expression of anger, Irene broke down, crying).

Irene: "I feel so bad for letting you down, but I can't keep letting you hurt me any longer. I'm not a bad person, in fact, I'm a good person. I deserve better."

Love Double: "I want to please you, but it doesn't work expecting so much of me. I have a right to be my own person.

Irene (still crying openly): "I love you, but I won't do it any longer. It's too much. Too much. I'm afraid all the time you're going to get mad at me. I'm going to stop trying to please you like this. It just doesn't work."

Anger Double: "I'm going to be happy with me with what I do" (also assisting her in her redecisions that she is okay and doesn't have to overplease).

Irene: "Even if you're not happy with me. No matter what, I'm okay. I'm just going to do what I can do. That's what matters, because I am okay as I am."

Love Double: "I can please me and still love you."

Irene: "I'll always love you, but I need to please me too and be happy with me. Even if you aren't. I will."

The multiple double method was instrumental in stimulating Joan to make a major step forward working through her mixed feelings and thoughts regarding her father. In the process, this helped her realize that she primarily needed to please herself rather than live for her father's acceptance, which was so difficult to get. It was also clear that her present Adult thinking and the therapeutic stimulation of healthy Adult thinking were integrated into her redecisions, as occurs in any redecision.

THE ROLE REVERSAL METHOD

Role reversal is used to increase empathy and understanding of the patient's significant others such as parents, siblings, spouse, children and close friends to connect to and better and more fully understand how one's significant others have affected one's thinking, feelings, behavior and life. This method also assists the therapeutic agent, acting, for example, as the patient's father, in learning what the patient's father is really like, what and how he feels and thinks and how he expresses himself. It is effective in improving relationships through improved empathy, understanding and sensitivity of others and in assisting to become more aware of how one looks to another person and is affecting this person through this person's eyes, ears and mind. Role reversal can also be used to achieve these objectives with nonsignificant others, as any method and approach can be utilized with.

Role reversal occurs when the patient steps out of him or herself and psychologically and socially puts oneself into the feelings, thoughts, mind and self of a significant other in one's life by becoming this significant other. It is essential to put aside one's feelings, thoughts and perceptions and only feel, think and perceive as the person one is role reversing with. In doing so, the patient moves into the chair or position that the person he or she is role reversing with was just in, as this person in most cases role reverses to become the patient moving into the chair or position the patient was in. Although used less frequently than a therapeutic agent, a group member, for example, in the role of the significant other in some cases rather than role reversing to become the patient, also remains in this role to double with the patient role reversing or takes an inactive role during the role reversing process. In such a case a therapeutic agent usually becomes the patient, asking pertinent questions of the actual patient as his or her significant other. As indicated, in some cases, the patient as his or her significant other will be doubled with or the person in the role of the patient, especially another group member, for example, will be doubled with to assist the role reversing process. The therapist needs to guide the role reversing process in the way which will most effectively stimulate the patient to deal with his or her issues.

When looking into and experiencing the inner feelings, thoughts and being of a significant other, such as mother or father, the patient is stimulated to look into such questions about the significant other as: "Why did Mom treat me so bad?" "Was Dad's work more important then me?" "Did Mom really want me?" "Why wasn't Dad ever happy with me?" "What did Mom really want from me?" "Why was Dad so angry?" or "Why did Mom drink so much?" When the patient is role reversing while reliving an experience, such questions are explored in the present tense.

Role reversal is not a cognitive and intellectual exercise. It is becoming one's significant other's feelings and thoughts and experientially becoming one's significant other. In doing so, the patient assumes and uses the name of a significant other, such as Mom, Dad, Bill or Mary, and expresses the significant other's feelings and thoughts in the first person using the pronoun "I". Significant others, such as parents, remain within our mind and personality structure, continuing to influence us despite our chronological age. Being able to take one's healthy Adult thinking into the mind of his or her parent in one's Parent ego state will give the patient an opportunity to become more clearly aware of the impact of such a significant other on one's feelings, thoughts and behavior. In doing this, the patient has an opportunity to step into the world and privacy of his or her parent's personality, becoming aware of and in contact with how, for example, mother's thinking, feelings, deceptions and messages have actually affected and influenced one's personality, mind and lifestyle. It is as though the patient has the opportunity to walk into a computer room that is his or her parent's self or one's parent in one's Parent. In doing so, the patient is able to experience and become aware of the program implanted into his or her Child ego state, which strongly influences his or her personality development, thinking, feelings and life and which one usually won't change unless effectively taking part in psychotherapy. As the patient experiences and connects to unhealthy feelings, thinking and decisions that have been transmitted into one's own self or Child, he or she then has the opportunity, by becoming oneself again, to more effectively decontaminate, diffuse, decode and reprogram his or her Parent contaminated Child which has created despair and dysfunction in one's life.

Only when the patient can feel, think and perceive as his or her parent did and experience what one's Parent has been negatively doing to him or to her can one "grab onto" one's unhealthy Parent from his or her wounded Child, with the assistance of one's healthy Adult, Parent and Child and take more control of the unhealthy Parent and its impact on oneself. It is necessary to get in touch with, feel and be in contact with the actual factors that have affected one's life before one can change their impact on oneself. Role reversal effectively provides this opportunity. Just talking about them and discussing them is not enough. It would be like talking about a problem in an automobile engine, knowing what to do but never getting in there to do anything about it. Of course, the healthy parental programming in one's Parent can be left intact to continue influencing the person in a healthy way. The patient is usually assisted to work on the impact of one parent at a time, though this is an overlapping process. Following is an example in group therapy of using role reversal in this way, with a therapeutic agent in the session in addition to the therapist. Here Betty, 21, was facing her mother's impact on her at age 5 when her mother overreacted to her for getting into trouble at Sunday school.

Therapeutic Agent as Mother: "How can you embarrass me like this? How can you do such a terrible thing like this to me? What is the matter with you?"

Betty: "I'm sorry, I'm sorry, Mommy" (crying, not knowing what she did wrong).

Therapist as Double: "I always have to be so perfect, why, Mommy, why do I have to be so perfect?" (preparing Betty to put herself in her mother's mind questioning her mother's motivation and treatment of her and then instructing Betty to repeat the question).

Betty: "Why do I have to be so perfect?"

Betty was then instructed to role reverse with her mother with the timing being essential. The therapeutic agent became Betty, repeating the question as Betty asked it. This step is optional, for in some cases a patient will become a significant other and respond immediately whereas in other cases, the patient will need this question repeated by the therapeutic agent.

Therapeutic Agent as Betty: "Why do I have to be so perfect?"

Betty as Mother: "I love you so much, Betty. When you were born, I knew you would be the light of my life. I looked to you to make my life worthwhile. I had so many hopes that you would give me what no one else ever gave me, that strength, courage and hope to make my life meaningful, that you could be what I never have been. That's why I have always had plans for you, to be proud of you, so I could tell everyone that my daughter is so special, good and smart. I have always let you know how terrible I would feel if you disappointed me or talked back to me. You've been the 'perfect' child so far. I've wanted you to live primarily for me, to please me, to give up your happiness for me and yourself for me. It doesn't matter if you're only five years old. You can't disappoint me."

This was her mother's theme message given directly or indirectly to Betty. In becoming her mother, Betty realized that at a very young age she was programmed to be used by her mother to be what her mother could never be, to be her mother's strength and clearly her mother's meaning in life. In this process, Betty's healthy Adult assisted her to role reverse with her mother. Betty's mother was not primarily concerned with Betty's welfare, but with her own narcissistic needs for her own satisfaction, status and approval through Betty's achievement and life. Once feeling, experiencing and realizing what her mother was doing to her, Betty was able to begin taking control of her mother's poisonous programming of her. Her first reaction, still as her mother, which is very typical, was that of tearful despair realizing how bad her mother hurt her. Though in her mother's self, her own self was interacting with her mother's self creating the tearfulness. She was then asked to role reverse back to being herself to further experience and express her feelings and thoughts toward her mother, with the therapeutic agent as her mother, to begin empowering herself to defuse and weaken her mother's impact on her.

Following this same process in a later individual therapy session, Betty relived her recall or what she believed it to be of her first contact with her mother immediately after she was born, including role reversing, becoming her mother to connect to her mother's motivation for becoming pregnant with her and then role reversing back to herself and working through her feelings and thoughts.

Role reversal can be helpful in answering other questions. For example, Nick, 28, in individual therapy, while reliving an experience as a child with the therapist as his mother, asked her if she wanted him without being stimulated by a double:

Nick: "Did you really want me?" (with the role reversing process then occurring without the therapist, as Nick, needing to repeat Nick's question).

Nick as Mother: "I wanted you to be a girl. I've been so disappointed you're not a girl."

At this point when the emotional intensity and message from his mother was very powerful, it was a key time to reverse roles again. At times the patient, as the significant other, will be asked to repeat such a message again, but often this isn't necessary because of the power of the message. At this time, the term *switch* was used, which is optional, to signal Nick to become himself, while the therapist became his mother repeating exactly what Nick, as his mother said. Rather than using the term *switch*, the therapist, also directing the session, may ask the patient, such as Nick, to become himself again.

Therapist as Mother: "I've really wanted you to be a girl. I've always been disappointed you're not a girl," (with the same feeling tone and mannerisms, as Nick, as his mother).

The therapist in this case can also further intensify this message of rejection.

Nick: (after a short pause, tearfully): "You don't love me because I'm a boy. I don't have a chance. I've never had a chance. You don't love me" (crying).

Nick from here continued his interaction with his mother, opening up to the point of a catharsis and then beginning to accept his mother's refusal to accept and love him as a male and that he was nevertheless, a good person. (An example of role reversal being used in a similar, but more extended way is given in chapter fifteen.)

Of primary importance is stimulating Nick, as his mother, to experience her damaging message of wanting him to be a girl and then role reversing back to himself to confront it. In cases when the message is less clear, the therapeutic agent as Nick, needs to ask more questions or make other remarks to further open up Nick as his mother, with her feelings and thoughts about him. Such questions may include: "Why aren't you ever interested in what I do?," "Why are you so critical?," "Why don't you listen to me?," "Why don't you spend any time with me?"

Role reversal is also useful when the therapeutic agent or person, as the significant other, isn't living out the feelings, thoughts and behavior of a significant other in an accurate way or needs more information to do so. When this occurs, the therapist will immediately ask the patient to become one's significant other to show the therapeutic agent or person what and how the significant other is feeling, thinking and acting. The time of this role reversal needs to be minimized to keep the reliving process moving smoothly and at an effective intensity.

Role reversal is also used to increase empathy and understanding regarding the significant other's life, feelings, thoughts and behavior. This can include information regarding how one's father felt about his or her siblings, parents, marriage, life and so on, in addition to the patient. In doing so, it can be used to prepare the patient to live out major past experiences. However, the patient should not get bogged down in too many specifics or unnecessary information.

Insight alone cannot change a person, but it can help the reevaluation and reprogramming process if not contaminated by the patient's denial, rationalizations and excuses regarding one's significant other and what occurred in his or her life. This is a common danger if the patient has not begun the decontaminating and reprogramming process through reliving his or her major life experiences. Examples include "My father couldn't help himself or didn't know any better the way his parents mistreated him," or "My mother had it so hard bringing all of us up by herself."

This type of informational and background role reversal may involve becoming the significant other for an extended period of time (more than five minutes), thinking and feeling as the significant other. Though intense, it doesn't usually penetrate the mind as deeply as when role reversal occurs more frequently within a short period of time, focusing on major themes and messages. It runs the risk of taking the patient further away from his or her own feelings and thoughts, than when using short role reversals looking for major themes where possible. The shorter role reversing process, focusing on the major themes and messages, often parental, in the patient's life, will stimulate the patient to be more in touch with one's own feelings and thoughts regarding these themes and messages. In doing so, the patient as his or her parent will be encouraged to express the parental theme or major message rather than the "exact" words, unless they can be recalled, with the therapeutic agent or person as the significant other then asked to repeat this. Of course, it may be difficult to recall the "exact" words anyway. What is imperative in the reliving process is for the patient to face his or her feelings and thoughts and the major parental themes and messages and not get bogged down looking for "exactly" what his or her parents said.

Despite the success of short term role reversal, it should not be overdone. Taking the patient out of oneself too frequently even for short periods of time still can inhibit the open expression of feelings and thoughts.

Though not a substitute for role reversal, an effective way of reducing long-term or too frequent short term role reversals is for the therapist to have as much information about the significant other as is possible regarding the major themes, messages, characteristics and background of the significant other and other data where possible.

The length of time for each role reversal or the frequency of role reversing needs to be as long or as frequent as is needed to bring out what is therapeutic, but as brief and infrequent as possible to keep the patient more in touch with one's major feelings and thoughts. This applies to any method used, but it is especially important in role reversal where the patient needs to move back and forth from being oneself to being one's significant other.

Another way to intensify the role reversal process and to stimulate further uncovering and opening up is to double with the person role reversing. For example, Brian, 16, in individual therapy, while reliving an experience as a child, role reversed and became his mother with the therapist doubling with Brian as his mother. This approach is used only when a patient, such as Brian, needs assistance opening up as his mother and where only a therapeutic agent is usually utilized as the double. In this case, Brian role reversed to become his mother in response to his question, "Why are you so mean to me?"

Brian as Mother: "I can't stand looking at you."

Double as Mother: "You're just in the way" (knowing some information about his mother and the dynamics of the situation, which was just enough to stimulate Brian to open up as his mother).

Brian as Mother: "You're a burden to me. I'm so tied down with you."

Double: "I wish you weren't around."

Brian as Mother: "I wish you were never born. I wish I never had you."

At this moment Brian was asked to become himself again, with the therapist remaining as his mother, repeating the same statements and opening up further to strongly communicate this message to Brian. Brian was now in a position to confront his mother with the essence of her rejecting messages that she had been communicating, to him throughout his life.

Role reversal can be effectively used to increase empathy and understanding as a mediating and conflict reducing method with one's significant others and can be helpful in the forgiveness process. This method can also effectively be utilized this way with nonsignificant others, but is not the primary focus of this discussion. However, when a patient is involved in reliving past experiences to rebuild from, this method should not be used this way prematurely. If used prematurely in this manner, it will inhibit the uncovering, expression, cleansing and letting go of feelings and thoughts and the reprogramming of one's thinking. Also, the patient is not helped by the need to be prematurely empathetic, excusing away the mistreatment of a parent or significant other. This avoids facing the painful experiences and wounds of one's past and maintains a pseudo-good, but hypocritical and superficially empathetic relationship with one's significant other, which is dishonest, not open, game dominated and not intimate. Once the rebuilding process has unfolded significantly, role reversal can be instrumental in giving the patient the opportunity to gain a better understanding of his or her significant others and possibly to move toward completion of the forgiving process without impairing own rebuilding. From this point on, sincere and open empathy can exist.

Role reversal is effective in family therapy in assisting to improve empathy and communication. For example, Barbara, 36, and Tom, 38, in joint marital therapy (individual family therapy), were having serious marital difficulties understanding and empathizing with each other. Barbara was very appeasing to the children and didn't want to face any type of problem. Tom, on the other hand, wanted to face the problems, but was very dominating and rejecting. Both of them needed to better empathize with each other and problem solve, with role reversal utilized to assist them. They were asked to role reverse, with Tom becoming Barbara and Barbara becoming Tom, and to interact as each other. Each was given instructions at the beginning of their role reversing:

Therapist to Barbara as Tom: "As Tom, feel as Tom, think as Tom and be Tom. Put your feelings and thoughts on the side" (and then gives these instructions to Tom as Barbara).

Therapist to Barbara and Tom as Each Other: "It is essential that when being the other person you don't mock or act out the negative qualities of each other, but only put yourself in the other's place, feelings and thoughts."

An excerpt from their interaction as each other is illustrated after both of them had some initial difficulty role reversing.

Barbara as Tom: "I feel you never want to face anything. You're always taking the kid's side. I'm made out to be the bad guy because I want my children to be disciplined. I feel the only way to get through to you is to be hard."

Tom as Barbara: "You think you're always right. No one can talk to you. The children and I are afraid of you. It has to be your way or we're wrong. I have to protect the children from you. So I give into the kids and sabotage you."

Barbara as Tom: "I feel pushed away in my own home. It hurts me and angers me. The only way I know how to take control and have any influence is to become hard and tough. My father ran his home successfully his way. Why can't I?"

Tom as Barbara: "I just can't take the conflict with you always having to be right and so critical. I just want peace. So if I let things go, you'll take care of them because if I take care of things you're never happy anyway. I can't even talk to you so I don't try to solve problems with you. I guess I learned this from my father as my mother was just like you."

Both were instructed to role reverse back to themselves to continue their communication with a better understanding of each other and themselves. The therapist gave similar instructions regarding how to empathize with each other, as when they role reversed, but this time they were being themselves communicating.

Therapist: "When Barbara opens up to you, Tom, feel Barbara's feelings, think her thoughts and be Barbara. Put your feelings and thoughts on the side until you have an opportunity to open up to Barbara."

The same instructions were then given to Barbara regarding Tom opening up to her. This method was effective in improving Barbara and Tom's communication and relationship, while also working individually on themselves and in other ways.

Role reversal in family therapy can also be helpful when a family member doesn't understand another family member regarding a specific issue and something is needed to break this block. In this case, George, a former high school basketball player, was having difficulty understanding why his 15-year-old son, Barry, didn't want to play high school basketball. In individual family therapy, to assist George to improve his understanding of his son, he was instructed in the following way.

Therapist: "Repeat after me. Barry, why don't you want to play on the basketball team? You'd make your father so proud."

George repeated the same question. The therapist then asked George to role reverse and become his son, Barry, with the therapist as George, repeating the question.

Therapist as George: "Why don't you want to play on the basketball team? You'd make your father so proud!"

George as Barry: (after some resistance) "I'd rather have fun and play basketball when I want to and not be pressured to play. You expect too much of me and its no fun because I'm so afraid to let you down. I'd be doing it for you, Dad, and not me."

At this point George's voice lowered, and he just "stopped" with much emotion, being caught off guard with this realization. After having time to begin digesting this, he was asked to role reverse and become himself again with his son Barry brought into the interaction.

George: "I'm sorry, Son. I didn't realize what I was doing. I'm sorry" (very upset with himself and how he had pressured his son).

Barry: "That's why I didn't want to play. You make me so nervous, Dad. It's not fun" (breaking into tears).

George: "I'm going to have to ask more questions and listen to you better. It's not my life, its yours" (embracing Barry. It took much therapeutic work, previously, for George to eventually allow himself to role reverse with Barry, but when he did, it was very helpful).

As in the last example, role reversal was effective in stimulating the patient to see how he or she looks in the eyes of another person and to better empathize and understand how he or she is affecting this person through this person's perception, feelings and thoughts. The mirror method used with role reversal demonstrates this, as described later in this chapter.

When role reversal regarding personal or family issues doesn't also involve the patient working through his or her past experiences, including dealing with one's upbringing, unresolved past issues will likely impair the role reversing process. This is primarily because denial and contaminated thinking and feelings won't allow the patient to role reverse with a clear mind and will make the patient resistant to look at anything in the other person he or she doesn't want to look at in oneself. This is why role reversal regarding present issues is more often utilized in conjunction with the patient working actively on facing issues in one's past which are impairing one's functioning. Of course, present issues will be worked on at one time, while past issues will be worked on at another time, although they will also be related. Role reversal can, sometimes improve empathy and understanding between family members where the reliving process isn't used, but less effectively and often temporarily.

Role reversal can also be used with friends, acquaintances, co-workers, employees, employers, customers, adversaries, and so on. In less intimate relationships when past issues affect persons less powerfully than when in intimate relationships, role reversal can be very effective without the reliving process. The empathy and understanding derived from such role reversal allow for a mutual and better understanding of persons.

Role reversal can be effective in developing empathy and understanding for specific groups. Putting oneself in the place of a gang member from the slums of a large city, a religious leader one doesn't understand, a Communist Chinese government official or a Third World leader will increase empathy and understanding and at least assist adversaries or conflicting parties to improve their relations and develop some type of working arrangement.

THE MIRROR METHOD

The mirror method is used as an active video replay to demonstrate to the patient how he or she behaves and appears to significant others, such as one's spouse or child or to other persons in his or her life. In fact, it goes further than a video replay, for as in real life action, it brings the patient face to face with one's dysfunctional and unhealthy attitude and behavior. It can also be used to mirror a positive attitude and behavior the patient is beginning to exhibit in order to reinforce it and further encourage it. However, its "videotaping" or replaying of unhealthy or rejecting attitudes and behaviors will be what is described here. The mirroring is acted out in the safety of the clinical setting and in no way does it ever involve inflicting physical harm of any kind on anyone. A therapeutic agent, for example, duplicates the attitudes and behaviors of the patient in a particular situation using the "same" posture, demeanor, body movements, actions, words, tone, volume, expressions, feelings, feeling level and thoughts that the person displays.

Although it is preferable for a co-therapist or auxiliary agent rather than the therapist to mirror the patient, this often is not possible, for such persons aren't available or cannot mirror the patient as effectively as the therapist. In other cases, another group or family member who was a victim of a similar unhealthy or rejecting behavior may effectively portray the patient, having experienced it first hand. At other times, the actual person victimized can effectively do the mirroring. The victim, role reversing and becoming the perpetrator, would have the opportunity to experience the perpetrator's thinking and feelings as the perpetrator was rejecting and contaminating him or her, becoming more aware of how this rejection affected oneself. In the same session, the perpetrator can also role reverse, becoming the victim, and experience as the person he or she victimized being mistreated by oneself. This method is effectively used in family therapy with the examples provided. The mirror method used in this way in the criminal justice, court and correctional settings with the victim and perpetrator role reversing or when the perpetrator role reverses to become the person he or she victimized with someone other than the victim acting out the crime has implications for crime prevention. The crime method described in chapter twelve discusses this subject in more detail. Another group member who was the perpetrator of a similar rejecting experience may also effectively portray the patient. This would be helpful in bringing such a person more in touch with his or her own rejecting behavior by living this out while mirroring another perpetrator. The choice of who mirrors the patient, as with other methods, depends on who is the best person to do so and who is available.

Effective timing is essential, and much therapeutic work may be needed before this method can be used. In other cases it can be utilized relatively early in therapy if a trusting relationship has been established between patient and therapist.

It is mandatory, and always important, that the person mirroring the patient's negative attitude and behavior have the patient's trust and not be a person the patient may misinterpret as ridiculing him or her. It is important to point out to the patient that he or she is not being made fun of and that this is being done primarily to further educate the patient regarding how he or she is coming across to others.

An example of the mirror method in joint marital therapy follows. Jerome, 27, a domineering and authoritarian husband, had the opportunity to perceive himself as he actually was—dominating and rejecting his wife Laura, 24. In his case, it was also necessary for Jerome to role reverse, becoming his wife, to experience as his wife being rejected by him and not just observing this situation. Frequently, this is necessary if a person is actually to experience and become aware of his or her impact on another person. Often the person is blinded to one's negative influence on others. The mirror method, often used with role reversal, breaks and cuts through the denial, finally letting the overly aggressive, rejecting or dysfunctional person experience and know how he or she is affecting others.

Therapist: "Jerome, please role reverse and become your wife Laura, while I demonstrate how you come across to her."

The therapist mirrored Jerome's behavior as it was an individual family therapy session with his wife, who was not ready to do so.

Therapist as Jerome: "You do what I say. I'm your husband, and if I don't want you to wear that dress, you won't wear it. No man is going to look at you the wrong way. You're mine. I want you the way I want you" (in a very tyrannical voice).

Jerome as Laura: "You're trying to own me. I'm not your property. You have no right to do this" (soon breaking out of his role as Laura surprised and shocked).

Jerome as Self: "I can't believe this is me. I have no right to do this to her" (becoming emotional).

In other cases, the mirror is used for a somewhat longer time, but only as long as is needed. Laura was then introduced into the session with the therapist doubling with her.

Laura: (Beginning to cry, but not saying anything).

Therapist as Double: "This is how you have been treating me."

Laura: "It's been like this for a long time. I have done just what you wanted, tearfully. I have to be just what you want. I feel like I'm in prison" (becoming angry, stronger and continuing to open up with both of them further realizing what her rights were).

Another way of using the mirror method in family therapy, where the perpetrator and the victim role reverse with each other, is described here. In multiple family group therapy, the therapist asked Michelle to become her 13-year-old son, Ben, in order to experience her guilt provocation, as Ben, and for Ben to become her demonstrating her attitude and behavior. This is very different from Ben putting himself in his mother's self, to feel her feelings and think her thoughts, for in this case he was videotaping and replaying her damaging attitude, behavior and messages to him. However, as a byproduct he had an opportunity to become more aware of his mother's feelings and thoughts. Utilizing Ben as his mother's mirror was helpful because he was her victim and was ready and willing to do this.

Therapist: "Michelle can you role reverse and become Ben, while Ben shows you how you affect him?"

Ben as his Mother: "You don't care about me. You don't love me. If you love me, why don't you listen to me after all I've done for you!" How can you do this to me? How can you hurt me so bad? How can you do this to me?"

Mother as Ben (first taking this in and then experiencing Ben's feelings and thoughts after some difficulty):"You make me angry, Mom! You make me so mad. I hate you when you do this!" (but still needing further assistance to experience her effect on her son).

To further demonstrate how Michelle was affecting her son, the therapist also doubled with her as Ben.

Double: "It really hurts me when you treat me this way."

Mother as Ben: "You really hurt me. You act like you don't care about me," (continuing for a short time and beginning to cry as Ben).

Once the point was made, Michelle (mother) was asked to become herself again, while Ben became himself. The therapist immediately doubled with Ben assisting him to open up, though in other cases a patient may open up immediately on one's own.

Therapist as Double: "You really hurt me, Mom. I'm so mad when you do this."

Ben: "You hurt me a lot when you do this to me. I feel very sad and mad. You confuse me" (starting to cry and continuing to communicate his feelings and thoughts, while his mother tearfully empathized with him).

The mirror method has also been used in demonstrating to the alcoholic or drug abusing person the impact of his or her unhealthy behavior on a loved one. For example, Jim, 34, was asked to role reverse in group therapy, becoming his 7-year-old daughter, experiencing himself, acted out by the therapist, intoxicated, drunk, yelling and screaming through his daughter's eyes, feelings and thoughts.

Therapist as Jim: "Leave me alone! Nobody can tell me what to do! I'm the man of this house! If I want to drink, I'll drink! If you don't get out of my way, I'll slug you, so leave me alone!" (to his wife, yelling louder and louder, simulating hitting his wife and then yelling at his daughter saying in a very loud and threatening voice) "You better stop your crying! You better shut up!" (slapping her and yelling more, of course just acting this out as the only therapeutic agent in the session, without physical harm to anyone).

Experiencing this as his daughter shocked Jim into tears and stimulated him to stop drinking, although this was only an early step in his rehabilitation. The mirror method, as other methods or approaches, can also be used in individual therapy, individual family therapy or multiple family group therapy, though, as with any method or approach, it must be used with discretion and sensitivity.

The mirror method can also be utilized when the patient is asked just to observe oneself rather than role reversing as a significant other. In this case, the patient is often resistant or not ready to role reverse to feel the feelings or think the thoughts of the person he or she is has victimized. However, this is a good beginning and effective in its own right, even if it is the only type of mirroring used.

It is sometimes more therapeutic not to use the mirror method if the patient is unable or unwilling to face oneself in this open demonstration of truth. If used when a patient isn't ready for it, as with any method, it presents the risk of further resistance, alienating the patient or possibly causing the patient to terminate therapy prematurely. Alternative methods can be used, such as gently explaining to the patient what he or she is doing with much support and sensitivity.

ANGER REDUCTION METHODS

Specific anger reduction methods are also utilized to stimulate the expression, working through and letting go of anger. Completely letting go of one's anger is impossible, but a therapeutic letting go of anger should be carried out so that it will no longer significantly impair the person's functioning. This letting go can apply to any type of feeling.

The Double Anger Release Method

In using the double anger release method the double demonstrates to the patient specific ways to express anger to stimulate the expression of anger regarding a significant other or situation the patient has had or has difficulty becoming angry with or about. This method involves asking the patient to repeat the same words and expressions in the same tone, volume and way in which the double does. As part of this method, the double may also initially need to show the patient what to express in content, verbally, as a warmup if the patient is especially "stuck" and inhibited regarding expressing his or her anger.

The skill of the therapist or therapeutic agent is often needed to most effectively use this method. However, a more advanced patient or group member or in some cases a capable family member who strongly relates to the patient can also be utilized. The family member is a different person than the one the patient is angry with.

An example is Art, 14, in group therapy, who was emotionally "stuck" and could not express his anger to his intimidating and rejecting father portrayed by a therapeutic agent, while reliving a major experience at a younger age, though able to express aspects of his sadness and unhappiness. Art needed to be warmed up briefly to the content of his anger before effectively opening up to his father, with the therapist as a double, using this method, demonstrating and modeling the expression of anger toward Art's father. The therapist became the double because he could most effectively use this method, while a therapeutic agent assisted him.

Double: "You make me mad. I have been afraid of you too long. I am not going to let you intimidate me anymore. I have a right to tell you how I feel. You have no right to intimidate me this way, to scare me like this. I am angry at you for this. I have a right to my feelings. I have a right to my views. I am mad at you! I am mad at you for bullying me around so long. I am so mad at you. I am so mad at you!"

This further connected Art to his anger for his father and his right to feel angry toward him, while preparing Art to confront his father directly this time in the reliving process. This warmup phase is not always necessary. The therapist then asked Art to repeat after him whatever he expressed until Art was able to do so independently.

Double: "I'm angry with you, I'm really angry with you!" (with Art repeating this).

Double: "I'm really angry at you. I'm so angry at you, Dad" (with Art repeating this).

Double: "I'm so mad, I'm so mad at you" (with Art repeating this).

Double: "I'm very mad at you. I hate you for what you're doing."

Art: "I'm very mad. I hate you. I hate you. I hate you more than I ever realized" (beginning to express anger on his own).

Double: "I hate you so much."

Art: "I hate you, I hate you! You never let me say anything. You don't respect anything I do. I can't stand it. It upsets me so much" (expressing his anger independently).

As Art was successfully jump started into expressing his anger more independently, the double was then utilized in its usual way with no further need for the double anger release method. From this point, the patient can soon be stimulated to express his or her anger at a higher and more open level using a mat to hit on; can more slowly accelerate one's expression of anger not using a mat at this time; or reach an effective level of anger expression not ever using a mat. With this method, there is usually minimal interaction with the significant other who angered the patient, portrayed by another person, until the patient has been jump started into expressing one's anger independently. The patient may then begin or continue to interact with and confront his or her significant other, acted or lived out by another person, while reliving a past experience, which Art was able to do in this session expressing his anger without using a mat which he would be ready to use in future sessions. In other cases, the patient may begin or continue addressing a significant other, portrayed by another person, in an open interaction in the present or past or from the present to the past when not specifically reliving an experience. This method can also be used in family therapy to prepare the patient to directly interact with and confront a family member or in other situations to assist one to express anger effectively.

The Anger Mat Release Method and Other Physical Anger Release Exercises

To further facilitate the more open expression of anger at a higher level and to encourage the "letting go" of anger, the anger mat release method is used. As with any method, it is essential that the patient be ready and willing to utilize it. The patient is encouraged to use a table with a mat on it. In some cases, the mat is placed on the floor if the patient requires more grounding and security, although I more frequently encourage my patients to stand to give them a greater sense of strength. While standing or kneeling, the patient is asked to raise his or her hands to the ceiling and to hit down on the mat with one's hands. If the patient is willing, but somewhat fearful and resistant, the double may first hit the mat to encourage the patient to do so or will hit the mat simultaneously with the patient. The patient is sometimes encouraged to strike the mat with open hands, symbolically letting go of one's anger in an open way, physically and emotionally, rather than with a closed fist, which at times may convey a revenge factor and even a holding onto factor. However, expressing anger with the fists is also a natural way of expressing anger and the way many persons will express it when enraged and possessing a high degree of anger. Eventually, a patient expressing anger in this way with his or her fists may choose to open up one's hands when striking the mat. On the other hand, it may not be necessary to distinguish between open or closed hands as long as the patient is physically expressing anger. How this is done and utilized with each patient is still open for further evaluation.

The patient is asked to feel his or her anger from the feet to the knees to the stomach to the chest to the throat and out through the mouth and then to start hitting down on the mat to begin or continue releasing one's anger. The arms and hands are raised as high as possible before hitting down on the mat to create a more powerful hitting process and a greater expression and release of anger. This process continues while the patient verbalizes such statements as "I hate you, I'm mad at you and you have no right doing this to me," until his or her anger is released effectively. It is as though one is climbing up a mountain, reaches the top, starts to come down and then eventually comes down all the way as he or she has gone through and experienced the catharsis. Letting go of and giving up "control," while still ultimately maintaining a basic level of control, increases the expression and releasing process. Once this process is completed, the patient usually feels an emotional burden or load lifted off his or her shoulders and a relief throughout one's physical and emotional self. In addition, other feelings such as sadness, fear and guilt may surface, allowing for a further working through of these feelings or may precede the working through of anger. Although feelings may occur concurrently, often a primary feeling is being expressed at a specific time, with this depending on the person. Usually, as anger is expressed authentically, guilt and fear are weakened. The specific working through of other major feelings besides anger is also necessary. (See the end of the section on the double method.) The release and working through of any contaminating feeling, especially anger, reduces the likelihood of hostile and inappropriate behavior.

While this process is occurring, the double may hit on the mat with the patient, also verbalizing with the patient. (See the multiple double method in this chapter.) At times, the double anger release method can be used as the double anger mat release method. In this case the patient will hit on the mat with one's hands exactly as the double does and verbally expresses exactly what the double expresses until the patient is jump started into expressing his or her anger more independently. At times the patient will be instructed to just hit on the mat, while the double expresses the feelings and thoughts associated with the patient's anger if the patient verbally expressing one's anger inhibits his or her expression of it. At other times, when further stimulation is needed, the patient will be instructed to express animal noises or to be an animal such as a wolf or tiger to express anger in a deeper and stronger way, with the double doubling as an animal or verbalizing what the patient is expressing. Though this approach may be needed, the patient's verbal expression of anger or any feeling is also essential.

Using the double in these ways, along with the mat, further strengthens the expression of anger, with there being little or no chance that the patient will regress as the patient is cleansing oneself of contaminating and poisonous anger. Again, the patient has to be ready and willing to use this or any method. Expressing anger without the mat, with the double's help, is an effective anger releaser, though usually less powerful.

Art was further encouraged to express his anger using the anger mat release method in a following group therapy session, when he was therapeutically reliving his father's rejection of him at another time as a child at a younger age than he relived in the previous session. However, the mat and hitting it can provoke strong feelings of fear and anxiety and resistance, for it is a powerful releaser of feelings and a stimulus to do so. Initially fearful, Art stated, "I am afraid I am going to lose control. I'm so mad at him, I don't know what I would do if I lost control. I'm scared. I'm scared of so many things." Also contributing to his resistance was his fear of being rejected by his father, letting go of his father, as he realized he would never have his father's love which he had wanted all his life, and being all alone. Often, a person holds onto one's anger to symbolically and wishfully hold onto the dream of being loved by the parent (angry rejecting parent in this case) who has never adequately loved him or her. When referring to the parent, in this context and throughout the book, it can apply to one or both parents, though one at a time. Even though the parent figure is held onto through anger, resentment and sadness, with such feelings frequently being repressed, this is often felt to be less painful and better than not having one's parent at all. Also, holding onto one's anger, which is often an aggressive and attacking feeling when held on to, encourages a feeling of more power and less vulnerability, though this sense of power is a myth as one remains dysfunctional with it. Facing the emotional pain and dysfunction of one's mistreatment stimulates the patient to let go of it and one's dysfunctional parent, which is a relatively scary though healthy process. However, the fear of facing one's psychological pain and being alone without a parent's love or even just without a parent or the dream of either is very traumatic and is something many persons will spend a lifetime avoiding. This is why there is significant patient resistance to using this method, at times, because of its power in uncovering repressed feelings, thoughts and experiences and making a major step forward toward letting go of the success of the dream or wish in the Child of having the parental love one never had in one's upbringing. (This issue of letting go is discussed in chapter nine regarding the letting go method.)

This method is illustrated with Art. Due to the complexity of using this method, the therapist doubled with Art and continued to assist Art to deal with his resistance while he relived this earlier childhood experience.

Double: "I'm afraid I'm going to hate him if I let go of my anger."

Art: "I really am scared. If I realize how much I hate him, I may want nothing to do with him and I've always wanted his love. I'm afraid to face I'll never get it. I'm really scared."

This process of assisting Art to deal with his resistance to expressing his anger continued for about ten minutes until he was ready to begin the releasing process standing by the mat and table with the double.

Double: "Am I going to go on living in this pain, in this hell so I don't have to face this?"

Art: "I know I need to release it. I'm so angry at him."

Double: "I'm feeling my anger more than ever. I can't believe how angry I am at him! I'm so angry at you" (now directing the expression of Art's anger toward his father).

Art: "I'm very angry at you! I'm so angry at you for all your criticism and put downs. I'm more than angry."

Art's father was then introduced into the process to further stimulate Art's expression of anger. A therapeutic agent, in the session in addition to the therapist, took this role. Art would soon use a mat on a table to express his anger.

Therapeutic Agent as Father: "You're such a disappointment to me. I'm so ashamed of you. You're always disappointing me" (looking at Art in a very disgusted way).

Art: "I hate you for this, Dad. It's not right. It's not right" (raising his voice as he becomes angrier).

Double: "I'm angrier than I could ever imagine. I'm going to explode I'm so mad." (Starting to slowly raise his hands and hitting on the mat) "Try this, Art."

Art: "I'm afraid. I'm scared. I don't know what will happen" (naturally exhibiting his resistance again which is not unusual).

Double: "Try it, I'll do it with you. We'll go at a pace you can handle. Now pick your hands up to the ceiling and hit down on the mat building up to as much and as hard as you can."

Art began to hit on the mat with his hands, with the double doing this with him. The pace began slowly to accommodate Art's anxiety and discomfort. It then began to pick up as Art began to hit on the mat harder and harder and soon got into "it", expressing his anger and rage which he had held onto. His father's "put-downs" continued in a timely way to continue the opening up process.

Father: "You're no good, Art. You'll never amount to anything. You're no good" (continuing to repeat this in a broken record way, which was the theme of his father's message).

Art (as his father continued doing this, he yelled out): "I hate you, I hate you!" (With the double assisting him he began to raise his voice louder and louder). "I hate you! I hate you! I hate you! I want to hit you. I want to punch you, I hate you" (and expressing other words of rage and anger).

Double: (growling and raving making animalistic noises of rage to further stimulate and reinforce Art's catharsis).

Although in this case it was helpful to double as an animal to maximize Art's expression of anger in this way, this is often not needed. Following the lead of the double, Art, at times also growled and raved as an animal, while yelling out what he was so enraged about, expressing, ventilating and letting go of a significant amount of raw rage he had been holding within himself. As he reached the peak of his anger release after about fifteen minutes of expressing his anger in this way with some pauses (this process varies from a few minutes to fifteen minutes or more), he started to come down the other side of the "mountain of his anger expression," stating he was a good person and started to cry intensely.

Double: "You hurt me so much. You hurt me so much."

Art (crying for at least ten minutes with no words followed by): "I did everything to please you, but you never were happy with anything I did. You never let me be myself. You hurt me so much. You'll never know what you could have had with me" (continuing to cry).

The expression of tears and despair is typical when this method is used, as indicated. In addition, other memories, feelings or thoughts will surface and come out as the mind is further opened up along with the physical release of body tension, the loosening of tightened muscles, a smoother breathing process and the weakening of one's defenses.

Art eventually reached a point where he felt more grounded, bringing his crying to a close.

Art: "I feel so relieved, that I'm seeing this clearly. You really haven't been a Dad to me. I have let you intimidate me so long, always afraid of what you would do or say. You've tried to rule me, to own me, to manipulate me, to use me. No more. No more. No one is going to do this to me again."

Double: "I'm going to be my own person."

Art: "That's right, I'm going to be my own person. I don't have to let you, Dad, or any one scare me again" (with a smile).

Double: "No one will scare me again like this. You petrified me" (communicating to him that he didn't have to allow himself to become so scared or intimidated in the way his father did to him, but not trying to convey he won't ever be scared).

Art: "No one will scare me. No one will. No one. Not in this way. I may be scared, but not petrified as I have been of you, Dad. No way. No way."

Double: "I am going to walk in faith and not in fear."

Art: "That's right, I am going to walk in faith and not in fear. I am going to believe in myself starting now" (integrating his thinking, feelings and himself further).

Double: "The last thing I'm going to express to you Dad is ..."

Art (still in his Child or younger self, with his Developing Nurturing Self, referred to as the Adult Nurturing Self for adults, assisting): "I still have love for you, Dad, but I won't have anything to do with you as long as you treat me like this. If you treat me well, I will have something to do with you. I want a relationship but one out of respect. Goodbye for now Dad" (continuing his integration and then returning to being 14).

Art then turned to his therapist embracing him and then to other group members who also embraced him, while the group cheered with applause of triumph.

If a patient needs a greater degree of security, placing the mat on the floor while utilizing it as described can also be effective.

The anger mat release method can also be helpful even if the patient is not initially feeling significantly angry on a conscious level. As Bioenergetic Therapy advocates, as the muscles loosen up and become less tight, as muscular tension decreases and one breathes more freely as the mat is hit, some of the patient's underlying anger and buried feelings and thoughts will often surface, often along with the uncovering of one or more experiences and conflicts in a way the patient usually can handle. The uncovering of another experience or experiences is usually related to the experience being relived, further supporting the opening up process and can be dealt with at another time if needed. The patient may initially feel uncomfortable doing this, but once hitting on the mat, he or she will usually feel relieved and more comfortable, relaxed and energized. In the process the patient will often feel less angry and depressed.

Lying down on a mat or bed and kicking with one's legs and feet on the mat or bed, while simultaneously raising one's arms and hands and hitting the mat or bed with one's hands is also an effective way of expressing and releasing anger. Kicking on the mat or bed with one's legs and feet alone or hitting down on the mat or bed with just one's arms and hands are other anger reduction methods. Although these lying down exercises are effective in helping people to express anger, they are especially effective for rape or molestation victims who are often lying down when being victimized as discussed in chapter fourteen. Also, women who are often stronger in the lower body area, may often feel empowered using their legs and feet to express and release their anger, in addition to using their upper body.

Other ways of physically expressing and releasing anger include hitting on a firm and safe mattress, cushion, pillow, punching bag or weight bag with one's hands, with appropriate protection when hitting on a punching or weight bag, or using a small thick bat-like object that is firm but not hard, a tennis racket or a strong towel to hit on a safe object such as a firm mattress or cushion or weight bag. Kicking exercises can also be effective in releasing anger.

The mat methods and exercises discussed in this section have been used regularly in Bioenergetic Therapy and to a certain extent in Psychodrama and can be effective in releasing anger when other methods have not succeeded or when the therapist is looking for a higher level of anger expression and release. The use of these methods and the way they are used, as with any method, depend on the patient and what is most therapeutic for that patient. These and any method must be used with utmost sensitivity regarding what the patient is ready for, needs, can deal with and is willing to work on.

CHAPTER 8

Other Rebuilding Methods

The therapeutic chair method, the visualization method and the blackout method are strong in their own way and helpful in stimulating the opening up process in certain situations. The therapeutic chair or auxiliary chair (as it is referred to in Psychodrama) and the blackout methods are psychodramatic techniques interpreted and further developed, as with other techniques from Psychodrama, where applicable for Rebuilding Therapy. The winning life method is helpful in opening the patient up to what needs haven't been partially or fully met. Joining the child within oneself (joining) and blending the past with the present (blending) are integrative methods that are helpful in demonstrating the working together of the ego states in the rebuilding process and relating the impact of the past on the present in specific situations, respectively. The visualization method, the winning life method, joining and blending have been developed for Rebuilding Therapy. These methods, as any Rebuilding Therapy method, utilize psychodramatic methodology when clinically used.

THE THERAPEUTIC CHAIR METHOD

The therapeutic chair method involves the patient visualizing his or her significant other such as one's parent, spouse, child or relative, or anyone else or situation that has significantly impacted him or her in an empty chair in whatever way the significant other, person or situation is perceived in the present or past and expressing one's feelings and thoughts to the visualized person or situation in the chair. The term *situation* refers to a specific situational experience and the person or persons and human factors of the situation affecting the person. Since the significant other is the type of person with whom the patient most frequently deals with, it is referred to when describing this and other methods, though not limited to this type of person if the patient is dealing with a nonsignificant other or a specific situational experience involving a nonsignificant other or others. The therapeutic chair is used when the patient is not ready or is resistant to face his or her significant other lived out by another person in the present or past or when the patient needs to visualize and experience one's significant other as "exactly" and as specifically as he or she believes is needed rather than utilizing another person as the significant other. The therapeutic chair stimulates the patient to target one's feelings and thoughts at the chair representing a significant other, for example. The patient can express his or her feelings or thoughts in the present to the significant other regarding a current situation, to the significant other from one's present chronological age back to the time the significant other mistreated or affected him or her or to the significant other as a child or in the past at the time the significant other mistreated or affected him or her. The patient can also perceive him or herself in an empty chair opening up to oneself at specific times in the present, from the present to the past or in the past. The patient is encouraged, as when other methods are used, to focus on a specific time he or she was affected or a key time representing other major times. However, if a patient isn't ready for this, he or she is encouraged initially to focus on a more generalized time period. The patient faces the significant other in the chair from a sitting or standing position—whichever is more therapeutic and realistic, based on the relationship and situation the patient is working on. The therapeutic chair can also be used as a warmup to prepare the patient to more intensively deal with the impact of a significant other on one's life in the reliving process or in other therapeutic ways.

Although this method is most often not as powerful as using a therapeutic agent or person to live out a significant other's impact on the patient, it can be effective in its own right. In the minority of cases, it is all the patient will be able and willing to deal with. In the following example of this method in individual therapy, Tony, 43, was having difficulty therapeutically experiencing and confronting his father's mistreatment while reexperiencing this as a child.

Tony: "I just can't face him. It's too scary, it's too scary facing him in person like this. I just can't. I'm not ready" (trembling).

Realizing at this time he wasn't ready to relive his father's rejection of him as a child with another person as his father, the therapist decided to use the therapeutic chair method.

Therapist: "I understand it is very difficult seeing your father lived out before you. Why don't you visualize or see him in this empty chair being the child you are again?"

Tony: "It would be too difficult, too hard, just too hard" (not ready to relive this).

Tony was then encouraged to return to the present.

Therapist: "Experience your father from your current age back to when you were a child at some age when he was mistreating you. Of course, if your father treated you similarly at other ages, you can face him regarding other ages also, which one experience represents, or you can look at all of the experiences together."

Tony: "I tried so hard to please you, but you were always upset with me. I could never please you. You always had to be right. You were never wrong. You always had to win with me and I was just a child" (from the present back to childhood).

The specific age in this case was not important, though in other cases it is. The therapist also functioned as the double.

Double: "It wasn't fair."

Tony: "It was wrong. I just wanted you to compliment me and you just criticized me" (raising his voice in anger).

Double: "It was like you were my enemy."

Tony: "You weren't a dad. You weren't a friend. You were against me" (his anger increasing).

Double: "You made me feel so bad."

Tony: "You taught me to hate myself, to feel stupid, that I can't do anything right."

Double: "That's why I have had so little confidence."

Tony: "I've never had you behind me, complimenting or encouraging me. No wonder I don't like myself. No wonder" (becoming angrier, while also looking sad).

Double: "I'm angry. I would have learned to like myself if you had encouraged me."

Tony: "I would have accomplished so much more. I'm mad at you. I'm so mad at you" (while continuing to look sad).

Double: "I'm also sad it turned out this way" (planting the seed for Tony to begin getting in touch with his sadness, if he was ready, while supporting what he was primarily feeling at this time).

Tony: "I am sad I didn't have a father-son relationship with you, that you hurt me this way. It's really too bad" (sadly). "I'm also angry, very angry you did this to me. Very angry."

Since Tony was more in touch with his anger than his sadness, he was encouraged to further work through his anger and to begin empowering himself, although he would have an opportunity to face and work through his sadness at another time. Although the expression of authentic anger is encouraged, it is also imperative to distinguish between authentic anger and defensive anger, the latter being a cover-up or defense against other feelings such as sadness, guilt, fear or also authentic anger.

Double: "I'm very angry at you. I hate what you did to me."

Tony: "I'm more than angry. I hate you for this" (going on with his expression of anger for the next ten minutes, while also expressing), "I'm not going to let you keep doing this to me. I'm not that bad. I do have a mind."

Double: "I'm not stupid. You just made me feel this way."

Tony: "I am not dumb. I have a good brain, if only I start believing in myself. I'm going to now."

Double: "I have a right to. I deserve better."

Tony: "I deserve a lot better and won't let you or anyone put me down like this anymore" (in a stronger and more confident voice).

Double: "I've made a lot of progress. I also realize I need to do a lot of work on overcoming your mistreatment of me" (planting the seed that he had more therapeutic work to do to overcome his father's rejection, including his sadness and improving his self confidence).

Tony: "I have a lot more work to do, but I'm proud of myself that I could even do this. I'm surprised. I didn't know I could do this" (relieved with a broad smile).

THERAPEUTIC VISUALIZATION: THE VISUALIZATION METHOD

This method involves the patient not using the empty chair, visualizing his or her significant other or anyone or situation that has significantly impacted him or her in front of oneself in the present or past in any way perceived and expressing one's feelings and thoughts to this person or situation. As with the therapeutic chair, the patient can express his or her feelings in the present to the significant other, from one's present chronological age back to the time the significant other affected him or her or to the significant other as a child or in the past at the time the significant other affected him or her. In addition, as with the therapeutic chair, the patient can visualize him or herself in a specific way opening up to oneself at specific times in the present, from the present to the past or in the past.

The visualization method can be used with a patient's eyes open or closed depending on the situation. When a patient in a state of relaxation with his or her eyes closed is reliving an experience, as described in chapter two, it is a much broader and usually more powerful process, though the visualization method is also a powerful method in its own way as is the therapeutic chair. In this case, the patient will have the opportunity in the present tense again to relive and reexperience an event, as needed, while other persons, as needed and is therapeutic, may or may not live out the role of significant others in an audible way.

Therapeutic visualization is used when the therapeutic chair, with its symbolic meaning, is too threatening to the patient, inhibits the visualization process needed to stimulate the patient to face a specific person, situation or experience or is not appropriate. As with the therapeutic chair, it is used when the patient isn't ready, is resistant or is uncomfortable in facing a therapeutic agent or person living out a significant other's mistreatment or affect on him or her or when the patient requests to see his or her significant other as "exactly" or as specifically as one believes him or her to be or was, but not represented in a chair. Therapeutic visualization may also be a method the patient or therapist prefers rather than using the therapeutic chair. The therapist will do whatever is necessary to avoid or reduce resistance, and if a method such as this can more effectively stimulate the opening up process, then it should be utilized. Eventually, the therapeutic agent or person living out a significant other's role can be introduced when the person is ready for this. In other cases, though in the large minority of situations, the therapeutic agent or person as a significant other will not be used.

This method is effective in individual sessions, as is the therapeutic chair, when the therapist is the only one available to double and to live out the role of a significant other or others. In individual sessions the therapist often needs to move from the role of double to that of the significant other and back to the double. Although the therapist in the role of a significant other, in this case, and switching in this way can be accomplished effectively once this is mastered and is the more powerful way to stimulate the patient, the patient will sometimes need the constant support of the therapist doubling with him or her and providing the needed stimulation in the process as permitted by the visualization method. Being able to stay by the patient's side without moving out of this role, which the visualization method allows, is what some patients need to have for the effective combination of stimulation and support. The therapeutic chair also provides this type of stimulation and support. As indicated, when a patient in a state of relaxation with his or her eyes closed is reliving an experience, the therapeutic process moves beyond the visualization method being a broader and usually more powerful process.

The visualization method, as the therapeutic chair method, is also effective in reducing or preventing overstimulation of the patient, when a patient needs more quiet, solitude and peacefulness in bringing out his or her feelings and thoughts. Such a case is with the excessively dramatic and overly active person who may be overstimulated by a therapeutic agent or person acting as a significant other and needs to first stop and get his or her feet on the ground to experience what is going on within oneself and externally before moving to the next level of intensity, as therapeutic. Having to visualize a significant other in a specific experience or in some way first requires stopping and looking at the situation. As with the therapeutic chair, this method is also helpful with inhibited or defensive individuals who are not ready to be stimulated by a therapeutic agent or person acting as a significant other, but who may at least be willing to begin facing his or her situation with this method. The visualization method can also be used interchangeably with a therapeutic agent or person acting as a significant other, as when using the therapeutic chair method.

An example of this method in group therapy is Roberta, 16, whose mother regularly ignored her as a child. The therapist functioned as the double.

Roberta: "I can't see my mother in that chair. That chair scares me anyway. It scares me."

After unsuccessful attempts were made to supportively desensitize her to the therapeutic chair method, the visualization method was tried, with Roberta agreeing to do this to begin experiencing her mother's impact on her as a child.

Therapist: "Roberta, visualize seeing your mother telling you as a child she is too busy to spend any time with you. I will double with you to help you recall Mom doing this. Feel free, if you choose, to keep your eyes open, though you can close them if you want to" (clarifying this option as realizing Roberta's initial resistance. Roberta kept her eyes open during this process as this was more comfortable for her).

Roberta: "I know she wasn't there for me, but it's hard to remember. This is uncomfortable" (though not saying she wanted to stop).

Double: "She was always too busy."

Roberta: "Her work, friends and activities were always more important than me" (and further discussing this).

Double: "I'm recalling one of these times."

Roberta: "I'm five years old and I want Mom to read me a story." (Her willingness to become a child was a breakthrough in itself with the visualization method encouraging this.)

Double: "Where am I? Where is Mom? What is happening?" (with pauses between each question).

Roberta: "I'm in the living room while she's dusting the furniture. I'm asking her to read to me and she tells me 'No, I'm too busy. I have housework to do and then I want to rest. Don't bother me now'" (not ready yet for someone to act in the role of her mother or to role reverse to be her mother, though she did start to cry).

Double: "I'm so sad. You just want nothing to do with me as I look at you and talk to you."

Roberta: "I don't feel you even love me. I feel I don't even matter to you. I'm always in the way" (and continuing to open up further to her mother, while continuing to cry).

At this point in the session, she was ready to face her mother portrayed by a therapeutic agent in this case. In doing so, she began working through her feelings and thoughts to the point where she began to realize she was a good person, had the right to be loved and was worthwhile.

Some patients will never be able or willing to go beyond this method, although the majority of patients will eventually allow themselves to deal with their problems at a higher level of intensity when supportively stimulated to do so. Whether used as a warmup for more intensive methods or as a primary approach, both this method and the therapeutic chair method can be intensive and independently effective methods.

THE BLACKOUT METHOD

The blackout method is used to decrease the person's anxiety, tension and discomfort level by increasing one's sense of privacy. In doing so, it further stimulates a more open expression of feelings and thoughts. It is effective working with individuals who are especially fearful of rejection, have difficulty trusting, require a sense of privacy and feel self-conscious when expressing feelings and thoughts in the presence of others. Although psychotherapy patients often exhibit these characteristics, this method is especially effective with those patients exhibiting these tendencies even more so. This method is also effective when the person is working through and expressing feelings of despair, sadness, grief, loss, aloneness and isolation. It is used primarily if the opening up process is blocked, inhibited or further stimulation is needed.

Dimming and brightening the lights is the most effective way of utilizing this method, for the level of darkness and lighting will be set depending on the kind and intensity of the patient's feelings and thoughts and what level will most effectively stimulate the opening up process. Dimming the lights gradually is a comforting and disarmoring experience, stimulating an increase in the patient's expression of feelings and thoughts.

At times, a drastic change from lightness to darkness can help stimulate a patient into facing the sadness or aloneness in his or her life, which the patient has had difficulty accepting or facing.

An example of this method in individual therapy follows. Fred, 27, and divorced, operated from a manipulative and bully position with others, never letting anyone get close to him. His wife leaving him was a tremendous shock to him, for he had always been in control over everyone and every situation in his life. As the room was darkened, he began sobbing and finally faced, as he had never done before, the sadness, isolation and emptiness he had been running away from throughout his life. At this point he finally realized how important his wife had been to him. As he was opening up regarding his divorce, he recalled at age 4 his father abandoning him and his family, stimulating him also to open up regarding this painful episode in his life. This was a significant breakthrough as he had buried this event for most of his life. The darkness gave him a sense of privacy, security and comfort which stimulated him to open up more effectively. After briefly verbalizing what he recalled, he clinically relived through the use of a relaxation exercise with his eyes closed and with the therapist's help portraying his father in an audible way and doubling with him, as needed, his father's abandonment at age 4 and began crying openly for his father, working this through in an effective way. This event had a significant impact on his life, leading him to make the decision that he would not get close to or need anyone, and stimulating him to become manipulative and sociopathic in the process. Previous experiences also contributed to this decision as usually occurs with other decisions.

The blackout method stimulated him to stop and more openly experience his wife and father's departure. Reevaluating his decision in his wounded Child, with the assistance of his healthy Adult, Parent and Child or Adult Nurturing Self, assisted him to decide that he did need people and intimacy. In his case, it was too late to reconcile with his wife, but he began his rebuilding process to eventually be able to develop a healthy and intimate relationship. He was not capable or willing to do this until he was stimulated through the blackout method to stop and look at himself, his feelings and thoughts and an important part of his past. In this example, the room was left darkened while Fred was in a state of relaxation, but could have been turned back to a comfortable lighting level in situations like this if a patient goes into a state of relaxation. The lighting was gradually turned back on as he opened his eyes after returning to a comfortable position of closure.

The blackout method can be a very powerful approach when the patient's eyes remain open and could have been used with Fred in this way. It may be the only method used in a session, a warmup for reliving an experience or experiencing a specific issue, or stimulation for further opening up while reliving an experience or dealing with a specific issue. The lighting is restored when and in a way it is therapeutic to do so.

THE WINNING LIFE METHOD

This method is utilized to portray and demonstrate to the patient that there are needs such as being loved, being intimate, having a family, being parented in a loving and healthy way, enjoying life, experiencing a high or success and being a winner which he or she hasn't experienced or didn't experience in a healthy way. The patient's unmet needs, unattained experiences or unfulfilled lifestyle are presented in a healthy and fulfilled way in contrast to what one has experienced or never has experienced to further bring out one's feelings, thoughts and psychological pain regarding this. Providing a contrast to the rejection and neglect the patient is reliving during a session is especially helpful in accomplishing this. This method stimulates the further exploration, uncovering, facing and working through of unmet and unresolved needs and the buried feelings, thoughts, emotional pain, experiences and wounds that were created by rejection, neglect and unmet nurturing needs. As this occurs, the patient may begin to cry or express sadness, despair or anger regarding what another child or person had or has which he or she didn't or doesn't have.

This method is also helpful when the patient denies that he or she missed having a loving or intimate relationship with a parent or a happy and fulfilling family life. Common statements of denial are: "I never had a father, so I don't really know what I missed," "I've made it alone this far, so I don't need anyone close to me" or "I've never had a close family. My life is fine without one." Once the patient experiences what he or she should have had a right to experience, opens the patient up to the possibility that this is also possible in his or her life in a realistic way in the present or should have been in the past.

Teaching these various scenarios to the therapeutic agent is quite helpful. The therapeutic agent or therapist will live out these situations, although it's often advantageous for more than one therapeutic agent to assist in living out these scenarios. However, the therapist will often have to live out these experiences alone as no one else is available. It is often not practical to utilize group members for this method for it frequently needs to be used spontaneously with little or no time for preparation or instructions. When another patient or group member can be utilized, this is encouraged, and when done so can benefit the patient by he or she identifying with this healthy interaction.

The interactions are short and quick, done in as brief a time as possible, making the major point and then taking the patient back to dealing with one's feelings and thoughts and the issues being worked on.

Healthy Interaction Between Parent and Child

The method works very effectively, when portraying the healthy interaction between a parent or parents and a child, while the patient is working through an upbringing issue. The first thing the therapeutic agent does in living out the role of each person is to announce who he or she is when using this method. This is described in the first example, though not illustrated in the examples after this regarding the use of this method.

Example One

Mother: "I'm Mom. I'm so glad to see you, Billy. How did school go today? I made some brownies for you" (living out being affectionate to him).

Billie: "I'm Billie. Hi, Mom. I had a good day, but I'm worried about a spelling test tomorrow. But it's good to be home. These brownies are so good. Thanks Mom" (smiling).

Mother: "I love to see you smile, Billie."

Billie: "I know, Mom. I'm so glad you're my mom."

Example Two

Arlene: "The kids at school are picking on me. They called me ugly. I thought Susan and Betty were my friends. I don't want to go to school tomorrow" (crying).

Father: "Come over here and sit down next to me. I know that must hurt a lot. Let's talk about it" (in an empathetic voice).

Arlene (acting as if she has just talked with her father): "Thanks Dad. I feel so much better. Maybe I can make some other friends. I'll go to school tomorrow" (smiling). "Thanks Dad" (embracing him).

Example Three

John: "I really blew it. I didn't get my chores done and lied about it. I'm really scared. I'm really going to get it from Dad."

Father: "John, we need to sit down and talk about what happened."

John: "I blew it, Dad. I didn't get anything done and I lied. I'm sorry" (crying).

Father: "I'm disappointed in you, John. Have you learned anything from this?"

John: "Yes, Dad" (crying). "I have to be more responsible and more honest."

Father: "I'm glad you learned something from this, but you know there is going to be a consequence. You're going to be on restriction for a day."

John: "I know, Dad. Thanks for being so understanding. I was so afraid you were going to yell at me and put me on restriction for a week. Thanks Dad" (relieved).

Example Four

Mother: "You're so loving, Joan. You're caring, you're sensitive, you're so imaginative, you're so smart, you're so pretty. You have it all. You're so special. I love you so much."

Joan: "You make me feel so good, Mom. Thanks, Mom, you're my best friend."

The same message to a male can also be used substituting handsome for pretty.

Feeling Good About Parents

Another way of using this method is when the therapist or therapeutic agent lives out being from one to three children, experiencing their satisfying feelings and thoughts regarding their parents, with each example immediately following the previous one. The following examples are for males, though any of these scenarios can be provided for either sex in modified ways. This can bring out what one has missed or is missing with his or her parents.

Examples for Boys

Boy One: "I have a father. He is so special to me. He hikes with me. He plays with me. He listens to me. He loves me."

Boy Two: "My mom is really cool. I can tell her so many things. I hope my wife will be cool like her."

Boy Three: "Daddy wrestles with me. He laughs with me. He teaches me. Sometimes he even gets mad with me when I'm not acting right, but I know he loves me."

The following examples, using this method in this manner with females, are illustrated. Again, these scenarios can be provided for either sex with modifications.

Examples for Girls

Girl One: "Whenever I have a problem, Mom is there for me. We can talk about almost anything. I love it when she shows me how to dress up. I love to go shopping with her and try on clothes. She's a great friend too, but she disciplines me when I have it coming to me."

Girl Two: "I love to sit by my daddy. He's so big and strong. My daddy won't let anyone hurt me. But he tells me I'm strong too and that I'll be special some day. He really loves me."

Girl Three: "My mom is such a good person. She's so sensitive and cares so much. I love to watch her cook and sew. She's a good boss, too, at work. She takes such good care of herself. She always looks good and she really stands up for herself. I want to be just like her."

Healthy Family Situations

Presenting healthy family situations regarding happy and healthy family interaction stimulates the patient to express his or her feelings and thoughts regarding family needs that were not or are not being met. As with any of these improvisations, they are lived out relative to the patient's needs.

Example One

Father: "It's wonderful being home with my family."

Mother: "This means more to me than any part of the day when we're all together like this."

John: "I know, Mom and Dad, that I can talk to you just about anything."

Susan: "We have our problems, we get mad at each other, but we work it out a lot of the time."

Example Two

Joan: "Can I sit between both of you and watch the fire?"

Mother: "Of course, Dear, come sit over here by Daddy and Mommy."

Father: "Come on, Joan, let's all sit together."

Joan: "I feel so safe and warm."

Example Three

Mother: "We have to sit down and talk about things, Everybody."

Father: "Let's go into the living room, children. We have some problems to discuss."

Mother: "I don't like how we have been getting along. We're fighting too much."

Father: "Everyone will get five minutes to say what is bothering them, and then we'll figure out how to start solving these problems."

Sally: "I'm glad we'll get a chance to talk about things."

Ed: "I'm glad Mom and Dad are going to listen to us."

Sue: "I have a lot to say."

It is also helpful to present healthy marital interaction as in the next two examples to bring out what couples are missing out on or are not experiencing in a healthy way.

Example Four

Delores: "Honey, can we sit down and talk about something that's really bothering me? I know that article you're reading is important, but I need you now."

Al: "Okay Dear, I'll be happy to. What's the problem?"

Delores: (acting as they have just spoke): "I'm so glad you listened to me. I feel better now Thanks, Honey, thanks" (relieved).

Al: "I'm glad I did too. I didn't realize I was bothering you so much. We both learned from this. I'd like to hug you, Dear."

Example Five

Sam: "I love being with you, Joan. I feel I can just be myself."

Joan: "I feel the same way about you, Sam. We're just so good for each other."

Sam: "I just smile when I look at you. You make me feel so good."

Joan: "I feel great making you happy and I know you want me to be happy too."

Sam: "I love you, Joan."

Joan: "I love you, Sam."

Grieving the Loss of a Person

Another use of this method is to assist the grieving patient to further open up regarding the death of a loved one or the breakup of a relationship. In doing so, the patient is presented with or stimulated to look at happy experiences that he or she had or missed out on with the departed person in order to further move along the grieving process. In the following example, Jean, 53, grieved the sudden death of her husband. A goal of this method is to make grieving a winning process.

Jean: "I miss him so much. We had so much together" (staring ahead, very sad).

Therapist as Double: "I remember some wonderful times when Bob was alive" (and then acting out very briefly a few good times Jean had with her husband, having obtained information previously regarding this).

Jean: "I miss those great times. We could have done so much more together" (crying and further opening up also realizing the happy memories she would always have).

At other times it may not be necessary to improvise a situation, as the double reminding the patient of a happy time or times with a departed significant other is all that is needed.

As indicated, this method can also be used to demonstrate joys, highs and successes in life in order to stimulate the patient to experience feelings and thoughts about experiencing this, while stimulating one to realize winning experiences are possible.

THE JOINING THE CHILD WITH ONE'S SELF METHOD

The joining the Child with one's self method, referred to as joining the Child with one's self or joining, is the process whereby the person's emotionally healthy and operative Adult, emotionally healthy Parent and emotionally healthy Child as the Adult Nurturing Self go back to join the wounded Child in one's self when reliving a rejecting or other major experience in a session. This process is demonstrated by the therapist or therapeutic agent and is then practiced by the patient when needed. It points out that the reliving process for the adult is not one in which the patient regresses to a childhood or adolescent experience exactly as one was without the assistance of one's Adult Nurturing Self. However, the reliving process referred to here involves reliving an experience at a younger age from the prenatal period through adolescence in one's wounded Child as it happened or can be recalled, while the patient's Adult Nurturing Self is with one's wounded Child assisting it and integrating into it for rebuilding to occur. In the large majority of situations, the patient has the ability to recall what happened in his or her life under the appropriate circumstances, though when referring to the prenatal, birth and early childhood experiences, in addition to directly recalling events during this period, I have added the possibility of the patient believing what happened, though usually connected to or symbolic of real life events that did occur, or a combination of one's recall and belief. The Adult Nurturing Self doesn't interfere with the person's reliving of an experience, but provides the security, support, teachings, nurturing, spontaneity, inquisitiveness, intuitiveness, creativity, sensitivity to one's needs, feelings, thoughts and pain, rationality and sense of reality needed to relive an experience, and while being with the person's wounded Child, while reliving an experience, will interact with one's wounded Child in the way needed in working through this experience. This interaction can be a more passive to more active depending on what is needed. The Adult in the Adult Nurturing Self is the controlling ego state and, when mentioned in the examples in this book, usually represents the Adult Nurturing Self. This process can also apply when an adult is reliving a rejecting, negative unhealthy or traumatic experience in his or her past adult life, as adults are often in a regressed and childlike state and in varying degrees during such situations. In addition this process applies to children and adolescents as it relates to their specific situations.

When joining one's wounded Child, it is important to do so in a supportive, nurturing, loving, spontaneous, sensitive, creative, rational and reality oriented way. The Adult is utilized to assess reality in the past, to validate one's feelings, thoughts and emotional pain that need to be cleansed and released and to assist one's wounded Child to reevaluate cognitively, rationally and realistically what has happened in the past and to make healthy redecisions. The healthy Parent, incorporating teachings from healthy parental figures, provides the support, nurturing, love and knowledge the patient needs to heal him or herself. The healthy Child provides spontaneity, inquisitiveness, intuitiveness, creativity, sensitivity and an ability to feel, empathize and understand one's wounded Child's needs, feelings, thoughts and psychological pain. Only the healthy parts of the three ego states will assist in the reliving process, the extent of which depends on the dysfunction and maturity of the person. Of course, the therapist, therapeutic agent, group and family members will provide additional support, nurturing and reality testing. This method is not necessary for a number of patients and in this case can just be explained as part of familiarizing the patient with the rebuilding process. It can be used with those patients who require further understanding of this process in an experiential way to warm them up to the reliving process. Either way it is a good description of the reliving process.

In utilizing this method, the therapeutic agent acts in the role of the healthy Adult, Parent and Child to demonstrate the role of the three ego states and their joining one's wounded Child and then does so as the Adult Nurturing Self, with the patient following doing this. The concept of the Adult Nurturing Self is a way of bringing together the healthy Adult, healthy Parent and healthy Child in the reliving process, made up of the three ego states. Some may choose to keep them separate ego states in this process, which is an acceptable alternative. This is illustrated with a therapeutic agent as the healthy Adult, Parent and Child and then as the Adult Nurturing Self speaking to the wounded Child in the patient regarding a parent's mistreatment.

Healthy Adult: (speaking to the wounded Child in oneself): "I am the healthy Adult in you and will join you to assist you to heal and rebuild yourself from your mom's mistreatment whatever it was. I will give you my maturity, perception, thinking and my sense of reality to assist you to face and overcome how Mom treated you. I will bring reason and reality into what happened to you as needed."

Healthy Parent (speaking to the wounded Child in oneself): "I am your loving, nurturing and caring Parent who will also join you to provide support, caring, love, protection and what I know to take care of and guide you, when needed, but I won't rescue you. I am a caring and understanding Parent, not an unloving Parent."

Healthy Child (speaking to the wounded Child in oneself): "I am your healthy Child who will encourage and support your feelings, thoughts and needs. I am concerned about you. I can feel. I am curious, inquisitive, spontaneous, intuitive, creative and sensitive. I can understand and relate to what you feel, think and need and will be helpful as you need me. I understand you've been treated bad and have deserved better."

Adult Nurturing Self (speaking to the wounded Child in oneself): "Together, I, your healthy Adult, healthy Parent and healthy Child as your Adult Nurturing Self will provide you love, caring, support, protection, maturity, knowledge, inquisitiveness, sensitivity, spontaneity, intuitiveness, creativity, and mature perception, thinking, judgment, reasoning and reality, as needed, to assist you to face, make sense out of and rebuild yourself from your mother's rejection and mistreatment."

The patient is then asked to live out being the healthy Adult, Parent and Child and Adult Nurturing Self talking to the wounded Child in oneself to assist in this joining process and then to experience being one's wounded Child, with the therapist or therapeutic agent as the Adult Nurturing Self. The patient can also practice moving back and forth from the role of Adult Nurturing Self to wounded Child, as needed. The therapist, as the director in whatever his or her role, in looking at the overall situation, is always in the role of an Adult Nurturing Parent, which is the same entity as the Adult Nurturing Self. (See chapter thirteen on reparenting.)

In summary, the Adult Nurturing Self, in the process of joining one's wounded Child, steps into the wounded Child's domain and while there will experience what the wounded Child is feeling and thinking, though not interfering and remaining a separate entity with three ego states, encouraging and supporting the wounded Child with its own strength to deal with one's rejecting significant other or others or experience. Once doing this, the Adult Nurturing Self, also with its strength and assets, will assist the wounded Child, as needed, in the reliving and redecisioning process. When working with a child or adolescent, this method is modified according to the needs of the patient, with the healthy Adult referred to as the Developing Adult and the Adult Nurturing Self referred to as the Developing Nurturing Self. The terms *Developing Adult* and *Developing Nurturing Self* are used as needed.

THE BLENDING THE PAST WITH THE PRESENT METHOD

The blending the past with the present method, referred to as blending the past with the present or blending, helps the patient to connect, relate and integrate past attitudes and behavior with current attitudes and behavior. Typically, people relive in their current relationships and lives the attitudes, patterns, habits and ways they learned from childhood, adolescence and past experiences. If the patient is having difficulty in current relationships because of past feelings, thinking, attitudes and behavior, stimulating him or her to clarify, become more aware of, connect to and own these past feelings, thinking, attitudes and behavior can be accomplished through the blending method. In doing so, the therapist or therapeutic agent will represent the patient as a child or adolescent and then as an adult repeating the same dysfunctional attitude and behavior. This method can be introduced by surprise to impact the patient in a major way.

An illustration in individual therapy is Brad, a 39-year-old married male who was very rebellious and argumentative.

Therapist as Brad (at 13 years old to his mother): "I'm Brad at 13 talking to my mother. I don't have to listen to you. You can't tell me what to do. I can do anything I want. No one tells me what to do."

Therapist as Brad (at 39 years old to his wife repeating this in very similar words and even in a firmer and more immature way): "I'm Brad today talking to my wife. You can't tell me what to do. I can do anything I want. No one tells me what to do. I do what I want to and that's the way it is" (walking away from his wife with disgust on his face as he rebels against her as he rebelled against his mother when he was 13 years old. As Brad realized this, he became surprised and emotional).

Brad as Himself: "I can't believe it. I can't believe how I'm treating my wife. I'm treating her just like I reacted to my mother. I have to grow up. I must get over my mother's treatment of me. I'll lose my wife if I don't" (tearful and distressed).

This was a major breakthrough for Brad as he connected to a major source of his problem which he needed to overcome through hard therapeutic work. Of course, patients may pose some resistance or express denial in dealing with such situations.

DEALING WITH DREAMS AND FANTASIES

Rebuilding Therapy also helps the patient to face and work through the impact of dreams and any aspect of fantasy life using the psychodramatic methodology.

J.L. Moreno (1952), Nolte, Weistart and Wyatt (1977) and Wolk (1996) have referred to the use of Psychodrama with dreams. Haskell described his use of the dream technique in stimulating a person to reenact a reoccurring nightmare, which led to what it was representing in reality and then provided the patient the opportunity to psychodramatically work out his or her actual problems.

The goal of this approach is to identify who the character or characters in the dream represent and to determine the meaning of the dream so that the actual problem, which the dream symbolizes, can be dealt with therapeutically. Rebuilding Therapy in working with the patient's dreams stimulates the patient in a lying or reclining position to drift off, usually in a relaxation exercise with one's eyes closed, into a state of "sleep" without actually sleeping. Then the patient reexperiences part of or the major aspects of the dream with his or her eyes closed in this same lying or reclining position. The patient will initially reexperience the dream without the character or characters in it portrayed by another person or persons in the session. If this isn't effective then another person or persons in the session can be introduced to portray the character or characters in the dream. The patient will usually only act or live out the dream with one's eyes open, with another person or persons in the session in the role of a specific character or characters in the dream, if reliving it with one's eyes closed is not effective in uncovering the meaning of the dream and what it represents in reality. Once it is known who the character or characters in the dream represent and the meaning of the dream is determined, the patient is then asked to open his or her eyes if the dream had been relived with one's eyes closed. At this point the patient is asked to act or live out the actual experience, conflict, problem, concern or fear that the dream represents with another person or persons in the session usually in the role of the significant other or others in the actual problem situation. The patient will also have the option of keeping his or her eyes closed and living out the situation that the dream represents, with or without the significant other or others in the actual problem situation acted out audibly by another person or persons in the session, until he or she is ready to open one's eyes. Then the patient continues to live this out clinically as just mentioned, or continues with one's eyes closed living out the situation. As when reexperiencing any type of situation, alternative ways of dealing with this therapeutically can be utilized, with the therapist being as creative as is needed.

Whenever a patient is actually fantasizing or wishing about something and it is helpful for him or her to look at its future impact on one's life, he or she will be encouraged to act or live this out in the session, as with any experience or situation as needed. The patient will therefore have an opportunity to determine how realistic his or her fantasy or wish is and whether it is worth pursuing in one way or another, while gaining some confidence to do so. (See chapter eleven for discussion of the future projection technique.)

CHAPTER 9

Letting Go and Breaking Free Methods

The cage method and letting go method are letting go, breaking away and freeing methods developed to release and free the patient from the bondage and shackles of one's psychological pain and turmoil due to one's life style, life situation or past (the cage method) or one's dependence on a need, wish or dream to be loved as one needed and desired as a child and adolescent (the letting go method). The funeral method is also a letting go, breaking away and freeing method assisting the patient to mourn and let go of a deceased significant other or the end of a relationship. I have developed these methods for Rebuilding Therapy using psychodramatic techniques and methodology, though due credit is given to M. Haskell's psychodramatic grieving work which I developed the funeral method from Kaminski's (1981) "Good-bye Technique" has legitimate goals for the grieving process. However, his examples in family therapy appeared too talk oriented and not as psychodramatic as they needed to be, though family members were eventually able to address their deceased family member to let him go. Relaxation is used with these methods as needed.

THE CAGE METHOD

The cage method demonstrates to the patient how he or she is imprisoned in one's self, living out life in a "cell of hell" in a state of helplessness and hopelessness, with the goal of setting the patient free from this cage. It can be used with anyone who lives within one's psychological armor with such feelings as despair, sadness, guilt, fear, anger, rage, helplessness or hopelessness. The invisible cage constantly encloses the person wherever he or she goes, whether alone, in a crowd or physically close to another person. Even when a person is as intimate with another person as one can be, he or she is still much less intimate than is possible because of the cage one inhabits. The cage separates the "person" from the love, joy, creativity, meaningfulness, fulfillment, satisfaction and spirit of life one can experience, despite who loves and cares for him or her or what attempts are made to convince the person of the existence of hope and light in the world. The outcome of living in one's cage can be psychopathology, chemical and psychological addictions, eating disorders, family dysfunction, isolation, emptiness and hopelessness that nothing will get better. Some situations reach the point where self destructive behavior, suicide or homicide seem to be the only options.

David, a 35-year-old bachelor, is an example of this lifestyle. David lived alone and had never been married. Although he tried to stay away from his own apartment to get away from his feeling of confinement, he lived in a cage wherever he went. He had been physically and emotionally abused by his father, while his mother did not protect his siblings and him. His childhood was an ongoing saga of rejection and horror; he was locked in closets for long periods of time, and he was at times thrown out into the street in the cold. He would be brought back into the home only when his savage father allowed him to return. Nevertheless, his spirit never really died. He always hoped for liberation, love, intimacy and meaning in life, while fighting off the tormenting fears that he would lose control and go crazy with the tremendous despair, rage, guilt, hopelessness, fear and horror with which he was imprisoned. In his attempt to stand up to his father to liberate both himself and his family from this tyranny and abuse, he became the scapegoat and family sacrifice.

David lived in constant fear that others would experience the imprisoned angry, depressed, insecure, fearful, guilty and enraged side of him and reject him, even though he was liked and had made much progress psychologically. This method was introduced in a group therapy session when it became clear that David, as he expressed himself, had been imprisoned for life in a cell of emotional pain that had impaired his functioning and fulfillment and which he had tried to hide from himself and others. The therapist functioned in the role of the double and perpetrator because he was the only trained person available and because of the complexity of this method. Relaxation was not needed in this case.

Double (starting the process): "People like me, but my other side is still haunting me. It's imprisoning me."

David: "My evil side is haunting me. It really is. I hate it. I can't stand it. I feel so guilty." (appearing in severe anguish as he began to put his hands on the top of his head, like the prisoner of war he really was). "I have this loving side and this evil side. I hate it. I can't stand it. I'm afraid I'm going to lose control. I just can't get away from it."

Double: "I'm really scared. I'm very scared."

David: "I know I'm going to go crazy. I must keep it in. I have to" (holding his hands more tightly on his head and moving to a corner of the room).

Double: "I must stay here. There is no hope for me. If I keep myself locked up, everyone and I are safe."

David: "It's safer here, locked in myself. It's safer. No one can hurt me and I can't hurt them."

At this point, it was clear that David's imprisonment stemmed from his childhood need to protect himself from the emotional pain and adverse effect of his father's abuse and mother's neglect. A number of decisions contributed to his imprisonment. David continued to hold his hands on his head leaning against the wall in the corner of the room, symbolic of the armored cell in which he had enclosed himself. To help him decide to begin freeing himself, David needed to be stimulated to relive a major theme experience, representing many other experiences, that contributed to his imprisonment, with no specific age as the abuse was so chronic. A theme experience represents a theme or frequent replay of a major scenario or situation in one's upbringing or life, in David's case representing and being an integration of many experiences when he was abused by his father. A theme experience can be a major experience which occurred representing other experiences like it or an experience that is acted out that didn't specifically occur, but in either situation represents a major theme or feature of one's upbringing or life. Although the theme experience in David's case was not specifically experienced, the messages in it and the related feelings and thoughts were experienced in a major way when he actually lived through many experiences when his father abused him. David was psychologically in the state he was in when his father beat him, and so it was appropriate to immediately stimulate the actual reliving of an abusive theme experience as a child. In other cases, this method can be introduced when one is reliving a specific rejecting experience. Knowing David's history, the therapist as his father lived out hitting David with a belt, smacking a belt on a mat on a table which was placed alongside David. Symbolic of the loud noise of a belt hitting someone, the hitting of the belt on the mat immediately brought back memories of his father beating him with a belt.

David (continuing with his hands on top of his head in the corner of the room): "Please stop, please stop, don't hit me anymore, please!" (as the therapist as his father continued to bang the belt against the mat reliving his father's beating him as a child).

Father (yelling): "You're no good. You deserve this. I told you to shut up. I've told you to keep your mouth shut, didn't I?"

David: "Stop it, stop it. Please, stop it!" (continuing to plead with his father).

The double, realizing David would initially be resistant, began stimulating David to realize there was a way out for him. The double referred to David's father in the third person as David wasn't at first ready to address him directly in the second person of you.

Double: "I can't stand him. I would do anything to get away from him. I'd do anything."

David: "It's never going to change. It's always going to be this way" (continuing to enclose himself, putting his hands more tightly on his head and starting to shake).

At this time, it was important to stimulate David to become more connected to and fed up with the pain he was experiencing before he would finally decide to fight his way out of his cell of pain.

Double: "I can't stand this. I don't like this. I hate this pain I'm going through. I hate it."

David: "I can't stand this, the pain is too much for me, too much" (his body shaking increasingly).

Father (yelling out): "You're no good David. You've never been any good" (continuing to smack the belt on the mat on the table).

While David continued to sit in the corner of the room trembling, the therapist began to encourage other group members to provide stimulation and support for David to get out of his imprisonment. The therapist did this coming out of his role as father for about ten seconds. The therapist's movement from one role to another was not confusing to David and the group as they had become accustomed to this in previous sessions. In addition, this is what a therapist needs to learn to do since he or she often does not have others to assist him or her in an optimal way.

Group Member One: "You can get out of there, David. You don't need to let anybody beat you anymore. You deserve a lot better. Get out of there."

Group Member Two: "Don't be so afraid anymore. You can let go of your anger. You don't have to hold on to that poison in you. You can free yourself" (stimulating him to externalize his unhealthy feelings and thoughts to take control of himself rather than allowing them to control him and encase him in his own emotional cell of hell).

The therapist portrayed his father as a sadistic "jail keeper" to illustrate the actual prison of abuse David lived in throughout his life. In addition to stimulating David, the therapist as his father was also appealing to the group to encourage David to stand up to his father and work through his feelings and thoughts, which they did enthusiastically.

Father: "You really don't know what kind of person he is. He's no good. He's nothing but trouble. He deserves to be in prison for the rest of his life. He deserves every smack, every belt mark, every welt I give him. You can't save him. No one can. He's doomed" (while smacking his belt on the mat symbolic of the abuse David constantly experienced).

David (becoming increasingly agitated, gently kicking on the wall indicative of his turmoil): "I can't do anything. I'm afraid. I'm afraid I'm going to lose control. I'm going to go crazy. I've always dreaded going crazy."

Double: "I have so much anger in me. I don't know what to do with it. I'm afraid of it."

David: "I'm very scared of it. I don't feel I can handle expressing it without going nuts."

Group Member Three: "Please, David, stand up to him. Don't let him continue hurting you. Please, I love you. I've done it. You can do it. I lived the same way as you and got out."

David: "I can't. I'm afraid. It's too much. The anger is too much. I'll go crazy. You don't know what I'd be like if I went crazy. I'd break up the room. I'm scared. I can't do it!" (becoming increasingly agitated and raising his voice).

Double: "I'll disintegrate. I'll fall apart" (assisting him to face and work through his fear).

David: "There won't be any more of me. I will disintegrate" (crying for a few minutes).

Double: "But I can't go on living this way. I need to get out of this cage. The only way to begin doing this is to begin letting go of these feelings."

David: "I want to, but I'm afraid. I'm so afraid" (his crying subsiding, but fearful).

Double: "Maybe it's just safer here. At least I won't lose control" (confronting his resistance and fear by stimulating him to look at it again).

As in other examples, although other group members doubled one at a time, the therapist's doubling is only described here. The therapist assumed the rejecting role of his father, as needed. This is a condensed description of what occurred, as with other examples.

David: "It's safer here. At least I don't have to lose control. I have something, even if it's this."

Double: "Maybe I have more control than I think. Maybe I can get out of this jail cell."

David: "I'm afraid. I'm scared" (still resisting).

Double: "It's just too scary. I'd rather live in this hell forever than try to get out of it and risk losing control. I'll just put up with it."

David: "I can't really put up with this anymore, but I'm scared. I'm so scared" (beginning to look more at how damaging his imprisonment has been to him).

Double: "Can it get any worse? Possibly I have nothing to lose."

David: "I hate this hell. I don't want to go through it anymore. It's terrible, it's terrible."

Double: "Then maybe I'll take a chance on myself and believe my friends (other patients) here."

David: "I'll go crazy. I will. At least here I know what to expect. I'm used to it."

Double: "I'll just put up with this hell. So what if I never fall in love, if I never have a family. I'll just continue to live this way" (confronting the impact of such a decision).

David: "I've never had happiness, so I'll never miss it. It's hopeless. I don't know what to do out there, how to live out there anyway. I don't know what love is. I don't know how to love anyone. Who'd love me? This is all I know."

Double: "But I hate living this way."

David: "I do hate it, I hate it! I can't stand it, but I can't believe it will get any better. I want to believe it. I want to, but I'm so afraid of being hurt out there, of failing."

Double: "I'll just stay in this hell forever, for the rest of my life."

David: "I don't want to. I don't, but I'm scared."

Father: "You're no good. You'll never amount to anything. You're going to stay here for the rest of your life" (hitting the belt on the mat still conveying the theme of abuse and hopelessness, stimulating David to stand up to his father to get out of his cage).

David: "I want to get out of here, I really do, but I'm so scared."

Double: "If I stand up to him, he won't have anything to do with me" (stimulating him to look at another part of his resistance).

David: "I won't have a father any more. He'll disown me. I don't want to lose him" (crying again).

Double: "But he's never been a dad to me, a loving dad to me. He doesn't have a clue how to. David, open up directly to your dad. It's time to."

David: "He's really no good to me." (And then directly expressing himself to his father) "You've never been a Dad to me. I've been holding onto you and putting up with you hoping to get your love. You don't ever give it to me" (continuing to cry).

Double: "I really don't have anything to lose. I should separate from you" (further stimulating the separating and releasing process).

David: "I've been afraid of losing you when I've never had you" (still crying).

Double: "I've never had you love me."

David: "I've never had you to love me and I'm realizing this. I'm really realizing this now" (his crying decreasing, while becoming angrier, but still fearful and hesitant).

Group member Two: "David, I love you. I'll help you" (beginning to cry and joining David). "You can't let yourself go on living this way. Tell him you hate him and that he's wrong."

David: "I hate you, I hate you!" (his anger increasing). "I know I must let go of this rage, I know I must get away from him, but I'm still afraid."

As David's anger level with regard to his emotional pain and despair increased, he was becoming empowered to work his way out of his hell. Becoming more open to his feelings helped him to face the psychological pain he was in and raised his anger and protest level in the process. He went back and forth for about ten minutes, being angry and fearful. During this time, with much encouragement from group members, while the therapist in a timely way acted as his rejecting father hitting the belt on the mat with the same messages, David reached the point where he successfully worked through a significant amount of anger and rage.

David: (hitting on the mat with his hands with some pauses with a group member who related to him doing this with him): "I hate you, I hate you. You're a monster. I'm not going to let you treat me like this. I'm going to get out of my jail. I'm getting out of my cell. I'm angry! I hate you!" (with the group cheering him on for more than ten minutes).

As he worked through and expressed his anger on the mat on the table, he broke down in tears of sadness and relief regarding what he had been through. Also, as David came down from his high level of catharsis and freed himself of much poisonous rage, sadness and pain, he reached the point where he was cognitively ready to free himself from his father's imprisonment.

Therapist: "Stand up as straight as you can, feeling your strong legs and feet under you, your strong arms, hands and body and the emotional strength within you."

Double: "You or no one has a right to do this to me" (the therapist resuming as his double).

David: "You have no right to do this to me. I don't deserve this. You're the problem not me."

Double: "Of course I don't deserve this. I'm a good person!"

David: "I'm okay! I'm a good person. I'm okay. I'm okay."

Double: "Louder David. There's nothing wrong with me. No one will ever treat me like this."

David: "There is nothing wrong with me. There certainly is nothing wrong with me. I won't let you Dad or anyone treat me like this again" (with more authority and confidence).

Double: "I don't have to be in prison any more. I'm out of here."

David: "I'm free, I'm free, free to be me" (smiling tearfully).

Therapist: "Is he okay folks? Does he deserve freedom, love and happiness?"

Group: "Yes! He is okay. He deserves everything good" (with much enthusiasm).

David: "I know, I know. It's about time. I'm going to be a winner. I'm not going to let anyone take advantage of me anymore" (as the group embraced him and congratulated him).

A unique aspect of this method is that it illustrated to David, in his wounded Child, his predicament of being a prisoner in a cage of hell, whipped by the memories, feelings and thoughts of his past. It became clearer to David what he needed to do, providing further direction, stimulation and hope to break out of his dilemma. It was a challenging journey for David enduring the emotional pain and "sweat" of working hard and intensively in therapy. He had been in Rebuilding Therapy for a few months and had been building up to this major psychological release and breakthrough, as is often the case with any major breakthrough, although the time varies when a patient first accomplishes this. Despite his progress in this session, David realized he still had further therapeutic work to do.

Although other Rebuilding approaches may appear similar to the cage method in helping people to break away and rebuild themselves from the rejection of the past, the uniqueness of this method is that it illustrates to the patient, through experiencing it, that he or she has been in a cage of hell and despair, symbolic of one's life, and needs to get out of it to find any meaning and satisfaction in life. It also provides the patient this opportunity, while not having to at times, as in this case, to relive a specific experience. In some cases this method may need to be used more than once for the same patient. As other Rebuilding methods, this method can be used effectively in short-term therapy.

THE LETTING GO METHOD

The letting go method (letting go) was developed to assist the patient to let go of and give up the success of the wish, hope or dream that one's parent or parents will ever love him or her in the way that the child and adolescent needs and wants one's parent or parents to love, nourish and bring one up, a major goal of psychotherapy. It is accepted that most persons will continue to have this wish to be loved by one's parent or parents in a nurturing, healthy, intimate and loving way even if they are eventually assisted to realize the success of it will never happen. For simplicity, when speaking of one's parent, unless the plural form is used, with regard to this method and throughout the book, I am referring to one or both parents or parent figures. Frequently, parents lack the ability and emotional health to love and bring up their children in a healthy way. Despite being rejected, abused, neglected, mistreated, beat up or molested, it is very natural to hold onto the hope of eventually getting the love one never received from one's parent as a child and adolescent. However, what this method tries to accomplish is to assist such a patient to realize, though he or she may maintain this wish, that it will never happen.

The patient takes his or her Adult Nurturing Self, as described in the joining method in chapter eight, back into one's wounded Child to assist the Child to give up the success of this wish after reliving and working through a key experience of rejection and unfulfillment or a theme experience representing experiences of rejection and unfulfillment. In this way, the patient's wounded Child has the reality of his or her entire life to convince it that such parenting and love will never occur. However, this goal meets with significant and severe resistance by most patients. In fact, this resistance is often why individuals and families prematurely terminate psychotherapy, not wanting to deal with this issue, and continue to maintain their dysfunction. Letting go of the success of this dream is essential to the patient's well being, for one will usually not let go of dysfunctional ways and will never grow up and become the person he or she can be unless this is relatively accomplished. In addition, one will usually remain depressed and angry indefinitely waiting for something to occur which will never happen. This unfulfilled hope and need is a primary motivating factor driving persons to seek out dysfunctional relationships with a spouse or others, who often become a parent substitute or extension for the wished-for parent one never had, with this parental substitute often as rejecting as one's original parent. The spreading of this "disease" of mistreatment to children and others has tragic effects from generation to generation. Even when satisfaction is found with a spouse, who is a substitute for a rejecting parent, the damage from the person's upbringing still cripples the person's functioning and potential, with this relationship never being what it could be.

It is also natural for the majority of persons to go back to their dysfunctional families looking for the affection and acceptance they never received and will never get. Grown adults allow themselves to be mistreated, criticized or guilt-tripped while spending time with dysfunctional family members. They do this as a regular part of their lives during holidays, other special occasions or when a relative is sick or near death, hoping for that ultimate acceptance that often never comes. Even when it does come for fleeting moments or eventually becomes part of a relationship with a formerly rejecting relative, it in no way makes up for the mistreatment inflicted on the person in the past or heals the related wounds.

Although this method focuses on letting go of the success of the wish of being loved in a healthy way as a child and adolescent, it can be used to give up the success of the wish of ever being loved by one's parent if this is applicable. When it is used, the patient has usually relived and worked through a number or many experiences, issues and conflicts in therapy regarding a rejecting parent or parents. Letting go is a difficult process and involves a lot of hard work, fortitude, courage, persistence, psychological sweat and determination. It may involve using this method more than once along with other therapeutic work. Prematurely using this method could have the effect of avoiding facing certain experiences, conflicts, feelings and thoughts that need to be dealt with before letting go is possible.

An example in group therapy is Joanne, a 41-year-old divorced woman who reached the point where she was ready to let go of the success of the wish her mother would ever love her in a healthy way as she wished for and needed as a child and adolescent and still strived for in her adult life. Joanne was severely abused and neglected by her mother. She learned and decided to be a victim because that was all she knew, hanging onto the hope that she would be loved by her mother or someone like her in a healthy or in any way. As a result, she selected individuals and situations that brought back memories of her childhood, as she looked for extensions of her mother and usually was rejected in the process. Although Joanne's mother was still rejecting her, with Joanne seeing her mother infrequently in this strained relationship, she still made some unsuccessful attempts to gain her mother's acceptance, adversely affecting her functioning in the process. Previously she had spent a number of sessions facing and working through the rage and despair she had felt regarding her mother, while also changing her thinking in a healthy way. She was at a crossroads in her life, knowing she needed to give up and let go of the fulfillment of her wish her mother would love her in the way her wounded Child hoped for and needed, and as a result of to let go of the belief her mother or any mother substitute would love her in a healthy way in the way she needed from her mother in her upbringing. Of course, this would be an ongoing process after the use of this method.

With the assistance of relaxation after working intensively reliving, as a child, a major experience typical of her mother's rejection and neglect of her, experiencing and letting go of a significant amount of anger on the mat and after about fifteen minutes of crying, Joanne reached a point where the letting go method was needed. As she was coming down somewhat from her crying, the therapist asked her to close her eyes again and specifically experience her wish to be loved and cared for by her mother not being fulfilled again at this time. The therapist could have also given her other alternatives such as experiencing any other key significant time or a theme experience representing the major experiences of her mother's rejection and unfulfillment of her needs during her upbringing. A theme experience is one that may or may not have specifically occurred and is an integration of the themes and messages of major or key experiences, as indicated. The therapist can introduce this method at whatever time is therapeutic. Sometimes this method can be introduced through the double method with the double stating "I'm never going to have the love and kind of mother I've needed and wanted as I grow up," referring to the patient experiencing this as a child. The patient's specific age may be identified, but may not be due to the context of the situation. While Joanne reexperienced this, the therapist asked a group member, who had mistreated her children, to lie on the floor as Joanne's mother, symbolizing the death of the success of Joanne's wish of having her mother's healthy love as a child and adolescent. The therapist then asked Joanne to open her eyes and look at her mother lying there in the "coffin" of the "fulfillment of hope for her mother's love," which Joanne did.

Therapist: "There is your mother lying there in the coffin representing the death of any possibility she will ever love you in the way you always wanted and needed her to as she brings you up. You've never gotten it, you don't have it and you never will have it. It's over. It's over. The fulfillment of this wish has always been dead. The hope of having your mom love you as other children have their mom's love them will never happen for you. You have all of your upbringing experiences to confirm this, being whatever age you are again as a child as you allow yourself to begin letting go of the success of this wish."

At this time, the therapist instructed the other group members to hum in a low volume "Rock of Ages" in order to stimulate the mourning process regarding the death of the success of Joanne's wish for the healthy love she wanted from her mother in her upbringing. This is optional depending on how much stimulation the patient needs to work through this issue effectively. It can be introduced at whatever time during the session it will be most effective. Other songs or music can also be used. Joanne broke down crying again as a young child, while bringing the reality of her entire life into her wounded Child that she will never have her mother love her in a healthy way as she needed and wanted as a child and adolescent. It was important for Joanne to begin doing this at a young age when the influences from the parent are so powerful. Even if the patient didn't start this process at an earlier age, this method would still be effective as long as additional therapeutic work would continue to accomplish the goal of this method. In either case, additional therapeutic work is still needed to accomplish this method's goal, the amount of which will depend on the specific patient.

Therapist as Double: "She never really loved me in a healthy way, she couldn't, she didn't. She's treated me terribly. She's neglected me and ignored me. I never had a chance. And I just wanted you, Mommy" (pointing to her mother lying on the floor symbolizing the death of the fulfillment of her wish for her mother's love) "to love me" (while encouraging Joanne to now directly confront her mother, while she was still as a young child).

The double in this case usually should be a therapeutic agent or the therapist with more specialized doubling needed in this situation. The therapist doubled being the only therapeutic agent available. The therapist then specifically took the role of therapist in the use of this method, though always a therapist, but in different roles as needed, and then returned to doubling for Joanne.

Therapist: "Now talk directly to your mother and your unfulfilled wish that she love and care for you in the way you want and need her to."

Joanne: "You don't even take time for me and I'm a little girl. You yell at me when I want to be with you. You're always sending me off to play not even wanting me around. You hardly hug me or kiss me and when you do it feels like you don't want to. You don't want to help me play house or dress Julie" (her doll, continuing to cry).

Double: "You say such bad things to me" (knowing this from Joanne's revelations).

Joanne: "You call me such bad names and tell me you wished you didn't have me sometimes. You slap me and spank me. You hate me, Mommy" (as she went on to open up further for about five minutes regarding her mother's mistreatment of her as a young child).

Joanne then moved to an older age. Moving around to different age periods is common when using this method for it brings together the patient's childhood and adolescence and in a number of cases the patient's entire life, further reinforcing the point that Joanne never really had a chance to be loved by her mother. The rest of the session would further confirm this.

Joanne: "I remember trying to please you at everything I've done. I've tried to please you in dancing, in school and helping you in any way to make you happy with me. Nothing worked. Nothing" (having moved to an older age period).

Double: "You haven't let anything work."

Joanne: "It's impossible. It's been impossible. You're never happy with me. Whatever I do, it's never good enough. I remember trying to please you with my dancing. I came home so happy one time with a second place trophy from a dance contest you didn't even come to. You said you were disappointed I didn't get first place and that dancing wasn't important anyway as I couldn't earn a living from it. You've never felt good about me. There's nothing I can do for you to love me" (sadly, as she continued to look at her upbringing days).

Double: "You really hurt me. You hurt me so much. You have been hurting me throughout my growing up" (pointing out that this mistreatment was a theme of her upbringing).

Joanne: "You've devastated me. You've broken my spirit. Nothing I ever do is right. I'm always wrong. I feel I'm just a big mistake to you" (in an angry voice bringing in her childhood and adolescent years in her Child).

Double: "Rather than looking for the good in me, you look for the bad in me. You always have."

Joanne: "That's all you do. You have never been happy with anything I'm happy with. You're constantly tearing it apart. Then when I act up or talk back to you, you slap me and hit me" (continuing to cry and becoming increasingly angry as she opened up further).

Double: "I hate you for this. You're crazy. You put red marks on me. You break my heart." (In a raised voice) "How could you do all this to me?" (assisting her to further express her anger).

Joanne: "You have no right, no right to hit me this way. Just because your father abused you, you have no right to abuse me. Never. You should go to jail. I've tried to stand up for myself for what's right and you slap me more" (speaking to her mother as a child with her Adult continuing to assist).

Double: "You have to be in total control" (indicating the present, though implying any time).

Joanne: "Anybody who disagrees with you, you yell at, you criticize or beat up. You're a witch, a crazy, crazy witch" (with anger and sadness).

Double: "There's no way you can ever really love me. You just don't have it in you."

Joanne: "I still don't know why I love you. It's crazy. How can I love somebody who treats me like this. You've treated me worse than a slave, worse than an animal. But I still have loved you. I would have done anything to have you accept me and you've done these terrible things to me" (still crying in her Child, and integrating her life into this).

Double: "I have never learned how to like myself."

Joanne: "If my own mother can't love me, who could love me?" (continuing to cry).

Double: "I've hated myself all my life, though I'm a child now again looking at my entire life" (encouraging her to bring in major aspects of her life, with the assistance of her Adult, though encouraging her to remain in her Child at a childhood age, where possible).

Joanne: "Oh, how I have hated myself. You started this. You mistreated me and abused me. Oh, I'm so mad at you for this. Now I'm finally realizing what you've done to me. You really, have abused me. All the wasted years, the giving in to others hoping they would love me, letting them do what they wanted to me hoping that maybe they would accept some of me. You taught me to be abused and I fell for it" (as she also moved back and forth from the past to the present, as occurs with this method).

Double: "And with these people, I was just trying to get a piece of you."

Joanne: "That's what I was doing. I was trying to get love through them."

Double: "It's been a dream, a wish."

Joanne: "It's been nothing more than a dream. You really hurt me. You've never been there for me. It's been a big lie. You really betrayed me" (sadly).

Double: "Because you should have loved me in a healthy way" (implying healthy love as even abusive parents often have or believe they have love for their children in a number of cases).

Joanne (crying): "That's what a mother is supposed to do, love her child. And you don't. You just mistreat me. I don't have a chance. I'm not the problem, you are. You are. I'm never going to have you" (her Adult continuing to assist her at this young age she was experiencing herself being).

Double: "I need to bury the possibility and success of the hope of having you love and care for me as I needed you to as a child and teenager in a healthy and okay way."

Joanne: "That's what I'm going to do. I'm going to bury the possibility that you will ever love me or could love me. And I'm going to overcome this."

Double: "I need to let you go and say good-bye to you as the mother I've needed."

Joanne: "That's what I'm doing. That's what I'm doing. I'm finally doing this. I'm ready to stop believing you'll ever love me and be a mother to me."

Double: "I could kneel down and touch her or stay where I am expressing my feelings of good-bye."

Joanne (kneeling down): "It's time to let you go. You have never really been there for me. You'll never be here for me. The possibility of you loving me the way I have wanted you to is over. All you've done is abuse me (integrating her mother's mistreatment throughout her upbringing with her Adult's assistance). I'm sad, I'm mad. I still want it, I know I can't have it. I'm a confused kid, but I know I have to let you go. I can't have what I've wanted growing up with you. I learned a lot from you regarding what not to do. I'm realizing I've always been a good person and I'm not going to be like you" (not referring to her mother by name as she had done for the most part in the letting go process).

In other cases a patient may refer to his or her mother as Mommy or Mom or refer to his or her mother by her first name depending on the situation.

Double: "When I grew up the first time, I became just like you in some ways."

Joanne: "This time around, when I grow up, I'm going to love my kids in the way they need. I won't be a victim or mistreat them or anyone. And I'm going to let someone love me too" (her Adult continuing to assist her).

Double: "It's so sad that you haven't loved me in a caring and sensitive way."

Joanne: "I'm facing this. I'm realizing this. You've never been a mother to me. Thank you for giving birth to me. But that's not enough for me. That's not enough." (After crying for about five minutes she picked up her head saying) "Good-bye, good-bye. I'm freeing myself of you" (not touching the group member representing her mother, where in other cases a patient may choose to in some acceptable way).

Double: "I'm beginning to let you go. This is a big step, but I have more work to do on this."

Joanne: "There will always be a part of me that will want you and desire you, but I know it won't happen. And I still realize I have more work to do to realize this forever. Good-bye. It's time for me to go on. Good-bye."

Joanne turned her head and walked away to the embracing of other group members as she cried further. She was freeing herself from the shackles of her mother's psychological bond, which she held onto in her quest to be loved. As the session ended, the therapist reached out to her letting her know, "I'm another parent figure. I won't take your mother's place. No one will. However, you have me now, have had me and can have other healthy parent figures like me if you choose to," with Joanne returning the embrace.

In having the opportunity to live this out in her Child, from where she needed to let go of the success of this wish, as much as this method could assist her in accomplishing this while having the major aspects of her upbringing in front of her with her Adult Nurturing Self's help, she was able to further experience her mother's impact on her and the need to let go of the belief her mother could have loved her in the way she needed and wanted as a child and adolescent. While this method was utilized, though she moved around throughout her upbringing years she was able to station herself sometime in her childhood to begin letting go of the success of the wish of having her mother love her as she desired and needed as a child and adolescent. As a result, she was able to begin freeing herself of this belief. This opened up the door for her to live a psychologically healthy life and to develop healthy relationships, not substitutes for the parent she never had. This included no longer allowing herself to be mistreated by her mother, mother-like persons or any rejecting person. Joanne no longer needed to wait "for something" she would never get and remain emotionally a child and dysfunctional in the process. She still had significant therapeutic work to do, although this was a major breakthrough. A patient may need the use of this method again or engage in whatever therapeutic work is needed to continue this process.

THE FUNERAL METHOD

The Funeral Method assists the patient to face, grieve, work through and eventually overcome the death or departure of a significant other or separation from a significant other resulting in the permanent end of the relationship. Though used more frequently to mourn the physical death of a significant other, it has been designed to grieve the end of a marriage, romance, relationship or in some cases the death or loss of a pet or job. When mourning the loss of a job, its human qualities are dealt with. As with any method, modifications need to be made relative to the specific situation. Often part of the grieving process involves dealing with some type of dysfunction, mistreatment or problems the grieving patient experienced with the departed person or situation, though often the patient has done a significant amount of therapeutic work regarding the departed person or situation and its impact on the patient before this method is used. However, in some cases the patient may have only been in therapy for a short time needing to grieve or currently grieving a recent death or departure. For the purpose of describing this method, it will be described in terms of its use grieving the departure or separation from a significant other in the patient's life, though it can apply to other situations as indicated.

The patient is first stimulated to briefly relive a typical major problem experience or experiences and then briefly a major happy experience or least not an unhappy experience, if possible, regarding the deceased or departed person, referred to as the departed person. The reliving process continues leading up to the last time or a last major time the patient had contact with this person, the actual dying process or experience (referred to as the dying process or experience when a person dies) or departure whether or not this was directly experienced, the announcement or news of the death or departure and then experiencing the departed person in a simulated coffin or in another way or ways representing the end of the relationship. The simulated coffin process is used more frequently when mourning the actual death of a significant other, but it can be used with some patients who are open to and can visualize, for example, a former living spouse or lover as dead in a simulated coffin. In some cases, the order of the experiences the patient relives will change, depending on what the patient needs and is ready for. Although it would be helpful to use all aspects of this method, the patient is only asked to experience what he or she is ready and capable of doing and what is therapeutic. The living out of the actual dying experience is especially optional, depending on the patient's needs and whether he or she is ready for this due to the power of such an experience. As when reliving any experience, the significant others related to the major issues regarding the departed person, as pertinent to the patient's grieving, will be acted or lived out by persons other than the actual significant others, if it is possible and therapeutic for the patient to address such significant others, as needed, in this situation. Utilizing persons to portray significant others besides the departed person, as needed, usually only occurs in group or multiple family group therapy where there are enough persons to do this.

The departed person is acted or lived out by a therapeutic agent, often not the therapist, when possible, when there is a death, especially when acting out the dying process and the situation after the death. Another group member or patient, if helpful for this other patient in relating to an issue in his or her life and ready for this, can also act out the role of the departed person, though a patient often would have difficulty acting out the dying experience, if this is needed. A family member or significant other of the patient also taking part in the session is not used in the role of the departed person, as he or she needs to be in a supportive and doubling role, in this case, and may be too emotionally involved and nonobjective owing to the nature of this situation. Pertaining to death, the person acting as the deceased significant other briefly lives out with the patient and others participating as significant others, as needed when this occurs, those experiences when the deceased person was alive, as described, leading up to experiencing the dying process, as needed, and the deceased person in a simulated coffin or in another way or ways symbolizing the end of the relationship, as the patient is ready. The person acting as the deceased person will lie on the floor or on a couch representing the death position, though usually more often on the floor for logistic reasons. The death position may be the deceased person's position he or she was actually in immediately after his or her death, even if the patient didn't experience this, which most often occurs, the simulated coffin experience where the deceased person is seen in a simulated coffin or in a position representing the patient's death in some other way. If for example the first two death positions were lived out, the reliving of these positions is done separately with the position the deceased person was in when he or she died usually preceding the simulated coffin position whether in the same session or different sessions, if needed. Even if the patient didn't actually experience a specific event, in this case regarding the deceased person's death, he or she was still living one's life while this occurred, having feelings and thoughts about this that still need to be addressed.

Though the therapist, as needed, can effectively function in the role of a significant other such as the deceased significant other while he or she was still alive, the therapist will usually not act out the dying process and the significant other's death as it becomes an even more complex issue when mourning the death of a loved one. This is because if the therapist's eyes are closed acting out the dying process and the situation after death, he or she would not be able to fully direct the session. However, further explanation is needed to support the need for the therapist to act out the dying process if he or she is best able to do this, while it is also best for the person acting out the dying process to be the same person portraying the deceased person after death. There are many cases that have demonstrated, as described, when if there is no other therapeutic agent available, or the therapist can live out the role of a significant other who the patient is addressing more effectively than others in the session, that the therapist should do so. This is because the effective acting out of a significant other's role, when utilized, as discussed in chapter six, is so important in stimulating the successful living out or reliving of a situation. Although ideally it is preferable to have someone besides the therapist living out the role of a significant other, especially when dealing with the significant other's death, the therapist needs to do what is in the patient's best interest. As a result, in very limited situations, when using the funeral method in a session with a patient who is ready and when it would be helpful, it is feasible for the therapist, as needed, to live out the role of a deceased significant other when he or she was alive and also after this during the dying experience and after his or her death if a co-therapist, also in the session with expertise in the use of the funeral method, could take over the therapist's role during the dying process and after the death. This would be necessary as the therapist portraying a deceased person's death with his or her eyes closed would not be fully able to monitor the therapy process and direct the use of this method in the session, as indicated, though with the expertise of a co-therapist the session could still progress effectively. The only exception to this when there isn't a co-therapist with expertise in the use of this method in the session, though there is a co-therapist or auxiliary agent in the session or usually at least a responsible person in the session, is when the therapist because of his or her acting ability and skill lives or acts out the dying experience in this case in a very quick but realistic way and remains on the floor as the deceased person for a very brief period (about five to fifteen seconds). In doing so, it occurs so quickly, for example living out being in an accident, having a heart attack or the end of a slow death, that the therapist as the deceased person can quickly get up and remove oneself from the situation and not lose overall direction of the session. In addition this further minimizes the possibility that the patient will be distracted by this process, if skillfully done. Also, the patient in this case has often been so strongly stimulated to reexperience the significant other's dying, that he or she is then so strongly concentrating on this situation that the therapist moving from living out being dead to being alive is usually not a distraction. Although the patient is in a strong state of concentration at other times when reliving a situation that doesn't involve death and the therapist or therapeutic agent moving from one role to another role, as needed, such as from the role of a significant other to that of a double, doesn't usually distract the patient, the importance of the patient being in a strong state of concentration and not being distracted when using the funeral method in this way needs to be pointed out. Again, the especially very small number of situations when this specific use of the funeral method should be utilized is when the therapist's ability to act out the dying process or experience is essential to the reliving process, while carrying out the procedures that have been described.

When it is not feasible or therapeutic for the therapist to act out the significant other's dying experience and the situation after death when it is best for the therapist to portray the departed person when he or she was alive, there are other alternatives. Such alternatives are utilizing another therapeutic agent to act out the dying experience and the situation after death or just the situation after death or another patient, who relates to the grieving process, to portray the deceased person, for example, in a simulated coffin. This is usually not distracting or confusing to the patient as the patient is very focused on what he or she is experiencing. Another alternative is using the visualization method stimulating the patient to experience the deceased person dying and after death or just the deceased person after death in some way or ways. When the visualization method is used, the patient can have one's eyes closed or open depending on the patient's needs, although closing one's eyes is usually more powerful. The therapeutic chair method can also be used to stimulate the patient to visualize the deceased person in some type of death position or positions after death. In addition, the importance of having alternatives such as this is that the therapist has other ways of using this method when he or she is the only therapeutic agent or trained person in a session.

When the patient experiences the departed person lying in a simulated coffin or in a death position in another way or in a position of departure such as being with a new lover, whether the departed person is portrayed by another person or not, the therapist or therapeutic agent may also speak as the departed person's spirit. In this situation, the therapist or therapeutic agent as the deceased person's spirit stands behind the grieving patient or out of sight of the patient raising questions the patient will need to answer in some way and expresses feelings or thoughts the departed person would express, if this was possible, to stimulate the patient to open up further. When a co-therapist or auxiliary agent acts out the role of the deceased person, including being the deceased person in a simulated coffin or in some death position, the therapist will usually function as the deceased person's spirit as in the upcoming example. When another patient or group member acts out the role of the deceased person in a simulated coffin or in some other death position or position of departure, the therapist or therapeutic agent will usually act as the departed person's spirit. At times, as needed, as with one person acting in the role of the deceased person when alive and another person acting in the role of the deceased person when and after he or she died, the patient is usually not distracted when different persons, for example, act as the deceased person in the simulated coffin and as the deceased person's spirit. The therapist in the role of the deceased person while he or she was alive, who doesn't live out the deceased person dying and the situation after death, may also be the deceased person's spirit. Bringing in the deceased person's spirit in this way can also be done when no one other than the therapist, for example, is representing the deceased person.

When the patient isn't ready to experience the acting out of his or her deceased or departed significant other by another person during any part of this process, then the therapeutic chair or visualization method can be used. More often a patient will have more difficulty experiencing the deceased person acted out by another person during the dying process and after the death. This method, as any method can be used in various ways or in a more limited way. Whenever a patient has difficulty and isn't ready to experience the deceased person in a lying down death position, this person can be portrayed in other ways such as standing or sitting with one's back to the patient, for example. The therapist can be as creative and therapeutic as is needed to reach the desired goals. (See chapter two regarding the use of relaxation which can be utilized with various methods as needed.)

The major goals of this method are to stimulate the patient to express, work through and let go of despair, sadness, guilt, anger and other feelings related to the person's departure; to have specific questions answered regarding the departed person's life and self, the patient's relationship with the departed person and its impact on him or her; to tell the departed person "things" one did not have an opportunity to; to learn from the departed person's mistakes and one's own mistakes in this relationship; to recall the good times and strengths of the departed person; and eventually to say good-bye to the departed person. Such goals and whatever is applicable regarding them can be utilized when grieving the human factors regarding the loss of a job or leaving or departing from some other situation.

An example of this method in group therapy is Alicia, 28, who was very despondent over her workaholic father's premature death after he suddenly died of a heart attack. He smoked excessively and was overweight. She never had a close relationship with him until the last year of his life, but it was never what it could have been. He provided her material things but not the loving closeness of a father. She briefly relived a major experience typical of her father's neglect of her, with the help of relaxation and opened her eyes while reliving this experience, and then relived a happy experience with her father in his last year of life. Following this she reexperienced one of her last major contacts with her father when she appealed to him to take care of himself, with a therapeutic agent, who was in the session in addition to the therapist, in the role of her father.

Alicia: "Dad, I wish you would take care of yourself. It scares me the way you smoke and don't care about your diet."

Dad: "I'm okay. I've been smoking all my life. I might as well enjoy my life while I have it."

Alicia: "But, Dad, it's going to kill you. You are overweight and you eat the wrong foods."

Dad: "I want to enjoy my life. No one is going to tell me what I can eat or do with my body."

Alicia: "But, Dad, I love you and I don't want to lose you. We finally have gotten close."

Dad: "Don't worry. Dear, everything will be okay."

Alicia (in soliloquy): "I love him, but I'm afraid I'm going to lose him. We finally have a close relationship. I don't know what I'll do if he dies. He's only 51 years old. I'm so afraid that he is going to die, that something will happen to him" (her eyes becoming watery).

Therapist as Double (being the most effective person in this role): "It even makes me angry."

Alicia: "It makes me very angry, but there is nothing I can do. He has been this way all his life and he is not going to change. Some people live until their 60's or 70's like him. Maybe he'll be one of those lucky ones. I can't think any other way or I'll drive myself crazy."

Alicia was then stimulated to relive the phone call she received from her hysterical mother telling her of her father's sudden death. The therapist asked Alicia to role reverse and become her mother.

Alicia as Mother: "Your Dad's dead. He died of a heart attack" (starting to cry openly). "He was looking so good. He even promised to stop his smoking. I thought things were going to get better. Now he's dead." (Alicia was then asked to return to being herself still crying.)

Alicia: "No, no, it can't be, it can't be. I was afraid this would happen, but I didn't want to think about it. I prayed he would live, but it's over, he's dead. I don't want to believe it" (sobbing).

While she was coming down from her crying after a significant catharsis regarding the news of her father's death, though still tearful she was then stimulated to reexperience the time she saw her father lying in his open coffin. Alicia was encouraged to move from one experience to another to maximize her expression, while not inhibiting her opening up from the previous experience and utilizing her opening up from the previous experience to stimulate her opening up in the next experience she relived. As Alicia briefly relived a typical neglectful experience and a happy experience, there was time to relive the experiences pertaining to her father's death described in this example. The therapist, always sensitive to the patient's needs, may determine that one or a few relived experiences is all the patient can handle. If this is the case it would usually be an experience or experiences directly regarding the person's departure. Often the simulated coffin experience or the departed person being in a position of death or departure are powerful in their own right. Acting out only a dying experience may be too powerful and overwhelming if just used on its own. The therapist or therapeutic agent, standing behind the patient or out of the patient's eye contact as the deceased person's spirit and interacting with the patient, as described earlier in the discussion of this method, is a powerful approach that can be used alone or with other parts of the funeral method.

If, in a death, it was a closed coffin, the patient is encouraged to see one's significant other through the coffin or is stimulated to experience him or her in an open coffin even if this did not actually occur. The open coffin is preferred because it more openly brings out the reality of the death. If the patient has an issue regarding why the coffin was open or closed, this can be dealt with or taken up at another time if necessary. Perceiving the deceased person in the "coffin", portrayed by an actual person, is encouraged because it is very important for the patient to see and experience the deceased person's physical body in the coffin before being buried or cremated to provide the concrete reality and "proof" helpful in facing and beginning to accept the person's death. Similarly, in grieving the loss of a nondeath relationship, perceiving the departed person in a simulated coffin further symbolizes the actual end or death of this relationship.

To begin reexperiencing her father in an open coffin, the therapist asked Alicia in a very unintrusive way to turn away, while the therapeutic agent who had been acting as her father when he was still alive, was asked to lie on the floor representing her deceased father lying in his coffin. In this case, Alicia did not need to experience the process of her father dying of a heart attack. In other cases, this has been helpful to the patient's grieving even when the patient didn't directly experience the dying and death process, as has been indicated. The therapeutic agent representing her deceased father lying in his coffin was sufficient to bring back this experience for Alicia. As she turned around seeing him lying there, she resumed crying in a more intense way with the therapist doubling. At this time or at another other significant time in the session, the therapist can also, as needed, instruct the other group members to hum "Rock of Ages" or another song to further stimulate the mourning process, although this wasn't necessary in this case. In individual therapy, the therapist can periodically do this between other roles.

Alicia: "Daddy, Daddy, why did you have to die? I loved you. We finally had a chance to become close and you left me. I am angry at you. I am so mad at you. I'm so sad. If only you would have taken care of yourself. I asked you, I begged you. You'd still be here."

Double: "I'm really angry with you."

Alicia: "I'm very mad at you" (raising her voice, yelling at him and continuing to cry).

Double: "I had you for such a short time."

Alicia: "You weren't there when I was young. Your life was your work. You didn't even know who my teachers were, what courses I was taking. I never had the father I needed."

Double: "And now you're dead, now you're gone."

Alicia: "I'll never have you. I had you for awhile and then you left again" (still crying).

Double: "I am angry at you. I'm so mad at you."

Alicia: "I'm very angry and I don't feel guilty anymore. I have a right to be angry. I really do" (as she continued to work through her anger and sadness for a period of time. As her sobbing became softer and slower, the therapist standing behind her representing her Father's Spirit, called out).

Therapist as Father's Spirit: "Alicia, Alicia, this is your Dad speaking. Just imagine what I could sound like if I could talk to you. Express to me anything you want to express to me, anything you need to express to me. Ask me anything you want to ask me. Go ahead, Alicia." (this was done to further stimulate Alicia to open up and to raise questions that she needed answers to, or some closure for, to resolve conflicts or issues regarding her father's death).

The therapist assumed this role because of its complexity. The concept of Father's Spirit, which I refer to as utilized by Haskell, is optional depending on the situation.

Alicia: "Why didn't you care about yourself?"

The therapist, as her Father's Spirit, reversed the question back to Alicia for she, as his daughter and the one grieving his death in the session, was the most likely person to answer the question accurately and other questions pertaining to his death, their relationship and his life. Role reversal could also be used, in this case, with Alicia becoming the Father's Spirit as needed.

Father's Spirit: "Do you really feel I didn't care for myself?"

Alicia: "Yes. You really didn't care" (expressing her frustrations regarding his self-neglect).

Father's Spirit: "Why don't you think I cared?" (the second part of the question).

Alicia: "I know Grandma pushed you and was never happy with anything you did" (crying). "It seemed like you always wanted to please her. But there was also something in you that didn't want to please her, which made you sabotage yourself. It was like you just didn't care about yourself. That's sad, Dad, because you were such a good man. Because of her, you never let yourself be yourself or get close to anyone. I am angry at her, but I'm angry at you, too, for letting it happen. I saw the good in you. I saw it in that last year we were close. I remember some really good times we had. They were great, but it was too short of a time. You didn't give me enough of yourself. I'm sad, but also angry with you Dad" (as she continued to express her anger and sadness regarding her father's neglect and soon stopped her crying).

Father's Spirit: "If you are still upset with me or are upset with me for anything else, please express it" (to assist her to continue opening up).

Alicia: "I'm upset with you for not being there for me for so long and neglecting yourself. When you were there, you were great" (and continuing to open up for a short period).

Another important part of grieving is stimulating the person to rid oneself of or to decrease any existing guilt if this exists. Alicia needed to continue letting go of her guilt, which was encouraged.

Father's Spirit: "Do you blame yourself for anything you did before I died?"

Alicia: "I felt very guilty for being angry with you and at times for not wanting to see you. I didn't feel I had a right to be angry at you as you were my father. However, I realize now I've always had this right. You hurt me very bad" (as she opened up further for a short time regarding this).

Father's Spirit: "I hope you can forgive yourself for something you don't have to forgive yourself for and just accept that you have had a right to be angry" (which hopefully her father would say as a reasonable person, if he could, or if she didn't feel he would to deal with this accordingly).

Alicia: "That's what I am doing. I am forgiving myself, though I really don't need to" (taking a deep breath with a sense of relief).

Father's Spirit: "Is there anything else that you blame yourself for regarding my life or my death?"

Alicia: "No, I believe I was a good daughter to you. If anything, you let me down. You weren't the father I needed when I was growing up. But I love you anyway. You were at least good to me in your last year. There were some good times" (crying again).

As she came down from her crying again, the therapist continued as her Father's Spirit.

Father's Spirit: "Is there anything else you want to express to me or ask me? Go right ahead."

Alicia: "No, that's it. That's it."

Father's Spirit: "We'll remember the good times we had, but be open regarding your frustrations with me."

There was now a brief silence with the therapist knowing it was time for Alicia finally to say good-bye to her father. And if this was not the time, it would soon become clear. Alicia had previously worked therapeutically on her relationship with her father and was ready to let go. When it is not time to let go, the mourning process needs to continue.

Father's Spirit: "It's time to let me go, it's time to say good-bye. If you need to come up to my casket and touch me or embrace me in some way, that's okay."

Some patients reach out physically to their deceased loved one, acted out by a therapeutic agent or person lying in the simulated casket, while others do not. However, the patient should be given the opportunity to do so. Touching the deceased person, whether it is holding one's hand or embracing him or her, is a way of making a last contact before letting go, while bringing out more of the reality of the death. Some patients find this physical contact very effective, while others are not ready or comfortable with such physical contact. However, giving the patient an opportunity for such physical contact gives one an opportunity to let go of his or her significant other in as realistic and "feeling" way as possible. Alicia knelt down to her father, represented by the therapeutic agent lying on the floor, and held him sobbing.

Alicia: "Good-bye, Dad. I really love you. I need to let you go. Good-bye. Good-bye" (crying again for a few minutes, and then physically getting up and separating from him).

Father's Spirit: "Good-bye, good-bye Alicia" (representing the departure of her father from her life).

After Alicia said good-bye to her father, the therapist opened and closed the door of the therapy room, further reinforcing her father's departure from her life. As Alicia began to stop crying the therapist physically reached out to her as a gesture of support. Alicia needed and wanted this, although some patients may instead prefer to be embraced by another group member or another therapeutic agent, or they may need more time to be by themselves.

Such a process can occur in one session if the patient has previously worked on this issue, but often more than one session will be needed, sometimes going over some or even much of what was worked on in a previous session. Even after saying good-bye the patient may find out that he or she needs further work on the grieving process and may need to use this method again.

In a number of cases this method will bring out additional feelings, thoughts, experiences or issues to deal with as other methods will. In this light, and as additional therapeutic work is still often needed, a patient may need to work more deeply on issues he or she had with the deceased or departed significant other, further work through the grieving process, as indicated, or work on other issues.

CHAPTER 10

Confronting Resistant and Sabotaging Behavior

The denial method, the hostility method, the spell method and the silent night method are confrontation methods to shock, confront and alert the often resistant patient into experiencing how his or her attitude and behavior are adversely affecting oneself and others. As with all methods the therapist needs to have the patient's trust when utilizing the confrontation methods. These methods are presented to the patient by surprise to catch the patient off guard in order to shock him or her into experiencing and feeling the damaging and sometimes destructive impact of his or her attitude and behavior on oneself and others. They may be repeated, as needed, in the way that is therapeutic, though the surprise factor may decrease to a certain extent. As with any method, the patient can reject using these methods at any time. Relaxation or relaxation exercises for the most part are not used when these methods are being utilized as the patients needing these methods are often outwardly resisting helping themselves. These methods can be used in some cases, while a patient is in a state of relaxation, when he or she for the most part is motivated to help oneself, but is resisting or has a blind spot in a certain area. These methods have been developed for Rebuilding Therapy using psychodramatic techniques and methodology. (Other confrontation methods are described in chapters eleven and twelve.)

THE DENIAL METHOD

The denial method portrays to the patient how he or she is avoiding facing one's feelings, emotional pain, thoughts, problems, conflicts, experiences, behavior or interpersonal relationships. It demonstrates the impact and poisonous effect of the patient's denial system and how it prevents one from facing the issues that are contributing to his or her problems, which are damaging and, in some cases, will destroy one's life unless faced, dealt with and treated. The goal of this method is to assist the patient to begin giving up his or her denial.

This method is especially helpful when a patient has little or no insight into what he or she is doing to avoid one's problems, with such avoidance further reinforcing the patient's pathology. At this point the therapist or therapeutic agent becomes Mr. Denial or Ms. Denial, depending on the patient's sex, and acts out what denial is and how it affects the patient. An example is Al, a 45-year-old married male whose denial is portrayed by the therapist as the only therapeutic agent in an individual session.

Mr. Denial: "I am Mr. Denial and I make all your pain go away. I also make all your problems go away. You're not going to have anything to worry about. Anytime there is any threat of pain, tears, sadness or that you're wrong, I stomp on it. I step on it immediately. Anyone who tries to bring it up, whether it be a friend, a brother, a sister, your wife, your son, your daughter or your therapist, I make sure you throw the blame or problems back onto them. I make you tell them that they're crazy, that something is wrong with them or that they have the problem, but I never let you ever believe that you have the problem or those feelings they claim you have. I am so effective that I even make your wife believe that she is wrong when in fact you're wrong. I do it in such a sneaky way she never knows you're doing this to her until it's done or some time later. I'm a magician at preventing you from taking responsibility for anything you do wrong or from facing anything that bothers you. Don't worry. I take care of you. So what if I lie to you. So what if I make excuses for you. So what if I even manipulate you into feeling you're feeling one thing when you are really feeling something else. So what if you don't even know I'm doing this to you. I even tell you that you are treating your wife well when in reality you are rejecting her and manipulating her. I make you tell her that you love her, when in fact you are bullying and manipulating her. So what if you won't know the difference, you'll put the blame on her. I make you guilt free. I make you provoke her to get mad at you to give you an excuse to be angry with her and blame her. I make sure that you're right about everything and that you can never do anything wrong. I always make you a winner in the world of battle. I give you an answer for everything. Don't worry, you can pull me out of your hip pocket anytime. As long as I'm in control, you'll never have to change. It is everyone else who will have to change. It will be just like you're living in Utopia. You're right and everyone else is wrong. I give you power. I even give you self-esteem. I make you feel that you're Mr. Universe and that you are God's gift to the world. I create such a fairy tale for you that you believe it, and you even convince others to believe it. I can develop such a good denial and excuse system for you that people will have difficulty seeing through it, at least for a while. If they do I'll give you justification to get them out of your life or make them feel they're wrong. I have all kinds of techniques that really work. So what if your life has just been a show to make yourself feel better and to avoid your pain because you're fearful to face it. So what if you don't allow yourself to be in love, to develop into your full potential or to live fully. So what if your drinking is ruining your life. So what if your wife leaves you because I won't let you face what is bothering you and that you need to change. Again just make sure you blame her. I give you an excuse and reason for everything. So let me control you. Give me ownership of you. So what if I take your soul from you. You won't know the difference anyway."

After initially laughing at this, denying this was him and putting up significant resistance, Al finally broke down:

Al: "I can't believe this. This is me. I don't want to keep lying to myself. I thought I knew what I was doing. I better start waking up. I'm really ruining my wife's life" (close to tears).

Double: "I am also ruining my life. I really am" (therapist also assuming this role).

Al: "I'm messing myself up bad. If I don't stop this garbage I'll lose everything, everything. I got it, how I'm affecting my wife and my children. I'm finally beginning to get it."

Once this is presented to the patient, he or she is usually awakened to how denial is contributing to one's dysfunction and its impact on oneself and others. It may not be necessary for this presentation of denial to be so long if the patient gets the message after a briefer presentation of it. Also, in other cases, it maybe helpful to stimulate the patient to confront one's denial lived out by the therapist or therapeutic agent. Asking the patient to role reverse and become his or her denial and then becoming oneself to confront one's denial is another form of this method. Role reversing and becoming one's denial may be used in addition or as an alternative to how it was presented here.

If denial doesn't work effectively avoiding, burying or hiding from one's problems, feelings, thoughts, emotional pain or past memories, then turning to alcohol, drugs or any addiction or escape are alternative forms of denial that Mr. or Ms. Denial will strongly support. This is illustrated in chapter twelve in describing the drug method.

THE HOSTILITY METHOD

The hostility method demonstrates to the very angry person, who holds onto his or her anger, the poisonous effect of hostility on oneself and others. It is a video replay of the person's anger and rage as utilized in the mirror method, but it goes further, focusing primarily on the person's hostility, how it is played out, how it affects others and oneself and the payoffs for not releasing it. The hostility method is effectively used with persons who are addicted to an angry and resentful way of life in order to maintain their psychological equilibrium. The goal of this method is to stimulate the patient to begin giving up this self-defeating behavior.

This method will now be described. Pam was a 44-year-old separated female who held on to her anger to protect against her internal conflicts and emotional pain and to feel empowered to deal with others, as is often the case. As she lacked awareness of the damaging impact of her anger on herself and others, she needed to be confronted with it. Pam had been married twice, with her last marriage breaking up because of her angry outbursts and chronic complaining and blaming.

Pam: "I'm so mad. He's always trying to screw me over. I'm going to get him. Nobody is going to mess with me. Who does he think he is? If he thinks he's hurt me, I'm going to hurt him a lot worse. I'll get him. I'll get him" (referring to her estranged husband).

The therapist became Pam's anger, as he was the only therapeutic agent in a group therapy session she was in, and as he could most effectively use this method.

Therapist as Her Anger: "I am your anger. I am your hostility. I am your rage. I'm really in control of you. You have no control of me. I take care of you and everyone else around you. No one's going to be able to touch me or get to me because I'm bigger than everyone. I'm strong. I'm powerful. If anyone messes with me I mess back with them. I criticize them. I blame them. I bully them. I don't have to hit them. My words will get them. This way no can hurt me. No one can hurt me with my power. I won't let anyone hurt you, Pam. No one will. You've been hurt enough. That SOB husband of yours, I'll take care of him. He'll be sorry he messed with us."

The therapist used the term *us* this time to emphasize the partnership of her hostility with her thinking and herself in order to stimulate Pam to take control of her anger rather than for it to control her. The first person "I" was used by the therapist to identify and emphasize the *identity* of the anger and hostility within Pam, which was of course Pam's anger and hostility.

Anger: "If you don't have me I won't be here to protect you. I'm your armor. I'm your strength. I'm your defense. Without me you're raw, you're vulnerable. I'm your best friend. You don't need to trust anyone. You have me Ms. Hostility."

After initially defending her anger in a dialogue with it, lived out by the therapist, she began to experience its impact on herself and others.

Pam: "I can't believe that you're a part of me (her anger), that I'm so mean, so desperate."

Anger: "You need me Pam. Without me you're weak. You'll get walked over the way your father walked over you. You have to stay tough. You can't trust anyone or they'll get you."

Pam: "You're that terrible side of me. I don't like you. You make me an ugly person."

Anger: "That's right. I'm bad. I'm mean. I'm ugly so no one will hurt you."

Pam: "But I don't want to be this way anymore. I'll take my chances without you because you mess up too many things for me. You push people away."

Anger: "You and I push people away. We're a team. We get them before they get us. That way we're in control. I'm you and you're me" (encouraging her to own her anger, as she had started to acknowledge this).

Pam: "You are me and I am you. I am a very angry person. And I don't want to be this way anymore. I do push people away with you. I push people far away with my anger" (increasingly owning her anger).

Because the therapist no longer needed to live out her anger, he became her double informing her of this, as is usually the case when the therapist shifts from one role to another. The therapist became the double as she needed his assistance as a double at this time and he could most effectively provide this.

Double: "My anger is poisoning me."

Pam: "My anger is ruining my life."

Double: "Being angry like this is no good for me."

Pam: "It's terrible for me. It's destroying me. My anger has been my enemy."

Double: "I'm taking control of it, of myself" (further integrating her anger as part of herself).

Pam: "I must take control of my anger or it will continue to control and sabotage me. I am taking control of myself. I don't want to be this way any longer. I don't want to be such a witch. I hate it. I hate me this way" (crying).

Pam decided to give up this side of her, but had much therapeutic work to do to reduce her anger level to the point where it would no longer impair her functioning. As with any method, the patient may resist more. As an alternative or in addition, the patient may be asked to role reverse and become his or her anger to experience what it is made up of, its poison, its "stink" and its impact on others and oneself. In doing so, the patient puts oneself into the eye of the storm to feel and touch it in order to assist in defusing and then decathecting it. The patient can role reverse back to being oneself to confront and weaken one's hostility, and continue this process and dialogue as long as is necessary.

THE SPELL METHOD

The spell method demonstrates to the patient how a significant other in his or her life still has a powerful effect on one's feelings, thoughts, attitude and behavior. This method is another therapeutic confrontation method, presented to a patient who is denying or resisting facing the impact of an important relationship, person or issue on one's life and how this is negatively affecting him or her. It is helpful when the denial method hasn't worked or when a more powerful method is needed to confront the patient's resistance. In doing so, the spell method, as other confrontation methods, is presented to the patient while he or she is not expecting it, catching him or her off guard to make the shock impact more powerful. The spell, for example, being the powerful and witchlike influence of a significant other, such as a parent, on the patient is presented to the patient by the therapist or therapeutic agent living out the significant other's influence on the patient. Presenting this influence, while the patient is not expecting it, allows it to penetrate the patient's strong defenses, bringing into one's consciousness the effect of this person on him or her.

An example is Martin, 53, who was having serious marital problems with his wife and was strongly influenced by his relationship with his guilt provoking and overprotective mother. He was not being sensitive, empathetic or loving to his wife, and he was mistreating her as his mother had mistreated him. In fact, he was spending excessive time with his mother with the excuse that he needed to look after her since there was no one else available to do so. In a joint marital therapy session with his wife Helen, 53, Martin was very critical of her. During the session, the therapist intruded with the spell method, acting as Martin's mother, while knowing he had the trust of the patient, as is needed when using any method, though especially with a confrontation method.

Therapist as Mother: "This is your mother, Martin, you know that Helen is really no good for you. You know that I'm the only woman in the world who really cares about you. Nobody can take my place. I always told you she was never good enough for you. She'll leave you if she has the chance. She really doesn't care about you. Martin, when it gets down to it, it's just you and me in this world who can really trust each other. Haven't I taught you this all your life. She's no good, Martin. She's no good. You know I'm the only one who will always be there for you. If you choose her over me, you'll kill me."

This message, as any parental message, is given directly or less directly through the parent's words, voice tone, attitude, mannerisms and behavior.

Helen (tearfully): "Yes, that's what is happening. I'm married to a little boy. And I hate it. I don't want to be married to a man who is married to his mother. I need to be number one to you, not her, or I'm going to leave you" (continuing to cry and expressing her distress and anger regarding this).

At this point, Martin was shocked and stunned, for he really did love his wife and had no insight into how he was rejecting her.

Martin: "But I love you, Dear. You're the most important person to me. I can't believe this. I was trying to be there for my mother. You know how she is. I didn't realize I was doing this to you" (sad and remorseful).

Mother: "Martin, don't listen to her. Don't listen to her. You've been such a good boy to me. You've lived for me and I'm the one who has always been there for you. Whether I'm dead or alive, I'll always be number one in your life. She is selfish and wants too much from you. No wonder you're so critical of her. How can you abandon me after all this? Go ahead and hurt me. Go ahead and let me down. Select her over me when I've always been there for you. Leave me all alone. Hurt me like everyone else, just like your father did. Kill me. Make my life worthless, because if you put her and yourself before me it will kill me and your guilt will be written all over my grave" (clearly demonstrating the guilt provoking spell she put on him, which had been so poisonous, damaging and potentially destructive to his marriage).

Martin began to confront his mother, with the therapist also assisting him as his double. Since this was an individual family therapy session, the therapist took the role of mother and double, being the only therapeutic agent in the session as usually is the case in individual family therapy and individual therapy.

Martin: "Mom, I'm not going to let you do this to me anymore. I'm not a little boy any more. I have a right to be my own person. I hate your domination. I hate it. I hate it. I really hate it" (as his anger level increased with each few words he expressed. He continued to work through his anger regarding his mother, interacting with the therapist, as his mother, and reaching the point).

Martin: "I won't let you control my life anymore. No more, no more. You'll never control my life again".

Double: "You don't own me."

Martin: "I'm my own person. I can live my life the way I choose to. It has nothing to do with whether I love you or don't love you. It's what is good for me."

Double: "You've never been happy with anything that I want for myself anyway."

Martin: "You're selfish. You're so selfish. You just want to control me. You want to own me. You don't really care about me. You just want me to make you happy. You just care about yourself."

Double: "My wife really cares about making me happy."

Martin (tearfully): "Helen really wants me to be happy. She really cares. I'm going to make her my number one priority" (tearfully turning to her as they both embraced).

The spell method was necessary in this case to stimulate Martin to realize how his mother was still casting a spell on him and his marriage, a spell she had cast on him throughout his life. Once experiencing this, he began putting his wife first. However, this was just the beginning of his effort to emancipate himself from his mother's spell. In other cases, a patient may have been further along in emancipating oneself from a dysfunctional parent. Often this method contributes to a major breakthrough with regard to the strong influence a significant other has on the patient in at least making one aware of it. At other times a patient may present more resistance when confronted with the spell plaguing him or her, again as when using other methods.

THE SILENT NIGHT METHOD

The Silent Night method is another Rebuilding Therapy confrontation method designed to stimulate the resistant patient, who does not want to face one's problems and pushes others away in the process, to look at the implications of his or her attitude and actions in damaging or in some cases destroying one's life. Like other confrontation methods, it is used only after other therapeutic procedures have been tried. It stimulates the patient to experience what he or she is missing out on in one's life, primarily love, meaning and intimacy, on the eve, day or night when families and persons are together and intimate. The song "Silent Night" is hummed by the other group members, therapist or available staff to create the atmosphere of Christmas Eve or Christmas Day. "Silent Night" can also be hummed by the therapist in an individual or individual family session. The patient is stimulated to be in whatever situation he or she would be in on Christmas Eve or Day if one's life would continue to worsen such as in a room by one's self, in an empty home alone, homeless on the streets, in a psychiatric hospital, in a jail cell or alone and isolated in other ways. Often the resistant patient rejects or withdraws from others claiming he or she does not need anyone, doesn't want anyone or doesn't ever want to be hurt by anyone or to trust anyone again. This person's attitude and outlook is that "I'm alone in this bad world and will always be alone. I don't need anyone. I don't need anyone to help me. I don't need any therapy. I'm fine alone and I want to be left alone." Being exposed to the Silent Night method will confront the patient with one's attitude, outlook and perception of life, stimulating the patient to ask: "Is this what I really want on a night and day when most people want to be with their loved ones?" Once exposed to this experience, the patient will often begin to realize that this is not what he or she really wants and that his or her resistance to involvement with others and helping oneself is done more out of fear than out of actual desire. Once the patient experiences and realizes this, he or she begins to understand what one is doing, is missing, is not getting, needs and wants. In doing so, the patient often becomes significantly more motivated to help himself.

An example of the Silent Night method will now be presented. Sara was a 35-year-old workaholic middle-management executive who had all the confidence in the world, at least she thought she did. She knew it all, had every man in the palm of her hand, didn't need anyone and was able to control anyone around her with her sexuality, appearance, intelligence and manipulative ways. Her father was an alcoholic and mistreated her, while her mother was a weak co-dependent person who neglected her. She decided at a young age that she would take care of herself on her own, would not ever need anyone and wouldn't trust anyone except herself. She had been through two marriages and was getting involved with a third man, John. Sara was having much difficulty with him because she needed to be in control and would not let her defenses down and relate to him intimately. Sara had recently had an argument with John, telling him that things needed to be her way. Sara informed him, "I am committed to me first and no one else, but I still love you. If you don't like it, then you can leave me." Her male friend, Tom, walked out on her, telling her he wouldn't put up with this any longer. Close to tears, she was in an individual session complaining about this turn of events, but still she did not want to give an inch regarding her need to control.

The session continued with Sara resisting therapeutic efforts, including refusing to face her father's mistreatment of her and being confronted unsuccessfully with the projected implications of her attitude and behavior up until the Christmas season, including being alone on Thanksgiving. The therapist assumed multiple roles since this was an individual therapy session.

Double: "It's the Christmas season. December 1st, 5th, 10th. It's December 15th. Tom's getting more serious with his new female friend. People are getting together, celebrating together, going to parties, buying gifts for each other, and preparing for the big day. It's a happy time, a joyful time, when people need people and let each other know this" (continuing to project the implications of her attitude and behavior and what she was missing).

Sara: "I don't need Tom. No man is going to control me. This is a bunch of crap! Christmas is a phony time. I don't believe in Christmas anyway. People smile because they are supposed to smile and give gifts because they are supposed to give gifts. It's phony. You're not getting to me. This is ridiculous" (laughing, but becoming angry and more emotional).

Double: "It's December 16th, December 17th, December 18th, it's December 19th. It's December 20th, Christmas is nearing, parties are everywhere. People opening up with each other, showing their loving sides to each other. Tom and Irene (giving his female friend a name) are making love together. He's going to introduce her to his family on Christmas Eve."

Sara: "Will you cut the garbage. Look, I've got other things to talk about. I've got to prepare for a presentation tomorrow. I'm wasting my time here with this mushy garbage you're throwing at me. I'm paying you so that I can learn how to get along in the world so men won't take advantage of me, so I can handle them the way I want to."

The therapist realized that this method was likely weakening her denial as she became more defensive and agitated and was using increasing energy to resist this process.

Double: "It's December 23rd, it's December 24th. It's Christmas Eve." (The therapist begins to hum "Silent Night" and intermittently saying) "It's Christmas Eve. Tom is introducing his female friend to his parents. People are together loving each other, husbands and wives, children, fiancees, friends, lovers. It's what life really can be like. It's what people hope for and really want. I wonder if Tom's parents like her" (and continuing to hum "Silent Night").

Sara: "I can live without Tom. So what! I make good money. I've got a good deal that I'm going to get. I'll never be alone on Christmas Eve. I'll find a man to be with. There are many men I could date. Anyway, love! What's that? Who needs it! I don't believe it exists" (and further opening up briefly to herself).

Double (continuing to hum "Silent Night" and joining her resistance to further confront her): "I'm sure, I don't need anyone. I have myself. And so what if I don't have Tom. He would control me anyway. So what if I don't get married. And children, they're just burdens. They get in the way. How can I have a career with a child? They will only tie me down and prevent me from doing what I want. Anyway, kids grow up, take advantage of you and leave you."

Sara: "Yeah, but kids aren't too bad, some of them are nice" (beginning to soften, as children were sentimental to her). "But I'm not the type for them anyway. I like them, but I don't think I would want to have them. I wouldn't be the mother kind anyway. I'm not that kind of woman. I'm a professional woman. I couldn't stay home and take care of children. I said I would never be a woman like my mother, giving up myself and letting a man and kids control me."

She began to become tearful as the therapist continued to softly hum "Silent Night," beginning to break through her defensive barrier and also continuing to double with Sara during pauses while humming.

Double: "So what if a man isn't loving me. All they do is manipulate me. I don't need to be lying in his arms. I don't need to be having any of his kids. That's not me. That's not me" (stimulating her to connect to her underlying needs for marriage, motherhood and intimacy during Christmastime when such needs often blossom).

Sara (pausing and beginning to cry): "That really is me. I really do want children. I do want someone to love me. I've been lying to myself. I've just been protecting myself. I'm just scared. I'm afraid. I can't be hurt anymore. I can't be hurt anymore. I want it, but I don't know if I want to go for it. That know-it-all bitch I portray is just my protection."

Double: "I'm afraid. I'm so scared" (and then continuing to hum "Silent Night").

Sara: "I really am afraid. I'm very afraid. But I'm like any other woman. I want to have children. I want to have a husband to love me, but I also want my success." (Crying for a few minutes and then saying) "Stop, stop!" (asking the therapist to stop humming "Silent Night"). "I got the message. I've only been fooling myself. I need to stop being so tough, so hard. It's not getting me anywhere just pushing people away. I want to love. There have just been so many 'hurts' in my life" (as she resumed her crying). "I just decided not to be hurt anymore."

At this point, she was given much emotional support by the therapist, as she continued to cry. As Sara regained her composure, as part of closure, there was a discussion of her future treatment goals as she had much therapeutic work to do. In other cases, where Rebuilding Therapy confrontation methods are used, the session may continue and return to what the initial goals were in the session or reach closure as with Sara.

CHAPTER 11

The Suicide Method

The suicide method is a confrontation method developed from my training with Haskell. It is used to therapeutically stimulate the suicidal patient to act out, simulate and experience the suicidal death process and its implications, without of course physically harming or killing oneself. The major goal is to stimulate the suicidal person to give up or significantly decrease the desire to kill him or herself by experiencing and finding out that death is not an acceptable alternative. It is used only after other therapeutic attempts have been made to reduce a patient's suicidal wishes and tendencies and the patient still remains a significant risk to harm oneself. This method is also an excellent assessment tool to evaluate the patient's suicide potential. Neither relaxation nor relaxation exercises are used to assist with this method, for the patient is usually in a very agitated state. It is not used or carried out if the patient chooses reliving an experience or engaging in another therapeutic procedure to reduce his or her suicidal potential as an alternative to using this method or changes his or her mind and decides to live before its implementation.

This method has been used in the large majority of times in hospital settings, where suicidal symptoms are more frequent. As with such methods as the crime and arrest methods, described in chapter twelve, the suicide method is used much less frequently than other methods only when the need arises, the patient is willing and ready to take part in it and the setting is conducive for its use. In hospital settings there is a higher level of security, protection and the resources the patient has needed if this method has not been initially successful, and even if it has been initially successful, the support, security and resources the patient has needed on a follow-up basis. The suicide method has been used less than 15 percent of the time on an outpatient basis, though its outpatient utilization will increase as inpatient mental health treatment continues to be less available and as strict outpatient security guidelines continue to be used and are further developed. Guidelines for using this method on an outpatient basis include the patient being accompanied to the session by a respected and responsible person, a secure plan providing for the patient's safety after this method is used, and the same person who accompanied the patient to the session or another responsible person remaining with the patient after the session until the patient is relatively safe. Remaining with the patient usually involves going home with the patient or to the place the patient came from before the session. This method can also be used with no preplanning. Every precaution is taken in this case to protect the patient's welfare and safety, including, if needed and possible, arranging for the patient to be with a responsible person and having appropriate follow-up after the session. A responsible significant other, who the patient has a good rapport with, is used for the support discussed above, when possible. (See the therapy team section in chapter two.)

When the suicide method is successful on an outpatient basis, hospitalization can be prevented with no significant interference with the patient's life, responsibilities and activities. When this method is not successful and the patient remains suicidal he or she is advised to sign oneself into a hospital. If the patient refuses to voluntarily be admitted into an inpatient facility or an equivalent treatment setting, then the patient should be put on an involuntary hold, if needed and possible. As outpatient treatment becomes the primary source of treatment for the seriously disturbed patient, including the suicidal patient, this method will have significant implications for the treatment of the suicidal patient on an outpatient basis.

This method has been successful the first time it has been used with more than 85 percent of the patients it has been utilized with on both an inpatient and outpatient basis. Success means that the patient has given up on his or her suicide plan and has strongly reduced one's suicidal ideation, and in some cases has given it up entirely. At least another 10 percent of the patients within a day to two weeks experienced the success of the first group of patients, though in some cases not to the same degree. I have received no information that any patient with whom this method has been used has killed him or herself. I have given some approximate figures regarding the use of this method due to the nature and type of method it is.

The patient is stimulated, with his or her complete approval, to act out his or her suicide in the safety of the psychotherapeutic session in the manner that had been planned or envisioned—for example overdosing, shooting one's self, hanging oneself, cutting one's wrist or asphyxiation. Once the patient has lived out the suicidal act, while of course not harming or killing oneself, he or she is then asked to lie down on the floor in the death position similar to how one would lie if the suicidal act was actually carried out. The patient is asked to close his or her eyes, once he or she has acted out the suicide and is encouraged to keep one's eyes closed until he or she gets up out of the death position. If the death is quick, such as from shooting or hanging, then it is acted out in this manner. If it is a slower death, such as cutting one's wrist, overdosing or asphyxiation, the patient has the opportunity to psychologically experience the slowness of his or her dying and one's eventual death. The time sequence for acting out the transition from life to death is not the exact one that would transpire in an actual suicide, for this would not be possible in the clinical situation, as when living out or reliving any experience. The important point is that the time used in a simulated experience or for any relived experience permits this process to affect the patient as it is intended to do.

The events following the acted out suicide are enacted as they would likely occur. If the patient is found by someone, this process is acted out just as one's relative, friend or loved one would respond to a suicide. For example, a therapeutic agent or therapist as a significant other such as a spouse, parent or child approaches the patient lying on the floor, acting out being dead, shaking the patient saying, "Get up! Get up! Why did you do it? Why did you do it? Get up! No! No! You're not dead! You can't be dead! No! No! Get up! Get up! Please get up!" As the significant other, the therapeutic agent or therapist acts out screaming and crying hysterically, "I thought you cared about me, I thought you loved me. How could you do this to me? You told me that things were going to work out and now you're dead, you're gone. No, no, it can't be. You can't be dead," shaking the "deceased" patient's body (of course still alive). "Please, please! How can you do this to me? How can you do this to yourself?" continuing to cry. Often, this will stimulate the suicidal person to openly cry and to want to get up and live as he or she begins to become aware of the impact of suicide, as shown in the example provided later in this chapter.

If this is not effective, other scenarios are acted out such as the paramedics arriving at the scene pronouncing the patient dead, taking the body to the morgue without the patient having to be physically moved, identifying the "body" at the morgue, holding the actual memorial service and funeral, the burial, or relatives and loved ones leaving and going on with their lives in ways they would in the months and years after the person's death. The last scenario is usually acted out with at least one of the other scenarios. Often, two scenarios are at least acted out, although sometimes one scenario is all that is needed. The experience of lying tightly packed in a coffin a "few feet" high and a "few feet" wide, "six feet" under the ground, may also be acted out. Although an actual coffin is not used, the patient's experience in simulating and acting out being in a coffin lying on the floor with a clean sheet on him or her, symbolizing the patient's death, can be very realistic and effective. The use of a sheet is optional, depending on the patient's needs. It is used in group or multiple family group therapy, in individual and individual family therapy when there is a therapeutic agent or responsible person besides the therapist in attendance in the session or sometimes on a limited basis in individual family therapy when the therapist is alone in the session with another family member or members. As indicated, acting out projected events and the lives of significant persons in the future after the suicide can be effective. For example, the potential widow of a suicidal patient is portrayed marrying again, having another child and being with her new family on Christmas Eve, with the group or therapist in individual therapy humming "Silent Night" to further confront the patient with the impact of suicide if carried out.

Once the suicidal patient decides to want to live again and get up from the floor, he or she is held down for a short period of time ranging from about twenty seconds to two minutes to "shock" him or her into the irreversibility of death. This part of the method is only used in individual therapy if another therapeutic agent or responsible person besides the therapist is present and in carefully selected situations in individual family therapy when the therapist is the only therapeutic agent available without another therapeutic agent or responsible person in attendance besides the family. This portion of the method is used more regularly in individual family therapy when there is another therapeutic agent or responsible person besides the therapist present and in group and multiple family therapy. Sometimes the patient will not be held down if not in the best interest of the patient, with the therapist relying on other parts of this method, as needed. At this time the patient is told firmly, "You can't get up, can't and won't come back and can't and won't live again if you die." It is clearly pointed out to the patient that you can't and won't get a second chance if you end your life. It is not unusual for the suicidal patient to say, "I can't breathe, I can't breathe, let me up, let me up," even though the patient is clearly able to breathe. Often, while being held down, the therapist as the Spirit of Death will whisper to the suicidal patient, "I am death and when you die, you never come back. You can't come back. You won't come back. I, Death, am irreversible. Death is irreversible. This is what you wanted and this is what you got. It's over. It's over. You should have thought about this in the first place. It's too late now. It's too late now." A strong attempt is made to shock the suicidal person into experiencing the implications of what suicide is all about, with the Spirit of Death contributing to this. The Spirit of Death approach is also used at other times as therapeutic, such as in the crime method in chapter twelve.

Again, the patient can reject any of the methods, procedures or approaches used at any point during the therapeutic process. As is the case before a living or acting out process starts, the patient is initially informed that if he or she wants to stop the overall therapeutic process in a session, or just doesn't want to take part in it any longer, during any portion of it, to say, "Stop Dr. Gass, stop" or whatever is initially agreed to in a specific way as the signal to stop the therapeutic process in the session, and his or her wish will be honored immediately. This is different from saying "I want to stop," followed by statements regarding wanting to live which is part of the method. In this case, the patient won't say, "Stop Dr. Gass, stop," but may say "No, stop," which is also associated with other messages about not wanting to be dead any longer. These statements include: "Take the sheet off me I've changed my mind," "Let me up. I don't want to do this any more or I don't want to lie here anymore. I don't want to kill myself," "I want to live, not be dead" or other statements of this type not including "Stop Dr. Gass, stop" or whatever was initially specifically agreed to stop the therapeutic process in the session. Again, this is different from being held down against one's will because one doesn't want to take part in this overall process or method, for the person in this case would say, "Stop Dr. Gass, stop" or something very similar. The patient by saying, "No, don't hold me down any more or let me up. I want to get up and live" or "I want to get up. I don't want to die anymore," is the essence of this method and demonstrates the patient's willingness to take part in it. As indicated, the patient has the ultimate control and can stop any part of the method or session if it is unacceptable to him or her. Thus, nothing is ever done against a patient's will, as is true with any method, with the therapist needing to be very alert and sensitive at all times to the patient's wishes to take part in any part of the session. (See chapters three and twelve for further discussion of this issue.) Again, the therapist may not choose a certain part of this method, such as holding the patient down if it is not therapeutic for the patient.

Eventually, after a relatively short period of time, about twenty seconds to two minutes as indicated, the patient is invited to get up, but the time that elapsed may have felt like an eternity to the patient. At this time the sheet, if used, will be taken off, or the patient him or herself will take off the sheet. When the patient gets up, he or she often feels like he or she just walked out of "death" and the "grave."

During the entire process, as in other parts of therapy, the patient is encouraged and stimulated, through the use of a double, to express one's feelings and thoughts. This stimulates the patient to become more aware of and further experience his or her feelings and thoughts regarding suicide, in order to take control of them and guide oneself out of the suicidal state.

When using this method, in the majority of cases, the double should be the therapist or a well trained therapeutic agent due to the life and death nature of the patient's condition. However, sometimes another patient in the group who has suicidal ideation and tendencies can be used as a double, but only if this is helpful for the patient doubling. In such a case, the double can help oneself through the doubling process or may eventually help oneself taking part directly in the process. The double is not increasing the suicidal risk by stimulating the patient to open up regarding his or her suicidal feelings and thoughts, which if the patient brings out are already there in the first place. Only when suicidal thoughts and feelings are brought to a conscious level can the therapist work with the patient to overcome these suicidal tendencies. The patient also has the right to reject anything the double states as in any case. If other thoughts and feelings related to suicide are covert or are not fully conscious, it is helpful for the patient and therapist to become aware of them to address them directly. The double will also encourage the patient to look at the disadvantages of suicide and to give oneself a new "lease on life." This is regularly done to assist the patient to start giving up his or her suicidal thinking.

Following the successful use of this method, the patient is usually given much support and space to make sense out of what has just occurred. If appropriate and the patient is ready, he or she will be asked to live out a future projection, a psychodramatic technique, described by Haskell, where the patient acts out how one wishes, hopes and expects to live sometime in the future, with the assistance of other persons in the group in the role of significant others or persons. Experiencing life in a fulfilling, meaningful and successful way is much more powerful and potent than just talking about it and is likely to increase the hope process in some way. A future projection can also be used regularly at the end of an intense reliving session or after a person works through a specific conflict.

When using this method, I have sometimes encouraged a patient who continues to be suicidal to remain on the floor in a simulated death position after a group or individual session has ended, when possible. In such cases I have continued to work with the patient, further attempting to stimulate the patient to reverse his or her suicidal decision and ideation. My attempts at such additional stimulation have usually been successful.

If the patient fails to get up after a period of time and no more time is left to work with the patient, he or she is abruptly and in a therapeutically "stern way," in some cases, asked to get up, conveying to the patient that "if you kill yourself death will be as ugly as this (referring to the simulated suicide) or in fact uglier." The patient is also informed, "Let's get on with it, you're alive. You're still not dead. So let's get up and get on with living. You at least had an opportunity to experience what death would be like, which hopefully will assist you to give up this idea. Now it's time to get on with the business of living." Then the patient is usually given close supervision and put on a high level of suicide precautions. The abrupt and stern manner, when used, is intended to further shock the patient into what he or she is doing by still wanting to be dead. The therapist will not be abrupt and stern if such a demeanor is not in the patient's best interest, and in all cases the therapist will always convey the utmost concern and sensitivity.

Again, when this method is unsuccessful on an outpatient basis, voluntary or involuntary hospitalization or residential treatment are the best options. If this treatment isn't possible, the patient should be encouraged to be with a responsible significant other or person and continue in outpatient treatment. If the therapist is not a psychiatrist, working closely with a psychiatrist or physician to safely prescribe appropriate medication in such cases may also be needed.

The following is an example of the suicide method, as utilized in group therapy on an inpatient basis with Julia, 37, married and the mother of two. It was determined that this method would likely be needed when Julia was openly expressing her suicidal ideation regarding her husband, Curt, leaving her for another woman. The therapist took the role of double due to the life and death nature of this situation.

Julia: "I wish I was dead, I have nothing to live for. Curt was my whole life and now he doesn't want me anymore. I'd rather be dead. I can't face the pain of him sleeping with another woman. I want to die" (crying).

Double: "It's so painful for me. I'm very sad. I hurt so bad" (stimulating her to face her pain to begin working her way out of it with the hope this would reduce her suicidal tendencies).

Julia: "I have nothing to live for. He was my whole life."

Double: "What about my children? What would happen to them?"

Julia: "No one would miss me anyway if I killed myself. The kids could live with him."

Double: "But Curt would neglect them."

Julia: "It just hurts too much to lose him. It hurts so bad. It's over for me. There is no life without him. It's over. I just don't want to be around any more. I want to die" (her despair overpowering everything else).

Another way of treating her suicidal ideation, rather than using the suicide method too soon, was to focus on its likely childhood origins aggravated by her husband's leaving. Although this was a long shot at this time, owing to Julia's crippling despair and hopelessness, this approach has been used effectively at times with suicidal patients and was tried in this case. In addition, as indicated, whatever other methods are available should be tried before using this method.

Double: "Curt's been the only person who has ever loved me. What it was like with my father was..." (the Double, knowing her husband was the only person who loved her in some way and that both parents rejected her, but that it would be best to focus on just one parent at a time, the parent who she could relate her feelings and thoughts to most openly at this time).

Julia: "My father didn't like me, and my mother loved my sister more. They didn't love me. I was all alone. No one cared."

Double: "I could never please them as I take myself back to a time when my father let me know I wasn't good enough. Maybe I decided to give up as a little girl because Dad didn't show love to me and my sister already had my mother. If I can face and begin to overcome how Dad treated me, then possibly I can begin to get over what happened to me as a little girl, which may also be contributing to me wanting to die now."

This was an attempt to clinically stimulate Julia to begin to face and deal with a likely major contributor to her poor self image and suicidal tendencies.

Julia: "That's over. He never loved me anyway. It's in the past anyway. There's nothing I can do about him. I just want to die. I just want to die."

Clearly Julia was only preoccupied with the loss of her husband and did not want to face the likely origins of her desire to die. She just wanted to give up. The therapist still made a few more attempts to convince Julia not to give up on herself.

Double: "Why don't I give myself a chance again? Maybe I'll be better off without him. Possibly, he never really loved me in a healthy way anyway."

Julia: "I've been giving myself too many chances. There is no hope for me. There's no hope for me. Without him I just want to die."

Now it was necessary to reintroduce the issue of her children, knowing how special they have been to her, with the hope that the suicide method still wouldn't be necessary.

Double: "I still have my children. I feel they could live without me, but they need me. I've been their primary parent and now I'm their only active parent as he left being a parent up to me. What will they really do without me? I know he won't treat them as well as I do" (appealing to her sense of responsibility, reality and concern for her children, even if this at least provoked guilt in her, to stimulate her to begin giving up her suicidal feelings and thinking).

Julia: "The kids would be better off without me. Let him finally take care of them. It's just too much for me. I want to die. I want to sleep forever. I am going to take the pills. I know I want to end it all and it will be all over. I just want out."

Double: "But that's the easy way out. Why am I allowing him to get to me like this?" (making a last ditch effort before using this method).

Julia: "I loved him so much. He was my life. I'm a loser and always will be. I don't believe anyone will ever love me. I just want to take the pills and never wake up again. I'm going to take the pills. There's no turning back" (adamantly).

At this time the therapist, knowing that this was the only course she was going to take, began using the suicide method to shock her out of her desire and plan to kill herself.

Double: "Why don't I just get on with it and take the pills to find out if this is what I really want, though I still have a chance to change my life" (encouraging her to simulate taking the pills, in whatever situation or location she would do so, without of course in reality taking them, but also still encouraging her to change her thinking before acting out or simulating her suicide).

Julia: "I'm going to get the pills" (determined to, while beginning to act this out at home).

Double: "Where are they?"

Julia: "They're in the medicine chest" (acting out going to the medicine chest and getting the pills).

Double: "Am I going to start taking them? Is this what I'm really going to do?" (continuing to stimulate the acting out of her suicide, but raising the question again if she really was ready to start taking the pills).

Julia: "I'm starting right now. I'm doing it."

Double: "Am I really, really sure this is what I want to do?" (still confronting her with her plan to die).

Julia: "Soon it will be over" (acting out putting the pills in her mouth).

Double: "How many I've taken are..."

Julia: "A handful."

Double: "I still have a chance to stop and call for help" (again stimulating her to reverse her decision).

Julia: "I don't want any help. I want to die. I want to die" (acting out taking more pills).

Double: "I just want to get away from it all."

Julia: "I'll be at peace away from it all."

Double: "How many I've taken now are..."

Julia: "Thirty five. I'm going to take more. I'm going to finish up the bottle."

Double: "I still have a chance to call the paramedics, to call someone. It's not too late. My children, my friends will be devastated if I die. It's still not too late" (still encouraging her to save her life and look at the implications of what she was doing).

Julia: "I want it over. I want to die. I want the pain to end."

Double: "Now no man will ever love me. My dream will never happen" (even at this point still encouraging her to save her life).

Julia: "I can't trust men. I'm not going to let anyone hurt me again. I don't want anybody to find me. I want to die. I want out" (acting out taking the rest of the pills).

Double: "I'm finally going to get what I want" (continuing to stimulate her to experience the suicide and dying process, which she needed to as she remained determined to die, despite the efforts to convince her otherwise).

Julia: "I'm getting away from all this hell."

Double: "What I'm feeling now is."

Julia: "I'm getting drowsier and drowsier."

Double: "I'm getting sleepier and sleepier. I'm feeling weaker and weaker. Soon it will be over. I'm beginning to fall off the chair to the floor."

The double then gently encouraged Julia to move down from her position on the chair and to lie down gently on the floor as she acted out the dying process. The double laid down with Julia to simulate her state of mind and the dying process, as Julia laid there quietly.

Double: "I'm dying, I'm getting weaker and weaker. I'm going into a coma. I'm taking my last few breaths of life. There is no way of coming back. Soon, it will be over. Soon, it will be over. I'm taking my last three breaths of life. Even though I'm dying I can change my mind, get up and give myself a chance to live and try again. I'm taking the third to last breath before death" (stimulating Julia to look at the seriousness of her suicidal decision and the thin line between life and death). "I'm taking my second to last breath before death. I'm taking my last breath of life. My last breath of life. I'm dead. I'm dead. It's over. It's over. I'm dead."

Julia had the opportunity to change her mind, even while simulating taking her last breath, and to decide to get up and live again. However, she allowed the process to continue acting out taking her last breath and dying while alone at home. Again, the patient at any time can reject the use of any part of this procedure. The double at this time was more active than Julia as she was lying down acting out the dying process, which is a quiet, somber and withdrawing state. At this point, the therapist got up from his doubling position lying on the floor and became the Spirit of Death in order to communicate what death was about. The therapist could also have remained on the floor in this role. The therapist assumed this role owing to the nature of this situation, although a well trained therapeutic agent other than the therapist could do so.

Spirit of Death: "You're dead! You're dead! It's over! It's over! You're never going to see your children again. It's over! It's over! No one will love you again. You will never see the clear blue sky again. You'll never enjoy any part of life again. It's over! It's over! You're dead. You're dead."

The Spirit of Death spoke in the second person in a frightening and depressing voice to confront her with the fact that she no longer had control of herself and her destiny and that an outside force, "death" now had control of her. In some cases, this shocks the patient into changing one's mind about wanting to die. In this case, it didn't. As she laid on the floor "dead," the therapist coming out of the role of the Spirit of Death instructed her:

Therapist: "Though you are dead and can't speak, if you could speak express whatever you are feeling and thinking."

Julia: "I'm glad it's over. I finally can have peace. I'm glad it's over. No one can hurt me again" (going on briefly regarding this).

Knowing that she would likely be shocked by her child's reaction to her death, the therapist, as her double, set up the situation for this shock. In other words, the therapist did not want the patient to be prepared for her child's probable reaction, which she wasn't.

Double: "My children will be fine without me. They will be better off without me" (joining her thinking and preparing her to be shocked by her daughter's probable reaction, which would be acted out by a therapeutic agent).

Julia: "I know they can live without me. They'll be better off without me. They'll be okay" (lying on the floor with a peaceful look on her face).

At this point, a therapeutic agent, in the session in addition to the therapist, acted as Julia's 9-year-old daughter Phyliss to shock her into experiencing the implications of what would happen if her daughter found her dead in her home. The therapeutic agent as Phyliss approached Julia lying on the floor, beginning to shake her. In other cases the therapist may have to act out this role too, which I often have had to therapeutically do.

Phyliss (yelling): "Mommy, Mommy, what happened to you? Why are you lying there like this? Mommy, Mommy, I love you! I love you! Mommy, what happened to you?" (acting out crying). "You're not dead, are you? Wake up, Mommy, wake up! Mommy, I want to show you my A on my science test. I'm so proud of myself. Mommy, Mommy, wake up! We were going to go shopping today. You promised to take me to the store. You promised. You promised. Mommy, wake up, please, Mommy, please! You're not dead, Mommy. You just must be sleeping. Oh no, you took these pills" (continuing to act hysterically upset). "Please Mommy, wake up! Wake up! Oh, I've got to call for help! I've got to call for help!" (acting out going to the phone and calling). "Please, please, send an ambulance over to help my Mommy. I think she's dead! She took some pills. Please! Please, hurry up, hurry up!" (continuing to cry in a very panicky way).

The therapeutic agent as Phyliss continued to cry over her mother Julia lying on the floor, periodically shaking her.

Julia (beginning to cry): "Oh no, oh no! I don't want to be dead! I want to get up! I want to get up! I love my daughter. I want to get up. I don't want to be dead anymore." (In other cases the changing of one's mind doesn't occur so quickly, and whatever also would likely have occurred is acted out until the person decides to give up the wish to be dead.)

At this time, the therapist with the assistance of a few other group members gently began to hold Julia down for about a minute and thirty seconds to shock her into experiencing the irreversibility of death. If holding the person down for even a short period of time risks the safety of the patient or anyone in the session, then this procedure would be immediately terminated as it would be if the patient requested this as discussed. A sheet was not put over her, for the death process had not gone long enough. She was encouraged to keep her eyes closed, which she was willing to do despite her desire to get up, indicative of her willingness to take part in this process. In other cases, for a person who opens one's eyes, but still allows this process to continue, the impact of what he or she therapeutically experiences is still very effective.

Spirit of Death (whispers back): "You can't get up. You can't open your eyes. You're dead. You're dead. You're never going to get up again. When you die you never come back. I'm death. It's over. It's over. You're never going to see Phyliss again or Bobby (son) again.

It's over. It's over."

Julia: "But I want to live, please! I've changed my mind. I want to live now."

Phyliss (screaming): "Mommy, Mommy, please! Get up, Mommy. Mommy, why did you do this?" (continuing to act out crying).

Spirit of Death: "It's over, you should have thought about this before you took the pills. You're dead. You're dead. It's over. It's over". (And turning to Phyliss) "Your mommy is dead. She will never get up again. You won't have her to be your mom again" (with the therapeutic agent, as Phyliss, continuing to cry).

Julia: "I want to get up. Please let me have my daughter. I want to see her. I want to live. I don't want to be dead" (still crying and actively taking part in this process).

Spirit of Death: "You'll never see her again. Sorry, sorry. It's over. You're never going to see her again. You're dead. You're dead. It's over. You can never get up and see her again. You're dead."

Julia: "This can't happen to me, this can't happen to me! Let me up! Let me up! I don't want to be dead. I don't want to be dead. I want Phyliss back. Please let me up!"

It was clear that Julia wanted to get up from the death position, but wasn't resisting the method, as this was evaluated very carefully. If she was resisting the overall method, she would have said "Stop Dr. Gass, stop" or whatever was initially agreed to, which would have been immediately honored. Her attempt to get up signaled her desire to live.

Spirit of Death (whispering back): "You should have thought of this. When you die, you never come back again. It's irreversible, it's irreversible. You're dead, you're dead. You'll never see Phyliss again. You'll never see Bobby again. You won't have a chance to bring them up, to see their development and success, to see them get married, to be a grandmother. You'll never have another chance again. You'll never have life again to live it as you could, to be what you could have been, to enjoy life as you could have, to bring up your children. It's over, it's over" (focusing more on her daughter and son as this was what was stimulating Julia to reconsider, though also focusing on convincing her to live for herself too).

As this process occurred, Julia continued to cry, trying to get up. After being held down, to clearly demonstrate to her the irreversibility of death, she was invited to get up, which she did, crying and reaching out to embrace the therapeutic agent as Phyliss. As she did this, she was informed by the therapist repeating the Spirit of Death's message:

Therapist: "You're lucky. You're very lucky. Because if you kill yourself, you never will come back. You'll never see this beautiful girl again, your wonderful son again. You'll never be their mother again. You'll never experience life. You'll never have that happiness and joy you sometimes hoped for. You'll never be what you could be, which is so possible for you. If you thought this was bad, then it will be many, many times worse than this, something you can never really imagine if you actually killed yourself."

Julia: "I don't want to die" (crying). "I don't want to hurt my children. I don't want to hurt those who care. I don't want to hurt myself. It's terrible. It's terrible. I don't want to go through that" (crying, clearly communicating the distastefulness and ugliness of the death process). "I want to live. I want to live for me and I want to live for my children. There's got to be hope for me."

Double: "I can pick myself up and go on."

Julia: "I can and I will get over this. I will."

Double: "There is a lot of hope for me."

Julia: "There's a lot of hope for me" (smiling as she then reached out to the therapist emotionally).

As part of her closure process, Julia was asked, in a future projection, to live out her wish of how she hoped to live some time in the future, which she was able to do. This gave her the opportunity to put some reality into what she was capable of accomplishing in the future.

This method gives the patient taking part in it an opportunity to experience the suicide and death experience, when in fact the patient is still alive, giving him or her the chance to decide if this is what he or she really wants. Again, the major goal is to stimulate the suicidal person to give up or significantly weaken the desire to take one's life. As indicated, I have never received any reports of any patient taking his or her life or making a suicide attempt after taking part in this method. When a person experiences the loss of something valuable, in this case one's life, though not actually, and what goes with this loss, life becomes much more desired and valuable. In addition, becoming more aware of how one can hurt another or oneself, which is irreversible and can't be taken back, such as by taking one's life, motivates the person to do whatever he or she can for this not to happen.

CHAPTER 12

Confronting Dangerous and Inappropriate Behavior

Various confrontation methods have also been developed to confront the implications of potential or law violating behavior. As with any of the confrontation methods, they have their origins in my Psychodrama training, which emphasizes reliving one's experiences for problem solving or living out one's projected future experiences to prepare for their probable impact and outcome. In this light, the person who has the opportunity to act out committing a crime or behaving inappropriately, without actually doing so, will experience the impact and consequences of his or her behavior on others and oneself. In doing so, hopefully, this will become a deterrent for such possible future behavior. With this in mind the drug, crime and arrest methods were developed for Rebuilding Therapy. Yablonsky wrote about a psychodramatic murder in which a gang member acted out a murder, including being confronted with its consequences in all of its aspects, its effect on his relatives and his psychodramatic sentencing to death in the electric chair. Badaines (1989) described a case in which she psychodramatically stimulated her patient to act out a murder, with the patient experiencing its impact and being sentenced psychodramatically to a long prison term. Both examples prevented a murder from occurring. Treadwell, Stein and Kumar (1990) described the substance personification technique in which the protagonist or patient chooses an auxiliary ego to personify the bottle, pill, needle or powder referring to Blume, Robins and Branston (1968) regarding this technique. Blume, Robins and Branston described a group member as an auxiliary ego personifying alcohol with this technique developed to demonstrate the impact of a substance, such as alcohol, on the person to stimulate the patient to "fight it" away.

The goal of the methods described in this chapter is to confront, shock and alert the law-violating, potentially law-violating, acting out or potentially acting out patient with the impact of his or her behavior or potential behavior on oneself and others. Relaxation or relaxation exercises are not used as a warmup or during the time when these methods are used owing to the resistant nature of such patients who could benefit from these confrontation methods. Again, as with other confrontation methods and with any method, the therapist needs to have the trust of the patient and his or her full approval. These methods may be repeated, as it applies to a specific method and situation, but may lose the surprise factor to a certain extent.

THE DRUG METHOD

The drug method is used when a chemically dependent person or a person developing a chemical dependency problem needs to experience the impact of drugs or alcohol on one's life when he or she is resistant to looking at or lacks insight into the chemical's impact on oneself and others.

A therapeutic agent or therapist surprising the patient becomes the actual drug, whether alcohol or another type of drug, demonstrating the drug's impact on the patient and others, while also using the denial method, as denial is a primary component of drug abuse. This same therapeutic agent can also function as Mr. or Ms. Denial, or when possible a second therapeutic agent can do so. A group member who has had a drug problem or relates to the patient in some way can also function as the drug or Mr. or Ms. Denial in certain cases. The term *drug* includes or represents one or more drugs that has a negative influence on the patient's life, though the specific or primary drug or drugs will be identified if known. Alcohol is also defined here as a drug. Following is an example of the drug method as used with Martha, a 24-year-old cocaine addict, who also abused alcohol. The therapist took the various roles as this was an individual therapy session and no other therapeutic agent was available, as is usually the case in individual therapy with the therapist alone with the patient.

Martha: "I like coke. It makes me feel good. It gives me a high I can't get anywhere else. I can work and still get along okay. And beer helps to relax me. Why should I give them up?"

Ms. Cocaine: "Hi Martha. I am Ms. Cocaine. You shouldn't give me up. You know I make you feel good. I stimulate you. I give you the high of your life. You don't have to think about your problems. You don't have to worry about your pressures. Just keep taking me and everything will be okay."

Ms. Booze: "Hi Martha, I'm Ms. Booze. And when you need to relax I'm here for you too."

Ms. Denial: "Hi, Martha. I'm Ms. Denial" (lived out also by the therapist as indicated). "It doesn't matter that you're unpredictable, yell at the kids and treat your husband lousy. Don't worry about your husband. He's just trying to control you. So what if he is angry a lot. He's just an angry guy who's trying to scapegoat you."

The therapist now took the role of Ms. Drug portraying the effect of cocaine and alcohol, moving back and forth between being Ms. Drug and Ms. Denial.

Ms. Drug: "Hi Martha. I'm Ms. Drug. I'm the cocaine and alcohol. Sleep with me. Be with me. I give you everything you need, confidence, the high you can't get any other way. You don't have to worry about problems taking me. You don't have to feel your sadness, your tension, your pain."

Ms. Denial: "I'm making sure you won't worry about the side effects even if it affects your thinking, feelings and effectiveness. So what if he leaves you? Big deal if you don't see your kids anymore. So what if you lose your job? Who needs to be a grown up? Who needs problems? Life's too hard anyway."

Ms. Drug: "Take me and I get you away from all that stress and turmoil. I make it go away."

Ms. Denial: "You have to do something that makes you feel okay. You can control it. You really don't have a problem with it. You can stop anytime you want to. And this thing about it affecting your thinking, alertness, judgment and such things as driving ability. You'll never be in an accident or hurt or kill anyone or yourself."

Ms. Drug: "I just numb you to everything and make you feel you're fine. And if I kill you, at least you can be put out of your misery."

Ms. Denial: "So what if your children and husband are devastated. So what if your kids don't have a mother or if Ron finds another woman. You won't know the difference anyway. You won't have any more problems" (emphasizing her escape from her problems and emotional pain to confront her with what she was doing, including the impact of it).

Ms. Drug: "So take me, snort me and then drink me. You'll have fun with me. I'll give you that high you're looking for. I'll relax you. I'll save you. I'll get you away from this hell you're in. The hell with all of them."

After fifteen minutes of resisting facing this reality, Martha broke down. She clearly needed to be exposed to this process before she finally realized how serious her problem was.

Martha: "Okay, the coke is destroying me. I'll lose everything if I continue taking it. I'm finally realizing this. I finally am" (emotionally).

Double: "I'll lose my husband."

Martha: "I don't want to lose Bob. I love him so much. He'll take the kids too."

Double: "I'll be all alone, all by myself."

Martha: "I don't want to be by myself. I don't want to lose my family."

Double: "I better stop or it will be too late. It will kill me."

Martha: "I don't want to destroy myself. I've been so foolish. I've been a fool" (very close to tears).

The primary goal of this method, to stimulate Martha to give up her use of drugs, was accomplished by giving her the opportunity to experience what her drug abuse and denial would do to her family and her. This method can also be used, giving the patient the opportunity to role reverse and become the drug and then one's denial to experience their impact on oneself and others or to further experience the impact of drug abuse regarding other consequences that could be experienced, including being arrested. The arrest method, demonstrating the impact of being arrested, is described later in this chapter.

THE CRIME METHOD

The crime method stimulates the patient who is likely or capable of committing a crime, behaving in an antisocial way, or threatening to do so, to clinically act out the crime or antisocial behavior in the safety of the clinical session to experience the impact of this action on others and oneself. Every effort is made to ensure the safety of everyone concerned. This method is used to reduce the probability or eliminate the possibility that a person will commit a crime or engage in dangerous behavior toward others or other's property. A person ready to commit a crime or an antisocial act usually does not consider its impact from a moral, ethical and humanitarian position to the extent necessary to prevent such an action. Of course, there are hardened criminals and sociopathic individuals who do not display a conscience. This method is geared to those with a conscience or even a partial conscience. The importance of experiencing a specific behavior, action, situation, event, feeling or thought is necessary in order to evaluate its impact on others and oneself. By experiencing this impact, the patient can touch and connect to it and fix a part of oneself, deciding not to behave inappropriately. It is used only after all other methods and efforts to reduce the risk of a crime or antisocial behavior have been tried.

The crime method is illustrated through the case of Steve, an 18-year-old patient in inpatient group therapy who wanted to kill Frank, a male friend, over Frank's friendship with Steve's former girlfriend, Sheila. Steve was enraged at Frank, blaming him for the breakup of his relationship with his girlfriend. Wanting revenge, he felt strongly about murdering Frank. After various therapeutic efforts were made to try to convince him not to harm Frank, it became clear that an additional intervention was needed to prevent a possible homicide. Realizing this, the therapist decided that Steve should have the opportunity to clinically act out murdering Frank so that he could experience the potential impact of such an action on himself and others. This opportunity was presented to Steve by the therapist in the role of a double. The therapist assumed primary responsibility for using this method and the various roles associated with it due to its complexity.

Therapist as Double: "Why don't I act out killing him? Why don't I experience what it would be like if I actually did this, before in reality I actually kill him?"

Steve: "I don't want to act this out. I want to do it. I want to kill that SOB."

Double: "However, if I kill him not only will his life be over, but my life will be over too" (still trying to convince Steve to change his mind. After further doubling with Steve, he reached the point where he was ready to act this out, though still resistant).

Steve: "I'll act this out, but this is just a game, a joke. I'll do it if you want me to."

Though resistant and claiming to view this therapy process only as a game, Steve agreed to pursue it, apparently believing at some level there was some hope it could help him. He soon got into acting this out in a serious way.

Double: "I'm taking myself to the place and time when I'm about ready to murder Frank."

The term *about* was used, in this case, to encourage a tentativeness regarding Steve's readiness to murder Frank rather than making it definite, in order to still give him a slight "out" or further chance to change his mind. In other cases, when clinically acting out the implications of an antisocial or law violating action, the term *about* won't be used in this context due to the nature of the therapeutic situation. The term *murder* was used to impress him further with his intended action.

Steve: "I'm standing outside his house with a gun. As soon as he comes out I'm going to blow him away. He won't have her. If I can't have her no one is going to have her" (getting into the emotion of killing Frank, holding on to a pen that was used as a gun. Steve was clearly ready to act this out trusting the therapist to help him).

Since a toy or prop type gun wasn't available, the therapist decided spontaneously to use what was available, which was a pen. If this method could have been planned, which was not possible due to the impromptu use of it in this case, a toy gun more closely resembling a real gun could have been used. Such a "therapeutic tool" should preferably be made available, if the therapeutic need arises. Fortunately, in this case the lack of a close substitute did not impair the process.

Double: "But what about myself? What about what will happen to me?" (still appealing to him).

Steve: "I don't care about me. It doesn't matter anymore."

Double: "What about his relatives? What about his parents? What will it do to them?"

Steve: "I can't care about his relatives. He doesn't have a right to live after what he's done to me. He has no right to live."

Double: "Well let's get on with it" (knowing that fighting his resistance was not working at this time, but not wanting to give up trying to convince him that murder was wrong).

Steve: "As soon as he walks out it's over for him" (more determined).

Double: "If I kill him I'll go to jail for a long time. I could even go to the gas chamber" (the type of execution at the time). "I'll never see my mother or sister again or anyone I care about" (still trying to convince him to reverse his decision to kill Frank and even bringing up the ultimate penalty, although this wasn't a likely outcome, to emphasize the gravity of such an action and the legal consequences for it).

Steve: "They'll all be better off without me. I'm no use to anybody anymore. Without Sheila I'm miserable, no good to be around. I don't want to live if I can't have her. I really don't care what happens to me. I just want him dead. I don't want Sheila to have him. If she doesn't want me she can't have him. They both won't have each other" (in a determined way).

Double: "Where Frank is ..." (knowing this was what Steve's attention was solely on at this time).

Steve: "He's walking out of the house. Here's my chance. I'm finally going to get him. I'll give him what he has coming" (holding onto the pen, as though a gun ready to use it).

Double: "I can still change my mind. Maybe my life isn't over. Maybe there's still hope for me. Why let Frank ruin my life?"

Steve: "I have nothing to lose. My life is over. Nothing is going to stop me. I have my chance and I'm going to blow him away" (with increased rage assuming a position ready to act out shooting Frank).

Double: "Let's do it. Let's get on with it" (knowing this was the only alternative left to change his mind).

Steve then acted out shooting Frank, with another patient who related to this, as Frank, acting out falling to the floor dead.

Steve: "He's dead. I got him. I've given him what he deserves" (continuing to verbalize his rage).

Double: "What I'm feeling now as he lays dead in front of me is..."

Steve: "I'm glad I did it. It's over. He deserved what he just got. He didn't deserve to be alive" (with simmering rage and little remorse).

To break through Steve's defensive armor, the therapist asked Steve to role reverse and become Frank, asking him to lie on the floor as his deceased victim. He initially resisted, but finally agreed while the other patient as Frank became his double. The therapist became Steve looking over Frank's body, as Steve had been doing in a guiltless and vindictive way.

Therapist as Steve: "You're dead. You're gone. You deserved everything you just got. It's so nice to see the blood flowing from your head" (continuing in this way, demonstrating to Steve what a vicious act murdering Frank would be and how Frank would look).

With Steve on the floor as Frank, the therapist then laid down beside him also doubling, while the other patient doubled on the other side of Steve as Frank.

Therapist Doubling with Steve as Frank: "Even though I'm dead if I could feel what I'm feeling lying here dead after Steve shot me, what I'm feeling is..."

Steve as Frank: "I deserved it. I deserved to be shot. I shouldn't have messed with Steve's girl" (resisting).

Therapist as Double: "I'm Frank, not Steve."

Steve as Frank: "I deserved it. I shouldn't have done what I did."

Steve continued to resist, not willing to put himself in Frank's place. Despite his resistance the therapist continued to try to stimulate him to change his homicidal thinking. In doing so, the therapist asked group members, one at a time, to represent Frank's parents and then his brother and younger sister acting out crying tearfully over Steve as Frank lying now in his simulated coffin. Still Steve continued to resist, with the therapist then asking one of the group members to portray his former girlfriend crying over Frank's death, screaming out how angry she was at Steve for killing him, that she made a good decision leaving Steve, that it was her responsibility for doing this and that her loving bond with Frank was much stronger now after his death. This was reinforced when Steve was asked to role reverse becoming Sheila. Although Steve did role reverse, he resisted this and other methods tried, including living out being arrested, going through the court process and being sentenced to the gas chamber. Steve was finally shocked into realizing that killing Frank was a bad mistake when he lived out his own execution and ended up in what he believed would be "hell." As Steve clearly believed in the concept of hell, the therapist instructed the patient who had been acting as Frank to portray himself dancing in heaven looking down on Steve in hell, while Sheila was instructed to cry out her love to Frank in heaven and her rage at Steve. At this point, while Steve lay on the floor living out his death in hell, he cried out:

Steve: "I never should have done this! I'm wrong. It didn't accomplish anything. I don't want Sheila to hate me. She loves Frank more and hates me more. And look where I am and where he is. I want out of here. I want out of here." (At this point the therapist as the

Spirit of Death, as in the suicide method in the last chapter, loudly whispered.)

Spirit of Death: "You're dead Steve. You're dead. It's too late. You'll never come back. It's over. It's over."

As Steve tried to get up no longer wanting to be dead, he was therapeutically held down by three group members for about ninety seconds to convey to him the irreversibility of death and the impossibility of getting out of the hell he would create if he murdered Frank. As he finally got up he tearfully expressed his sadness and remorse about what he had planned to do. As with the suicide method or any other method or approach, he had the option to refuse continuing with this process with the same guidelines followed.

Steve: "I thought this would be the right thing to do, but now I realize how wrong I would have been. I lost my girlfriend and that was my own doing. It had nothing to do with Frank" (as he continued to cry).

The session ended with Steve receiving a significant amount of therapeutic support with a good prognosis that he would not harm anyone. Although a murder had been prevented, a significant amount of therapeutic work remained ahead for Steve. The projected execution may seem an unrealistic outcome for an 18 year old, but he needed to be confronted with the potential penalties, which hopefully would prove a deterrent for him throughout his life. Although he didn't specifically relate to the impact of the gas chamber, he did relate through his belief to the concept of hell. In some cases, the impact of the gas chamber when using this method has indeed been effective. The gas chamber was presented as the mode of execution because this was the sole type of execution used in the state where I practice at the time of this example. When using this method, the therapist can use whatever mode of execution or penalties exist in his or her geographic area of practice.

In other cases the potential murderer, robber, rapist, molester, child abuser, or other potential type of criminal is likely to see the light before Steve did. In my practice, the patient often decides to give up the potential crime when he or she first experiences its effects on the intended victim and oneself. In other cases, the patient may need to experience from being arrested to going through the court process to being incarcerated to being executed before changing one's mind about carrying out the crime. Of course, the projected outcome will be relative to the situation and what the patient needs. Hopefully, assisting the person to experience the impact of the crime or antisocial behavior will prevent one from carrying it out, although for some people nothing works. When the patient can't be deterred, every effort should be made to protect the intended victim within the guidelines for psychotherapists and existing law in the clinician's particular geographical area.

THE ARREST METHOD

Whereas the crime method can include the arrest method, it focuses initially on challenging the conscience and reasoning of the less hard-core person. The arrest method, by the patient being stimulated to clinically act out being arrested, focuses on the more hard-core person with a less developed conscience to stimulate this type of person to experience the impact of external reality (jail). It may be what the hard-core person needs to wake him or her up from the denial of where criminal or antisocial behavior will lead.

The arrest method is used only after all other methods have failed. Being arrested and going to jail is a traumatic, ugly experience, and is ordinarily enough to shock anyone with any sense of reality into making a behavior change.

Although the right of the patient and parent or parents, when applicable, to approve and disapprove of the therapy process and methodology has been discussed in chapter three, while it is also addressed in chapters eleven and fourteen, it needs to be addressed again when using confrontation methods such as the arrest and crime methods. In addition, although the patient and, when applicable, the parent or parents are informed as treatment begins of the Rebuilding Therapy process and its methodology and give their approval to it, they need to also be informed if possible at other times during the course of therapy, if needed, about specific methods and approaches such as the arrest, crime and suicide methods which may be used shortly within one to two weeks. As they are informed again of such methods, the patient and the parent or parents, when applicable, are also informed of their right to reject such methods at any time as they are informed at the beginning of treatment. In some cases when the therapist has a good trusting relationship with a patient and, when applicable, with a parent or parents, the therapist may need to use a confrontation method such as the arrest or crime method without recent approval (a week or two or less) from the patient and, when applicable, from his or her parent or parents, if such methods as the arrest or crime method need to be used during the course of the session to immediately prevent a patient from behaving in a dangerous or inappropriate way which would have adverse effects on others and oneself. When using the crime or suicide methods, the patient still must approve of the use of such methods before they are utilized in a session and as indicated can stop the therapeutic process at any time. Even when there is a surprise factor when using the arrest method alone or as part of the crime method, and when using a method involving any type of surprise, the patient at any time can stop the process. As has been discussed in chapter eleven, it is especially helpful to regularly inform the patient before the living out or acting out process starts in a session, to say "Stop Dr. Gass, stop" or whatever is initially agreed to in a specific way as the signal to stop the therapeutic process in a session if the patient chooses to terminate the use of a method or the therapeutic process in the session. This certainly applies when the therapist may be planning to use the arrest or crime method in a session or even if this wasn't planned. The wording "Stop Dr. Gass, stop" or whatever is initially agreed to in a specific way as the signal to stop the therapeutic process in a session especially applies to situations where a patient when living out or reliving an experience or working therapeutically in some way in a session would use such terminology as "Stop this, I don't want you to do this any longer or stop this, I hate what you are doing to me." In doing so it distinguishes the patient's willing participation in the therapeutic process, while such methods as the arrest, crime or suicide methods are used or the patient is reliving an experience when such statements may be made, and the situation when the patient no longer wants to take part in the therapeutic process in a session. In fact, even while such methods as the arrest, crime or suicide methods are being used or during the course of the session, when applicable, the patient is also informed he or she can stop the therapeutic process from continuing in a session by saying "Stop Dr. Gass, stop" or something very similar specifically which was initially agreed to. When the patient is informed of this while the therapy process is going on, it is done in a manner which won't significantly impair the effectiveness of the method or the therapy process. Whatever the situation the patient will always have the option to terminate any part of the therapeutic process in whatever way he or she communicates this, though the therapist can develop ways for this to always be an option.

An example, in group therapy, in an inpatient setting, is Jack, a 16-year-old amphetamine abuser and dealer who had everything going for him—looks, talent and personality. His denial system was sophisticated, elaborate and strong, to the point where he had an answer for anything, justifying anything he did and believing his own rationalizations, excuses, projections and distorted thinking. He fully believed that he would never be arrested and that he could go on manipulating and taking advantage of others. While sitting in a group session, he was "going on" about his lifestyle, bragging about it and how he wouldn't give it up for anything. As he began talking about his amphetamine use and his selling of drugs before his admission to the inpatient program he way in, the therapist decided the arrest method was needed since no other method had been effective with him and as he was a high risk to be arrested. The session then proceeded. The therapist assumed the roles of an undercover police officer and the Spirit of Juvenile Hall due to the complexity of this method.

Jack: "I have everything covered. No one is ever going to catch me. I have a few dealers I use. I trust them totally. The pigs will never suspect me. I know when to use, when not to use and I take just enough not to be addicted to it. I have control of the uppers, I have control of the pigs. I have control of everything. No one is going to get me. No one's going to get me."

Therapist as an Undercover Officer (shocking him without any warning as he began to act out Jack's arrest): "You're under arrest! You're under arrest! Get down! Get down!" (as Jack was told in a "tough like" manner to lay down on the floor as might happen in an actual arrest). "Get your hands behind your back! Anything you say will be held against you" (while giving him his rights in a stern police-like manner). "Get your hands behind you! If you cause any problems I'll make it rough on you" (acting out handcuffing him and the arrest process).

When using the crime or arrest method, in acting out touching and frisking the patient with men only, the hands, arms, shoulders and back are touched and with women just the hands, arms, and shoulders are touched if needed. The patient must agree to this process and can end it any time he or she chooses under strict guidelines (as discussed in the suicide method in the last chapter and in chapter three). The touching portion of this method is only used in individual therapy when there is at least a responsible person besides the patient and therapist present, and in individual family therapy on a very limited basis when there is no therapeutic agent or responsible person besides the therapist present. The touching part of the crime or arrest method is used more frequently in individual family therapy when at least a responsible person besides the therapist is present and in group and multiple family group therapy where, besides other group or family members, a therapeutic agent in addition to the therapist is more likely to be present, though more often in multiple family group therapy. At the start of therapy a patient is informed that as long as he or she agrees, one will be touched only in the acceptable areas described here and only when needed and serving therapeutic purposes. The extent of how stern and police-like the therapeutic agent or therapist becomes depends on the setting. The therapist is more limited regarding the use of this type of method in an individual session because no one usually is there to support what he or she is doing and is somewhat less limited in an individual family therapy session, especially less limited when or at least a responsible person besides the therapist is available. The arrest method and methods such as the crime and suicide methods are used more freely in group and multiple family group therapy as other patients or family members and a therapeutic agent or responsible person, when available besides the therapist though more likely in multiple family group therapy, are available to provide support and assistance in the use of these methods. Careful discretion is used when utilizing family members of the patient to assist with these methods in some way. Other responsible persons also can serve as witnesses that the therapist is ethically assisting the patient. (See the section on the therapy team in chapter two.) The session continued.

Jack: "What do you think you're doing? You can't do this to me!" (shocked, but allowing himself to take part in the process, whereas if he wanted to stop he would have said, "Stop Dr. Gass, stop" or something very similar as he had been informed he could).

Undercover Officer: "Oh yeah, I'm doing it to you. I'm arresting you. I'm a police officer. I'm putting the cuffs on you. You're going to juvenile hall and you're going to get prosecuted. You thought you knew it all. You really didn't. You've got a lot to learn."

Jack: "You can't do this to me. No way. You can't" (still agreeing to take part in this process as he was responding to the therapist as the police officer arresting him).

Undercover Officer: "You've broken the law. You've made your last deal. You've conned your last con. It's over, it's over. You're going to be spending the night of the big football game in juvenile hall. It's over. it's over."

Jack: "Please, let me go, let me go. Stop it!" (starting to cry). "I don't want to be arrested. I don't want to go to jail."

Undercover Officer: "It's too late. It's too late. You should have thought about this in the first place. You're going to juvenile hall and you're going to be put away for a long time. You're not getting off easy this time. It's over. It's over."

The therapist could have stopped at this time, for it appeared that Jack was clearly facing the implications of his inappropriate law violating behavior. On the other hand, he was a chronic lawbreaker with a strong sociopathic characterological structure, but hadn't been caught. As a result the therapist chose to go further, including shocking him into experiencing what juvenile hall life would be like.

The therapist as the police officer then acted out putting Jack in the back of a police car and the conversation en route to juvenile hall, further shocking him into what it is like to be arrested.

Undercover Officer: "You've had it, you've really had it! You should have thought about it before. Who knows what's going to happen to you there? There's some big time bullies in juvenile hall–murderers, robbers, sexual perverts and just plain mean people. They may even want to play around with you a little and if you don't cooperate they'll hurt you bad."

Jack continued to cry, asking to be released and saying he would never do it again. The usual juvenile hall process was then lived out, including being fingerprinted in a manner in which it would actually be done. The session then moved to his incarceration in juvenile hall, with the therapist also in the role as the Spirit of Juvenile Hall, to further convey the juvenile hall atmosphere and environment.

Therapist as the Spirit of Juvenile Hall: "You have no control. You're at the mercy of the juvenile hall guards and the other kids and really it's those kids you're at the mercy of. Some of them are very mean. You're really at their mercy. In fact, if you're not careful they can really hurt you" (in a fear provoking voice).

Jack: "I didn't want this, I didn't want this" (becoming increasingly afraid).

Spirit of Juvenile Hall: "Sorry, sorry, this is what you're going to get. Sorry."

Inmate Leader and Juvenile Hall Inmates (therapeutic agent as inmate leader and group members as inmates after given specific instructions by the therapist to further convey the juvenile hall atmosphere and environment): "Hi Jack. How ya doing? Glad you're here. We heard you saying you know everything, that no cop can get to you. Well, let me tell you something. We're going to get to you. We're going to have a good time with you" (pushing him back, though not hard, toward another juvenile hall inmate who pushes him to another inmate as would likely happen. Each group member was instructed to act tough, but in no way physically to hurt Jack).

Juvenile Hall Inmate II: "We're going to really mess you up. We're going to initiate you. You'll be sorry you ever got arrested. You're ours" (in a very mean way).

Jack: "No, no, please, no, no, please, no, don't do that to me, no, no" (increasingly fearful).

Juvenile Hall Inmate III: "Shut up, we're going to have a good time with you."

Jack: "No, no, please don't hurt me. Please I don't want any trouble" (even more upset).

Spirit of Juvenile Hall: "There's nothing you can do, Jack. You're really at their mercy now. You should have thought about this before. It's too late. It's too late" (giving him a short period of time to experience what was happening). "This is what you get" (continuing).

Jack: "Please, stop. Please. I can't handle this. I can't handle this. Please don't hurt me" (still responding to this process, his agitation level still increasing).

Jack was not rejecting this method, and, as mentioned, a patient can terminate a method or approach anytime by saying "Stop Dr. Gass, stop" or whatever is initially agreed to. The therapist, also, is always sensitive to when to stop the process of this or other confrontation methods and when the patient just doesn't actually want to take part in a specific method any longer or has experienced "enough". The patient always is in ultimate control and can terminate any part of the therapeutic process at any time.

Juvenile Hall Inmates: "You better shut your mouth" (continuing to push him around and making motions to beat him up, though of course not harming him in any way).

Jack: "No, no, please, no, no, I'll do anything, please leave me alone, please, please, please! They're going to hurt me. They're going to hurt me. No, no!" (screaming in fear).

Therapist, still as the Spirit of Juvenile Hall (knowing that Jack had enough stimulation and confrontation, raised his hand stating): "OK, we're going to let you go, but if you continue acting as you have and get arrested, it will be a lot worse than this. A lot worse than this."

Jack: "Okay, okay, you gave me the message, I got it, I got it. I have the message. I didn't realize what a fool I've been, what I could have done to myself. It's not going to happen again. It's not going to happen again. Thank you. Thank you" (crying).

Group Member One: "I'm glad you're finally taking a look at it. There was no talking to you."

Group Member Two: "There was no talking to you. You thought you knew it all."

Jack: "I know I did. I know I did. Somebody should have done this to me a long time ago. I could have been arrested. I could have been killed. I can't believe it. I can't believe it."

The arrest method, being part of the crime method, can go further, living out the highlights of a court trial and incarceration, including the impact of these events. This method is brought to a close whenever it is clear that the patient has been emotionally confronted to the point where he or she is experiencing effectively the impact of his or her behavior.

CHAPTER 13

The Reparenting Method

For the development of a healthy self, reparenting is an important and essential method during the course of the therapeutic process as it is needed. Reparenting is the process of reparenting and nurturing the wounded Child in a healthy way after originally being parented in a dysfunctional way and incorporating the healthy parenting persons and reparenting into one's Parent. Although reparenting has been part of Rebuilding Therapy, incorporating it in a specific way and as a specific method is a rather recent development. Reparenting was developed by Transactional Analysis clinicians including Schiff, Wilson, Osnes and James. It is also an outgrowth of Rebuilding Therapy's way to teach patients to treat and bring themselves up again in a loving and healthy way. Presently it is primarily used with adults and in some cases with adolescents. When using this method specifically, the therapist or therapeutic agent becomes the therapeutic parent who, in the role of the Adult Nurturing Parent, nurtures, therapeutically loves, compliments, supports, guides, teaches, reassures and parents the patient in a healthy way. The patient also uses his or her Adult Nurturing Parent to reparent oneself in Rebuilding Therapy's self-parenting process. Although a therapist or therapeutic agent generally functions in this role throughout therapy, reparenting has been developed as a specialized method in a limited way as described in this chapter, though it is more than a limited method when provided in the rebirthing method described in chapter fifteen. Reparenting can also be provided as the major focus of a session, but it has not regularly been used this way. Reparenting, is often used with relaxation as needed and, as any method, approach or process, is used within the parameters of the patient's wishes, needs, problems, functioning, capability and situation.

The Adult Nurturing Parent of the person assisting in reparenting or of the patient in self-parenting, which is the same entity as the Adult Nurturing Self (see chapter eight), is made up of the healthy Adult, healthy Parent and healthy Child ego states with the Adult being the controlling ego state. Both entities are identical depending on whether one is in the reparenting or redecisioning process. The reparenting process is carried out through the specific reparenting method described in this chapter, that is in the process of further development, and through the attitude, actions, behavior and messages of the therapist, therapeutic agent and others such as group or family members in the session, which should occur in any therapy. The attitude, actions, assistance and work of the therapist, therapeutic agent and others in the session to help the patient make healthy redecisions and to strengthen oneself emotionally in this process also involves reparenting in varying degrees.

The developing reparenting method of Rebuilding Therapy is relatively limited, but it serves in the way it needs to in the rebuilding process. The therapist or therapeutic agent becomes the therapeutic parent, therapeutic mother or father or another parent person or mother or father person. The patient is informed of the reparenting process and of the therapist's or therapeutic agent's role in this and that the therapist or therapeutic agent won't take the place of the patient's actual parents. Reparenting is used, as needed, after the patient has clinically relived an experience or when the patient gets "stuck" and is unable to carry out the reliving process, with reparenting assisting the patient to eventually resume doing so. As relaxation is utilized, as needed, to enhance the opening up process to assist the patient to clinically relive an experience, the relaxation process, also as needed, stimulates the patient to be more responsive to reparenting. Reparenting can also be a primary focus of the session, though used less frequently in this way. Reparenting is used only as needed, as any method or approach is utilized.

This reparenting process incorporates a part of the therapist or therapeutic agent as an Adult Nurturing Parent into one's Parent, while owning this as part of oneself and one's Parent and strengthening oneself and the Parent in the process. In this way, the patient and his or her wounded Child is reparented with the parenting and messages of the therapist or therapeutic agent. As this occurs, the patient's wounded Child is reparented and nurtured in a healthy way, reinforcing and strengthening the cathartic, redecisioning and rebuilding process in the Child if reparenting follows redecisioning and prepares the wounded Child for redecisioning if reparenting occurs before the redecisioning process. Also, as this process occurs, the patient's Adult and Child is also strengthened. As the reparenting process is introduced to the patient, it can be carried out throughout the period of therapy and afterward independently by the patient, with the patient's healthy Adult, Parent and Child as the Adult Nurturing Parent doing the self-reparenting or self-parenting. In doing so, the patient has the opportunity to reparent oneself in a healthy self-parenting way. Thus reparenting involves inserting new and healthy parenting and teachings into one's Parent, while one's wounded Child is being reparented in a nurturing, healthy and reality-oriented way. This is not a complete reparenting, but is a partial reparenting, the degree of which depends on the specific situation.

An example of reparenting in group therapy is with Toby, 48, immediately after he relived and worked through a rejecting and neglectful experience and worked toward making a redecision as a child, with the reparenting usually done at the age the patient last relives. Also to be noted, is that a patient can work toward making more than one redecision within the limitations of the session. The reparenting in this case was more generalized for this was what Toby needed. The therapist functioned in the role of the therapeutic parent in both examples where reparenting is described in group therapy in this chapter, as the therapist was the only therapeutic agent in the example that will now be described and was most capable of utilizing this method in the later example. The co-therapist and auxilary agent, also being therapeutic agents, can also effectively use this method.

Therapist as Therapeutic Parent: "I'm a therapeutic parent, but I can't take your parent's place. You're such a special child. I really admire you. You are so special. I love you and respect you as a person. You're going to be something very good when you grow up. You're going to really amount to something. I'm your friend. I'll be here for you. I'll listen to you. I'll support you, I'll guide you, I'll teach you. Even though you have been hurt, neglected and mistreated this in no way means you're bad. You're a very good child, an intelligent person, a creative person, a lovable person, capable of doing anything you want to do. I know it may be hard to trust me or to let me care for you. I'll be here anyway to assist you, as long as you allow me to. Life isn't going to be easy, but I will be here for you, to support you, to cheer for you, to protect you, and to spur you on. I'll also be here to set limits for you. You have a lot of challenges to face, the rejections in your life, the disappointments and the neglect. I'll be here to assist you to face these experiences, to overcome them and to become the person you can be rather than allowing these times to hurt you and continue to wound you" (preparing him for future therapeutic reliving experiences).

The therapist or therapeutic agent as the therapeutic parent can use whatever wording is helpful. In addition, the therapeutic parent can reeducate the patient on whatever subject area is helpful to the patient. Also, as the patient's Adult is participating in this process, it assists the patient to understand what is being communicated when being reparented as a child, again.

As part of the reparenting process, the therapeutic parent can hold the patient in a nurturing way if the patient is ready and in need of such physical touching, though specific guidelines need to be followed as discussed in chapter fourteen.

Reparenting can be used soon after a patient relives, as a child, a specific type of rejection such as guilt provocation working toward making a redecision not to allow anyone to guilt provoke him or her, with the reparenting specifically supporting this redecision. For example, Rebecca, 21, in individual therapy right after reliving and working through this type of experience as a child, went through a brief reparenting experience.

Therapist as Therapeutic Parent: "I'm a therapeutic parent, but I'm not taking your parent's place. You're a good person. You're not responsible or to blame for Mom's life, happiness or mistakes. This is up to her. I don't want you to ever feel this is your responsibility. You're not guilty for her problems and feelings. And you have a right to be angry and upset about this. You have a right to live, to have your own life, to laugh, to have fun, to be a child and to be you. I'm here for you with your good points and mistakes." (Following the therapeutic agent's reparenting, the patient who is ready can follow with self-parenting as will be described.)

If the patient, for example, remains stuck with guilt, cannot decide to give it up and continues to think in an unhealthy way while reliving a guilt-provoking situation, then reparenting can be helpful in strengthening and warming the patient up to redecide to give up this guilt. The therapist or therapeutic agent's role in this case, as with Rebecca, is to support and reeducate the patient into realizing that he or she has a right to be angry and upset when one's rights, feelings and thoughts are violated as a person. Once this is accomplished, the patient is in a better position to resume the reliving process or to reach closure, which is good preparation for the next session.

The reparenting method can also be used when the patient is emotionally stuck in a significant state of despair, hopelessness or self-destructiveness to assist the patient to continue with the reliving or therapeutic process or to experience effective closure. This can occur when, for example, Ellen, in group therapy reliving an event as a child, was sobbing helplessly: "I'm no good. No one cares about me. No one loves me. Why go on living? I want to die," remaining in this state after further therapeutic efforts were made to assist her to come out of it. Reparenting in this case can be helpful at the age the patient is reliving. Such reparenting should not suffocate the patient's feelings and thoughts or rescue the patient. The reparenting method in this case started with the therapist as the therapeutic parent.

Therapist as Therapeutic Parent: "I am another parent person, Ellen, but I'm not your mother or father. I'll help you get out of this hole, this blackness, this hopelessness you're in. I'm going to give you affection, confidence and hope. I'm not here to take your problems away from you. You'll still have to solve them, but I am here to give you concern, care, security and affection which will help you realize that there is someone else in your life who cares about you" (repeated to further reinforce this and then) "You're really not bad. You're okay and you don't need to give up. You have a lot of strength and healing power. You're a very good person. You have a right to live. I'm with you."

The therapist or therapeutic agent may go on in this way for a short time, if needed, until the patient is ready to resume the reliving process or whatever he or she was therapeutically working on. When the patient can't go on any longer in a session and needs closure, the therapist or therapeutic agent will provide this. In some cases, the therapeutic agent may continue with: "If it's all right with you, I'm going to just hold you and let you experience my concern and support, though not as your mother or father, but as a therapeutic parent." The holding may be for this entire period or intermittently during this time, depending on what the patient needs and is ready for. This process continues for about five to twenty minutes depending on the need, while the therapeutic agent also talks supportively and in a nurturing way with the patient. Sometimes the therapeutic agent, in any case of reparenting, may also hum or sing some soothing music or play such music on a tape recorder or cassette to enhance the reparenting process in a way depending on the situation. There are some cases where holding or embracing the patient is not appropriate, especially when the therapist is alone with one patient or the patient is not ready for this. An alternate approach in such cases is encouraging the patient to visually experience being held or embraced. (See chapter fourteen for guidelines regarding holding, hugging, or embracing a patient.) The time period for reparenting when the patient is able or appears capable of continuing with the reliving or therapeutic process is briefer—from about one to seven minutes. In this case, the patient is usually not physically held which will give the patient the space needed to return to the therapeutic work he or she was doing. Various reparenting options are available.

Two therapeutic agents (therapist and therapeutic agent) can provide reparenting to the patient, one as the therapeutic mother and the other as the therapeutic father, as the patient is ready for this. However, at this time, often due to a lack of another therapeutic agent in a session and the more limited nature of reparenting in Rebuilding Therapy, it has often been effectively provided by one therapeutic agent. Sometimes, though in the large minority of situations, two therapeutic agents have been used in the reparenting process, as needed.

In the closing parental remarks, the therapist or therapeutic agent is setting the stage for the patient to bond with the therapist or treatment team on a stronger and more therapeutically intimate basis or for the first time in a significant way, though there usually is some type of bond between the patient and therapeutic agent in order for reparenting to occur. The stage is set therefore for continued sessions during which the patient will have an opportunity to clinically relive and work through those negative experiences he or she still needs to effectively rebuild oneself from or to engage in whatever therapeutic process he or she is ready for.

The recommended length of time for reparenting, as indicated, should be from about one to twenty minutes in any one session, except when reparenting is the primary modality in a session. When a session is needed primarily for reparenting, the therapist or therapeutic agent takes more time to parent and provide a nurturing and loving parenting experience for the patient. This type of reparenting is selectively used when the patient is in need of such an experience and is willing to experience it. Rebirthing is a type of reparenting, being a primary focus in a session (see chapter fifteen).

Self-reparenting, developed by James (1974), and referred to as self-parenting in Rebuilding Therapy, is also encouraged, as adapted to Rebuilding Therapy, through the patient's internal self-parenting, support groups, classes, reading and seeking out a healthy mentor or mentors or parent figure or figures. An important part of self-parenting in Rebuilding Therapy is first telling oneself what one's healthy Adult, healthy Parent and healthy Child contribute as it applies to the reparenting process and then integrating them as one's Adult Nurturing Parent, as one does with the development of the Adult Nurturing Self. The patient should have a basic knowledge of the Adult, Parent and Child before doing this. As with the Adult Nurturing Self, this is only practiced as a specific exercise as when taught in the joining method, as needed, and, in this case, in the reparenting method, as needed, with the Adult Nurturing Parent and Adult Nurturing Self being a working part of the reparenting and redecisioning process, respectively. As indicated, the Adult in the Adult Nurturing Self or Adult Nurturing Parent is the controlling and managing ego state. Once this integration occurs, self-parenting can occur. Each time the person's Adult Nurturing Parent talks to one's wounded Child or self in a self-parenting way, one's Parent is strengthened incorporating the strengths of the healthy

Adult, Parent and Child in the Adult Nurturing Parent operating at this time. Of course, the weaknesses of any one of the person's ego states can contaminate the self-parenting process, but is not the focus of this discussion focusing on the healthy parts of the Adult, Parent and Child in the Adult Nurturing Parent. This is why, when possible, it is so important to do redecisioning work before reparenting to significantly decontaminate and strengthen the ego states.

A self-parenting exercise can help a person make such affirmations to one's wounded Child as: "You are a good child," "You're a smart child," "You're a handsome or pretty child," "You're a loving child" or "You're getting down on yourself too much. Okay you blew it, but everyone does and so let's learn from this." Such self-parenting affirmations can be made to one's overall self substituting the term *person* for the term *child.*

An example of teaching self-parenting is provided by the therapist or therapeutic agent who, acting as the Adult Nurturing Parent in the patient, specifically demonstrates a way for the patient to reparent oneself, as needed. The patient then practices this speaking as one's Adult Nurturing Parent to one's wounded Child or self to utilize for his or her own self-parenting. The patient is first reacquainted with what the healthy Adult, Parent and Child is, as needed, and then what the Adult Nurturing Parent is before this procedure is utilized, as in the joining method regarding the Adult Nurturing Self in chapter eight. Often, at this time, the patient does not need to be reacquainted with what the healthy Adult, Parent and Child is. If this is needed, the patient will then live out being the healthy Adult, Parent and Child before living out being the Adult Nurturing Parent. This procedure is modified in individualized ways when working with adolescents. The terminology in this case is changed to the Developing Adult and the Developing Nurturing Parent from the Adult and Adult Nurturing Parent in the adult, respectively.

Therapeutic Agent as Adult Nurturing Parent: "I'm the healthy Adult in you. I'm the healthy Parent in you. I'm the healthy Child in you. I'm the Adult Nurturing Parent in you. You have so much potential in you. You are such a good child or person" (depending on whether addressing the person's overall self or wounded Child). "You are not bad. You're going to be okay. Even if you don't make the progress or changes you want to or need to, give yourself a break and encourage yourself rather than being too hard on yourself. Don't punish yourself for what has happened to you in the past, which wasn't your fault and you were an innocent victim of. Don't punish yourself for mistakes or what you could have done differently in the past. Look at them as learning experiences, to learn from rather than beating yourself up about" (referring to an emotional beating). "You have enough problems and enough stresses and challenges. Don't make it harder by putting yourself down. Use your good mind to change your unhealthy thinking to healthy thinking. You have so much energy, spontaneity, intuitiveness, creativity, love and talents which you can develop in you. Treat yourself well. Love yourself and you'll guide yourself in a way that is good for you and everyone around you. So I'm here for you. I'm really here for you."

Again the wording of the reparenting can be modified to meet the patient's needs. The wording of self-parenting can also be provided in the first person plural such as "Don't punish ourself for what happened to us in the past. We have enough stresses and problems." Although the wording may be redundant to a certain extent in the different cases, this is what is needed in the various situations to reeducate and reparent the patient in whatever way is helpful.

The patient, now ready, is then asked to practice this process on his or her own, being the Adult Nurturing Parent, talking to the wounded Child within oneself to live out this self-nurturing process. The therapist or therapeutic agent can also demonstrate a way for the patient as his or her Adult Nurturing Parent to nurture his or her more mature and healthy Child or any part of the self. The patient can then practice and utilize this type of self-parenting. The patient can regularly learn to self-parent by consciously modeling the parenting of the therapist or therapeutic agent or other healthy and respected parental figures.

A form of reparenting also occurs during the redecisioning process, when the patient's Adult Nurturing Self and the Adult Nurturing Parent of the therapist, therapeutic agent and others in this session assist the patient's wounded Child, as needed, while each time this happens their influence and messages are inserted into the patient's Parent. The healthier the Parent the more effectively it, as part of the Adult Nurturing Self, can assist the wounded Child in the redecisioning process and the person in his or her overall functioning. Reparenting, also, in strengthening the Adult and Child, contributes to a healthier Adult and Child in the Adult Nurturing Self. This also is helpful in redecisioning and in the person's overall functioning.

Although the major focus of Rebuilding Therapy is on redecisioning in the wounded Child, it supports use of the reparenting process and is open and supportive of the discussion of reparenting in chapter five. This is the case as long as reparenting encourages and supports the redecisioning process, which usually needs to occur before effective and lasting reparenting can occur (see chapter five). Reparenting can be an important adjunct, as needed, to the redecisioning process, and once effective redecisioning is achieved, it can be effectively accomplished on a long-term basis without being overpowered by the wounded Child with its unhealthy feelings, thoughts and decisions.

CHAPTER 14

Reliving the Experience

Stimulating and assisting patients to relive their past major experiences in the living out stage phase involves a significant amount of skill, timing, creativity, empathy, sensitivity, leadership and creative acting ability. This stage, taken and developed from the action phase of Psychodrama, powerfully stimulates the patient to relive experiences that have impacted his or her life.

It is not possible to immediately stimulate and assist the patient to relive or reexperience a major experience. Rather, the patient needs to be warmed up and slowly stimulated at a pace that the patient can handle to reach the relived experience. In the process, a person's unhealthy defenses, including fears, excuses and rationalizations, need to be dismantled gently, while the fear of facing a past unresolved experience must be desensitized and decreased step by step. It is essential to encourage the patient to maintain a modified defense system and some degree of control and direction of his or her destiny. When people fear losing control, they becomes defensive, resistant and lose confidence in the therapist just as they formerly lost confidence in their rejecting or nonempathic parent. However, as the patient opens up, he or she will soon find out that one is in more control.

All aspects of the session, including all methods and approaches used, must meet with the patient's approval. A patient who actively works on an issue or issues in his or her life decides and agrees to do so on one's own, though of course, he or she may be encouraged to do so. Often a patient doesn't need specific encouragement to actively work on an issue due to the stimulation in the group. The patient can choose to terminate participation in the session at any time (see chapters three, eleven, and twelve for further clarification).

Despite an effective warmup, the patient must still be led gently into the eye of the original experiential storm. In some cases, a patient can more quickly be stimulated to relive a major experience effectively, which usually occurs with patients who have been in therapy for a while.

The patient can be stimulated in a number of ways to relive a major experience in his or her life. When the patient has been in a previous or sessions, the warmup (which is kept to five or ten minutes in individual therapy and ten to twenty minutes in group therapy) may consist of a discussion of what the patient has been feeling, briefly what has been happening in the patient's life and what the patient wants to or needs to work on. Such a discussion is usually shorter in a group session. After the warmup, the patient may begin talking out loud about his or her situation. Then as a key word, phrase or problem is mentioned, the alert therapist will ask the patient to go back to a time and place when the significant experience was occurring. This can be done with the therapist encouraging the patient with his or her eyes open in a psychodramatic way or closed in a relaxation exercise or in relaxation, which is equivalent to and interchangeable with hypnosis. Without specifically talking out loud about one's situation, a patient can be stimulated in a relaxation exercise or in relaxation to age regress back to a specific time as a child or adolescent to a past major experience. Another way in a group therapy session of warming up patients to the living out stage is for a number or all of the patients to age regress with a relaxation exercise to a time, usually in their childhood or adolescence, when they were significantly impacted and affected. The patient who is ready, willing and most intensely beginning to relive an experience will then begin to actively relive this experience. The other patients are supportively informed they can come back to their experience at another time in this or another session, and to return to the present and open their eyes to participate with the patient in the session, as needed, or to at least support the patient. The other patients, already warmed up to the living stage, are in a good position to double with the patient, to even live out the role of a significant other of the patient, to enter the living out stage later in this session, if possible, or at least are more prepared to do so in another session. Patients age regressing in a relaxation exercise back to a previous experience, without reliving this experience, and then returning to the present does not adversely affect them, with this process also occurring for a number of group members when relaxation isn't used when a patient in a group session relives a life event.

Relaxation exercises or relaxation, as needed, are often used, as in Hypnodrama, to stimulate the most effective age regression, uncovering, reliving and opening up. There are also patients who effectively age regress, without relaxation, in a psychodramatic way with this process used as therapeutic. Patients are encouraged to age regress to their childhood or adolescence to give them an opportunity to relive whatever they are ready to, though they will be encouraged to go back as early into their past as is therapeutic. For those patients who are ready to do so, they are encouraged to go back to anywhere from the prenatal period through adolescence when dealing with issues from their upbringing. In some cases when a patient is ready to explore a certain time period or a specific experience or problem in a specific time period, he or she will be encouraged to age regress to this period. The importance of focusing on the patient's needs and what he or she is ready for is essential. In addition, reliving an experience can stimulate a patient to relive an earlier or another experience in the same session. A patient can usually relive from one to three life events in a session, or in some cases a fourth event, though when using the funeral method this may include, at times, a patient reliving from four to six experiences where the reliving of some experiences is brief leading up to the experiences involving dying and death. If it is advantageous for the patient to continue the reliving process in a session to further open up and rebuild, and the patient has done as much work in reliving an experience as is possible or cannot progress any further while reliving an experience, he or she is encouraged to relive a related experience, an experience like it or one contributing to the feelings and thoughts he or she has just been experiencing in the experience just relived. After reliving one experience in a session, a patient is for the most part encouraged to relive an earlier experience or, in some cases if the patient is unable or isn't ready to go further into the past, to relive a major experience at an older age if in the latter case the person will open up further. In such a case when moving to an older age, the patient may not only benefit from reliving an experience at this age, but may progress to the point where he or she is ready to go further into one's past than he or she could at the start of the session. A patient at times can make a major breakthrough while reliving one experience in a session. A breakthrough experience can also occur after a patient relives one or few experiences in a session. Most relived experiences, as the patient is open and ready to take part in the living out stage and is effectively stimulated in the reliving process, are major experiences even though they may not all be breakthrough experiences. If there is not a major breakthrough when reliving an experience, a situation that occurs a number of times, what is important is that the patient opens up to the best of his or her ability and that such relived experiences, as any relived experience, leads to the reliving of another experience and further opening up, as needed in the rebuilding process. Each relived experience in a session usually is a major part of an event that occurred, and usually involves some type of opening up and reevaluation, as part of the redecisioning process, with experiences often being related leading up to a therapeutic breakthrough experience when there is one, with redecisioning being incorporated into the patient in a major way at this time. Even when there isn't a therapeutic breakthrough in a session it can set the stage for one in the next or a future session. Usually during the course of therapy there are a number of therapeutic breakthroughs when therapy is progressing successfully.

Sometimes introducing a related major message from an experience which the patient doesn't specifically relive in a session, can be a powerful stimulus assisting the patient to express feelings, thoughts and emotional pain from the experience or experiences just relived or being relived in the session. This can be introduced while a patient is reliving an experience or right after an experience is relived to further emphasize, reinforce or support the message or messages from the experience or experiences the patient has relived or is reliving in the session or to bring out a message or messages from the experience or experiences the patient has relived or is reliving in the session that the patient hasn't become conscious of up to this point. This approach can also be introduced to stimulate the patient's expression of feelings, thoughts and emotional pain from experiences relived in previous sessions or never relived, in order to stimulate the reliving of an experience. In addition, it can be utilized when a patient isn't ready or is resistant to reliving an experience or when it isn't the time for the patient to relive an experience. (See chapter six for a discussion of this approach.)

Whatever is needed to stimulate the opening up process is encouraged, as the patient is ready. For example, sometimes the therapeutic chair or visualization method is used, or a patient is encouraged to switch from being oneself to being a significant other or others, usually to the role of one significant other, and back to being oneself while reliving an experience, if the patient isn't ready to face having a significant other or others acted out by another person or persons. This process of switching back and forth from being oneself to being a significant other will occur as long as is therapeutically needed in the session, as with any approach.

What is discussed for group therapy can apply with modifications, as needed, to individual therapy, individual family therapy and multiple family group therapy. Of course, a therapist can creatively work with a patient in whatever way is therapeutic, with variations occurring in assisting patients in the living out stage. A patient is also stimulated to relive experiences in one's adult life, if needed. When working with children or adolescents, stimulating the reliving of an experience is adapted to their age and situation.

The patient should not be led in any direction that is not accurate. Nor should it be suggested or even hinted that the patient had an experience or was treated in a way he or she did not experience. Regarding the accuracy of the reliving process, I do not believe the therapist can stimulate the patient to recall what didn't happen, for all that is being stimulated is what is in the patient's mind and memory recall. This has been my experience in doing uncovering work for more than twenty years.

An appropriate way, for example, to proceed when not knowing if a patient was mistreated is:

Therapist: "Slowly go back, back to a time when Dad was treating you in a typical way or was being the way he usually was with you."

When the patient is aware of or is beginning to recall a major rejecting or neglectful experience with a significant other, such as one's mother, the therapist may use more specific words to arrive at this time.

Therapist: "Allow yourself to go back, back, back in time to a time when your mother was mistreating you or was upsetting you in some way."

Once the patient arrives experientially at this time, the therapist will proceed as follows:

Therapist: "It's beginning to focus in, it's becoming clearer, clearer and clearer as you arrive at the time right before it begins to happen to you. You're feeling it, experiencing it, living it."

From here, the therapist will stimulate the patient to relive the experience as it happened.

An example of how an experience is relived involves Mary, a 31-year-old married woman who was assisted in group therapy to rebuild herself from the emotional damage of her father molesting her at age 12, which she knew about. Mary allowed herself to lie down on a mat and was stimulated through relaxation with her eyes closed to age regress back to a time when she was molested. (An example of a portion of a typical relaxation exercise is described in chapter fifteen.)

Therapist: "Let yourself go back to a time right before your father approached you sexually" (counting back in years to this time, while Mary was in a state of relaxation).

Although Mary and the therapist knew she was going back to her father's molestation of her, every effort was made not to mislead her. It is essential not to proceed too quickly and to continue warming up the patient to the reliving process.

Therapist as Double: "How old I am is ... Where I am is ... Who is here is ... What is happening is ..." (with the therapist doubling, encouraging Mary to open up).

Mary: "I'm twelve years old" (in other cases a patient may approximate her age). "I'm in my room, lying in my bed, praying my father won't come after me."

Double: "What the room is like is ..."

Mary: "It's dark and scary."

Double: "Do I smell anything?" (stimulating her senses).

Mary: "No."

Double: "Do I hear anything?"

Mary: "Not yet."

It is important to stimulate the patient to recall the environmental surroundings for this may help the patient to recall more aspects of the experience and in further detail. In addition, it is essential not to get bogged down in excessive detail for the patient's feelings and thoughts created by the experience need to be primarily stimulated.

In this example, the therapist assumed a number of roles with the assistance of the co-therapist, owing to the nature of the situation and the inherent complexity of the molestation situation. The co-therapist was capable of taking direction of the session at any time, though the therapist in any role always must maintain direction of the session. Although ideally the therapist should primarily take the role of director with a co-therapist or auxiliary agent often living out specific roles of significant others such as the perpetrator with the therapist's assistance, as needed, this is often not feasible as another therapeutic agent may not be available, and when available, the therapist still is best able, as in this example, to function in the role of the perpetrator.

Double: "What I'm feeling is ..." (with the therapist at this time doubling to assist her to move most effectively into reliving this situation).

Mary: "He really scares me. I'm afraid if I don't let him do this to me that he won't love me anymore and maybe might even hit me. If I let him touch me and play with me, at least he won't hurt me and he does treat me nice after if I do this with him. He treats me better than anyone in the world, even better than Mom. A lot of the time, she doesn't even pay attention to me." (When her father treated her well it was the primary affection she received in her highly dysfunctional family.)

Double: "At least he pays attention to me."

Mary: "He is the only one who cares about me and sometimes it feels good, but it confuses and upsets me" (as she further opened up in a soliloquy).

Double: "It really confuses and upsets me. I also feel guilty" (trying to stimulate the patient into her ambivalence regarding her father's ongoing molestation of her).

Mary: "I do feel guilty, very guilty, but it also feels good, but I'm also scared of him."

By stimulating Mary to reexperience her mixed feelings regarding her father molesting her, she was further warmed up to experience the actual molestation she went through or a significant part of it. The more warmed up a patient is, the more open the patient will become. The therapist then stimulated the passage of time until the major event was relived.

Therapist: "The seconds start passing by" (pause). "The minutes start passing by" (pause). "More and more time passes by as I'm" (the patient knowing that this refers to her) "going to the time when something begins to happen" (in this case stimulating the reliving of the experience).

Of course, reliving an experience in a session takes much less time than it took for the original experience to occur. However, the therapist is skillful in using the time available to impact the patient as is needed. It is essential to keep the experience flowing, which the therapist did doubling with Mary.

Mary: "There's nothing I can do. He's going to get me again. He's going to get me again!" (starting to cry and tremble with fear).

Double: "Where Mom is ..."

Mary: "She's playing bingo."

Double: "Gone as usual."

Mary: "She's let me down again. She's never here when I need her" (crying).

Double: "What's happening is ..." (continuing to ask questions or making statements to stimulate the reliving of the experience).

Mary: "He's walking toward my bed. He's getting closer and closer" (with her beginning to curl up as a small child starting to cry hysterically).

Double: "The seconds pass by and time passes by. What is he beginning to do to me? What is he doing to me?"

Mary: "He's beginning to touch me. He's beginning to put his hands on me" (continuing to cry).

Double: "What he is doing as he touches me is ..."

Mary: "He is starting to take my nightgown off. No, leave me alone. Leave me alone" (crying, and, of course, still wearing her clothes while her rights were therapeutically respected).

Double: "There's nothing I can do. I'm helpless."

Mary: "I'm all alone and there is nothing I can do as he continues to take my nightgown off. He's telling me that if I don't shut up, he won't love me anymore and will make it harder on me. He is confusing me, telling me he loves me and he is all I have and I'm all he has. I don't understand. I don't understand."

At this point the therapist asked Mary to role reverse to become her father so that he could more accurately and specifically find out what her father said, felt and thought regarding molesting her. This provided the therapist with information to more accurately and authentically live out the role of Mary's father molesting her. This also gave Mary the opportunity to further connect to and understand her father's thinking and feelings, that was helpful in further recalling what occurred.

Mary as Her Father: "Mary is so special to me. She gives me the love Joyce (wife) doesn't give me. If it wasn't for her I'd be so alone. And I gave her love too. I'm all she's got and treat her so well. Her mother neglects her and is always so busy. I love to touch her. She's my little wife. She's so soft and pretty. She's sexy too. I love to make love to her. She knows this is Daddy's way of loving her. She doesn't say no like her mother and it's so easy with her. She complains sometimes, but does what I ask her to do. She knows if she didn't how mad I get and how bad I'd treat her. Then where would she be. Anyway, I'm teaching her how to be a woman, how to love a man. I know she even likes it. I make her feel good sometimes. Even though it hurts she knows she's doing this for me. Mary will never tell her mother because she knows I will blame her and that this would break up our family. So I know she'll continue to be Daddy's special little woman. She won't ever hurt me." (Mary went on further for a short period of time as her father to provide what information, understanding and recall the role reversal process encouraged.)

Once she did this she reversed back to being herself, with the perpetrator, her father, introduced into the session with the therapist in this role. The therapist functioned as the perpetrator because he was best able to act this out, and in doing so to provide the patient with the most therapeutic opportunity to relive and resolve this situation. The skill of acting or living out this or any role of a significant other includes knowledge and sensitivity of what and how the significant other feels and thinks, knowledge of the significant other's behavior and acting ability. A therapeutic agent besides the therapist would have been used in this role if it would have maximized the patient's therapeutic experience. I have had to function as the perpetrator, in many cases, when patients have relived various types of abuse and mistreatment, as no one else has been available to do it or to do it as effectively as I. I could choose not to assume this role, but it has been instrumental in stimulating the patient to open up and further recall events. In doing so I have learned how to maintain direction of the therapy process, with or without another therapeutic agent or responsible person in the session, while being flexible to come out of this role, when needed, to provide support or stimulation in other ways. In addition patients usually respond effectively to this and the therapist assuming various roles and responsibilities, as in need of what will work most effectively in therapy. The patient while having trust and confidence in the therapist will often allow the therapist to stimulate him or her therapeutically as strongly and intensely as needed, which certainly occurs when the therapeutic situation calls on the therapist to act in the role of the perpetrator. The makeup of those persons in the session and the type of session are also important when therapeutically working in specific ways. Strict guidelines are also needed, including when the therapist does or doesn't act as the perpetrator or significant other. (See chapter six regarding the living out of significant other roles.)

Though, certainly not limited to this situation, especially when a patient is reliving a molestation or sexual abuse experience, as was the case in this example, it is preferable to have another therapeutic agent or responsible person in the session besides the therapist and other group or family members in a group session, besides the therapist in an individual therapy session or besides the therapist and a family member or members in an individual family therapy session to provide increased protection against liability and a lawsuit, in addition to the therapeutic assistance or support he or she provides. It is often not possible, however, to have this type of support owing to the lack of availability of a therapeutic agent or responsible person. At least in group and multiple family group therapy, the group and family members offer the therapist some protection against liability. Depending on the specific family, there may be a more limited type of protection from liability provided by another family member or members, though this needs to be carefully evaluated. However, the therapist often has no choice but to operate alone if therapy is to be carried out. As a result, every effort should be made to lower the liability risks, as indicated. Therefore in individual therapy, the therapist when alone with the patient and in individual family therapy when alone with a family member or members, unless a family member or members could be a responsible witness or witnesses, should not act out as the perpetrator any type of molestation or sexual abuse or even speak as the perpetrator when the patient relives being molested or sexually abused. In this situation the therapist instead can encourage the patient in relaxation with one's eyes closed to relive being molested or sexually abused without the role of the perpetrator acted out by another person. The therapist in this case will assist the patient to do this through doubling and questions and statements, as when assisting a patient to relive other experiences in this manner. In such a situation the therapist can provide stimulation and support doubling with the patient and in other ways. The only exception in very limited situations, after careful assessment, with a very advanced adult patient who has been in therapy for a while, is highly motivated, and where very structured guidelines are established to protect the patient's welfare beyond what is usually done is it feasible for the therapist when alone with the patient, without touching even an acceptable area of the body, to act out the role of the molester or sexual abuse if the patient relives being molested or sexually abused. In addition, for the most part with a child under age thirteen and with some adolescents without adult family members in a session, a therapist should not act out as the perpetrator any type of abuse or rejection when alone with the patient in individual therapy, when alone with patients in group therapy, and in individual family therapy when alone with a family member or members, unless a family member or members could be a responsible witness or witnesses. In multiple family group therapy when there may be children from ages nine to twelve involved with their families, there is usually a therapeutic agent or responsible person in the session in addition to the therapist.

In individual therapy, the therapist when alone with the patient should never touch the patient, even in socially and culturally acceptable areas due to the litigation risk. In addition, in individual family therapy, the solo therapist alone with a family needs to be cautious about touching patients or family members even in acceptable areas. The only type of touching that is recommended when alone with a patient is shaking his or her hand. The only time a solo therapist alone with a patient should hug or embrace a patient should be after the session in "eye contact" of another responsible person, that could include clinic or facility staff or a patient or family member who could be trusted to state that this was an acceptable hug or embrace and who wouldn't be adversely affected or jealous if witnessing this.

Although it is obvious that the therapeutic agent is acting in the role of perpetrator, for therapeutic and liability reasons the therapeutic agent should regularly announce his or her role to the patient before assuming it, no matter what type of mistreatment is involved. In acting or living out a molestation, the therapeutic agent in the role of perpetrator must be extremely careful not to violate or touch any sexual areas of the body and should have the patient's approval to touch any nonsexual area of the body, as in any case. In addition, the therapeutic agent must proceed very carefully when touching nonsexual areas of the body and should only do so to facilitate the reliving process and stimulate the more open expression of feelings and thoughts. Touching should be limited to touching the patient's shoulder, arm or hand, which are relatively safe areas if the therapist has a good rapport with the patient. Patients who have been molested or sexually abused often respond as if they are being molested when touched in acceptable areas during the reliving process.

The patient must also be comfortable with or at least a willing participant regarding the physical position he or she takes in the acting or living out of a past experience. Encouraging the patient to be as close to the position he or she was in at the time of the incident or experience will add to the more accurate and effective living out of the patient's feelings and thoughts associated with this incident or experience. When sexual abuse or any experience is reenacted, the patient always keeps all his or her clothes on and never shows or reveals the private areas of the body. Sometimes a patient may choose or agree to lie down if the act occurred in a lying position, as it did with Mary, or may choose to be in a lying position even if the mistreatment did not occur this way. At other times, the patient may instead choose to sit or stand while the experience is clinically relived, even though the patient was in a lying down position when, for example, he or she was molested.

In continuing this process, the therapist as her father repeated in a similar type of voice and with similar words what Mary as her father lived out. The wording and statements given by Mary role reversing in the role of her father were the major messages of his feelings, thinking, verbalizations and behavior which Mary was able to recall as her father. Picking up on this, the therapist as Mary's father verbalized and acted out these major messages of her father's feelings, thinking, verbalizations and behavior. The therapist or therapeutic agent can simulate the perpetrator abusing the patient through actions ranging from just verbalizing along with the use of facial and bodily gestures to acting out verbally and in action what happened in the patient's view, depending on what is most therapeutic. Of course, the therapist or therapeutic agent does not in reality violate or harm the patient in any way. Mary was also informed that she should correct any inaccuracies acted out by the therapist, as is always the case when the role of a significant other is acted or lived out by another person. Mary was in a state of relaxation with her eyes closed, reliving this experience in this way up to this time and verbalizing what occurred as described. As her father was physically introduced into the situation, with the therapist as her father, she was asked to open her eyes to visualize him, which she did, with this adding to the reality of the situation and the opening up process. This did not take her out of a state of relaxation or hypnosis, but further focused her concentration while increasing the therapeutic stimulation she was receiving. The patient may sometimes continue to keep his or her eyes closed to live out what happened, with the therapeutic agent acting out the perpetrator's role audibly to further enhance the reliving process if this is what is therapeutic. In some cases the patient may only be ready to relive an experience with his or her eyes closed and verbalize what he or she is experiencing without a therapeutic agent or person in the role of a significant other. At other times, it may be therapeutic for the patient to open his or her eyes later in the living out part of the session, with it continuing as described here. (See the section on hypnosis or relaxation in chapter two.) In still other situations, a patient can also effectively relive an experience without using relaxation or hypnosis. The session continued.

Father: "I'm all you have and you're all I have. Without you I don't know what I'll do. You must do this for me. You can't let me down. Don't you want me to love you? If you do, let me touch you and let me do whatever I want to you." (The therapist as her father briefly touched her hand, which stimulated Mary to cry further.) "You know this is Daddy's way of loving you. In fact, who loves you the way I do. You know your mother is too busy doing other things. She's always gone. This is special. This is what a daddy does with his daughter. It will make you feel so good. Let's finish taking your nightgown off. We've done it before and you've made me so happy" (in a very manipulative voice and then moving away from Mary in near view to soon begin to act out as Mary's father having intercourse with her).

The therapist as Mary's father moving away from Mary to soon assume the position he would take to simulate having intercourse with her as a 12 year old did not take Mary away from reliving this experience as she was very much into reexperiencing this situation. As indicated, of course, Mary kept her clothes on throughout the session as any patient would. The co-therapist became the double and then referred back to Mary to continue getting an accurate account of what she was reexperiencing.

Double: "What is he now doing to me?"

Mary: "He's taken my nightgown off and is getting on top of me. I feel his nude body against me. He is starting to hurt me. I can't say anything now when he is doing this because I'm afraid he'll hit me or get mad at me" (continuing to cry).

Double: "There's nothing I can do."

Mary: "I'm helpless. It's so dark and scary." (continuing to cry). "I'll just have to let him do whatever he wants to me. I know he wants to come inside me. I've had to give in before and I'll make the best of it. He's coming inside me now. There's nothing I can do. He's in me now telling me how good it feels and how bad Mom is."

Again, her description of the situation takes much less time than the actual time it took for her father to molest her.

Father (communicating out loud in a scary voice, while lying on the floor in near view of Mary, simulating having intercourse with her, with, of course, his clothes on and not touching Mary. At this time, the therapist as her father did not need to touch Mary in any acceptable body area, for his briefly touching her hand and his acting out having intercourse with Mary when she was 12 in view of her was all that was needed to stimulate her to most effectively relive this situation): "It's feeling good. Oh, it's feeling so good being inside you. I want to love you. You make me feel better than your mother. She's mean to me, cold to me, but you're different. You're so soft, so warm. I know you really care about me. Don't you know how special you are to me? Oh this feels so good and I know you won't fight me too much because you know I can get really mad and mean if you resist me. You say mean things to me sometimes and get mad, but you always give in and I know you will again. You know if you don't how bad I'll treat you."

The therapeutic agent or therapist can act this out in a more limited way. Another alternative is for two therapeutic agents, one being her father and another being Mary, in Mary's view, to simulate Mary being molested with their clothes on, of course. The session continued.

Mary (thinking out loud while reliving her father having intercourse with her): "I wish he would leave me alone, but sometimes it feels good and in some ways it feels like he cares about me. At least this way he pays attention to me, even if it does hurt." (After pausing briefly she moved into the pain she was experiencing). "It hurts. Oh it hurts so bad, it hurts. I'm in so much pain" (moving into crying helplessly for about five minutes and then returning to her acceptance of the situation. Her crying was the type of expression leading back to a giving up type of acceptance). "It's not so bad. There's nothing I can do anyway. At least he is paying attention to me, loving me in his way. At other times, when he just touches me, it feels much better. At least then it doesn't hurt."(She continued briefly about how her father treated her well at times when he wasn't molesting her, her fear of losing her father's 'love' entirely if she didn't take part in this incestuous relationship with him and having no one besides her father as her mother wasn't available to her. However, she soon returned to the sickness of the situation.) " But I'm so confused. I know what he is doing is wrong. I feel bad, I feel dirty. I don't know what to do. I wish I was dead. I can't take this. I can't take this!" (beginning to cry again).

Double: "I'm so confused. I feel so hopeless. This makes me so sad. Why can't he love me like a normal father? Why does he have to treat me like this?"

Mary: "It's the only way he can love me, so I accept it, but I hate it. I feel so dirty, so bad. I tell him sometimes how I don't like it and I even get mad, but he doesn't care. I can't tell Mom as he would hate me and I would ruin the family. I'd rather be dead than go on this way if this is the only way I can get love" (crying for about five minutes in a weak and hopeless way, wanting to die).

At this point, it was essential to stimulate Mary to begin making a change in her thinking from wanting to die to wanting to live and overcoming this traumatic time in her life. Her death wish as a child strongly related to the hopelessness she felt because of her father's sexual abuse of her and contributed to her serious suicide attempt before she became involved in treatment. Clinically reliving and then overcoming her father's molestation of her was her primary hope for healthy change as this issue affected her. As she was emotionally stuck, in order to strengthen and prepare her to effectively relive this situation the co-therapist assumed the role of therapeutic parent to support and encourage her to confront her father. Although the situation she was reliving was temporarily put on hold, Mary still was in touch with her feelings and thoughts regarding being molested by her father, while being briefly supported and encouraged in a reparenting way. Mary was asked to keep her eyes open to visualize the co-therapist as the therapeutic parent, though in other cases a patient could close his or her eyes in a reparenting situation. Also though not necessary, in this case, Mary's progress wouldn't have been hampered if the therapist had taken role of therapeutic parent, for Mary had become accustomed to working with her therapist functioning in various roles.

Co-therapist as Therapeutic Parent (sitting beside Mary with her hand on Mary's shoulder in the role of a therapeutic parent): "I'm another parent person in your life who is here to support you and guide you. I'm not a replacement for your mother or father, but I'm here to help you out. This time it is different. I am with you and I am assisting you. It's not your fault what he is doing to you. Give yourself another chance. Don't give up. It's primarily up to you, but I'm with you."

Mary: "But I'm so bad. If my own dad treats me this way, how are other persons going to love me? If he can't love me in the right way, then no one will love me in the right way" (crying).

Therapeutic Parent: "There are other men who are different than your father. There are good men in the world too. Your father has problems. He's a very disturbed man. What he says is not accurate. It's not right. It's very wrong. It's very sick" (emotionally).

Mary: "But it still hurts. It hurts so bad. I just want to get away from everything. I want to die" (continuing to cry).

Therapist as Double: "Then no one can hurt me again. It just hurts too much" (pause). "But if I die, I lose out on life and he goes on" (encouraging her to look at both sides).

Mary: "It hurts too much. It really hurts. I want to try, but how do I know if I can trust you?" (turning to the co-therapist in the role of therapeutic parent).

Therapeutic Parent: "It's the chance you need to take. If you don't trust someone, then you very likely won't see any hope and may kill yourself. You're a good person. Give yourself a chance."

Mary, integrating her Adult thinking into the situation and realizing she had made two serious suicide attempts and that the therapy team was there to assist her, decided to give herself another chance as this process continued briefly. However, the decision to no longer want to die would strengthen and materialize as the reliving process continued. In other cases it may be more difficult to remotivate a patient.

Mary: "I'm not going to give up. I'll try, but I'm so sad. I feel so bad that he is doing this to me" (her crying subsiding with her not feeling as hopeless).

Mary needed to allow someone back into her life to reparent and support her briefly before she could again fully reexperience her father's sexual abuse and rebuild herself from it. She was then asked to close her eyes, which she did, to further connect to her strength, courage and healing abilities and then to again take herself back to the experience when her father was raping her where she left off before going into the brief reparenting exercise she had experienced. She was soon again able to reexperience the abuse and pain of her father raping her, crying strongly about this for about ten minutes, while the therapist again in the role of her father made remarks and noises audibly simulating having intercourse with her to stimulate Mary to open up, but not overwhelming her.

Mary (still crying): "I'm so sad, he's hurting me so much," (continuing to express and work on her feelings and thoughts in the first person until ready to begin confronting her father).

Co-therapist as Double: "Open your eyes and take him on now as you experience him having intercourse with you. You're abusing me Dad" (encouraging her to confront her father with the therapist as her father again acting out, in view of Mary, having intercourse with her. The therapist as Mary's father continued to act out having intercourse with Mary to maximize her expression of her feelings and thoughts in this situation).

Mary, with her eyes open, first addressed him directly regarding her sadness and then moved into her anger. Whether anger or sadness is expressed first depends on the person, with both feelings often overlapping. Though she was still struggling, she fought not to give up. The statements or messages provided by the therapist as her father to Mary's statements, pertaining to some or a number of which she may not have made to her father in actuality but which she was now making in reliving this situation, were what her father possibly would have said if she confronted him with these statements. Mary may not have made these statements to her father in actuality fearing his reprisal or was not even conscious of them or her feelings and thoughts related to them. Even though in this session these were possible statements her father would have made to statements Mary may have never originally made, her father had already in actuality provided such messages to Mary, directly or implied, and had impacted her in the process, which she now had the opportunity to confront and rebuild herself from. This interaction was encouraged during the reliving of Mary's father having intercourse with her because this was a powerful and effective way to stimulate Mary to reexperience the impact of her father's sexual abuse and to work on rebuilding from this.

Mary: "It's not right. It's wrong what you're doing to me" (beginning to fight back, though a struggle for her).

Double: "I'm not going to die because of you."

Mary: "But it's so hard. I feel so bad. I feel so dirty" (still feeling weak).

Double: "It's very hard, but I can overcome this."

Mary: "I know I can't give up anymore, but I feel so weak."

Father: "But you love me and make me feel so good. Why fight it, I'll make you feel good."

Mary: "It's not right what you're doing. You're taking advantage of me. You're sick."

Father: "But I love you. This is what you're made for. It feels so good being inside you. You like it. You know you do. You've liked it a lot. You know you have. It makes me feel so good. You can't disappoint your Dad. You would hurt me so bad" (in a manipulative and guilt provoking way).

Mary: "You're crazy. You're nuts. I only give into you because I'm afraid of you, because I'm so scared."

Double: I like it sometimes when you make me feel good physically, like other girls my age would like it" (informing her that feeling good at times when being sexually abused was not abnormal).

Mary: Sometimes I do feel good, like any other girl would. But it's not right. It's sick what you're doing to me. Why do you do this?" (increasingly realizing she did nothing wrong and raising an important question as her Adult continued to assist her).

Mary was then asked to role reverse to become her father to answer this question further. The therapist role reversed becoming Mary asking this question, with Mary as her father answering it. This further connected her to the messages her father had given her, while again having an opportunity to further experience, as her father and in his mind, the sickness and poisonous of his messages and abuse he inflicted on her. Mary then role reversed back to being herself and the therapist role reversed back to being Mary's father again simulating having intercourse with Mary. The role reversing process was done in a manner to keep the reliving process moving without interrupting the therapeutic effect the therapist, as Mary's father returning to acting out having intercourse with her, would have on her. The session continued with Mary's father continuing to intimidate her.

Father: "If you resist while I'm doing this, I won't pay any attention to you anymore. I'll treat you like crap. You'll be sorry. You'll be very sorry" (in an intimidating tone which was a psychological way to manipulate and force Mary into this situation).

Mary weakened again, but with the help of the double became stronger as she continued again to confront her father. She reached the point when the double further stimulated her.

Double: "I have more strength than I realize. I'm not going to give up."

Mary: "I won't. I won't give up. I'm tired of being sad and weak. "I'm not going to let you break my spirit again. I want to live now (as she continued to interact with her father with the double's help).

Mary's redecision to live and not die was materializing in a significant way.

Double: "It's not fair. I deserve better. It's not right what you're doing to me Dad" (mobilizing her anger and strength to confront her father).

Mary: "I'm angry. You're using me. I'm going to finally tell Mom" (becoming stronger and beginning to feel her anger).

Father: "You'll be sorry. I'm just loving you. I'll tell her how much you like this. That you wanted me. And she'll believe me."

Mary: "I didn't know any better. I felt you were loving me. Now I'm realizing you're taking advantage of me."

Father: "And if your mother believes you, she'll kick me out of the house. I'll go to jail and the family will break up because of you. You won't be able to live in the nice house you live in. You won't have all those things you're all use to. You'll really be sorry" (in a guilt provoking and intimidating way).

Mary briefly continued to interact with the therapist as her father, with Mary's father continuing to intimidate her. With the help of the co-therapist as a double Mary became stronger, reaching the point:

Mary: "Now I'm realizing how perverted you are. You're so sick. You're out of it. You make me feel so dirty, so ugly, so bad. You don't love me, I'm going to tell Mom and you won't stop me. I won't let you. No more" (more determined and angrier).

Double: "I'm very angry. I'm mad at you Dad."

Mary: "I'm very mad" (her voice rising). "You have no right doing this to me. It's not right, it's not fair" (becoming angrier and angrier).

Double: "I'm so mad at you. You're a beast doing this to me."

Mary: "This is wrong Dad. This is wrong. I hate you. I really hate you" (enraged).

At this point, while still lying down on the mat, Mary was asked by the co-therapist, who had been doubling with her, to psychologically push her father "out of her" to terminate his raping of her by pushing a pillow, representing her father, away from her a number of times, which the therapist as Mary's father, no longer simulating having intercourse with Mary, held in front of her. This was repeated while she sat up and then stood up. Once she was able to do this in a strong and forceful way, she was supportively escorted over to a table with a mat on it to further work through her anger and other feelings using the anger mat release method described in chapter seven. In other cases the patient may remain lying on a mat, continuing to relive the position taken in the actual molestation; may continue to take whatever position agreed to initially; or may move into a position that is more conducive for the expression of anger and other feelings. If the patient remained lying on a mat, he or she could kick one's feet and hit one's hands on the mat together, just kick one's feet on the mat or just hit one's hands on the mat (see the anger mat release approach in chapter seven). Mary was then stimulated to begin working through her anger and other feelings.

Co-therapist as Double (beginning slowly hitting on the mat to model for Mary and instructing Mary to begin doing the same): "I'm so angry at you."

Mary: "I'm mad at you. I'm bubbling. I'm more than mad at you."

Double: "I hate you."

Mary: "I hate you, I hate you for betraying me" (beginning to hit the mat with her hands in the process).

Father: "I'm just loving you. You've been so special to me making me so happy. You'll be sorry for treating me like this. You'll really break up the family and I'll go to jail for a long time. And it'll be your fault. It will be your fault."

Mary began raising her voice, hitting the mat with her hands harder each time expressing, working through and letting go of a significant amount of rage that had been contaminating and poisoning her.

Mary (continuing to yell out): "I hate you, I hate you. I am so mad at you. You have no right doing this to me. I'm not a bad person. I'm a good person. I hate you. You're a monster, I hate you. I'm not going to kill myself over you" (hitting the mat with her hands and verbally letting go of her anger for about the next fifteen minutes, while also expressing her sadness and other feelings with the help of her double).

Mary didn't hit the mat continuously, but she did so with some pauses to catch her breath. After she reached the peak of expressing her anger, she started to break down crying, "I'm a good person. How could you betray me like this! How could you!"

Double: "I've loved you. I loved you, I really loved you. You betrayed me."

Mary: "I only wanted to love you" (she cried out). "I would have done anything to love you and you did this to me. I hate you. I hate you!"

Double: "You're not going to do this to me anymore. I'm not dirty or bad. I'm a good person."

Mary: "I'm not bad. There's nothing wrong with me. I am a good person. I'm a very good person" (reprogramming her thinking and redeciding in her Adaptive Child that she was okay, which was possible because of her catharsis decontaminating and cleansing herself of her anger and sadness and other feelings as she was able to. The catharsis and redecisioning occurred in her wounded Child with the assistance of her Adult Nurturing Self).

Although Mary's reprogramming and redecisioning was becoming stronger, she still needed to further experience, express, release and decontaminate herself of her anger, sadness and other feelings to continue reprogramming her thinking regarding this situation. Further sessions are often needed when working to heal and rebuild from a situation like this or other rejecting situations. Of course, the more serious the abuse or rejection, the more therapeutic work is needed. In future sessions, another major part of the rejecting experience may need to be relived or the same part of the experience may need to be relived again. Only the major part or parts of any experience are relived, eventually representing the entire experience. In addition, the reliving of one experience like this can represent the reliving of similar experiences. The session continued.

Double: "I don't deserve to be treated like this."

Mary: "I don't deserve this type of treatment. I don't" (breathing a sigh of relief).

Double: "I deserve to be loved, to be treated well."

Mary: "I do deserve to be loved. I deserve it a lot" (beginning to smile).

Double: "And I'm not going to do anything to prevent myself from being loved. No more. I'm going to trust and let someone love me."

Mary: "No more, no more. One day I'll find someone who can love me, and I will trust someone. I have to. I need to. I want to" (still in her Child and soon naturally moving back to her chronological age).

Mary had worked her way naturally out of her state of relaxation, which had facilitated the reliving process. Though she opened her eyes, closed them again briefly and reopened them during the session, she remained in a state of relaxation until completing her therapeutic work. This state involved a relaxation of her defenses and a heightened state of concentration and focusing of attention blocking out stimuli in her present environment which would have impaired the reliving process, the reexperiencing of her feelings, thoughts and pain and her redecisioning. Although a patient can effectively achieve this state when psychodramatic or Rebuilding Therapy methods and approaches are used without a formal relaxation exercise, relaxation along with psychodramatic or Rebuilding Therapy methods and approaches often assists the patient to operate at a deeper level in the mind and more effectively in the reliving process than with relaxation or psychodramatic or Rebuilding Therapy methods and approaches alone. In other cases where the patient's eyes remain closed, in a state of relaxation throughout the session, the therapist can assist the patient out of this relaxed state, though the patient would come out of it naturally, anyway. The use of relaxation in addition to its use in this example is also described in chapter fifteen and can be used as is needed. (See the section on hypnosis or relaxation in chapter two and the section on hypnosis and Hypnodrama in chapter five.)

At this point, the therapist and co-therapist embraced Mary warmly, making some closing remarks designed to encourage her and give her direction. The session moved into further closure with sharing and support from other group members, the therapist and the co-therapist. It is essential that all participants in a session, especially the working patient or patients, reach a psychological state of comfort and safety as the session draws to a close. This reliving process was very therapeutic for Mary, stimulating her to get to the core of a major issue in her life and changing her thinking, decisioning and outlook in a healthy way, though further progress still needed to be made.

CHAPTER 15

Life in the Womb and During Birth: The Prenatal-Birthing-Rebirthing Method

A. Thompson (1984) a teacher of gifted children, described a psychodramatic rebirthing experience she had beginning at the point where the previous terror of her actual birth experience began. This time she had the opportunity to reenact her birth, being welcomed into the "world" with reassuring gentleness, warmth and rejoicing. This was in sharp contrast to her actual birth which was long and difficult, after which she was kept away from her mother for two days. She reported that she no longer felt rejected, that she was wanted and that she was given herself, the self that perhaps had never been born. Several months later she claimed being different reporting that previous to the rebirthing experience she tuned into especially the negative thoughts of others, "but now I can feel their love and acceptance as well" (p. 29). This method is similar to the rebirthing method described later in this chapter. However, there was an important difference. Ms. Thompson did not first have the opportunity as part of the healing process, unless this just wasn't discussed, to relive her difficult birth experience and any significant prenatal experience recalled or believed or imagined to have happened. Once, and only after this process, is the person ready for the rebirthing method as one's inner wounded Child, if not treated, will eventually overpower any gains made.

Mellor reported the rebirth of a person on his own time into a warm and accepting environment, relying on this experience to increase his confidence in order to reexperience his own traumatic birth. Janov (1970 and 1991) has done significant therapeutic work in effectively assisting patients to relive and overcome their traumatic births. Barnett claimed that hypnosis, in working with prenatal and birth experiences, was effective in changing negative feelings related to these experiences to positive feelings in a large number of the cases. Barnett also briefly described examples in which hypnosis was effective in assisting to bring about marked improvement where negative prenatal experiences, including traumatic experiences, were related to significant psychopathology. To assist in the healing process, Barnett pointed out the value of applying adult wisdom and understanding, while the patient is in hypnosis, in effectively treating negative prenatal and birth experiences. Though Barnett's findings are worth looking at, further examination of his work and the work of other therapists regarding the effect of psychotherapy when dealing with prenatal and birth experiences certainly needs to be undertaken.

With the fifteen adult patients in clinical sessions I have worked with on prenatal and birth experiences, these experiences have had a significant impact on their psychological development and functioning. This is a very small number of patients worked with compared to the very large number of patients worked with where other Rebuilding Therapy methods and approaches have been utilized. However, the nature and type of work done during the prenatal and birth period makes it important to point out the number of patients worked with related to prenatal and birth issues. Despite the intensive rebuilding therapeutic work of these patients on postbirth experiences, their negative prenatal or birth experiences and related messages from their parent or parents appeared to continue to affect their psychological functioning in a negative and dysfunctional way. To deal with these problems during this period, which likely exist repressed within the person significantly more than is addressed, I have utilized the prenatal-birthing-rebirthing method. In using this method, I have worked with each patient from about one to four sessions, assisting them to clinically relive negative or traumatic prenatal or birth experiences or both, which usually have included prenatal experiences when birth experiences have been relived in these cases, so that they could ventilate, express, work through and cleanse themselves of contaminating feelings and thoughts and reevaluate and reprogram their primitive and elementary thinking and decisions related to these experiences, followed by a therapeutic rebirthing experience when needed and possible. This method is usually employed after a person has done a significant amount of postnatal therapeutic work. However, through relaxation, some patients in age regression have gone back to this period rather early in therapy and have dealt with this time in their life therapeutically, followed by postnatal therapeutic work. Often prenatal, birthing and rebirthing work is done with the same patient, though a patient may not need to relive his or her birth if it wasn't a rejecting or traumatic experience. In other situations when the prenatal environment was a positive and psychologically healthy one and there was a negative or traumatic birth experience, this needs to be relived clinically.

Nowhere in the literature have I come across studies or therapeutic work of psychodramatic or Rebuilding Therapy methods being utilized to deal with psychological issues from the prenatal period through the birth process, though if it exists I welcome reviewing it.

THE PRENATAL-BIRTHING-REBIRTHING METHOD

This method, comprised of the prenatal, birthing and rebirthing methods, has been used effectively with patients in Rebuilding Therapy who were not wanted, were felt to be a burden and discomfort to their parent or parents, whose parent or parents wanted to abort them or give them up, were emotionally disturbed, had a chemical dependency problem, weren't mature enough or prepared to care for them or experienced significant physical, marital or family problems during the prenatal period through the birthing process or when the birthing process was negative or traumatic.

Usually, a victim of this process appears to think and make decisions on a primitive and elementary level, such as: "I don't want to be born," "I want to die," I'm no good," "I'm a burden," "I'm unlovable" or "I'm going to stay by myself. The outside world is hostile and bad. I won't bother anyone and I won't trust anyone." Such a person may be born with one or more of such prebirth decisions. The prenatal environment or birth process or both, in these cases, often has had a very adverse effect on the patient's psychological development and functioning or appears to have had such an effect. Such psychological damage can most effectively be reversed and even repaired through reliving and reexperiencing the trauma and rejection of the prebirth experiences, which is the prenatal method, or of the birth process, which is the birthing method, and rebuilding oneself from this as in other age periods. The rebirthing process, which is the rebirthing method, is often encouraged after working through a prenatal or birth issue to give the patient a second opportunity to come into the world with confidence, hope and trust and feeling and believing he or she is the winner one has always been. Often when there was a negative prenatal experience or experiences there was a negative birth experience in some way, though this is not always the case (see chapter four).

Though appearing likely, possible and realistic, when the patient actually recalls prenatal experiences, usually from about six months from conception and older in the womb, or birth experiences, this period is open to further evaluation along with the methods used. Even if the patient is reexperiencing what one believes happened in the womb or during birth, which is another possibility to directly recalling what occurred, it usually relates to a specific event or situation that did occur or represents or is symbolic of what occurred. It is also possible there is a combination of direct recall and the belief of what occurred prenatally or during birth when a patient is reliving this time period. The reliving process, as described throughout this book, offers significant possibilities for growth and rebuilding through the cleansing of repressed feelings and thoughts, the release of emotional pain and the reprogramming of one's thinking at whatever level, depending on one's development. The Adult Nurturing Self, with the Adult in control and representing the Adult Nurturing Self, joins the wounded Child to provide the reality and reasoning of the Adult, the nurturing and teachings of the healthy Parent and the spontaneity, sensitivity, intuitiveness and creativity of the healthy Child, and in the process interprets and communicates in the wounded Child what is happening, while not taking away from the reliving and reexperiencing process in the wounded Child. Of course, the part of the Adult, Parent and Child that assists is healthy or as healthy as the person has access to, while the rebuilding is a relative rebuilding and healing. When the Adult is specifically referred to, the healthy Parent and Child are assisting in the reliving process as needed. Although I haven't worked with children and adolescents regarding prenatal and birth issues, this reliving process with modifications can be utilized. (See the living out stage in chapter two.)

The prenatal-birthing-rebirthing method is usually performed with the assistance of relaxation to stimulate the patient to clinically relive one's prenatal or birth experiences, and to experience the therapeutic rebirthing process if needed. In this case, the patient keeps his or her eyes closed reliving one's situation while in the womb or during the birth process and may or may not open one's eyes at the time of his or her rearrival into the world. Often the patient doesn't initially know prenatal or birth factors affected his or her functioning, though sometimes this was initially known. In the majority of cases when using this method, the patient will be encouraged to regress into the womb and in other cases will regress back into the womb without any therapeutic suggestion to do so.

THE PRENATAL METHOD

Edna, a 45-year-old married woman and mother of two children, had experienced a rejecting and traumatic childhood. She had not been wanted, was severely mistreated by her mother, molested by her father and then psychologically abandoned by him and sadistically scapegoated by her family as the "black sheep". It was imperative to explore her prenatal life and birth process to determine what damage occurred there and then to rebuild herself from this. Edna was stimulated through relaxation to relive a part of her prenatal life. Through relaxation, with her eyes closed, the therapist took her back in an age regression to one year of age and continued to stimulate her to age regress into her mother's womb. The patient informs the therapist, usually with a finger signal, when the significant experience was reached. Edna was asked to put herself in a fetal position on the couch before the relaxation process began to approximate her position in the womb, knowing and agreeing this area was going to be explored. In cases where it isn't initially clear that the patient would be reliving an experience in the womb, the patient is initially in a relaxed physical position he or she chooses and then eventually moves into the fetal position, if possible. The counting back in years and months can be done in the first person to personalize the age regression process with the therapist functioning as a double, or it can be done in the third person with the stimulation of age regression being an individualized process. When the therapist functions more specifically as the therapist, he or she is referred to as therapist rather than double, as in any session. In this example, the therapist assumed various roles for this was an individual session with the therapist alone with the patient.

Therapist as Double (continuing to slowly count back in time): "I'm a year old. I'm ten months old. I'm eight months old. I'm six months old. I'm four months old. I'm three months old. I'm two months old. I'm one month old. I'm three weeks old. I'm two weeks old. I'm one week old. I'm six days old. I'm five days old. I'm four days old. I'm three days old. I'm two days old. I'm one day old. I've just been born. I've just been born. I'm in mom's womb, her stomach. I'm a little, little child in Mom's stomach. I will raise my left pinky, the littlest finger on my left hand when I get to a place inside my mother when she had a very strong and important effect on me or when something important happened to me" (reminding Edna again to give this signal when she reached this important time). "I'm nine months from the time I was produced. I'm getting smaller and smaller, younger and younger. I'm eight months from the time I was produced. I am seven months from the time I was produced," with the double going slowly and pausing regularly to encourage the patient's interaction, with Edna appearing to stop at about seven months from conception.

When earlier than about six months from conception, which will usually not be the case, the therapist no longer needs to refer to the specific number of months from conception or from when the child was produced and may use the statements "I'm getting smaller and smaller, younger and younger" (with appropriate pauses), "I am arriving at a time inside Mom's stomach when something very important and significant is happening to me." In case the patient bypassed a significant time in the womb, if a significant time could be any time in the womb or if the patient doesn't acknowledge a specific age or time after the therapist stimulated the patient to go as far as the patient can go or the therapist believes is beneficial, then the therapist doubling as the patient, may say "I'm going to whatever age, time or size inside Mom's stomach when something important and significant is happening to me." Even when a patient goes to a specific time, it may represent more than one to a number of times or experiences. If the patient goes to an age that he or she recalls or believes occurred before six months from conception, the therapist still needs to assist the patient to face and work through what this issue is or represents. For the most part, Rebuilding Therapy focuses on postconception from about six months from conception and older in the womb, often appearing to be about six or seven months and older from conception in the womb in my therapeutic work. As indicated, the prenatal period is fertile ground for future research and exploration.

Although it is helpful to be as precise as possible it was not essential to know Edna's exact prebirth age, though an attempt was made to approximate it. However, as this method is further developed it may be necessary to reevaluate this matter.

Double: "Though I can't talk as an unborn child, let my current Adult self communicate what I as an unborn child am feeling and thinking. Where am I? What is it like where I am?" (with appropriate pauses stimulating Edna to identify where she is and what it is like to begin the reliving process in the womb).

Edna: "It's dark, it's dark" (as her Adult communicated her feelings and thoughts as a fetus, or at least what Edna believed she was feeling and thinking).

Although the Adult in Edna was speaking for her, a significant part of Edna in her Child was experiencing what it was like in the womb or what she believed it was like, or a combination of these factors. The reliving of life in the womb is done while the patient's eyes are closed as indicated.

Double: "What position am I in? What am I doing?"

Edna: "I'm just here, just here. I'm floating, floating" (with a sad, painful look on her face as she lay in a fetal position tightening up in discomfort).

Double: "What I'm feeling is ..."

Edna: "I'm sad. I'm sad. I don't want to be here. I wish I wasn't here" (starting to cry).

Double: "I feel bad, very bad."

Edna: "I feel terrible. I wish I wasn't here. I'm causing problems."

Double: "What problems I'm causing are" (doubling in question form for Edna to clarify what was happening to her).

Edna: "I'm not sure, but it's not good."

Therapist: "Become the person you're in, your mother. Go into her mind to feel what she is feeling, to think what she is thinking, go inside her mind" (to clarify what problems her mother felt she was causing).

Role reversal allowed Edna to go into her mother's self and her newly developing Parent to experience, through her mother's mind, her mother's messages regarding her feelings and thoughts about Edna as a fetus with Edna's Adult speaking for her as her mother. These are the messages she may have received from her mother as a fetus on a primitive and elementary feeling-thought level. As indicated, these messages are either recalled or believed or imagined to have occurred or in some cases, any combination of these factors.

Edna as Mother: "I hate this. I hate this. God, not another one. I don't want this one. I don't need this kid. I have two beautiful daughters. Why do I have to be pregnant with another child? I'm only doing this because of my husband. He wants a boy. It better be a boy as he won't get any more children. But I really don't want to be pregnant. I don't want to be pregnant. If there was a way to get rid of this child I'd do it. I'd rip it out of me. This baby is nothing but a burden to me. It's just a piece of garbage to me. I hate it. I hate it. I don't want this baby."

Therapist: "Become yourself again Edna and I'll become your mother" (as this was an individual therapy session and the therapist needed to function in all necessary roles).

Mother: "I hate it. I hate it. I don't want this baby" (repeating the last statement made by Edna as her mother and going to another significant message). "I wish I could get rid of it. I wish I could rip it out of me."

Edna (crying): "I don't want to be born. I want to die. I don't want to go out there and not be wanted. He doesn't want me as a girl and she just doesn't want me. I don't want to be hated. I just want to disappear" (curling up even further and crying weakly and hopelessly).

To determine if her mother's feelings and thoughts had changed further in her pregnancy, Edna was stimulated to move briefly to eight months from conception, to nine months from conception and to before the birth process with no change. Edna was then encouraged to move back to seven months from conception with this approximate time period representing her mother's attitude about her in the womb.

It would have been helpful if Edna had been directly aware of her father's feelings and thoughts regarding her mother's pregnancy of her. However, this wasn't pursued at this time owing to the nature of the situation. Edna at least appeared to be aware through her mother that her father wanted a boy as interpreted by her Adult. It is also possible, as when reliving any experience, that Edna already had information available to her, such as her father wanting her to be a boy. As will be described, Edna did get an opportunity to reexperience her father directly in another session after she was born.

As Edna verbalized what she was reexperiencing and realized she was a girl, she couldn't have been reliving this experience in the womb just as she did originally, alone as a fetus. As indicated in chapters two and eight, no one totally relives any life event alone as a child again, but does so with the Adult Nurturing Self assisting the patient in the reliving process without significantly interfering with the reexperiencing process and the experience's actual impact on the person. If this situation is contaminated by untruths, however, it can impair the reliving process, although this has not appeared to be a problem in the age regression work I've done with patients. In addition, whatever the patient reexperiences, whether directly recalling it or believing it occurred or a combination of these factors, it usually comes from a source of reality regarding what actually occurred. The Adult will clarify reality rather than add something major that didn't occur. What was most important is that Edna felt and realized she wasn't wanted for who she was, as her Adult further clarified the situation, while she had the opportunity to clinically relive this experience and its messages and rebuild from it.

Mother: "I don't want this child. I wish I could get rid of it."

Edna: "She can't stand me. I'm just a burden to her. I'm making her life worse. I'm not the boy Dad wants. She will be better off without me. I want to die. I want to die" (continuing to cry with, of course, her Adult interpreting this situation).

Double: "I feel so bad. I'm so sad. Mom doesn't want me" (stimulating her to stay open to her feelings contributing to her desire to die and then to work her way out of this, while encouraging her just to focus on her mother's rejection at this time, as this had been the primary focus of the session. It was also important not to overstimulate her).

Edna: "I'm bad. I must be no good if she doesn't want me" (continuing to cry).

Double: "I just can't stand myself. I'm so bad" (stimulating her to deeply experience her self-hate and its origin and its related sadness).

Edna: "I'm just no good. I'm a big burden. I'm bad. If she says I'm bad, then I must be bad."

Double: "I'm so sad. I'm so sad."

Edna: "I'm in so much pain. I'm so sorry. I'm no good. I'm so sorry. I'm letting you down Mom. I feel hopeless. I feel bad. I'm very sad" (continuing to cry).

Double: "She doesn't even know me. She's not even giving me a chance."

As she was working through and cleansing her mind of her sadness, Edna was being stimulated to become more open, though resistant at this time, to the irrationality and craziness of her mother's messages, rather than just blindly accepting them. The double was doubling about her mother in the third person as Edna was very isolated in the womb and wasn't ready to directly confront her mother yet.

Edna: "She has to know. If she says I'm bad, I must be bad. I must be very bad. She wants to get rid of me I'm so bad. She hates me, she hates me. She won't ever love me."

Double: "But she hasn't even seen me. She doesn't even know if I'm a boy or a girl."

Edna: "She feels I'm bad. I'm a burden to her. I'm just causing problems" (continuing to cry).

Double: "She doesn't even know who I am. She's never seen me" (encouraging Edna to continue reevaluating her mother's messages to her and how absurd they were as her mother didn't know who she really was).

Edna (after a short silence): "She's never seen me. She doesn't know me" (further expressing herself about this as she begins to look at this situation and starts to feel her anger).

Double: "It's not my fault she really doesn't want me. You don't know me. You know nothing about me. You have no idea who I am" (stimulating Edna to begin confronting her mother).

It doesn't matter whether one is in a prenatal or postnatal period regarding confronting one's parent in his or her Parent, for it must be done to defuse the poisonous parental message that is communicated.

Edna: "You can't know me. You've never seen me" (becoming angrier).

Double: "It's not fair. I need to confront her."

Edna: "It's not right. It's wrong. It's wrong" (her anger increasing).

Double: "I'm angry. I'm mad. This isn't right."

Edna: "I'm angry. I'm furious. How can you be so mean, so selfish and not give me a chance?"

Although some may think it is impossible or inconceivable for a fetus to have such feelings and thoughts, even on a primitive and elementary level, the literature and the number of patients recalling or believing that prenatal experiences have occurred or a combination of these factors has demonstrated the reality of this situation, though further research is needed. Moreover, whether Edna felt and thought this in and from the womb, whether recalled or believed to have occurred or a combination of these factors, it was her reality that she needed to address to heal and rebuild herself from.

Double: "I hate you for this. I'm so mad."

Edna: "I do hate you for this. I hate you. You're an ugly person" (her anger level increasing).

Double: "I'm just a little innocent baby who hasn't hurt anyone."

Edna: "I've never done anything to you, I'm just a little baby, a little baby."

Double: "It's not my fault you don't want me. It's your problem."

Edna: "I'm just a little child. I didn't ask to be here. I'm here because of you, not me."

Double: "I'm so mad. I'm mad. I'm really mad."

Edna: "I am mad. I'm mad. I'm so mad at you. I deserve to be given a chance" (becoming angrier).

Double: "I have a right to be given a chance. I'm very mad."

Edna: "You should give me a chance. It's wrong that you don't. I'm mad at you. I'm so mad. I have a right to be given a chance" (expressing her anger more strongly).

Double: "I have a right to be born."

Edna: "I do have a right to be born. I'm not a bad person. There's nothing wrong with me."

Double: "You have no right depriving me of my life."

Edna: "I have a right to live. I'm mad at you for what you've done, for what you're doing. I really hate you. I hate you. I hate you."

Double: "I hate you. I hate you so much."

Edna: "You're really a mean, bad person. You're crazy. You're nuts. I hate you so much for not wanting me, for not wanting to give me a chance" (her anger increasing to a higher and higher level).

As Edna continued to express and work through her anger, feeling empowered, she reached the summit of her anger, breaking down crying in sadness, empowerment and relief beginning to realize she was a good person who had a right to be born. The session continued with Edna crying out her grief and continuing to strengthen herself.

Edna: "I'm so sad that you don't want me, Mom, that you don't want me."

Double: "You're missing out on a lot not appreciating me."

Edna: "It's really too bad that you don't appreciate me."

Double: "I'm a lovable, intelligent, pretty little girl."

Edna: "I am a smart person. I'm even pretty too. I'm so sad that you can't appreciate me" (soon terminating her crying and continuing to become stronger).

Double: "But I'm going to be born. I'm going to give myself a chance to go on despite you."

Edna: "Yes, I do want to be born. I really want to give myself a chance" (and continuing to open up further expressing more hope and determination).

Edna was encouraged to return to the present with integration, support and closure provided, as in any session. As she opened her eyes, she was relieved and proud of herself. In later sessions, which will be described, she addressed the birth process and experienced being clinically reborn in a psychologically healthy and loving way. In other cases, the patient may be stimulated to move to another related major experience or experiences in the womb in the same session, as in postnatal work, if the patient doesn't go through a healthy and strong catharsis and cognitive reprogramming in the experience just worked on, has the strength to work on another experience and there is a need and the time to. Sometimes, though less frequently, a patient can have two cathartic experiences in one session.

Although helpful to determine the specific prenatal month the patient is reliving, it is not necessary, as indicated. What is most important is that one experience or a second or third experience represents the theme of what occurred in mother's womb as in postnatal work, although in postnatal work it is easier to determine the patient's age when the experience occurred.

ANOTHER SESSION: THE BIRTHING METHOD

The same rejecting prenatal theme continued through and after birth. As she had made significant progress dealing with this, in the next session the therapist stimulated Edna, in relaxation with her eyes closed, to age regress to a time when she was approaching birth to prepare her to reexperience her traumatic birth. The therapist again assumed various roles as this was an individual session. Edna initially felt much ambivalence regarding wanting to be born related to her mother's resistance to having her. However, after encouragement from the therapist and because of her previous progress, she agreed to go through the birth process. As Edna began to reexperience her mother going through labor, she was asked to role reverse to become her mother going through labor to further connect to her mother's feelings and thoughts and to ensure she was accurately reliving what occurred as communicated by her mother, or at least what she believed this to be.

Edna as Mother: "This is killing me. This is killing me. I can't handle it. I feel like this baby is going to rip me to pieces. It's too much. It is ripping me apart. I wish I never had to go through this. It's not right. This child is ruining my life. I hate it, I wish I wasn't having it."

Therapist (to Edna): "Become yourself and I'll be your mother."

Mother: "This is killing me. This baby is killing me. It's ripping me apart. You're killing me, you're ripping me apart. You're ruining my life. I wish I wasn't having you" (communicating the message directly to Edna).

Edna: "It is my fault. It is my fault. I'm the one putting you through this. I'm the reason why. I'm bad. I'm no good" (now directly opening up to her mother, though regressing back to her condition in a previous period).

Double: "But I decided I was good and I had a right to be born" (referring to the last session). "I need to continue believing and feeling this. My mother's physical pain and her attitude are because of what happens when a child is being born and because she doesn't want me. It's not my fault. I'm an innocent victim of this. I need to give myself a chance and not let her make me give up."

Edna (after blaming herself for a while and thinking of giving up again, she soon fought back with her previous progress assisting her): It's so hard, but I know I can't let her destroy me. I'm going to do what I have to do" (with her Adult continuing to communicate for her as a fetus in the reliving process).

With the assistance of the double, Edna relived her very difficult and stormy birth and being born, experiencing and working through in a highly cathartic and intensive way her feelings, thoughts and pain, including her fear, guilt, turmoil, sadness and anger related to this, and then directly opened up to her mother beginning to take some control of her mother's rejecting messages. In doing so, she was working in the most effective way for her to give herself another chance, with her Adult Nurturing Self's assistance as is the case in reliving and redecisioning, further changing her thinking from "I'm no good" to "I'm okay" and from "I don't want to be born" to "I want to be born and I want to live" as she entered a hostile world of rejection. However, she was still psychologically wounded to a significant extent and needed to do more therapeutic work in this session, as part of the birthing experience, which included therapeutically dealing with the unloving and unaccepting reactions of her parents. She was encouraged to keep her eyes closed, even after she relived being born into the world. Edna was encouraged to relive her traumatic birth and delivery and immediate postbirth experience with her eyes closed due to the nature of the experience, the very young age period she was reliving and because an actual birth involves touching from those involved once the child is actually delivered, which couldn't be done in an individual session such as this, with no other therapeutic agent or responsible person in attendance.

Edna: "I'm going to try, but it's going to be hard" (as she was born).

Therapist as Physician: "You have a beautiful girl. She looks smart too. You ought to be very proud of her" (communicating what an objective person, such as a physician, would say to her parents).

Mother: "I'm in too much pain. I don't want to even look at her. I didn't ask for this."

Edna: "She wants nothing to do with me. She can't stand me. She hates me" (crying for a few minutes).

Edna was then asked to become her father regarding his response to her birth. Although her father's response to her birth would be relatively clear from the previous information, it was helpful to live out his response as Edna recalled it or at least believed it happened through role reversal to further connect to it.

Therapist: "Become your father and respond to your birth as he did."

Edna as Father: "Oh no, it's a girl. What am I going to do with another girl? I was hoping for a boy. I wanted a boy. I'm so disappointed. What am I going to do? It's not fair. It's not fair."

Therapist: "Edna become yourself again and I'll be your father."

Edna (soon reaching the point): "He doesn't want me. She hates me. They both don't want me around. This is too much. I don't want to be here. I want to die. I want to go away. I'm unlovable. I'm no good. I'm no good" (crying reverting back to her hopelessness, despite her previous progress, although her progress in this session up to this point and progress in. other sessions would eventually contribute to her rebuilding effectively from this).

Edna was assisted to continue facing, experiencing and working through the impact of her parent's rejection on her immediately after she was born to the point where she was ready to begin overcoming this painful experience. She cried significantly, continuing to grieve not being wanted by her parents. During this time she was reminded that she had made considerable progress before in previous sessions and during the living out of her birth in this session and shouldn't back off. It was clear Edna needed to go through further catharsis and cognitive reprogramming in this session owing to the nature of what she needed to relive. Edna also had the strength to do this, which was necessary for her to accomplish this. As this was anticipated, the therapist left time for this which does occur at times when needed and possible, though specifically mentioned in this case.

Edna (reaching the point): "I'm sad. I'm hurt, but I won't give up" (no longer crying).

Double: "I have a right to live. I have a right to live even though you don't want me Mom and Dad" (stimulating her to begin protesting and feeling her anger).

Edna: "I have a right to live. I do. I do. This isn't right the way you feel. It's very wrong."

Double: "This is wrong. You should give me a chance. I have this right. I'm angry."

Edna: "I am angry. I didn't ask to be born. But since I'm here, I just want to be loved. You're not giving me a chance. I am angry, very angry" (her anger increasing).

Double: "I hate you for this. I deserve a chance and I'm not going to let you prevent me from living a good life."

Edna: "No more. I deserve better than this. I'm mad. I'm so mad. I have so much hate. I hate it. I hate how you haven't accepted me Mom and Dad. I hate you. I hate you. I have a right to be loved and treated well" (and then continuing to express and work through her anger and deciding to live a healthy, productive and happy life. Of course, this was a decision she needed to further develop and strengthen, as with any new decision. As she reached this point, she again expressed her sadness regarding her parents' lack of acceptance, though expressing hope this time regarding herself).

Double: There is hope for me. And I really am a good person."

Edna: "There are a lot of good things about me. I'm a good person. I'm realizing this, really realizing this. I'm going to give myself a chance to live a good life. I really am" (with a smile as she continued to strengthen herself).

The therapist also provided her a reparenting experience to strengthen her confidence, outlook and self, and prepared her for the next session when she would have the opportunity to be reborn psychologically in a loving and healthy way.

Therapist as Therapeutic Parent: "You certainly do have a right to live a good life. You're a good child, a smart child, a pretty child. You've already made it through life the first time around. However, this time as you rebuild yourself, you have the opportunity to live a happy and better life as you continue to work on overcoming the rejecting experiences in your life, which you are facing again in part now and will face again in therapy regarding other experiences you will have the opportunity to heal yourself from. It will be difficult. However, you will do it with more confidence and hope because of your hard work and the success you've experienced facing and overcoming these early times of mistreatment and other experiences of mistreatment you've also worked on" (referring in the latter case to postnatal experiences she formerly worked on in other sessions previous to her prenatal, birthing and perinatal experiences she had worked on described in this chapter up to this point). "To further strengthen you in your next session, you will have an opportunity to be born again in the way you had a right to be born, with the love, acceptance and welcome you should have received."

Edna was then stimulated to return psychologically to a comfortable, safe place in the present, from where she originated the session and went into a state of relaxation. She opened her eyes taking a deep breath appearing more confident and strengthened. Any patient, whether going through relaxation or a relaxation exercise or not, is always encouraged to return to a comfortable and safe place or state of mind at the end of a session. She was given a significant amount of support, encouragement and closure. When working individually with patients such as Edna without another therapeutic agent or responsible person in the room, the therapist should not hug, hold or embrace the patient for liability purposes, despite the significant therapeutic value of appropriate physical touch when needed. Hugging or embracing a patient after an individual session, when the therapist is alone with the patient, is encouraged for supportive reasons when at least another responsible person is in eye contact of this interaction. (See chapter fourteen regarding the issue of holding, hugging or embracing a patient.)

A REBIRTHING EXPERIENCE: THE REBIRTHING METHOD

In a following session, Edna was given an opportunity to be reborn therapeutically, bringing her into the world with confidence, strength and hope, and further decreasing the negative impact of her prenatal life and birth experience. Through relaxation, with her eyes closed, Edna was again taken back into the womb when she was approaching birth, with a description of this session provided in digest form as other examples. Since this was also an individual session, with the therapist again alone with Edna, the therapist assumed the various roles.

Double: "Where I am is ... What's it like where I am is ..."

Edna: "It's dark. It's very dark. I'm floating. I'm floating" (pause). "I'm inside mom."

Double: "What am I like?"

Edna (pause): "I'm a little, little baby."

Double: "How long have I been inside her? A little time, a long time?"

Edna: "A long time. A long time."

Double: "What I'm feeling is ..."

Edna: "I'm really scared. I'm very scared."

Double: "What I'm scared of is ..."

Edna: "I'm afraid to come out. They don't want me. They're not going to treat me well, but I don't want to stay here. She hates me and hates having me here. I'm mixed up" (crying).

Though making progress in previous sessions, Edna still was responding appropriately to her rejecting environment. She would work her way out of this effectively, which would have been difficult to do if she hadn't made her previous progress.

Double: "I'm confused, but what am I going to do? What am I going to do?" (stimulating her in an encouraging and determined way to look at her free will and ability to act on it now, while reliving being in the womb previous to birth especially after the previous progress she had made).

Edna: "I'm so scared. I don't want to go out there and be hurt by them. I don't. I don't."

Double: "But I can't stay in here. I don't have any control over being born. I will soon be coming out of this person."

Edna: "It's not fair. It's not fair. I'm not a bad person. I didn't ask to be here. It's not right" (in a sad and angry tone).

Double: "I deserve better than this. I have a right to be loved."

Edna: "I do have a right to be loved. I'm a good person. I'm realizing this more than ever before" (indicative of her progress). "I feel so helpless as there isn't anything I can do about all this. I feel so bad" (crying indicative of her confusion at this time).

Double: "There is something I can do about this."

Edna: "There's nothing I can do. I'm stuck here. I'm stuck" (still a usual process to go through, despite her previous progress).

Double: "I can let myself be born with confidence and strength and as the good and loving person I am. I've let myself be born in a stormy way as a winner and then faced the rejection I was born into as a winner" (referring to the previous session).

Edna: "They don't care about who I am. They don't even want to get to know me" (referring to her parents). "They just don't care. It's so wrong. It's so wrong" (continuing to cry and becoming angrier).

Double: "It's very wrong. I have a right to be mad, very mad."

Edna: "I'm very angry. I'm an innocent child. I want to be loved and they're never going to love me, but I want to get through this" (her Adult speaking for her, while being in her Child as occurs in age regression).

Double: "Though they won't love me, I have the strength to be born in a healthy, confident and happy way this time" (continuing to assist Edna to prepare for a healthy psychological birth).

Edna: "I want to be born. I don't want to be blamed for causing Mom's pain. I can't help it, what she goes through. She can't stand me. She doesn't want me. She blames me for everything. I can't help what I am. It's not my fault" (still responding to the rejecting environment she was in, though in a stronger way than previously. She was no longer crying, though crying is not an indicator of weakness).

Double: "It's not my fault. It's not right, Mom. I'm angry at you" (stimulating her to begin directly expressing her anger to her mother again).

Edna: "You have no right to keep me from wanting to live. I have a right to live."

Double: "Nobody can take this from me, including you."

Edna: "I won't let you stop me from living. I have a right to live" (in a stronger voice).

Double: "I do have a right to live. I also have a right to be born."

Edna: "I do have a right to be born. I want to be born. I do want to be born."

Double: "I'm going to be born. I am. This time I'm going to have the opportunity to be born with love, acceptance, confidence and hope. I'm going to have the birth I always should have had to give me the welcome and chance I have a right to have. It won't be your love, Mom or Dad, but love from a parent person."

Edna: "I do have this right to let myself be born with hope and love, even if it isn't your love" (referring to her parents).

Double: "This is going to give me a new lease on life. A new beginning."

Edna: "I'm ready to be born. I'm scared, but I'm ready. I want to give myself a chance. I do."

Double: "I have a right to."

Edna: "I do have a right to be born. I have a right to be born. I want to be born now" (in an even stronger voice).

Double: "And I'm going to let myself be born now with the love, respect and acceptance I have a right to have" (reinforcing her desire to be born).

The therapist became Edna's therapeutic mother, living out and simulating giving birth to her this time in a healthy and loving way. Although ideally a female therapist or therapeutic agent should clinically rebirth the patient, I, as a male, have not found this to be a significant problem in the therapeutic rebirthing experiences I, as therapeutic mother, have directly assisted patients to experience. Far more important than the sex of the therapeutic mother is the loving, respectful and caring manner in which the therapeutic rebirth is done.

Therapist as Therapeutic Mother: "I'm looking forward to having you. I can't wait to see you. I can't wait to hold you, to touch you, to love you. I'm starting to feel the contractions" (beginning to breathe as a mother would beginning labor).

The living out of a simulated labor and delivery is of course significantly shorter than an actual labor and delivery. However, what is most important is the impact and effect of the therapeutic birth on the patient. The simulation of the labor and delivery usually lasts about five to twenty minutes, often about five to fifteen minutes followed by the immediate postbirth experience. In Edna's case, it took about ten minutes. The therapist, as therapeutic mother, continued to live out a mother going through labor. Edna continued lying in a fetal position, living out the birth process again but this time being born with love and acceptance. The therapeutic mother communicated the love that Edna had the right to experience. Although this did not make up for what she suffered through during her original birth, it was an uplifting, confidence, trust and hope building experience.

Therapeutic Mother: "You're so special, Edna. I'm finally having you. I'm going to see you so soon" (simulating a mother's pain in labor). "It's painful, but it's worth it. You're worth it. Oh, you are worth it. You're so special. I know you're special even though I haven't seen you. I feel it. I know it. You're so special. You're so special. I love you so much" (continuing to live out a mother going through the deep breathing process and pain of labor to the point of delivering. As this process continued) "You're coming out. You're coming out. I can't wait to see you."

Edna continued to lie in a fetal position experiencing the rebirthing process, not saying anything, while internally experiencing the loving and accepting process of her rebirth. This is the typical patient response during this process. The surrogate mother continued to breathe heavily while continuing to verbalize.

Therapeutic Mother: "You're coming out. This is so wonderful. This is so wonderful. This is a miracle. I've been waiting for this moment for so long. You're coming out. I know you're going to be so special."

This process continued with the delivery and with a physician giving Edna over to the therapeutic mother being lived out, with the therapist also portraying the physician. After the patient is therapeutically born again, the therapeutic mother actually holds the patient or the patient is encouraged to visually experience being held, depending on the situation and the amount of intimacy the patient can handle. Since Edna was in an individual session, alone with the therapist, she was encouraged to visually experience, with her eyes still closed, being held as a small newborn child receiving the love and affection of her therapeutic mother. As she visualized and experienced herself being held by her therapeutic mother, the therapist as her therapeutic mother continued to provide greetings, acceptance and affection. If there had been at least another responsible person in the room, it would have been feasible for the therapeutic mother to have actually held Edna, which is preferable. Again, the decision not to hold or embrace a patient, as in this case, is for liability reasons.

Therapeutic Mother: "I love you. You're such a special little girl. You're so bright. You're so intelligent. You're so wonderful. You're so pretty. What a beautiful child you are. Your specialness will continue throughout life. You're going to be whatever you choose to be.

I care about you so much. You're so lovable. You're so special. You're so strong. You're so beautiful" (continuing to welcome and greet Edna into the world, with the surrogate mother then singing a lullaby to Edna further communicating love and acceptance to her. The singing, humming or playing of a lullaby on a cassette is optional, though very effective in communicating a loving and accepting message).

At this point the therapeutic father is introduced, with the therapist also in this role.

Therapist as Therapeutic Father: "Oh you're so wonderful. I'm so glad you've come into the world. I love you. You're so special. You're so smart. You're so beautiful. You're such a strong little girl. I'm so glad you're here. You are wonderful and will always be, whatever you become" (also encouraging Edna to visually experience her therapeutic father holding her as he continued to greet her in a loving way into the world).

The therapeutic mother was then reintroduced. Only the therapeutic mother is involved, if involving the therapeutic father would be too much for the patient at the same session. In such a case, the therapeutic father could be introduced in another session. In this case, the therapeutic mother and father were involved at this time, with the therapist in both roles.

Therapeutic Mother: "You're going to make it in this world. You have the ability, talent, strength and courage to do so.

Therapeutic Father: "Even though we can't take the place of your natural mother and father, I want you to know how really wonderful you are. You have a right to a good life."

Therapeutic Mother: "You really do. You do have this right."

Double (short pause*)*: "What I Edna as a newborn am feeling is ..." (the therapist doubling).

Edna: "I am feeling so content. I'm peaceful. I feel loved. I feel accepted" (with a mellow and satisfying smile on her face). "I feel rejuvenated. I have a chance now. I'm okay."

Double: "I am a winner. I am a winner. I am."

Edna: "I am a winner. I'm going to make it now in my life. I really am."

Double: "I have many challenges and rejecting experiences to work through" (letting her know she still had much therapeutic work to do), "but this time I will deal with them with more hope, confidence and strength."

Edna: "I will. I will. I realize I have a lot to face. I'll face what I have to face" (continuing in this positive way for a brief period).

Therapist: "You have that chance now, Edna. You have a great chance now to continue to rebuild yourself and become what you can be, though you're wonderful right now. A very special person. Now let yourself go to where you came from in the present at the beginning of the session, in that peaceful, comforting and rejuvenating place."

Edna again returned to a comfortable and secure state of mind experiencing integration, support and closure and opening her eyes as she was ready as the session drew to a close, as needs to occur in any session. This experience gave her an opportunity to reenter the world with more confidence, strength, dignity and a feeling of acceptance, which she could utilize positively in her future therapeutic work and life experiences, significantly improving her prognosis.

CHAPTER 16

Rebuilding the Family

Utilizing Rebuilding Therapy methods in a family therapy context can be referred to as Rebuilding Family Therapy or Rebuilding Therapy in the family unit, with *Rebuilding Family Therapy* being the term utilized. Rebuilding Family Therapy, as other family therapies, is provided in individual family sessions where one nuclear family is involved or in multiple family group sessions where approximately three to eight nuclear families are involved in a group therapy situation. The same Rebuilding Therapy methodology and approaches used in individual or group therapy are used in family therapy as needed, including relaxation or relaxation exercises as needed. Talk therapy approaches are used, as needed, as in individual and group therapy.

Guldner (1982), describing his use of multiple family psychodramatic group therapy, appeared to rule out the use of a patient's family member in the role of double or as a significant other (a different family member who affected the patient in some way), which I advocate in limited situations when the patient and family member are ready for this and can both benefit from this process. (See chapter six regarding the involvement of family member in the role of a significant other.) Starr (1959) presented a good, though simplistic, use of Psychodrama in individual family therapy employing the double and role reversal with family members in the role of each other.

Family therapy is often necessary in working with the adult patient, for the nuclear family (spouse or nonspouse partner, children or other involved significant others) often influences and reinforces an adult's problems. With the child and adolescent patient and in some cases with the young adult patient (ages 18-25), family therapy is always needed, as the nuclear family (parents, siblings or other involved significant others) usually creates and certainly influences and reinforces a child and adolescent's problems and in some cases, a young adult's problems. While an adult patient's problems are usually created in the family of origin, this family unit is often not involved owing to the ongoing dysfunction and resistance of specific family of origin members to involve themselves in family therapy. Though involving the family of origin or a family of origin member or members is encouraged at times, it would be encouraged more if possible. The term *family member* refers to any significant other including a spouse, nonspouse partner, a blood relative, a relative through marriage or an involved person such as a close personal friend or relationship. In this sense the terms *family member* and *significant other* are interchangeable.

THE REBUILDING FAMILY THERAPY PROCESS

Rebuilding Family Therapy is utilized as an adjunct or primary treatment modality, while in some cases the boundaries of whether it is an adjunct or primary treatment modality are blurred by the nature of this process. This occurs as it reaches outside the family therapy process into the domain of individual and group therapy to assist specific family members to improve their functioning, while in other cases, when used as an adjunct to a patient's treatment, it becomes a powerful modality in its own right.

While Rebuilding Family Therapy focuses on present interaction and communication modes, using such methods as the double, role reversal and the mirror, it goes a step further than most other family therapies, stimulating the family members, as needed, to face the impact of their past experiences and upbringing on themselves and the entire family unit. The impact of the past on the present is clearly taken into account, which has a potent effect on family interaction and functioning as well as individual functioning.

Too frequently, family therapy is primarily practiced in the present, with its proponents believing that the family members learning of techniques and skills in empathizing, communication and assertion to deal with present family problems is sufficient for effective and intimate family relations. There is some validity to this for some families in crisis situations and on a short-term basis will make effective progress by just focusing on present issues. However, this will frequently be temporary, for unresolved experiences and conflicts from the past will often overpower, contaminate and negatively affect whatever communication, interaction and relationship skills are learned in the present. Once a family member has had an opportunity to begin facing, working through and overcoming one's upbringing, past negative experiences, conflicts or dysfunctional relationships, he or she will be able to decontaminate him or herself of such feelings as rage, anger, despair, sadness, guilt and fear and of poisonous and unhealthy thoughts, release psychological pain and change one's thinking from such decisions as "I'm unlovable" to "I'm lovable," from "I won't trust" to "I will trust," from "I don't need anyone" to "I do need love," and so on. Based on this process, such a family member is likely to interact more intimately and effectively with other family members as he or she gives up dysfunctional, unhealthy and nonintimate ways of living. Once this occurs, then methods such as the double, mirror and role reversal can more effectively help improve family communication, assertiveness, empathy and intimacy.

Each family member often plays a dysfunctional role in a dysfunctional family unit contributing to a dysfunctional and unhealthy family equilibrium. The conflict, disharmony, manipulation, fighting, rejection and neglect hold the dysfunctional family together. When a family member in therapy becomes healthier, this poisonous bond is often threatened, encouraging the dysfunctional family members to reject and resent this family member who threatens to break up this equilibrium, as unhealthy as it is. If other family members remain dysfunctional, the growing family member has a choice to "fight" with his or her family members, to regress back to one's dysfunctional family ways or to separate from the family. This is why all family members, as needed, should be involved in the family therapy process in order to better understand what the patient is going through and how he or she is growing, to assist family members, in addition to the designated patient, to begin to overcome negative experiences and conflicts that are impairing their functioning and to encourage family members to perceive the growing family unit in a positive and supportive way. As such, family members also become working or designated patients. When the entire family is the initial presenting problem, all participating family members are designated patients. As this process occurs, family communication, empathy, interaction and intimacy can significantly improve, as indicated. The entire family or at least the major persons in the family must grow with the patient or family growth, improved communication and intimacy won't result. However, it is often idealistic to expect all family members, who need to, to work intensively in therapy, with it being more realistic to expect varying degrees of participation and progress from other family members. Nonetheless, it is important to point out the optimal therapeutic process with the best prognosis and then to determine what is possible.

Family therapy, especially multiple family therapy, is often a powerful assessment and diagnostic indicator of individual and family pathology, as well as family strengths. The strength of multiple family therapy as an assessment tool lies in the multiple stimuli in this process, including the designated patients, other family members and families with their motivation, strengths, resistance, problems, pathology and experiences, which are capable of bringing out clearly and further the conflicts, dysfunction, assets, experiences and resistance of the participants and of even those persons who are not actively participating. Often, all "things" and dynamics come together in family therapy, though more often in multiple family due to the number of interacting stimuli and factors. Family therapy is also effective in assessing those family members who have appeared to be making more progress than they actually have through the resistance or pathology the family therapy process can bring out in such persons. Of course, when these factors are brought out, they are dealt with therapeutically. As such they are potent indicators and therapeutic stimulators assisting the participants to open up further and to become more aware of their resistance and defenses.

The stimuli and dynamics of the multiple family group therapy process may threaten some persons where they don't want any part of this process, even if they haven't attended. For example, a mother who attended individual family therapy regularly refused to attend multiple family group sessions as she feared that the other group members, by working on their past experiences of rejection, would stimulate her to become aware of unresolved conflicts related to an ongoing sexual affair she had had with her stepfather from ages 10 to 13. In other cases, some family members who do take part in multiple family group may be resistant to face their problems, emotional pain or past negative experiences at the level and openness they can be brought out in this process. Group therapy also brings out such dynamics due to the multiple stimuli and issues its participants bring out. Denial of one's feelings thoughts, pain and problems and resistance to facing these are chronic obstacles to improving individual and family functioning.

Family members who resist family therapy and in facing their issues and problems will most likely continue to control and manipulate pathologically and relate in dysfunctional and nonintimate ways with other family members. They will make rationalizations or excuses regarding their resistance, when the primary reason for their resistance is their fear of facing their past painful experiences and current problems. The tragedy is that such resistance will further aggravate and worsen family dysfunction.

THE WARMUP IN MULTIPLE FAMILY GROUP THERAPY

The therapist initially warms up the group, including a fifteen to twenty minute warmup talk the first time, to prepare the families for the intensive therapeutic process they will become involved in. The type of warmup and the therapist's specific wording depend on the makeup of the group, with the co-therapist or auxiliary agent usually available to assist.

The therapist discusses various family issues that need to be dealt with, emphasizing how important it is for family members to communicate more openly and empathetically and to relate more intimately. For example, regarding empathizing, the therapist points out the importance of role reversing and feeling another family member's feelings and thinking his or her thoughts informing the group: "Become your parent, your son, your daughter, your wife, your husband, your partner, your sister, brother or any important person in your life as he or she is opening up to you. Put your own feelings and thoughts on the side. His or her feelings and thoughts are most important at the time he or she is opening up to you. Give him or her your entire attention and energy. Let him or her know in some way you're listening. If your family member says that his slacks are "white" even though they're black, then let them be "white". It does not mean that he or she is right or wrong. It just means this is what he or she is feeling or thinking. The issues are not those of agreement, but of understanding. If one person wins, you both lose. You both or all need to be winners. It is also important to realize that when someone close to you is angry or upset with you, it doesn't mean that he or she doesn't love you. It means that he or she is expressing frustrations and concerns that are bothering him or her about you, with the hope of working out the problem. When your loved one stops talking to you, that's when you really need to worry. As long as someone close to you is talking to you, there is hope. He or she still has enough confidence in you to reach out to you, to appeal to you to listen and understand and possibly to change what you are doing which has upset him or her."

The therapist also emphasizes the importance of the past, one's upbringing, the influence of parental messages and of grandparents and relatives, and briefly discusses the Parent, Adult and Child ego states, their interaction and their relation to making decisions. Specific examples of dysfunctional parental messages and their relation to unhealthy decisions may also be provided. In addition, the therapist emphasizes the importance of addressing current individual and family problems. The therapist discusses such methods as the double, role reversal and the mirror, living out the role of a significant other and involving other group or family members in this process when beneficial. (See chapter six and seven regarding involving other group or family members in the role of a significant other and such basic methods as the double and role reversal, respectively.) If the patient working on a specific issue becomes too confused or overwhelmed with, for example, the doubling process, other group or family members will be asked to stop doubling or to decrease the amount or nature of the doubling. The group is informed that the therapist or therapeutic agent will double whenever it is in the patient or family member's best interest. No more than two persons will double at one time, but most often one person will be the primary double. The therapist also discusses the importance and implications of not leaving the session prematurely, as in any session, although the patient always has the option to do so. Whatever other instructions are needed will be provided.

This discussion may be provided for a new family in individual family therapy or for new families in multiple family therapy. At times families will be exposed to this discussion or a part of it again, although repeating it is minimized, unless helpful. When one or two families are introduced into an ongoing group, usually less than three, then these families may receive this warmup on an individual or mini-group basis. This initial fifteen to twenty minute talk seems long, but it is needed to introduce the families to this family therapy process and to prepare to work on their issues. Optimally, it would be best to focus on all the factors presented in this discussion, although this is often not possible or practical owing to such factors as types of patients, problems, families, length of treatment and setting. A warmup discussion of this nature with specific modifications can also be used in individual and group therapy.

Following the warmup talk, each family member is asked what he or she needs to work on regarding family or personal issues from the present or past. The family members, including the patient, are asked what they need to work on rather than what they want to work on in order to move through any resistance to not wanting to deal with an issue. Families and family members may be asked to work on specific issues or may volunteer to do so, but they always have the option not to work on an issue directly or to stop their involvement in the therapeutic process in the manner already described. When a family member works on an issue he or she is working therapeutically as a patient. Anyone taking part in family therapy is in actuality a patient.

Multiple family group therapy, as group therapy, has families or participants moving in and out of the group as needed. However, families or family members are still able to bond with each other, often being exposed to the same participants for at least three or four sessions of an average of about six sessions per family.

AN INFORMAL FAMILY

The multiple family therapy group, as a group therapy group, is also an informal family in which the unrelated group members are therapeutic brothers, sisters, friends and so on with each other, providing whatever support and stimulation are needed. Of course, actual family members are encouraged to provide support and stimulation to each other, as needed. Family members in multiple family group therapy, as group members in group therapy, are also encouraged to be supportive to each other outside of the group process. The difference is that group members who are not in the same family are not encouraged to become personally involved with each other. This kind of support can include two unrelated members sharing telephone numbers to provide encouragement and support for each other on the phone. Two examples of the family therapy process follow.

MULTIPLE FAMILY GROUP THERAPY: AN EXAMPLE

John, a 36-year-old workaholic businessman, under the camouflage of a college educated professional appearance, neglected his family, had a very bad temper, was authoritarian and was psychologically abusive to his wife and children. John was taking part in a multiple family group therapy session in an inpatient setting with his 35-year-old wife, Judy, and two children, Allan, 14, and Cynthia, 12. John had a history of being physically and emotionally abused by his mother. His father was a passive co-dependent person who rarely stood up to his wife (John's mother), allowing her to tyrannize the family out of his own sense of insecurity. John hated his mother's mistreatment and vowed never to become like her. The session was comprised of six families, all of whom were dysfunctional having difficulty communicating, relating intimately and exhibiting interactions characterized by mistreatment, rejection and neglect. Each family had one dysfunctional adolescent, who was the initially designated patient in an inpatient adolescent treatment program. The only inpatients in the group were the adolescent patients such as Allan. John and his family were the first family to work on their issues in the session. As with any example, this example has application to other settings such as outpatient and partial hospitalization settings.

The part of the session for John's family started after the warmup with John and his family sitting in a circle with the therapist and the co-therapist. There was no need for the use of relaxation or relaxation exercises in this session. The co-therapist was utilized to double, to live out the role of John's mother and to provide support for the family group members. The therapist directed and did what was needed. It is preferable to have a co-therapist available in multiple family therapy and if one is not available, then an auxiliary agent. In cases where this isn't possible, the skills of the therapist are used to effectively direct and guide the group alone.

John: "I really want things to get better. I don't like how we're living. No one in my family wants to talk to me. I'm here trying to help myself. How about the rest of you?" (sadly).

Therapist as Double for John: "I really wish you would talk to me."

The therapist being a male and the co-therapist being a female, started doubling for the same sex partner since this arrangement, in this case, was initially more supportive for John and his wife, Judy. However, the co-therapist also doubled with Allan later in the session. The sex of the double is usually not a significant issue, with the ability and sensitivity of the double being most important. Other group members were also encouraged to double, but not to overwhelm John or Judy or their children. As throughout the book, only the doubling of the therapist and therapeutic agent is described, unless specifically stated otherwise.

John: "I wish you would communicate with me" (looking at his wife sitting quietly).

Co-therapist as Double for Judy: "I'm afraid to say anything really personal or deep to him. He scares me. He's got a terrible temper, but I better tell him. Now's the chance" (knowing Judy's fear to communicate with John).

Judy: "I'm afraid, I'm afraid what will happen when we get home. No one knows what he's like. No one knows what he's like" (breaking down crying, still not directly speaking to John).

Double: "What he's like is ..."

Judy: "He scares us. We're all scared of him. He's not around most of the time. He's married to his work. And when he is around he is a monster, an SOB."

Double: "Tell him."

Judy (crying):"You really scare us. The children and I are afraid of you. We never know when you're going to yell and make us feel guilty. We're even afraid you may hit one of us. We can't take it anymore. You say such terrible things to us. It's like living in hell."

Double: "It is hell for us."

Judy: "It is hell. That's what it is. It's hell. I hate it. I hate it. I don't want to live like this any longer. You can't keep ignoring us and treating us so bad."

Double: "You're not loving us. You're mistreating us."

Judy: "You're beating (emotionally) us up and I won't put up with it any longer" (still crying).

The children, Cynthia, 13, and Allan, 15, began to break down crying, with the therapist and co-therapist doubling with Allan and Cynthia, respectively.

Co-therapist as Double for Cynthia: "I hate it when he yells. It makes me so sad. It really scares me."

Cynthia: "I'm afraid of him" (continuing to cry).

Double: "I'm going to tell him."

Cynthia: "I'm afraid of you, Dad. I'm scared of you. You treat us so bad sometimes. You yell at Mom and us so loud and say such bad things to us."

Double: "It hurts me."

Cynthia: "It makes me sad Dad and you do such few things with us" (crying).

Double: "What else I feel is ..."

Cynthia: "I wish you would stay away when you're like this" (continuing to cry. Allan's crying increases).

Therapist as Double for Allan: "I'm so sad. I'm afraid Mom and Dad are going to break up. They're going to get a divorce."

Allan: "I hate all this. Dad, you treat us so bad. You scare me. I get scared when you start yelling. You hardly ever do things with me or go to my games. I wish I was dead. I have nothing to live for. I wish I would have killed myself when I tried before. I wish I was dead. I hate living. I hate it! I hate it!" (continuing to cry. Allan had previously made an unsuccessful suicide attempt, overdosing on pills).

Judy: "You have to do something John. I'm not going to take this anymore. You have to face what is bothering you, or I'm leaving you. And I'm serious" (her crying subsiding).

Co-therapist as Double for Judy: "I'm not changing my mind. I mean it" (encouraging her to be firm).

Judy: "I won't change my mind. You're going to finally have to help yourself. I'm not putting up with this. No more" (firmly).

John: "I'm doing everything I can. I'm here. If you would all give me a chance, everything would be okay. Just give me a chance" (very worried but appearing more concerned about himself at this time).

Judy: "You still don't seem to fully understand how you have hurt all of us. You still seem concerned with yourself."

John: "I know you're all upset with me. I've been listening."

Judy: "You need to face the what caused your problems."

Double: "The persons in your life, in your upbringing who have affected you."

At this time the session was beginning to focus on John's past and upbringing to get to the core of his problems and improve his empathy of what his family has been going through with him. Encouraging John to role reverse with Judy or one of his children, to become one of them, could have been another way to help him better empathize with his family's feelings, thoughts, pain and needs. However, this method would have been limited in this case by John's wounded Child and defenses impairing his ability to empathize with his family. It was essential for John to get to the causes of his problems for actual healing to occur, which also would increase his empathy and insight of how he impacted his family. Role reversal could be used at a later time when his mind would be more open to the feelings, thoughts, pain and needs of others. The session continued.

Judy: "You know your mother has had an effect on you."

John: "I love my mother. She's a very good woman. She taught me everything."

Judy: "She drank and abused you and your sister. And your father let this go on. You refuse to face it. And you're just like her."

John: "I won't put up with this anymore. You're not going to talk about her this way."

Judy: "You either face how she and your father have affected you or I'm leaving you."

John: "You're not being fair. My mother is a good woman. She did her best with me. I deserved what I got from her."

The therapist continued doubling with John to reduce his resistance, to stimulate John to open up regarding his mother's rejection and then to go back to a time when his mother actually rejected him.

Double: "She was a very good woman" (trying to stimulate John to begin thinking about his mother and joining his resistance).

John: "I love my mother. She wanted the best for me. She worked so hard as Dad didn't make enough money. When she was home, she was always busy doing something for us" (his father, brother and himself).

Double: "She was strict, she was hard on me, but she meant well."

John: "Oh, she was strict, she was really strict. Boy, was she strict. But I can't blame her. I acted up bad sometimes. And she did so much for us always working so hard, even when not at her job. I can't get mad at her."

Double: "I remember one time when she was really tough with me" (stimulating John to further recall his past).

John: "Oh boy, do I!" (further looking back into his past).

Double: "She loved me, but that was a real tough time" (reassuring John that his mother loved him in her own way and inferring she could make mistakes in a tough time. This also helped to reduce John's defensiveness, while opening him up to look at his mother's mistakes).

John: "It was tough. She went through a lot. But, she slapped me around. I remember one of those times when she did. I'm remembering this now. I am. It's coming back" (pausing many times as he opened up about this with increasing emotion).

Double: "She really hurt me when she did that."

John: "I didn't expect her to treat me that way. It hurt me a lot. She also had a way of making me feel guilty and wrong and really bad around her" (his face looking somber and beginning to become angry).

Double: "She really made me mad."

John: "She made me very mad. I felt like hitting her that one time. In fact, I almost did" (becoming angrier).

Double: "I'm recalling this time, as I go back, back, back in time" (saying this slowly) "right before this time she hit me, when she started becoming upset and angry with me. It is becoming clearer and clearer to me as it begins to focus in. I'm here, I'm here. How old I am is ... Where Mom is ... Where I am is ... What's beginning to happen is ..." (pausing between questions).

John: "I'm 10, she's coming into my room. I know she's mad. She's got my report card in her hand. I'm really scared. I got a D in math. I know she is going to go crazy about this."

John's return to this experience at 10 was representative of and similar to earlier rejecting experiences with his mother, with his reliving of this experience being a psychological reliving of a number of these earlier rejecting times.

Double: "She hardly spends any time with me and when she does I can never please her" (introducing the issue of his mother's neglect, though more in a secondary role to his mother's physical and emotional abuse which he was more ready to face at this time).

Although John's family was upset with his neglect of them, they were initially demanding that he stop abusing them emotionally. However, he would also have to directly face his mother's neglect and his neglect of his family.

John: "Mom's always so busy and she's so hard on me. I got an A, three B's and a D and she is going to go after me for the D. I'm scared. She looks angry. But I understand. She works hard and I keep letting her down."

Double: "She's hit me before, I'm afraid she'll do it again." (At this point, the therapist encouraged John to recall his mother previously abusing him, as a warmup for what John was going to reexperience this time.)

John: "She really has belted me around before. She has hurt me bad" (thinking out loud).

Double: "One thing you never do is cross her."

John: "And I did it again. I'm scared. How stupid can I be, letting her down like this."

The co-therapist then took the role of John's mother. The therapist continued as John's double. In describing the therapist and co-therapist roles, it is clear that these roles have application to individual, individual family or group therapy, as has been discussed.

Mother: "I have your report card, John. I'm very disappointed in you. You know how badly I was wanting you to get an A in math. You know how hard the competition is going to be later on in life when you want to go to college. You know how hard I have to work to help make ends meet. You know what this means to me for you to become the doctor or engineer I know you could be. I'm very disappointed. I'm so hurt. I'm also very angry at you. I'm very angry at you" (her anger increasing).

John: "I'm really scared. I'm very scared" (shaking).

Double: "I'm afraid she's going to hit me. I really am."

John: "I'm really scared. She's starting to come up to me, and she's starting to raise her hand to me" (thinking out loud).

Mother: "I told you how it would feel if you screwed up again. I've had it with you. You're never going to amount to anything getting a grade like this. Damn you!" (as she started to slap him). "Damn you, what's wrong with you? You're a disgrace to me. I'm always busy working so hard for you. You've hurt me so bad" (continuing to live out slapping him. Of course, she was simulating slapping John and in no way was hurting him).

John: "I did the best I could, but maybe I didn't, Mom. I'm sorry, I'm sorry Mom. I'll do better next time. Maybe you're right."

Double: "I know I blew it."

John: "I'll try much harder next time, I really will. I know I could do better" (trembling with fear feeling disgraced).

John's mother disgraced him and punished him, leaving him feeling guilty inadequate, fearful, sad, angry and mistrustful and then making dysfunctional decisions regarding this in the process. He also was burying and internalizing his anger and despair from his upbringing, which he lived out in his life in a dysfunctional way and transferred onto his wife and children. John's Adaptive Child also decided for John to model himself after his mother as a way of coping with his childhood environment. "If I'm tough like Mom, no one can hurt me. I can do the same to others," coming from his Adaptive Child. Other Adaptive Child decisions and behaviors were also developed from his mother's mistreatment which he also needed to make in order to survive, including "I won't let anyone get to me," "I'll be in control," "I won't trust" and "I'll be busy all the time and work like Mom." John's Adaptive Child responded by having John build a wall of armor around himself, becoming a tough, hard workaholic to protect himself against others' mistreatment and his belief that he would be mistreated again. His Adaptive Child, in trying to make it more comfortable for John to live with his mother's rejection, also decided to rationalize, justify and even condone her behavior with such thinking as, "I deserved it. She's doing this because she loves me and wants the best for me. She wants better for me than she had for herself," "She can't really help it as her father hit her and threw guilt on her" and "She can't spend much time with me as she's working hard for the family," along with other justifications that can be made together or as separate thoughts.

In order to reverse this cycle, which was carried on from generation to generation and would likely continue, it was essential for John to break away from his mother's rejection and his belief that his mother's behavior wasn't so bad and was even okay. This would be accomplished by John experiencing the rejection, neglect and emotional pain that his mother inflicted on him, how it affected him and the dysfunction of this situation and overcoming this. As he would begin doing this in therapy, he would have the opportunity to stand up to his mother, expressing and cleansing himself of contaminating feelings and thoughts regarding her mistreatment, releasing emotional pain, changing his thinking and unhealthy decisions and beginning to separate from her influence. In doing so, he would likely no longer put up with his mother's or anyone's rejection. Through experiencing his mother's abuse, which he inflicted on his family, he would also experience, feel and realize to a greater extent that his mistreatment of them was not okay. The therapist knew he needed to continue stimulating John to further face and deal with his mother's rejection, rather than just accepting, suppressing or repressing it or just complaining about it and remaining angry, sad, guilty, miserable and wounded and modeling himself after her.

Double: "I love her. I wish she wouldn't do this to me, but I know she's right. She works so hard and I don't try hard enough" (joining his denial in the third person as John needed some time to look at this in a soliloquy).

John: "I deserve it. I deserve it. I really let her down. I really let her down. I deserve it."

Double: "I'm just no good, I'm no good."

John: "I'm really no good. She loves me, works so hard for me and I should do everything I can to please her. I really let her down getting that D."

By joining his self-blame, the double continued to stimulate John for a short period of time in a soliloquy to look at his denial, self-punishment and acceptance of his mother's abusive treatment and neglect and then to directly confront his mother, which continued to be a challenge for John.

Double: "I hate you for what you are doing to me. It's not right. I hate you."

John: "I can't hate her. She's my mother. I love her" (still defending his mother, though the doubling of the therapist would soon pay off for John).

Double: "You're abusing me. I'm not going to take this from you anymore."

John: "But she's my mother and I messed up. Isn't that right?"

Mother: "You've devastated me John. You knew what my reaction would be to you. You deserve everything you're getting" (continuing to live out slapping him to bring him back to directly experience his mother's abuse).

John: "That's right. You told me what would happen if I messed up."

Double: "No one has a right to abuse me this way."

John: "But she has to discipline me, to teach me" (thinking out loud).

Double: "This is abusive, this is wrong."

John (after thinking for about thirty seconds): "Maybe, maybe this isn't right. Maybe you don't have this right, Mom, maybe you don't" (beginning to directly confront his mother).

Double: "I should be treated better. I don't deserve this abuse."

John: "You could treat me better, not be so hard on me, but she's my mom and she has to teach me" (reverting back to justifying his mother's abuse).

Double: "She is just giving me what I deserve. It's really okay for her to hit me like this. It's really okay" (joining John's resistance to facing his mother's mistreatment, while also stimulating John to finally look at the absurdity of justifying his mother's abuse of him).

John: "But I've done something wrong. If I didn't get that D, Mom wouldn't have had to lose her temper with me and feel so bad." (However, after a short silence and relooking at the situation) "You could treat me different Mom, you can. You really can. What you're doing is not fair, it's wrong" (beginning to confront his mother again).

Double: "I'm angry at you, Mom. You have no right treating me this way."

John: "You don't have the right to treat me this way. It's not right. It's not right slapping me this way. I am angry. This is wrong Mom" (beginning to feel his anger).

Mother: "I can do anything I want to you. I'm your mother. Don't you talk back to me" (living out slapping him again, responding as she would have if John would have confronted her in this way as a child).

As his mother abused him in this way as a child and likely would have continued to respond in this way if John confronted her as he was now but didn't do so in the past, it was necessary for John to live out this experience to give him the opportunity to rebuild from the wounds of his mother's abuse. Even if John's mother would have possibly responded more viciously if he confronted her, the messages of her abuse were of primary importance. As a result of the information the co-therapist had about John's mother, she accurately responded to John as his mother would have responded. If this wasn't relatively accurate, John could have corrected this, which he and all patients are encouraged to do. Having information regarding the situation is helpful, though not necessary.

John: "No you can't. I won't put up with this. I won't. You can't do this to me" (becoming angrier and stronger).

Double: "I'm very mad at you. I did try, but next time I will do better. Hitting me like this is wrong, very wrong."

John: "My grades weren't that bad except for the D."

Mother: "You deserve what you're getting. You know how much it means to me, how proud I've always been of you. You've hurt me terribly. You're going to pay for this."

John: "You care more for yourself than you do for me."

Mother: "I just want what is best for you. Now shut up or I'll hit you again. Don't you understand? Don't you know who I am?"

John: "You're selfish, Mom. You have no right treating me like this. Stop it. Stop it."

Mother: "Who do you think you are? Who in the world do you think you are?" (in a very angry way).

John: "I'm your son and I'm mad at you, very mad at you. You have no right doing this, to me, your son, treating me this way, no right" (his anger still increasing).

Double: "I'm very mad at you. I hate you for what you're doing to me."

John: "I can't hate her. She's my mother" (his guilt taking over again as he starts to back down).

Double: "I can hate her for what she's done and love her too. I love you, but I also hate you" (assisting him to realize he can maintain the security of loving her, while also hating her or hating what she did and encouraging him to confront her again).

John (after briefly, in a soliloquy with the double's help, looking at his guilt and his needs as a child): "I love you, but I'm realizing I also hate you. I do hate you. It's not right treating me this way. And I don't have to feel guilty for being mad at you" (raising his voice, becoming angrier and angrier).

Double: "You hardly have any time for me and treat me very bad when you do" (reintroducing her neglect as part of her overall mistreatment).

John: "You don't have anything to do with me and when you do you treat me terrible. How can you do this to me? It's wrong" (acknowledging this further).

Double: "I'm going to hit the mat on the table" (beginning to do so as a model and catalyst for John). (And saying) "I'm angry at you, Mom. I'm mad at you, Mom. I hate you, Mom."

John: "I do hate you, Mom. You're selfish, Mom. I hate you" (beginning to hit the mat with his hands and then stopping). "I'm afraid, I love her. I don't want to let her down anymore. I don't want her to hate me" (continuing to express his ambivalence).

Mother: "You certainly are hurting me again like you always do. You'll be sorry. You should be afraid" (in an angry, guilt provoking, emotionally rejecting manner).

John: "I don't want to hurt you anymore, Mom. I know I've hurt you bad. I'm really scared and confused. I'm very confused."

Double: "I don't want her to hate me for being mad at her, but she overdid it with me" (joining John's resistance, but stimulating him to realize he still had a right to be mad and feel healthy anger and hate for his mother. The double did this in the third person as John needed to think about his ambivalence again in a soliloquy).

John: "I don't want to hate her and I'm so afraid she won't love me anymore, but I'm mad. I'm so mad that I'm scared of Mom getting angry at me and that I'll get so mad back at her that I won't ever want to see her again" (thinking out loud in this way for a short time).

Double: "I have a right to feel a lot of hate for you the way you have treated me" (stimulating John to confront his mother directly again).

John (after a short pause): "You're a witch, Mom. You're mean and have no heart the way you treat me. I hate you so much for this. I hate you."

John soon began feeling more comfortable experiencing his anger for his mother. He returned to hitting the mat with his hands for about ten minutes, with some pauses, while also verbally expressing his anger, reaching the peak of his anger and then decelerating into tearfulness. While he was hitting the mat, the co-therapist as his mother continued to make rejecting remarks to him and again acted out slapping him to confront him further with his mother's abuse, which along with the therapist doubling with him stimulated him to open up very effectively.

John (continuing to express himself, crying): "It's not fair. It's not fair. I wanted so bad to please you."

Double: "Now I realize, it's your fault. It's not my fault. I'm just a victim of your abuse. You have no right treating me this way, even if I disappoint you."

John: "Instead of talking to me and encouraging me, you get mad at me and hit me. You don't even compliment me for doing well. You've let me down, you've hurt me bad" (still crying).

Mother: "I'm just trying to teach you. You drove me to this. You drove me to this."

John: "But you bully me. I'm finally realizing this. It's wrong. It's very wrong. You can't do this to me anymore. And the way you treat me is not my fault. It's your fault."

Double: "And you've spent so few good times with me."

John: "Most of your attention has been negative attention" (crying harder).

Mother: "But I do everything for you and the family. How can you say this to me?"

John: "I am saying this to you. Quit the excuses, Mom. I'm seeing you more for who you are. You were everything I wanted to be. I thought your way was the right way. It's not. No one has the right to bully others and not spend time with their kids. You can't treat me this way, Mom. I've been a victim of you. You can't neglect me. You can't if you want my love, if we're to get along. It has to be different" (as a child still crying and opening up in his Child, as he had been, with the help of his Adult Nurturing Self and then beginning to relate his past to his present, as he naturally returned to the present, as regularly occurs). "And I'm realizing I've treated others this way too."

Double: "I've treated my wife and kids the way you treated me. I didn't hit them the way you hit me, but I've been very mean to them which is just as bad as hitting them."

John (becoming even more tearful): "Just as you treated me I treated my wife and children. I became just like you. I was you. No one could tell me I was wrong" (crying more heavily).

Double: "I've been hard, really hard."

John: "I've been a bully. Now I realize what I've done. I really hate myself for it. How could I have hurt Judy and my children like this? I'm very sad, very sad" (as he continued to cry openly).

Double: "I've ignored all of you as my mother ignored me."

John: "I'm realizing this. I've been more concerned with my work. It's been most important to me" (though needing to become aware of his neglect of his family at this time, this was an issue he needed to further focus on in future sessions).

Double: "But I need to forgive myself. I need to learn from this and go on."

John: "It will be hard. I don't want to mistreat my family any longer. I want to just love them. I will try to forgive myself. I just hope you can forgive me" (turning to his family).

At this point, his children embraced him, realizing their father had made a major breakthrough and now realized that he needed to change, as they cried together. His wife then tearfully embraced him realizing there was now some hope. Then the entire family embraced for the first time in a number of years.

John (as they all eventually sat down, tears still coming from their eyes): "I wish I would have known this before. I wish I wasn't so defensive. How could I have treated you all like this? How could I ignore you so much? I'm really mad at myself. Everything you've all said is true. I'm really understanding it because I finally understand and feel how my mother treated me. I never wanted to look at this before. It was too painful."

Double: "I had no way of knowing what you were feeling, when I mistreated you. I was numb to it" (assisting John to continue coming down and integrate what he had experienced and learned, while assisting him to begin letting go of his guilt).

John: "Now that I have felt what it is like to be treated so badly, I'm beginning to know what it has been like for all of you" (speaking to his family and feeling a need to emphasize this as he related more to this).

Double: "I also thought she was right, and that's the way a parent brings up children."

John: "I didn't want to hear about or look at how my mother treated me. The pain was too much. The sadness was too great. If I hid from it, I didn't have to face it. And my anger was out of control. But I didn't think it was."

Double: "But I just continued the cycle by not facing it."

John: "What a tragedy. What a tragedy" (putting his head down in despair, but in relief). "I don't want you to be afraid to speak to me anymore, though I know it's going to take time. I hope you'll give me a chance" (continuing to address his family).

Judy: "I want to give you a chance, but I've given you so many chances. This time I feel there's more hope as you are helping yourself, but I'm scared, very scared you will hurt us again and ignore us again" (still tearful).

John: "I understand, but I really am committed to changing this time. I also hope you, Cynthia and Allan, will give Dad a chance."

Cynthia: "I want to, Dad, but you can't yell at me anymore. I'm afraid, but I want to try. Please don't yell at me anymore. You've made me so sad."

John: "I won't let you down. But, I'm scared too. I'm afraid I may not change in the way I need to, but I'm going to work hard at it" (trying to reassure her, though fearful also). (Turning to Allan) "Can you give me another chance, Allan?"

Allan: "I don't know. I want to trust you, but I'm afraid. I'm very afraid. How do I know you're not going to yell at me or some day smack me or promise to spend time with me and then not? It's going to take some time. I want you to be my friend. I've always wanted a dad, but I've never had one" (crying).

Co-therapist as Double for Allan: "You're going to have to be patient with me, Dad."

Allan: "I need time. I've been hurt a lot. I really have."

John (tearful): "I know. We have a long way to go. And I know I need a lot more help in working out my problems."

Therapist: "It's just the beginning. You all still have a lot of sadness and anger to get over regarding your life and a lot of rethinking to do."

John: "At least it's a good beginning" (relieved).

Therapist as Double for John: "I'm going to have to be very patient as you all try to give me a chance to let me back in your life. And I'm thinking of going into my own individual therapy" (stimulating John to do this).

John: "I need therapy and I'm going to face whatever I have to face. It's going to be tough. I definitely will take part in my own therapy. It is essential."

This session ended with John and his family knowing that much more work remained to be done, including resolving their present problems and that each one needed to work on themselves, though John was the primary focus at this time. What was accomplished was beyond the family's expectations. It supported the importance of family members facing the impact of their past if they are to function effectively, productively and intimately in the present with their loved ones. In this case, the family's future was at stake, including John's involvement in it.

INDIVIDUAL FAMILY THERAPY: A FOLLOW-UP SESSION

After John had made his significant breakthrough, a follow-up individual family therapy session was held shortly after the previous session. This session was held in the same inpatient setting as the multiple family group therapy session described in the previous example and, as other examples, has application to other settings. This session focused on the family's present interaction and conflicts, for it was essential to immediately assist the family to deal with these issues owing to the enormous stresses affecting it. Though the last session was a major breakthrough, Judy, Allan and Cynthia were still very angry, hurt and sad and fearful of being rejected by John again. They still needed to open up to him and he still needed to listen and more deeply empathize with them. Relaxation or relaxation exercises were not needed in this session, as in the previous session. A description of an excerpt from this session is presented to illustrate the use of Rebuilding Family Therapy in dealing with present issues and problems. The session focused on John's need to be right and his difficulty empathizing with and not respecting the feelings and thoughts of the other family members. The therapist, being the only therapeutic agent available, functioned in the role of double for each family member. After a brief warmup of about five minutes regarding the issues to be worked on, the session proceeded. Since no one initially opened up after the therapist's encouragement, the therapist became the double for everyone.

Double: "What I'm feeling is, what I'm thinking is, what I want to discuss with my Mom is, with my Dad is, with Cynthia is, with Allan is, with John is, with Judy is, what's been bothering me for some time is, what angers me is, what scares me is, what saddens me is, what worries me is" (stimulating all of the family members to begin thinking about what they wanted or needed to discuss, pausing between each question-statement).

Judy: "Though the last session was great, I'm still afraid that if we're really open to you, you will hold it against us and act like you were attacked. It worries me" (addressing John).

John: "You need to give me a chance. I'm going to try to listen. I'm trying to face my problems now."

Judy: "But you've never listened before. I know that you're trying, but I'm still scared. And how do I know you'll stay in therapy for yourself."

Allan: "I'm afraid too, Dad. You always think you know everything."

Cynthia: "You don't ever listen to me. You always think you're right, Dad. I hate the way you put us down."

John: "Please give me a chance. I'm going to try to listen. I'm really going to try to listen. I promised you all that I would. It's going to be hard, but I'm going to try."

The therapist began doubling with Judy, knowing that she would open up most spontaneously and stimulate the children to do so in the process.

Double: "You yell and scream, but you also have neglected us."

Judy: "You've been in love with yourself, John. We haven't been important to you" (starting to cry). "Your work has been your love, not us. You really haven't been married to me. You haven't really been a husband, a partner or a father. And you've treated the kids and me terrible" (her voice rising, very emotionally and tearfully as she expressed her anger and sadness for the next ten minutes).

Judy then turned to the children, while John was tearful, telling them they needed to tell their father how they felt, even though the last session was very helpful. A modified form of role reversal could also have been used where John would have doubled for Judy while she was opening up, though only used in very specific situations. Though the double in effect becomes the person he or she is doubling with, in this case this would be a type of role reversal. He could have also doubled or in this sense role reversed with his children. However, this was not needed at this time as John was listening more emphatically and was beginning to work on himself personally. The therapist began doubling with Allan, believing that he was ready to open up and would further stimulate his sister.

Double: "I'm very sad, Dad. Other things have been more important to you than me."

Allan (crying for about five minutes and then saying): "I feel like you hate me, Dad. You never want to be with me, and when you are, you treat me lousy."

Double: "Other kids' dads come to their games. You hardly come. And their dads don't yell like you."

Allan: "Your work is more important than me. You'd rather be at work than love me. You care more about making money than me. You treat other people nice, but not us, calling us names and scaring us. I'm so afraid you're going to hit me" (becoming angrier and angrier at his father). "I wish you were like the other dads. I hate you, Dad. I hate you. Mom was right about wanting to divorce you" (breaking down and crying further continuing to express his sadness, also).

Although the last session was a major breakthrough, it was not surprising that Allan had much sadness and resentment to express and work through. The therapist led Allan over to the mat on the table as he needed to further externalize his anger for his father. This would be helpful in reducing the probability of Allan becoming suicidal again, while increasing the possibility he would forgive his father.

Double: "I'm so angry at you, Dad. I'm mad at you. I hate you. Hit on the mat like me."

As the therapist demonstrated hitting on the mat, Allan began to hit on the mat and did so with his hands with some pauses for about eight minutes. While also verbalizing his anger, Allan worked through a significant amount of anger to the point where he expressed with the double's help.

Allan: "No more. I'm not going to die. I'm not going to kill myself over you. I'm going to live. I'm going to live."

Double: "I deserve better. I deserve a lot better Dad. I'm a good person. I deserve to have a dad."

Allan: "I'm not a bad person. I deserve having a real Dad, a Dad who won't fly off the handle, who won't scare me, who will have time for me. And it's your fault you won't spend time with me. You have a lot of problems, Dad. You need counseling. You do. It's not my fault you've treated me so bad. It's your fault" (feeling relieved and empowered while his father listened in a tearful and empathetic way).

As Allan opened up, Cynthia intensified her crying. The therapist had a choice. He could continue the interaction between Allan and his father or encourage Cynthia to open up. The therapist decided that as Cynthia was opening up and would further support and stimulate Allan, who had reached a position of strength, it was best for her to continue doing so rather than waiting for her father and Allan to further work out some of their differences. The therapist realized that some type of closure was needed between Allan and his father before the end of the session and planned to do this. The therapist then began doubling with Cynthia.

Double: "I feel just like Allan. You care more about your work and yourself than us. And you act like we're not even your family."

Cynthia: "You don't come to my soccer games, and the other girls have their dads there. I'm not that important to you, Dad. You care more about your friends and those people at work than you do about us" (putting her head down and crying).

Double: "It hurts. It hurts a lot, Dad."

Cynthia: "I'm so sad. I feel like I don't even have a father. And when you're around you treat us bad, worse than animals. You yell, scream and say bad things to us. Allison's dad doesn't scare her. He goes to all her games and takes her places. Not like you, Dad. It's too lonely without a dad. I wished I lived in another family. Sometimes I feel just like Allan. Sometimes I want to die too. It just hurts too much. My body hurts. I'm so sad. It's like I really don't even have a dad. I'd rather be dead. I'd be better off if I were in heaven. God would take care of me. It just hurts too much being alive. It hurts so bad not having a dad" (sobbing).

Double: "I really want a dad to do things with, to root for me at my games, to teach me, to respect me, to talk with me, to be a friend to me" (not focusing at this time on her wish to die as this was not unexpected in this type of family, she didn't have a history of suicidal tendencies and the entire family was in therapy).

Cynthia's thinking about dying wasn't taken lightly, however. There was a plan to assess this further before the session ended or after the session. Focusing on her unfulfilled needs and sadness regarding her father was what she needed at this time and would help reduce any significant suicidal ideation.

Cynthia: "Allison has that kind of dad, but I don't. I wanted that kind of dad for so long" (continuing to cry and expressing and working through a significant amount of sadness regarding her father).

Cynthia reached the point where she realized she should go on living even if her father didn't change. She began to realize she was okay, while her father and the other family members listened in a tearful and sensitive way.

Allan began to embrace his sister as she finished her crying in his arms. John and Judy also cried, with the next step being for John to reply to his children's and his wife. Allan returned to his seat in tears, but coming down from this, as was Cynthia. John began to look at each family member and addressed his family tearfully. He expressed to them, with the therapist's encouragement, that he realized even more how foolish he was and how lucky he was to still have a family, that they had every right to feel as they did, that he felt terrible about how he treated them and that he was scared they might never forgive him. The therapist also realized that Cynthia had done as much therapeutic work as she could in this session and needed some loving closure from John, if she would accept this. With the therapist's encouragement, John then made some reassuring remarks to Cynthia, who responded with some reluctance, but soon warmed up somewhat to John as he embraced her. This, at least, provided some closure for them, although they needed to address each other further in another future family session. The therapist then encouraged John to speak to Allan and reach some closure with him. Their interchange reached the point where Allan expressed:

Allan: "I'm not sure you're going to change, Dad. I love you, but I'm afraid to give you a chance. I really am, but I want to. I'm very mixed up about you" (tearfully with a pause following this).

John: "I realize I need a lot of help and I'm going to work hard to change myself to be a better dad and husband."

Judy: "It's good you want to change, but you must stay in therapy if you're to remain in the home. It won't be any other way."

The session continued with John and Allan discussing how they hoped their relationship would improve with both of them tearfully embracing. Judy and John made some positive closing remarks and embraced, but clearly she was still angry at him. The entire family, after briefly discussing some goals to work on, embraced as a unit. Physical embracing is an effective way to promote family bonding and closure, but it is not encouraged if family members are not ready for it or refuse it. While this session was another step forward, considerable therapeutic work still needed to be done in this family. The therapist also assessed Cynthia further after the session, determining that she was not a risk to harm herself, but certainly in need of continued treatment, as were the other family members.

Rebuilding Family Therapy can also be effective in marital therapy or other types of family therapy. In individual marital or relationship therapy (with persons who are not married) the therapist, whenever applicable, will double with both partners, ask them to role reverse with each other, utilize the mirror and other methods and encourage the reliving of past experiences when needed. (For other examples of Rebuilding Family Therapy, see the double, role reversal and mirror methods in chapter eight and the spell method in chapter twelve.) As with any aspect of Rebuilding Therapy, talk therapy is integrated into the process as needed. Rebuilding Family Therapy can also be effectively utilized with just present family conflicts. However, as with individual problems, for more significant, greater and more lasting change to occur in a healthy direction, past experiences and issues, as needed, should be faced, dealt with and resolved.

CHAPTER 17

The Place for Rebuilding Therapy

REBUILDING THERAPY: SHORT-TERM TO LONG-TERM TREATMENT

Rebuilding Therapy, which includes Rebuilding Family Therapy, has a place in the mental health and chemical dependency fields as an innovative, uncovering and reconstructive therapy that can be effective on a short to long-term basis depending on the degree of pathology and dysfunction and the amount and type of reconstructive work the patient needs and wants. Of course longer term therapy, when needed, gives the patient more of an opportunity to utilize Rebuilding Therapy, as with other modalities, to assist the patient to make more significant and more permanent changes. Any treatment method and approach is always geared to the patient's and family's needs and what one is ready for and willing to participate in. As a result there are times when Rebuilding Therapy methods and approaches are used minimally and other times when just talk therapy approaches are utilized.

Adult Outpatient Treatment

The following general outcome observations and evaluation for adult outpatients without chemical dependency problems have been based on overall observations of Rebuilding Therapy without doing any statistical studies, as have other general outcome observations and evaluations made in this chapter. Though any type of session for any age category is usually on a weekly basis, the frequency of sessions, whatever the length of treatment, can be varied as needed, or, especially during the latter part of treatment, spread out further as needed. Rebuilding Therapy has the power to make significant breakthroughs regarding present issues, conflicts and relationships within six weekly outpatient individual sessions, blending the past with the present and using Rebuilding Therapy methods and approaches, when needed, along with talk therapy approaches. Sometimes, when it is known Rebuilding Therapy will be limited to six weekly outpatient individual therapy sessions, reliving work, modified to this time period with effective closure, can also make a significant breakthrough assisting the patient to begin healing from a major experience and related experiences with effective redecisioning beginning. In this case, the reliving work, only when the patient is ready, can usually occur in the third to fifth session, with adequate preparation for the patient to continue what progress he or she has made without continued therapy. There are cases when a therapist will refer a patient for outpatient reliving work for a specific experience and related experiences. In such a case Rebuilding Therapy can assist the patient, often in about two to six individual therapy sessions, for example, to make a major breakthrough with effective redecisioning developing. In other cases, a patient can do reliving work with effective redecisioning developing in, for example, six to eight Rebuilding Therapy group therapy sessions as an adjunct modality to non-Rebuilding Therapy individual therapy. In such cases, the referring therapist can continue to assist the patient with the progress made. Often the redecisioning process can begin to develop significantly in about six weekly outpatient individual therapy sessions of longer term therapy if the reliving process or reliving of past experiences has been started in about the third session. Rebuilding Therapy can also begin making major personality breakthroughs, including the redecisioning process developing significantly, in about twelve weekly outpatient individual therapy sessions along with, as needed, weekly outpatient group therapy sessions which start in about the fourth to sixth week. Personality changes usually require reliving major experiences and redecisioning. As needed, Rebuilding Therapy ranging from about twelve weeks to six months of outpatient therapy, preferably one individual therapy session a week and then also, as needed, one group therapy session a week starting from about the seventh to twelfth week of therapy, can provide major breakthroughs regarding personality changes with significant redecisioning and changes of lifestyle. As needed, when provided for more than six months on an outpatient weekly basis, preferably one individual therapy session a week and then also, as needed, one group therapy session a week starting from about the seventh to twelfth week or later of therapy, Rebuilding Therapy offers significant opportunity for even more profound redecisioning, personality and lifestyle changes.

There also needs to be room for modifications of the treatment plan which can include a patient eventually taking part primarily in group therapy with periodic individual therapy sessions. There are also cases when individual therapy, as individual family therapy, is the only treatment modality available or where a patient or family is not willing, receptive or ready to taking part in group or multiple family group therapy. Integrating family therapy, as needed, on an adjunct basis when individual or group therapy are the primary treatment modalities, will significantly improve the prognosis for the adult patient and any patient and will benefit family members.

Rebuilding Therapy has application in working with chemically dependent adults on an outpatient basis to assist in improving coping, adaptive and relationship skills and rebuilding from the dysfunction and mistreatment in their past. In doing so, in addition to dealing with present life problems and issues, along with active family involvement, as needed, and participation in AA, CA or NA, Rebuilding Therapy can address with a large number of patients, as is needed and they are ready, issues from their upbringing and past after a successful detoxification program and drying-out period. For those patients who are ready, many months do not have to pass, as usually does, before doing this. Once a successful detoxification and drying-out period has occurred, general outcome observations and evaluation provided for adult patients without chemical dependency problems can apply to a number of chemically dependent persons taking part in Rebuilding Therapy.

Predicting psychotherapeutic treatment outcome involves many variables and is a difficult and complex process being an entire area of expertise in itself. As a result, despite the general outcome observations and evaluation for adult outpatients, success in treatment and the length of successful therapy for any patient varies depending on the patient's condition and problems, the nature of the rejection and dysfunction experienced, the extent of the rebuilding process needed, the kind of change the patient wants, is motivated for and is capable of making, the patient's utilization of therapy, the involvement of the family as needed, the therapeutic process, the therapist and the treatment team, if a treatment team is available, the involvement of other resources and the patient's financial and health insurance resources. With regard to the patient's financial and health insurance resources, every attempt is made to work with the patient financially relative to his or her finances and resources, while encouraging and expecting the patient to contribute to and meet his or her financial obligations as possible.

Outpatient Treatment for Children, Adolescents and Some Specific Young Adults

General outcome observations and evaluation are even more difficult and complex for children, usually age nine and over, and adolescents and, in some cases, for young adults when family therapy is always needed when there is a family, which is usually the case. In addition, other factors such as the instability or dysfunction in their upbringing and family which they may be going through and differing maturational levels make observations and evaluation more complex. Owing to the complexities of evaluating treatment outcome for children, usually ages nine to twelve, adolescents and some young adults, the discussion in this section is of a general nature relative to treating patients in this age category.

The usual length of outpatient treatment can be from about six weeks to four months of usually at least weekly sessions for the most part, though in some cases it can be longer. As with adults, present coping, adaptive and relationship skills are effectively worked on throughout therapy, as needed, with reliving work also effectively done as needed.

Reliving and redecisioning work with this population, usually when their parents are also involved themselves in this process or at a minimum are at least supportive of it, can often effectively start in about the third weekly individual session or later, as the patient is ready, which may include individual or individual family therapy. Group or multiple family therapy, as needed, can also effectively contribute to the reliving and redecisioning process after about the sixth individual session.

Though Rebuilding Therapy has been provided with the adult population in the majority of the cases, it has also been utilized effectively with many adolescents and some young adults and their families. Usually an adolescent and some young adults are in treatment for a shorter period of time than adults as their personality functioning is more fluid and less developed than the adult's personality functioning, where redecisioning and personality changes are not needed on as deep a level as with adults. Additionally adolescents and some young adults due to their maturity level don't see the need for growth and rebuilding as do adults. When it is known therapy will be for six weekly outpatient individual therapy sessions, there are some adolescents and young adults who can effectively relive experiences, in a way modified to this time period usually from the third to fifth sessions, with some redecisioning effectively developing and with effective closure. When the adolescent or specific young adult does relive experiences on an outpatient basis, he or she can make significant improvement in psychological functioning with significant redecisioning in seven to twelve weeks of weekly individual therapy sessions along with, as needed, weekly group therapy sessions which start in about the seventh week. More profound and deeper changes in psychological functioning can occur in Rebuilding Therapy when outpatient treatment, as needed, continues for more than twelve weeks of weekly individual therapy sessions along with, as needed, group therapy sessions which start in about the seventh to ninth week of therapy. Individual family therapy can be substituted for individual therapy, as needed, while multiple family group therapy can be substituted for group therapy, as needed. An adolescent or young adult may just be involved in individual therapy and individual family therapy, at times just in multiple family group therapy, or just in group therapy after a specific number of individual therapy sessions along with some type of family therapy. The type and frequency of sessions, whether individual therapy, group therapy, individual family therapy or multiple family group therapy needs to depend on the specific patient and family as in any age category. This patient population especially responds effectively to group therapy and multiple family group therapy where therapeutic support and stimulation are available, though individual therapy and individual family therapy are also effective with this age group. As chemical dependency problems for some adolescent and young adults are often intertwined with psychological and family problems that can be addressed right away as long as the patient is no longer abusing chemicals, the treatment focus for these patients in a number of cases can be similar to what has been described, with some modification in addition to AA, CA or NA.

What has been discussed for adolescents and some young adults has application to children, usually ages nine to twelve with specific variations depending on the specific patient and family. Though I have used Rebuilding Therapy methods and approaches infrequently with children, in comparison to adolescents and adults, those children I have utilized this methodology with have responded effectively, including reliving experiences with some effective redecisioning. The duration of treatment has often been shorter than with the adolescent population, with children often needing less reliving work for effective redecisioning and changes as their personality functioning is even more fluid and less ingrained than the adolescent population. Children can also easily relive experiences being less defended than adolescents and adults. On the other hand, their maturity level at times makes it difficult for children to understand the value of the reliving process. Their treatment plan needs to be especially variable, depending on the child and his or her family in this age group.

As with adults, Rebuilding Therapy methods can be used with children, adolescents and some young adults referred to in this section, as needed, along with talk approaches even when the patient isn't ready for the reliving process. Improvement for the patient in this age category usually depends on the healthy changes made by family members in addition to the patient, though as in any case there may be some exceptions. Success in therapy and the length of successful therapy, in addition to the involvement of the family, varies depending on similar factors as for the adult population.

Outpatient Family Therapy

Integrating family therapy into the individual or group therapy process can be very helpful toward an improved prognosis, as indicated. For example, utilizing individual family therapy as an alternative for individual therapy or multiple family group therapy as an alternative for group therapy, as needed at certain times during the treatment process, or adding these modalities when helpful, can contribute to improved individual functioning and an improved family unit and prognosis. The value of multiple family group therapy and individual family therapy as an adjunct to group therapy and individual therapy was described in chapter sixteen. Used in an adjunctive way, both family therapy modalities are powerful therapeutic processes in their own right. As a result, while strongly assisting and strengthening the therapeutic and change process as Rebuilding Family Therapy did in the examples in chapter sixteen, it can also effectively be used as the primary treatment modality. There are also times, for the same family, when Rebuilding Family Therapy may move from an adjunctive role to a primary treatment role or from a primary treatment role to an adjunctive role, depending on the family and family member's needs.

When regularly utilized as the primary treatment modality, individual Rebuilding Family Therapy can be effective on a short-term basis from about six to twelve sessions, usually on a weekly basis. As indicated, the frequency of sessions can be reduced, especially during the latter phase of treatment. Rebuilding multiple family group therapy also can regularly be used effectively as the primary treatment modality on a short-term basis from about six to twelve weekly sessions. The value of multiple family group therapy to stimulate and support family members and families to work on their issues is enormous. Multiple family group therapy can be very helpful along with individual family therapy in selected cases.

When used on a short-term basis as the primary treatment modality Rebuilding Family Therapy's focus is primarily on current communication, interactional and family coping skills. Reliving and redecisioning work for some family members, as it relates to the current family dynamics can begin in short-term family therapy. However, for certain families to make stronger and more lasting changes, which includes redecisioning and personality changes in varying degrees for specific family members, longer term family therapy beyond the short-term model is needed, often along with individual or group therapy for these specific family members. Although the change process usually increases and becomes more lasting as the length of family therapy increases, as needed, along with individual or group therapy for specific family members, the length of successful family therapy also depends on similar factors which the length of successful individual and group therapy depend on. As with any treatment modality, certain family members and families may resist or refuse to take part in family therapy. The complexities of family therapy, as with individual and group therapy, make it very difficult to predict the successful length of treatment, though an attempt has been made to offer some general outcome guidelines.

Redecisioning and personality change can occur in varying degrees for specific individual family members as past experiences related to specific family dynamics are relived as part of the family therapy session, as needed at the time. This assists in improving the individual and family functioning of the family members, while encouraging, stimulating and supporting other family members to do the same. However, as family therapy often needs to focus on present family dynamics, communication and relationship factors to improve current family functioning, the process of redecisioning and personality change in the family therapy session, though still important, is often slower and less extensive than in individual or group therapy. This is why when family therapy is the primary treatment modality, individual or group therapy, as needed, along with family therapy offers the best prognosis for change as a significant amount of reliving and redecisioning work is done in the individual and group therapy process. The amount of reliving and redecisioning work in the family session, as it relates to current family issues, when family therapy is an adjunctive modality depends on the needs of the family and family members.

Even when the reliving process is not part of family therapy, integrating and blending the past with the present using Rebuilding Therapy methods and approaches, along with talk approaches, to improve family interaction and functioning can contribute to an effective treatment outcome, though not as significant or long lasting as when reliving and redecisioning are part of the overall treatment process, when needed.

When used as an adjunct to treatment or the primary therapeutic modality, Rebuilding Family Therapy offers family members the opportunity to successfully resolve present family problems and issues, and also, as needed, with the assistance of individual or group therapy as needed, to effectively work on the impact of the past on individual functioning and family interaction.

Inpatient Treatment

For the adult patient, when inpatient treatment usually ranges from three to seven days for crisis resolution, the focus of treatment can effectively be on present personal and family issues with the involvement of the family as needed. In such cases redecisioning work is left for outpatient treatment. In those infrequent cases when a patient can be treated for at least five days on an inpatient basis that doesn't involve treating chemical dependency, then some reliving and effective redecisioning work can effectively be started for certain patients. For adults with chemical dependency problems the inpatient stay is often for three to seven days focusing primarily on detoxification, with further treatment left for outpatient work.

Inpatient treatment for adolescents and for some young adults usually ranges from one to two weeks with intensive involvement of the family. Though managed care may push for shorter stays for adolescents with chemical dependency problems, their dysfunction, as indicated, also involves serious psychological and family problems that can often be addressed right away along with involvement in AA, CA or NA.

Inpatient treatment for children, usually age nine and over, also with intensive family involvement, usually ranges from two weeks to two months or more.

The focus of inpatient treatment for children and adolescents and for some young adults is often on present coping skills and family dynamics, with the impact of the past also dealt with as needed. Reliving and redecisioning work can be effectively done, usually if parents are themselves involved in the reliving and redecisioning process or at a minimum are at least supportive of it, as discussed.

As needed, Rebuilding Therapy methods and approaches, along with talk therapy approaches, can be effectively used with the patient and family on an inpatient basis for crisis intervention and short-term therapeutic work.

Alternatives to Inpatient Treatment

Rebuilding Therapy can make significant contributions for children, adolescents and adults in effectively resolving problems in a cost-effective way in partial hospitalization and structured outpatient treatment settings (i.e. three hours a day three or four days a week). The development of Rebuilding Therapy programs in these settings has significant potential as the need increases, while reducing the need for inpatient treatment in many cases. Usually treatment in such settings is from about two weeks to two months or more. The development of short-term residential treatment when in-house treatment is needed is another effective treatment alternative.

A BREAKTHROUGH THERAPY

Rebuilding Therapy can actually break through and get to the causes of problems, which is usually one's past experiences and upbringing or, in some cases, singular major life traumatic events or experiences. In the process, it can repair the damage created by such causative factors. It provides an active reliving, uncovering, cathartic, ventilating, expressing, opening up, cleansing, cognitive reprogramming, redecisioning and rebuilding process. In this way it allows the patient to connect to, access, touch, rearrange, modify and change his or her unhealthy thinking resulting in healthy behavioral change, rather than just thinking about changing one's thinking and behavior or making a cognitive or philosophical interpretation or evaluation of it.

REBUILDING THERAPY: ITS APPLICATION IN MENTAL HEALTH AND CHEMICAL DEPENDENCY AND BEYOND

Although Rebuilding Therapy has been used primarily with the adjustment disorder, neurotic, chemically dependent and personality-disordered populations, it has much potential for the schizophrenic and psychotic populations. By stimulating the schizophrenic or psychotic person to walk into his or her delusional system, it may provide greater access and connection to what this process is about, what it represents and the psychological factors in one's upbringing, past, self and family contributing to it. The psychotic patient in varying degrees will also have the help of his or her own Adult with its rational and reality-oriented thinking that is still operative to a certain extent, the healthy part of one's Parent that is still functioning with its nurturing and teachings and the healthy part of one's Child that is still functioning with its sensitivity, intuitiveness, creativity and spontaneity. In addition, the schizophrenic or psychotic patient will have the assistance of the therapist or therapeutic agent in order to make sense out of his or her world, while also having the caring, teaching, modeling, creative, intuitive, empathy and reparenting skills of the therapist or therapeutic agent. In group therapy other patients with the therapist's or treatment team's direction can also be helpful. Such a process, along with Rebuilding Therapy methods and approaches, as useful, and psychiatric medication gives the schizophrenic or psychotic patient the opportunity to modify his or her thinking and behavior in a more reality-oriented and healthy way and in some cases to return to an independent self-sufficient lifestyle with some meaning and fulfillment or at least to make some progress. (Sacks, Bilaniuk and Gendron's *Bibliography of Psychodrama* lists a number of references regarding the use of Psychodrama with the psychotic and schizophrenic populations.) Rebuilding Therapy also has application with the mildly neurologically impaired person, which can be discussed at another time.

Rebuilding Therapy has a place in other fields including corrections, criminal justice, law enforcement, religion and pastoral counseling, the workplace, education and in the municipal, county, state, national and international arenas related to psychological, social, cultural, political and religious conflict resolution and psychological growth. Although it hasn't been utilized in these areas, it can be done so effectively. (Sacks, Bilaniuk and Gendron's *Bibliography of Psychodrama* also lists references regarding the use of Psychodrama in areas such as criminology, education, industry, teaching, pastoral counseling and religion and politics.)

REBUILDING THERAPY IN LAW ENFORCEMENT, COURT AND CORRECTIONS

Rebuilding Therapy has a place in the law enforcement and juvenile and criminal court systems on a preventative basis. Its confrontation methods, as crime prevention tools, are designed to shock and connect the delinquent or criminal with the impact of law-violating behavior on others and oneself. Law enforcement agencies, in some cases, already have programs in which potential delinquents are taken through the system acquainting them with jail, juvenile hall or the arrest process.

In the correctional system, Rebuilding Therapy can be helpful in the prevention of crime and in the rehabilitation of offenders. Being a methodology, having a visual, active, experiential and concrete component, it can be effective in dealing with the concrete, visual, tangible and black and white aspects of the delinquent and criminal mind, which cognitive talk therapy alone in its abstract, intellectual and philosophical way has difficulty doing. The delinquent and criminal's strong denial system of blaming, projecting and rationalizing needs to be constantly shocked, confronted and addressed for the delinquent and criminal to look at the impact of his or her behavior on others and oneself. Educating the criminal and delinquent regarding his or her impact on others and oneself is a prerequisite to teaching him or her to effectively solve problems, relate to others and get what he or she wants in a nondelinquent way. Rebuilding Therapy also gives the criminal or delinquent the opportunity to face, express, ventilate, work through and let go of contaminated anger and rage, which if held on to may result in further acting out behavior. This does not mean that most of a delinquent and criminal's anger will be eradicated, but by decreasing his or her anger level the probability of future delinquent behavior will decrease. For those inmates who choose to involve themselves in Rebuilding Therapy to repair themselves from their past rejection and the wounds from their upbringing, the carrying out of the opportunity to do so can be rewarded with added bonuses for shorter prison terms if the inmate is successful. An inmate's engaging in Rebuilding Therapy has significant implications for crime prevention in the future. Significant segments of the adult inmate population likely cannot be rehabilitated, but there still are significant other segments that can be. On the juvenile level, the majority of delinquents can be rehabilitated inasmuch as they are younger and their delinquent and sociopathic personalities have not become as deeply ingrained as in the adult criminal population.

REBUILDING THERAPY IN THE INNER CITY

Rebuilding Therapy also has a place in the inner city, assisting opposing groups such as gangs and police to reduce their mutual resentments and prejudice, to improve their understanding and to find more effective ways of relating to each other. A brief example could include a group session with a limited number of gang members and police officers. This could first involve assisting specific gang members to reenact a major experience with the police, where one gang member, for example, Stan, reenacts a conflict he had with a police officer, with one of his buddies, Buz, in the role of the police officer. This would give Stan an opportunity to ventilate and express some of his own anger, while Buz would have the opportunity to better understand the feelings and thoughts of the police officer. In addition, Buz "in the police officer's shoes" would better empathize with how he appears "in the officer's eyes." Stan could also role reverse, becoming the officer, to increase his understanding of the officer, while Buz becomes Stan ventilating his anger to the police officer. Both of them would then go back to their original roles, with the process continuing until Stan has expressed and worked through his anger sufficiently and then practices, through role training, a positive way to relate to the officer. In the process, Buz also learns to more effectively relate to the police. This would be a good crime prevention experience for both Stan and Buz. While the gang members are engaging in this process, the police officers would be observing, better understanding the gang members and their experiences with the police. The police officers would then engage in the same process, while the gang members observe the police, hopefully developing a better understanding of what a police officer experiences when dealing with gang members. After this process, both groups would sit down, dialogue, and, with increased empathy for each other, work towards gaining a better understanding and working relationship, which could include further role training to practice more effective ways of relating with each other.

REBUILDING THERAPY IN OTHER ARENAS

This same process, as in the previous section, or with other Rebuilding Therapy methods and approaches can be utilized with any opposing groups, factions or entities ranging from religious groups to cultural groups to political groups, with any conflicting parties in business and industry or any organization and with any adversarial and conflicting entities or factions in the local, state, national or international arenas.

The use of Rebuilding Therapy in the international and world arenas, where it can make a significant contribution to world peace and improved relations between nations has realistic possibilities. Relating to this is a presentation I made in 1980 at the National Conference of the American Society of Psychodrama, Group Psychotherapy and Sociometry in New York. In this presentation, I worked with supporters of the Palestinian Liberation Front and supporters of Israel, who, though bitter enemies, were struggling to improve their relations as they are presently. Each group was given an opportunity to reenact major experiences they had suffered through being victimized by the other group, the Israelis by the PLO and the PLO by the Israelis. The Israeli supporters worked through some of their anger, while also role reversing with their Palestinian foes to better understand what it was like to be a Palestinian, including what the Palestinians felt and thought about the Israelis, their turmoil and problems and being a Palestinian victim of the Israelis. The Palestinian supporters were given the same opportunity to work through some of their anger and to role reverse becoming an Israeli to better understand what it was like to be an Israeli just as the Palestinian supporters did. In the latter part of the session, both groups were given the opportunity to dialogue for a better understanding. Such a process could also be augmented through role training, with both groups practicing more effective ways of relating with each other.

Rebuilding Therapy can also be used within the United Nations to assist nations to reduce tensions, improve understanding and develop better working relations. Living out therapeutically the conflicts between opposing nations places nations in the reality of the actual conflicts, without actual violence or conflict, giving nations the opportunity to look at problems more closely, connect to their problems and in turn effectively repair them.

REBUILDING THERAPY IN RELIGION

Rebuilding Therapy also has significant potential in pastoral counseling and religion. Religion operates largely on the strong belief that faith in God or some divine power brings greater personal fulfillment. In believing that God's influences are all-powerful and can convert and change the lifestyle of the God-obedient person into a meaningful and constructive one, religion often does not address the importance of therapeutically treating the wounded Child and person. When there is no healing in the wounded Child, the wounded Child, under the direction of the impaired Parent, frequently causes persons to resist religious and Godly influences and to misinterpret what is ministered to them. In essence, Rebuilding Therapy and other breakthrough psychotherapies are needed in the religious process, for without such intervention, a clergyman ministering to his or her congregation is doing so incompletely working with many wounded individuals with impaired defense systems. Accordingly, God or any greater power cannot then penetrate, reach and teach the person in the manner which is possible.

WHERE REBUILDING THERAPY GOES FROM HERE

Rebuilding Therapy will continue to be that of a breakthrough psychotherapy in the mental health and chemical dependency arenas. While Rebuilding Therapy will continue to assist persons to rebuild themselves from the damage of the past in a major way with significant and lasting personality changes, it can also make effective contributions assisting persons to live more productively in the present, without having to make major personality changes. Though such progress will be more limited and often more temporary than when reliving and redecisioning is done, this progress will still be substantial compared to other therapies focusing on present issues and functioning. Rebuilding Therapy is much shorter in duration and considerably less expensive than the longer term analytic therapies, while offering managed care significant opportunities to provide psychotherapy in a more efficacious and cost-effective short-term way.

In addition to Rebuilding Therapy's use in mental health and chemical dependency, which has been the primary focus of this book, Rebuilding Therapy is being recommended in a number of arenas and on a number of fronts, having far-reaching implications. Such recommendations will provoke considerable controversy, though clearly requiring further consideration and evaluation. The cost of such proposals would be significant, although enormous cost savings in the long run could occur. Even more important is reducing the conflict, turmoil and dysfunction in individuals, families, groups, cities, states, nations and the world and working toward individual, family, group, national and international progress, fulfillment and peace. As Rebuilding Therapy develops and grows, formal research is called for to assess its effectiveness, as should be the case with any treatment therapy or change agent.

The methods and approaches described in this book have application wherever there is human conflict. The importance of feeling, experiencing, connecting to and touching one's problems and issues; expressing, working through and letting go of suppressed and repressed rage, anger, sadness, guilt, fear and other feelings; releasing emotional pain; understanding differing and opposing views, opinions, beliefs, persons and groups in an experiential way; reexamining thinking, decisions and belief systems; and dialoguing and practicing more effective ways of living and relating to others offers tremendous opportunities for problem resolution and less conflict.

Bibliography

Anand, K.J.S. and Hickey, P. R. (1988). "Pain and Its Effects in the Human Neonate and Fetus," *Pre- and Peri-Natal Psychology Journal*, Vol. 3, No. 2, pp. 103-123.

Badaines, A. (1989). "Murder! (She Said!)," *Journal of Group Psychotherapy, Psychodrama and Sociometry*, Vol. 41, pp. 179-180.

Barber, T. X. (1969). *Hypnosis: A Scientific Approach*, New York: Brunner/Mazel.

Barnett, E. A. (1987). "The Role of Prenatal Trauma in the Development of the Negative Birth Experience," *Pre- and Peri-Natal Psychology Journal*, Vol. 1, No. 3, pp. 191-207.

Batchelor, E. S., Dean, R. S., Gray, J. W., and Wenck, S. (1991). "Classification Rates and Relative Risk Factors for Perinatal Events Predicting Emotional Behavioral Disorders in Children," *Pre- and Peri-Natal Psychology Journal*, Vol. 5, No. 4, pp. 327-341.

Berne, E. (1961). *Transactional Analysis in Psychotherapy*, New York: Grove Press.

Berne, E. (1963). *The Structure and Dynamics of Organizations and Groups*, Philadelphia: J. B. Lippincott.

Berne, E. (1964). *Games People Play*, New York: Grove Press.

Berne, E. (1966). *Principles of Group Treatment*, New York: Grove Press.

Berne, E. (1967). "Transactional Analysis," in H. Greenwald, ed., *Active Psychotherapy*, pp. 119-129, New York: Atherton Press.

Berne, E. (1972). *What Do You Do After You Say Hello*, New York: Grove Press.

Blatner, A. (1985). "The Dynamics of Catharsis," *Journal of Group Psychotherapy, Psychodrama and Sociometry*, Vol. 37, pp. 157-166.

Blume, S. B., Robins, J., and Branston, A. (1968). "Psychodrama Techniques in the Treatment of Alcoholism," *Group Psychotherapy*, Vol. 21, pp. 241-246.

Campos, L. P. (1970). "Transactional Analysis of Witch Messages." *Transactional Analysis Bulletin*, Vol. 9, No. 34, pp. 51-57.

Chamberlain, D. B. (1980). "Reliability of Birth Memories: Evidence from Mother and Child Pairs in Hypnosis," Read at 23rd Annual Science Meeting of the American Society of Clinical Hypnosis, Minneapolis.

Chamberlain, D. B. (1983). *Consciousness at Birth: A Review of the Empirical Evidence*, San Diego: Chamberlain Communications.

Chamberlain, D. B. (1990). "The Expanding Boundaries of Memory," *Pre- and Peri-Natal Psychology*, Vol. 4, No. 3, pp. 171-190.

Chamberlain, D. B. (1992). "Is There Intelligence Before Birth," *Pre- and Peri-Natal Psychology Journal*, Vol. 6, No. 3, pp. 217-238.

Church, D. (1988). *Communicating with the Spirit of Your Unborn Child*, San Leandro, Calif.: Asian Publishing.

Coleman, T.R. (1976). A Comparative of Certain Behavioral, Physiological, and Phenomenological Effects of Hypnotic Induction and Two Progressive Relaxation Procedures (Doctoral Dissertation, Brigham Young University). Dissertation Abstracts International, (University Microfilms No. 76-2561).

Del Casale, F., Munilla, H. L., Del Casale, L. R., and Fullone, E. (1982). "Defective Parenting and Reparenting," *Transactional Analysis Journal*, Vol. 12, pp. 181-184.

Edmonston, W. E., Jr. (1977). "Neutral Hypnosis as Relaxation," *American Journal of Clinical Hypnosis*, Vol. 20, pp. 69-75.

Edmonston, W. E., Jr. (1981). *Hypnosis and Relaxation: Modern Verification of an Old Equation*, New York: Wiley.

Edmonston, W. E., Jr. (1991). "Anesis," in S. J. Lynn and J. W. Rhue, eds., *Theories of Hypnosis, Current Models and Perspectives*, pp. 197-237. New York-London: Guilford Press.

Ennes, J. M. (1950). "The Hypnodramatic Technique," *Group Psychotherapy*, Vol. 3, No. 1, pp. 11-54.

Erickson, M. H. (1980). *Innovative Hypnotherapy by M. Erickson, The Collected Papers of M. Erickson on Hypnosis*, Vol. 4, E. L. Rossi, ed., New York: Irvington.

Erickson, M. H. and Rossi, E. (1979). *Hypnotherapy: An Exploratory Casebook*. New York: Irvington.

Erickson, M. H., Rossi, E., and Rossi, S. (1976). *Hypnotic Realities*. New York: Irvington.

Farber, E. A., Vaughn, B., and Egeland, B. (1981). "The Relationship of Prenatal Maternal Anxiety to Infant Behavior and Mother-Infant Interactions During the First Six Months of Life," *Early Human Development*, Vol. 5, pp. 267-277.

Feher, L. (1981). *The Psychology of Birth*, New York: Continuum.

Feldman, Y. (1981). "The Problems of Interuterine Anxiety: Its Consequences and Resolutions." Modern Psychoanalysis, Vol. 6, pp. 75-78.

Feldmar, A. (1979). "The Embryology of Consciousness: What Is Normal Pregnancy?" in D. Mall, and W. Watts, eds., *The Psychological Aspects of Abortion*, pp. 15-24, Washington, D. C.: University Publications of America.

Ferrant, Graham. (1986). "Cellular Consciousness, Aesthema," *Journal of the International Primal Association*, Vol. 7, pp. 28-39.

Fodor, N. (1949). *The Search for the Beloved*, New York: Hermitage Press.

Frank, L. K. (1966). *On the Importance of Infancy*, New York: Random House.

Gellert, S. D. (1974). "Regression Analysis," *Transactional Analysis Journal*, Vol. 4, No. 4, pp. 42-44.

Gellert, S. D. (1976). "Key Scenes," *Transactional Analysis Journal*, Vol. 6, No. 2, pp. 144-146.

Gill, M. M., and Brenman, M. (1959). *Hypnosis and Related States; Psychoanalytic Studies in Regression,* New York: International University Press.

Gilmore, T. M. (1989). "The Tomatis Method and the Genesis of Listening," *Pre- and Peri-Natal Psychology Journal*, Vol. 4, No. 1, pp. 9-27.

Givens, A. (1987). "The Alice Givens Approach to Prenatal and Birth Therapy," *Pre- and Peri-Natal Psychology Journal*, Vol. 1, No. 3, pp. 223-229.

Goodlin, R. C. (1979). *The Care of the Fetus,* New York: Masson Publishing.

Goulding, M., and Goulding, R. L. (1979). *Changing Lives Through Redecision Therapy*, New York: Brunner/Mazel.

Goulding, R. L., and Goulding, M. (1976). "Injunctions, Decisions and Redecisions," *Transactional Analysis Journal*, Vol. 6, No. 1, pp. 41-48.

Greenberg, I. (ed.). (1977). *Group Hypnotherapy and Hypnodrama*, Chicago: Nelson-Hall.

Grof, S. (1985). *Beyond the Brain: Birth, Death and Transcendence in Psychotherapy,* Albany, N. Y.: State University of New York Press.

Guldner, C. A. (1982), "Multiple Family Psychodramatic Therapy," *Journal of Group Psychotherapy, Psychodrama and Sociometry,* Vol. 35, pp. 47-56.

Harris, T. A. (1967). *I'm OK, You're OK*, New York: Harper & Row.

Haskell, M. R. (1975). *Socioanalysis: Self Direction via Sociometry and Psychodrama.* Long Beach, Calif.: Role Training Associates of California.

Hendricks, G., and Hendricks, K. (1987). "Techniques for Dealing with Prenatal and Perinatal Issues in Therapy: A Bodymind Perspective," *Pre- and Peri-Natal Psychology Journal,* Vol. 1, No. 3, pp. 230-238.

Hilgard, E. R. (1977). *Divided Consciousness: Multiple Controls in Human Thought and Action*, New York: Wiley.

Holloway, W. H. (1972). "The Crazy Child in the Parent," *Transactional Analysis Journal*, Vol. 2, No. 3, pp. 32-34.

Holtby, M. (1976). "The Origin and Insertion of Script Injunctions," *Transactional Analysis Journal*, Vol. 6, No. 4, pp. 371-376.

Humphrey, T. (1978). "Function of the Nervous System During the Prenatal Life," in U. Stave, ed., *Physiology of the Perinatal Period*, Vol. 2, pp. 751-796, New York: Plenum Medical.

Jacobsen, B. (1988). "Perinatal Origin of Eventual Self-Destructive Behavior," *Pre- and Peri-Natal Psychology Journal*, Vol. 2, pp. 227-241.

James, M. (1974). "Self Parenting: Theory and Process," *Transactional Analysis Journal*, Vol. 4, No. 3, pp. 32-39.

James, M., and Jongeward, D. (1971). *Born to Win*, New York: New American Library.

James, W. H. (1969). "The Effect of Maternal Psychological Stress on the Foetus," *British Journal of Psychiatry,* Vol. 115, pp. 811-825.

Janov, A. (1970). *The Primal Scream, Primal Therapy: The Cure for Neurosis*, New York: G. P. Putnam's Sons.

Janov, A. (1991). *The Primal Scream,* Wilmington, Del.: Enterprise Publishing.

Kahler, T., and Hedges, C. (1974). "The Miniscript," *Transactional Analysis Journal*, Vol. 4, No. 1, pp. 26-42.

Kaminski, R. C. (1981). "Saying Good-bye: An Example of Using a 'Good-bye Technique' and Concomitant Psychodrama in the Resolving of Family Grief," *Journal of Group Psychotherapy, Psychodrama & Sociometry,* Vol. 34, pp. 100-111.

Kellerman, P. F. (1984), "The Place of Catharsis in Psychodrama," *Journal of Group*

Psychotherapy, Psychodrama and Sociometry, Vol. 37, pp. 1-13.

Kirsch, I., Mobayed, C. P., Council, J. R., and Kenny, D. A. (1992), "Expert Judgements of Hypnosis from Subjective State Reports," *Journal of Abnormal Psychology*, Vol. 101, No. 4, pp. 657-662.

Klaus, M., and Kennell, J. (1972). "Maternal Attachment: Importance of the First Post-Partum Days," *New England Journal of Medicine*, Vol. 286, pp. 460-463.

Kluft, R. P. (1984). "Treatment of Multiple Personality Disorder," *Psychiatric Clinics of North America*, Vol. 7, pp. 9-29.

Kluft, R. P. (1992). "The Use of Hypnosis with Dissociative Disorders," *Psychiatric Medicine*, Vol. 10, No. 4, pp. 31-46.

Kluft, R. P. (1993). "The Physician as the Perpetrator of Abuse," *Primary Care: Clinics in Office Practice*, Vol. 20, pp. 459-480.

Kohn, H. B. (1984). *Clinical Applications of Hypnosis: A Manual for the Health Professional*, Springfield, Ill.: C. C. Thomas.

Laing, R. D. (1982). *The Voice of Experience*, New York: Pantheon Books.

Lake, F. (1982). *Tight Corners in Pastoral Counseling*, London: Darton, Longman & Todd.

Liley, A. W. (1972). "The Foetus as a Personality," *Australian and New Zealand Journal of Psychiatry*, Vol. 6, pp. 99-105.

Lowen, A. (1967). *The Betrayal of the Body*, New York: Collier Books.

Lowen, A. (1970). *Pleasure: A Creative Approach to Life*, first published in the United States by Coward-McCann, and later published by Penguin Books, New York, 1975.

Lowen, A. (1975). *Bioenergetics*, New York: Penguin Books.

Lynn, S. J., and Rhue, J. W. (1991). *Theories of Hypnosis: Current Models and Perspectives*, New York-London: Guilford Press.

Maldonado, J. R., and Spiegel, D. (1994). "The Treatment of Post Traumatic Stress Disorder," in S. J. Lynn and J. W. Rhue, eds., *Dissociation: Clinical and Theoretical Perspectives*, pp. 215-241. New York-London: Guilford Press.

Marnie, E. (1989). *Love Start: Prebirth Bonding*, Los Angeles: Hay House.

McGee, B. A. (1973). "The Treatment of the Two Faced Parent," *Transactional Analysis Journal*, Vol. 3, No. 2, pp. 41-45.

Mellor, K. (1980). "Reframing and the Integrated Use of Redeciding and Reparenting," *Transactional Analysis Journal*, Vol. 10, No. 3, pp. 204-212.

Mellor, K., and Andrewartha, G. (1980). "Reparenting the Parent in Support of Redecisions," *Transactional Analysis Journal*, Vol. 10, No. 3, pp. 197-203.

Meltzoff, A. N., and Moore, M. K. (1977). "Imitation of Facial and Manual Gestures by Human Neonates," *Science*, 198, pp. 75-78.

Moreno, J. L. (1939). "Psychodramatic Shock Therapy: A Sociometric Approach to the Problem of Mental Disorders." *Sociometry*, Vol. 2, pp. 1-30.

Moreno, J. L. (1940a). "Mental Catharsis and the Psychodrama," *Sociometry*, Vol. 3, pp. 209-244.

Moreno, J. L. (1940b). "Psychodramatic Treatment of Psychosis," *Sociometry*, Vol. 3, pp. 115-132.

Moreno, J. L. (1946). *Psychodrama*, Vol. 1, Beacon, N. Y.: Beacon House.

Moreno, J. L. (1950). "Hypnodrama and Psychodrama," in I. Greenberg, ed., *Group Hypnotherapy and Hypnodrama*, pp. 159-169, Chicago: Nelson-Hall.

Moreno, J. L. (1952). "Psychodramatic Production Techniques: The Technique of Role Reversal, The Mirror Technique, The Double Technique and The Dream Technique Transcript of a Didactic Session," *Group Psychotherapy*, Vol. 4, pp. 243-273.

Moreno, J. L. (1968). "The Validity of Psychodrama," *Group Psychotherapy*, Vol. 21, p. 3.

Moreno, J. L. (1975) "Mental Catharsis and the Psychodrama," *Group Psychotherapy and Psychodrama*, Vol. 28, pp. 5-32.

Moreno, J. L., and Ennes, J. M. (1950). *Hypnodrama and Psychodrama*, Beacon, N. Y.: Beacon House.

Moreno, J. L., and Moreno, Z. T. (1956). "Psychodrama," Vol. 2, *Foundations of Psychodrama*, Beacon, N. Y.: Beacon House.

Moreno, J. L., and Moreno, Z. T. (1969). "Psychodrama," Vol. 3, *Actions and Principles of Practice*, Beacon, N. Y.: Beacon House.

Moreno, Z. T. (1959). "A Survey of Psychodramatic Techniques," *Group Psychotherapy*, Vol. 12, pp. 5-14.

Moreno, Z. T. (1965). "Psychodramatic Rules, Techniques and Adjunctive Methods," *Group Psychotherapy*, Vol. 18, pp. 73-86.

Moreno, Z. T. (1975). *A Survey of Psychodramatic Techniques*, Beacon, N. Y.: Beacon House.

Moreno, Z. T. (1978). "The Function of the Auxiliary Ego in Psychodrama with Special Reference to Psychotic Patients," *Group Psychotherapy, Psychodrama and Sociometry*, Vol. 31, pp. 163-166.

Moroney, M. K. (1989). "Reparenting Strategies in Transactional Analysis: A Comparison of Five Methods," *Transactional Analysis Journal*, Vol. 19, No. 1, pp. 35-41.

Nash, M. R., and Lynn, S. J. (1986). "Child Abuse and Hypnotic Ability," *Imagination, Cognition and Personality*, Vol. 5, pp. 211-218.

Netter, P. (1982). "Unwanted Pregnancy as a Cause of Childhood Development Disorder," *Z. Geburtshife Perinatal* (West Germany), Vol. 186, No. 5, pp. 256-262.

Nolte, J., Weistart J., and Wyatt J. (1977). "Psychodramatic Production of Dreams: The End of the Road," *Group Psychotherapy, Psychodrama and Sociometry*, Vol. 30, pp. 37-48.

Orne, M. T. (1964). "A Note on the Occurrence of Hypnosis Without Conscious Intent," *International Journal of Clinical and Experimental Hypnosis*, Vol. 12, pp. 75-77.

Osnes, R. E. (1974). "Spot Reparenting," *Transactional Analysis Journal*, Vol. 4, No. 3, pp. 40-46.

Ottinger, D. R., and Simmons, E. (1964). "Behavior of Human Neonates and Prenatal Maternal Anxiety," *Psychological Reports*, Vol. 14, pp. 391-394.

Perline, I. H. (1968). "Group Hypnotherapy: A Brief Survey," in I. Greenberg, ed., *Group Psychotherapy and Hypnodrama*, pp. 29-35, Chicago: Nelson-Hall.

Pontelli, A. (1992). *From Fetus to Child*, London: Routledge.

Reading, A. E. (1983). "The Influence of Maternal Anxiety on the Course and Outcome of Pregnancy: A Review," *Health Psychology*, Vol. 2, No. 2, pp. 187-202.

Riley, C. M. (1988). "Fetus Communication: A Workshop on How to Teach Pregnant Mothers to Communicate with their Unborn Children," *Pre- and Peri-Natal Psychology Journal*, Vol. 3, No. 2, pp. 77-86.

Roedding, J. (1991). "Birth Trauma and Suicide: A Study of the Relationship Between

Near Death Experiences at Birth and Later Suicidal Behavior," *Pre- and Peri-Natal Psychology Journal*, Vol. 6, No. 2, pp. 145-170.

Sacks, J. M., Bilaniuk, M. T., and Gendron, J. M., eds., (1955). *Bibliography of Psychodrama*, New York: Psychodrama Center of New York.

Salk, L., Lipsitt, L. P., Struner, W. Q., Reilly, B., and Levat, R. H. (1985). "Relationship of Maternal and Perinatal Conditions to Eventual Adolescent Suicide," *The Lancet*, Vol. 1, pp. 624-627.

Sarbin, T. R., and Coe, W. C. (1972). *Hypnosis: A Social Psychological Analysis of Influence Communication*, New York: Holt, Rinehart & Winston.

Schiff, J. L. (1969). "Reparenting Schizophrenics," *Transactional Analysis Bulletin*, Vol. 8, No. 31, pp. 47-71.

Schiff, J. L., with Dax, B. (1970). *All My Children*, New York: Jove Publications.

Schiff, J. L. with Schiff, A. W., Mellor, K., Schiff, E., Schiff, S., Richman, D., Fishman, J., Wolz, L., Fishman, C., and Momb, D. (1975). *Cathexis Reader: Transactional Analysis Treatment of Psychosis*, New York: Harper & Row.

Scott, E. M. (1968). "Hypnosis Without Conscious Intent in an Alcoholic," *Quarterly Journal of Studies on Alcohol*, Vol. 29, pp. 709-711.

Scott, E. M. (1977). "When Psychodrama Can Slip into Hypnosis," in I. Greenberg , ed., *Group Hypnotherapy and Hypnodrama,* pp. 303-306, Chicago: Nelson-Hall.

Spiegel, D. (1981). "Vietnam Grief Work Using Hypnosis," *American Journal of Clinical Hypnosis*, Vol. 24, pp. 33-40.

Spiegel, D., and Cardena, E. (1990). "New Uses of Hypnosis in the Treatment of Post Traumatic Stress Disorders," *Journal of Clinical Psychiatry,* Vol. 51 (10 suppl.) pp. 39-43.

Spiegel, D., and Cardena, E. (1991). "Disintegrated Experience: The Dissociative Disorders Revisited," *Journal of Abnormal Psychology*, Vol. 100, No. 3, pp. 366-378.

Spiegel, D., Detrick, D., and Frischholz, E. (1982). "Hypnotizability and Psychopathology," *American Journal of Psychiatry*, Vol. 139, pp. 431-437.

Spiegel, H., and Spiegel, D. (1978). *Trance and Treatment: Clinical Uses of Hypnosis*, New York: Basic Books.

Starr, A. (1959). "Psychodrama with a Family," *Group Psychotherapy*, Vol. 12, pp. 27-31.

Steiner, C. (1966). "Script and Counterscript," *Transactional Analysis Bulletin*, Vol. 5, No. 18, pp. 133-135.

Steiner, C. (1974). *Scripts People Live*, New York: Grove Press.

Stewart, A. M. (1955). "A Note on the Obstetric Effects of Work During Pregnancy," *British Journal of Preventative Social Medicine*, Vol. 9, pp. 159-161.

Stuntz, E. C. (1972). "Second Order Structure of the Parent," *Transactional Analysis Journal*, Vol. 2, No. 2, pp. 59-61.

Supple, L. K. (1962). "Hypnodrama: A Synthesis of Hypnosis and Psychodrama: A Progress Report," *Group Psychotherapy*, Vol. 15, pp. 58-62.

Sutcliffe, J. P. (1960). "'Credulous' and 'Skeptical' Views of Hypnotic Phenomena: A Review of Certain Evidence and Methodology," *International Journal of Clinical and Experimental Hypnosis*, Vol. 8, pp. 73-101.

Thompson, A. G. (1984) "Rebirthing Through Psychodrama." *Journal of Group Psychotherapy, Psychodrama and Sociometry*, Vol. 37, No. 1, pp. 27-32.

Treadwell, T. W., Stein, Steven, and Kumar, V. K. (1990). "A Survey of Psychodramatic Action and Closure Techniques," *Journal of Group Psychotherapy, Psychodrama and Sociometry,* Vol. 43, pp. 102-115.

Turner, J. R., and Turner, T. (1993). "Prebirth Memory Therapy, Including Prematurely Delivered Patients," *Pre- and Peri-Natal Psychology Journal*, Vol. 7, No. 4, pp. 321-332.

Udolf, R. (1981). *Handbook of Hypnosis for Professionals*, New York: Van Nostrand Reinhold.

Van de Carr, F. R., and Lehrer, M. (1988). "Prenatal University: Commitment to Fetal-Family Bonding and the Strengthening of the Family Unit as an Educational Institution," *Pre- and Peri-Natal Psychology Journal*, Vol. 3, No. 2, pp. 87-102.

Van den Bergh, B.R.H. (1990). "The Influence of Maternal Emotions During Pregnancy on Fetal and Neonatal Behavior," *Pre- and Peri-Natal Psychology Journal*, Vol. 5, No. 2, pp. 119-130.

Van Husen, J. E. (1988). "The Development of Fears, Phobias and Restrictive Patterns of Adaptation Following Attempted Abortions," *Pre- and Peri-Natal Psychology Journal*, Vol. 2, No. 3, pp. 179-185.

Vaughn, B. E., Bradley, C. F., Joffe, L. S., Seifer, R., and Barglow (1987). "Maternal Characteristics Measured Prenatally Are Predictive of Ratings of Temperament 'Difficulty' on the Carey Temperament Questionnaire," *Developmental Psychology,* Vol. 23, pp. 152-161.

Verny, T. (1977). "The Psychic Life of the Unborn," Fifth World Congress of Psychosomatic Obstetrics and Gynecology.

Verny, T. (1994). "Working with Pre-Natal and Peri-Natal Material in Psychotherapy," *Pre- and Peri-Natal Psychology Journal*, Vol. 8, No. 3, pp. 161-186.

Verny, T., and Weintraub, P. (1991). *Nurturing the Unborn Child: A Nine Month Program for Soothing, Stimulating and Communicating with your Baby,* New York: Delacorte Press.

Ward, Alan J. (1991). "Prenatal Stress and Child Psychopathology," *Child Psychiatry and Human Development*, Vol. 22, No. 2, pp. 97-110.

Watkins, H. H. (1986). "Treating the Trauma of Abortion," *Pre- and Peri-Natal Psychology Journal*, Vol. 1, No. 2, pp. 135-142.

Weitzenhoffer, A. M. (1953). *Hypnotism: An Objective Study of Suggestibility*, New York: Wiley.

Weitzenhoffer, A. M. (1989). *The Practice of Hypnotism*, 2 Vol., New York: Wiley.

Wilson, T. E., Momb, D., Hunt, R. D., and Heiber, R. G. (1982). "Reparenting Young Schizophrenic People," *International Child Welfare Review*, Vol. 55, pp. 31-38.

Wilson, T. E., White, T. L., and Heiber, R. G. (1985). "Reparenting Schizophrenic Youth in a Hospital Setting," *Transactional Analysis Journal*, Vol. 15, pp. 211-215.

Wolberg, L. R. (1964). *Hypnoanalysis*, New York: Grune & Stratton.

Wolk, D. J. (1996). "The Psychodramatic Reenactment of a Dream," *Group Psychotherapy, Psychodrama & Sociometry*, Vol. 49, pp. 3-10.

Woollams, S. J. (1973). "Formation of the Script," *Transactional Analysis Journal*, Vol. 3, No. 3, pp. 31-37.

Yablonsky, L. (1976). *Psychodrama: Resolving Emotional Problems Through Role Playing*, New York: Basic Books.

Zeig, J. K. (1988). "An Ericksonian Phenomenological Approach to Therapeutic

Induction and Symptom Utilization," in J. K. Zeig and S. R. Lankton, eds., *Developing Ericksonian Therapy: State of the Art,* pp. 353-375, New York: Brunner/Mazel.

Zeig, S. K., and Rennick, P. J. (1991). "Ericksonian Hypnotherapy: A Communications Approach to Hypnosis," in S. J. Lynn and J. W. Rhue, eds., *Theories of Hypnosis: Current Models and Perspectives,* pp. 275-300, New York-London: Guilford Press.

Zitrin, A., Ferber, P. and Cohen, D. (1964). "Pre and Paranatal Factors in Mental Disorders of Children," *Journal of Nervous and Mental Disorders*, Vol. 139. pp. 357-361.

Zuckerman, B., Bauchner, H., Parker, S., and Cabral, H. (1990). "Maternal Depressive Symptoms During Pregnancy and Newborn Irritability," *Journal of Development and Behavioral Pediatrics,* Vol. 11, No. 4, pp. 190-194.

Author Index

Subject Index

About the Author

MICHAEL GASS is executive director of The Rebuilding Therapy Center in Anaheim, California. He is a licensed psychologist, clinical social worker, and marriage, family, and child counselor and a certified practitioner in Psychodrama, Sociometry, and Group Psychotherapy.

www.ingramcontent.com/pod-product-compliance
Ingram Content Group UK Ltd.
Pitfield, Milton Keynes, MK11 3LW, UK
UKHW041641031026
15587UKWH00001B/413

9 780275 953294